Good As Lily

minx

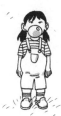

GOOD AS LILY

Published by DC Comics,

1700 Broadway,

New York, NY 10019.

The stories, characters and incidents mentioned in this book

are entirely fictional.

Printed in Canada.

DC Comics, a Warner Bros.

Entertainment Company.

ISBN: 1-4012-1381-2

ISBN: 978-1-4012-1381-7

COVER BY DEREK KIRK KIM

Good As Lily

Written by Derek Kirk Kim

Illustrated by Jesse Hamm

Lettering by Jared K. Fletcher

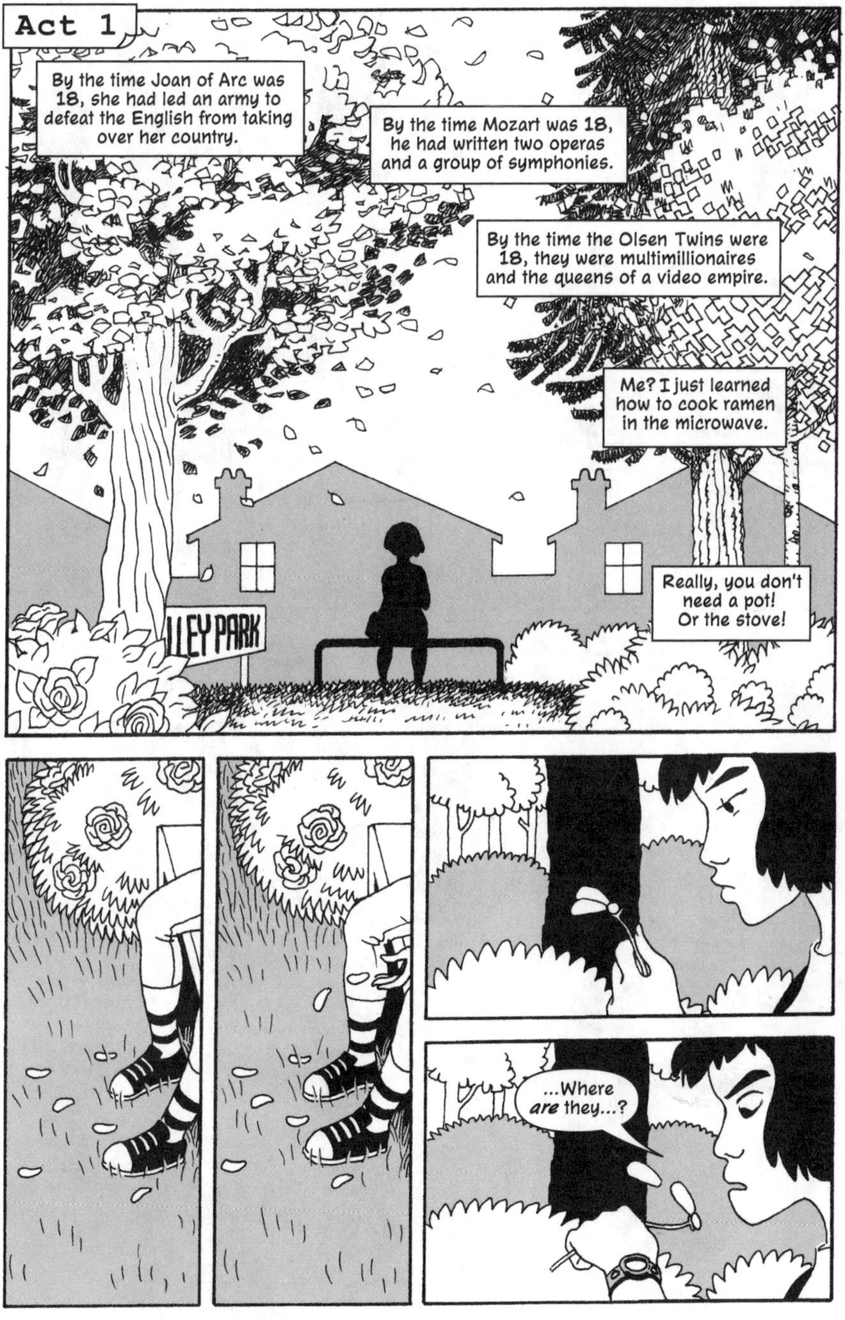
Act 1
By the time Joan of Arc was 18, she had led an army to defeat the English from taking over her country.
By the time Mozart was 18, he had written two operas and a group of symphonies.
By the time the Olsen Twins were 18, they were multimillionaires and the queens of a video empire.
Me? I just learned how to cook ramen in the microwave.
Really, you don't need a pot! Or the stove!
LEY PARK
...Where *are* they...?

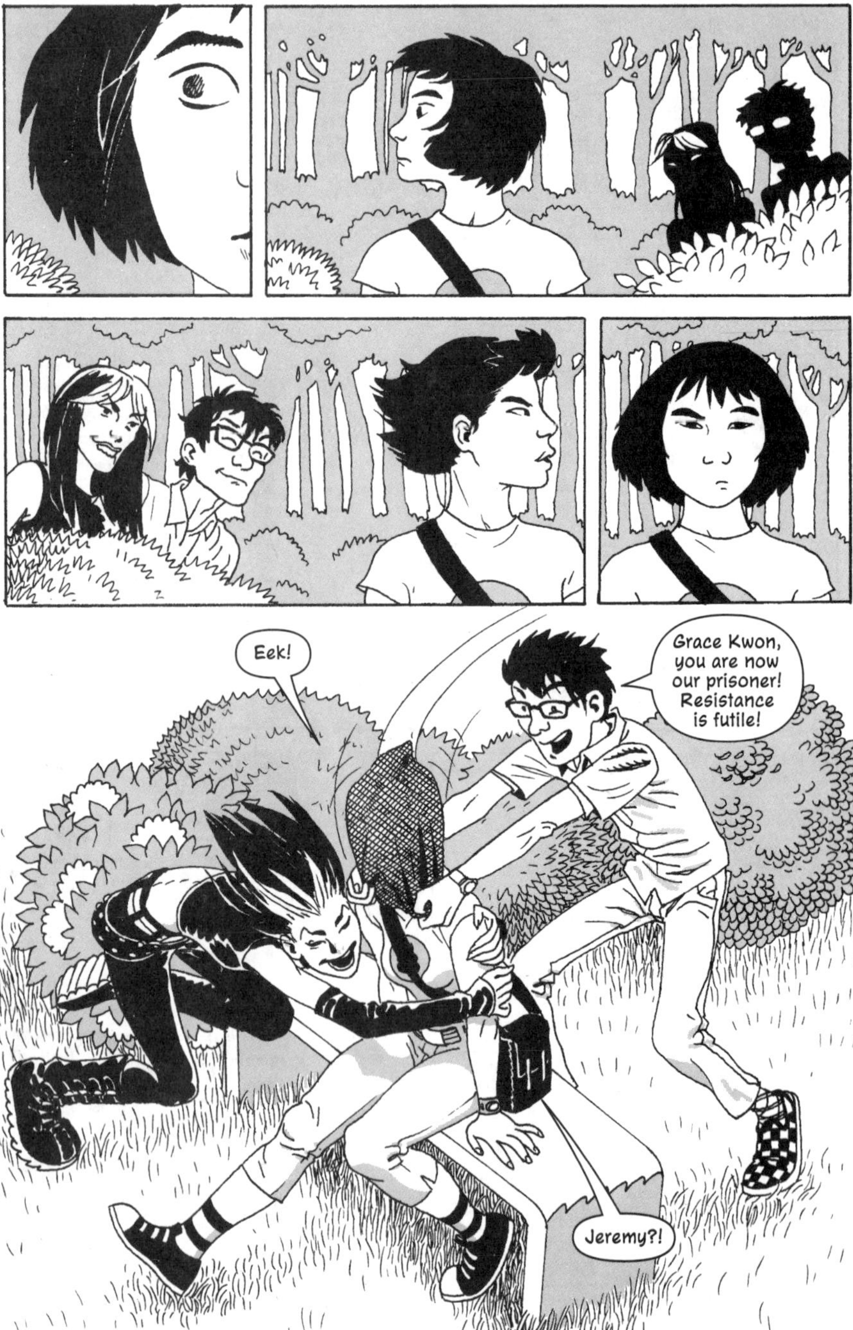
Eek!
Grace Kwon, you are now our prisoner! Resistance is futile!
Jeremy?!

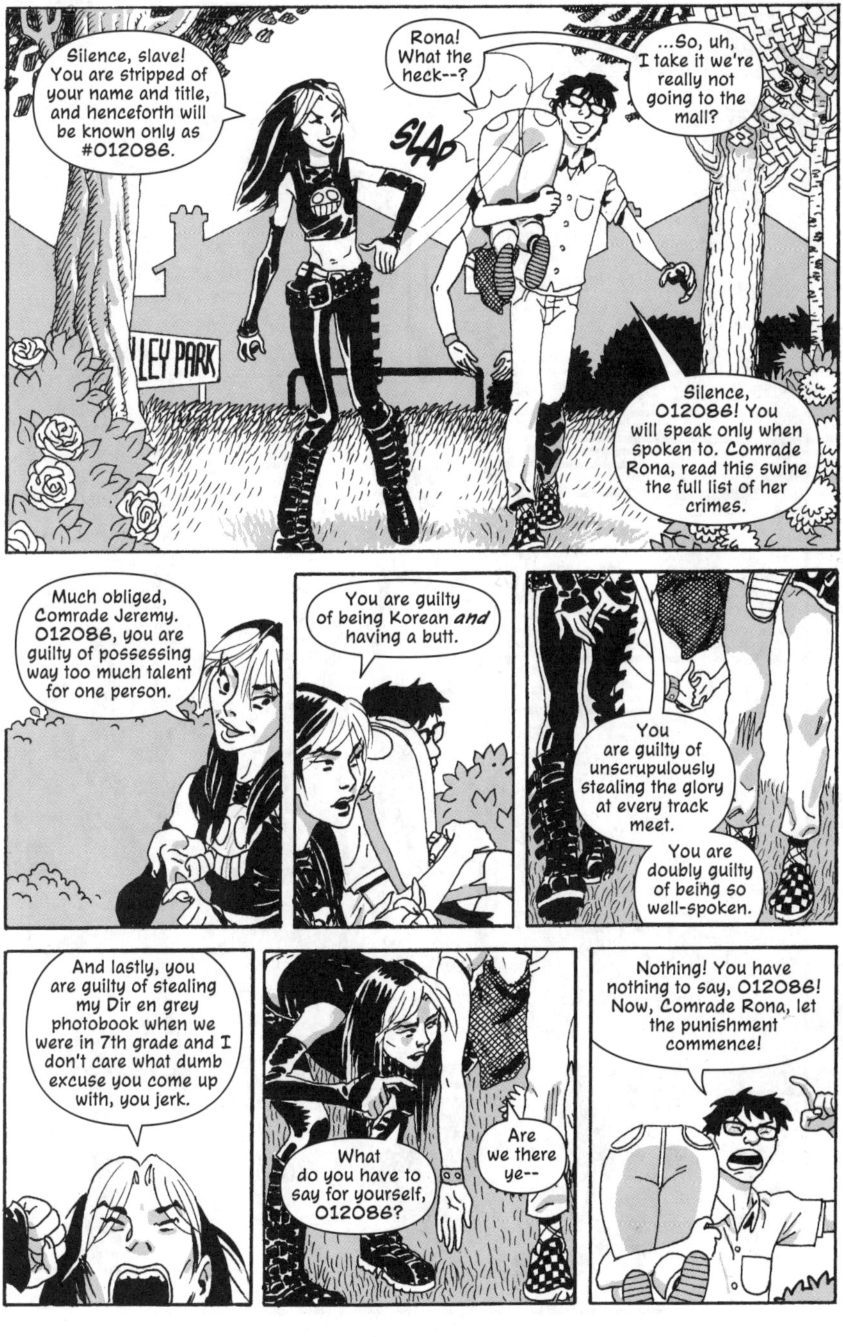
Silence, slave! You are stripped of your name and title, and henceforth will be known only as #012086.
Rona! What the heck--?
SLAP
...So, uh, I take it we're really not going to the mall?
LLEY PARK
Silence, 012086! You will speak only when spoken to. Comrade Rona, read this swine the full list of her crimes.
Much obliged, Comrade Jeremy. 012086, you are guilty of possessing way too much talent for one person.
You are guilty of being Korean *and* having a butt.
You are guilty of unscrupulously stealing the glory at every track meet.
You are doubly guilty of being so well-spoken.
And lastly, you are guilty of stealing my Dir en grey photobook when we were in 7th grade and I don't care what dumb excuse you come up with, you jerk.
What do you have to say for yourself, 012086?
Are we there ye--
Nothing! You have nothing to say, 012086! Now, Comrade Rona, let the punishment commence!

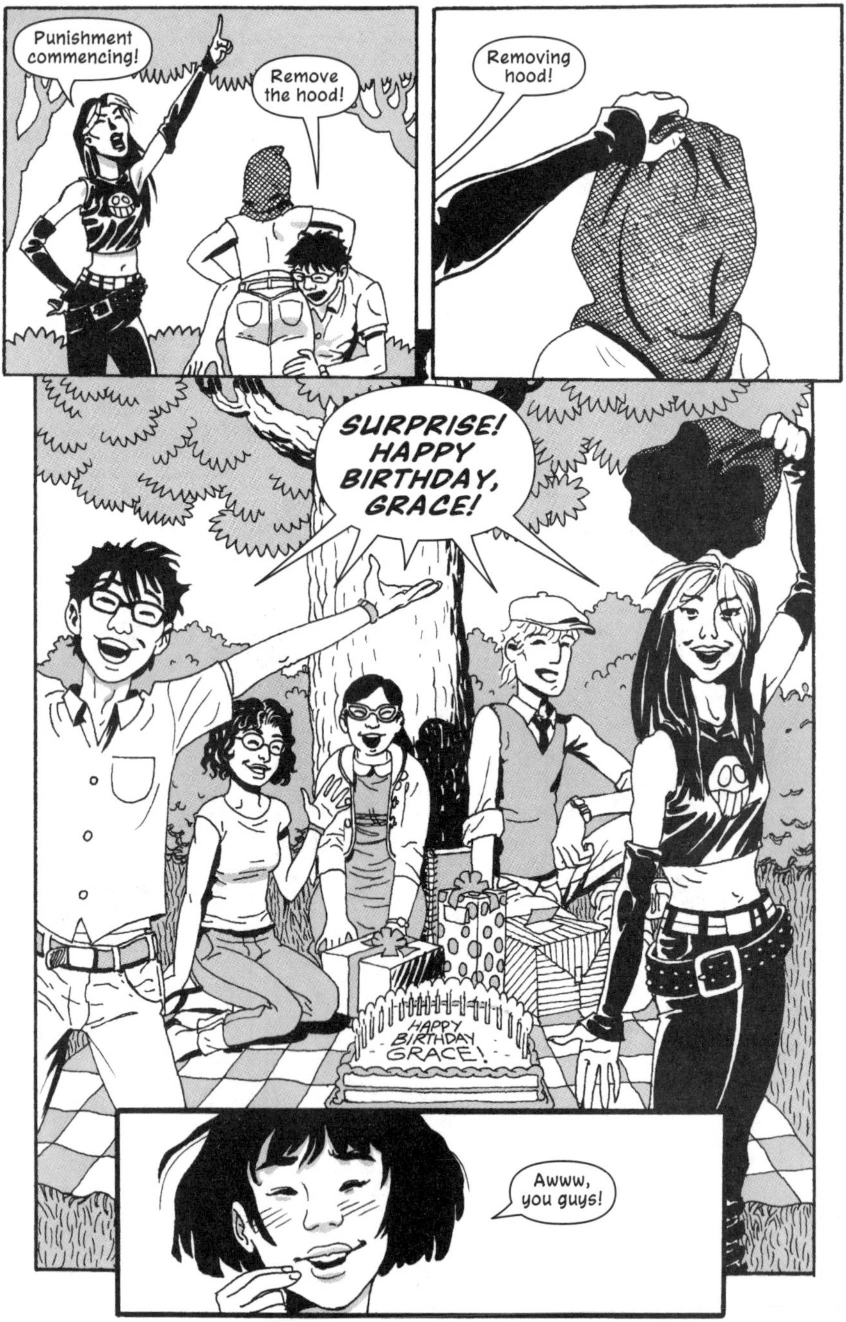
Punishment commencing!
Remove the hood!
Removing hood!
SURPRISE! HAPPY BIRTHDAY, GRACE!
HAPPY BIRTHDAY GRACE!
Awww, you guys!

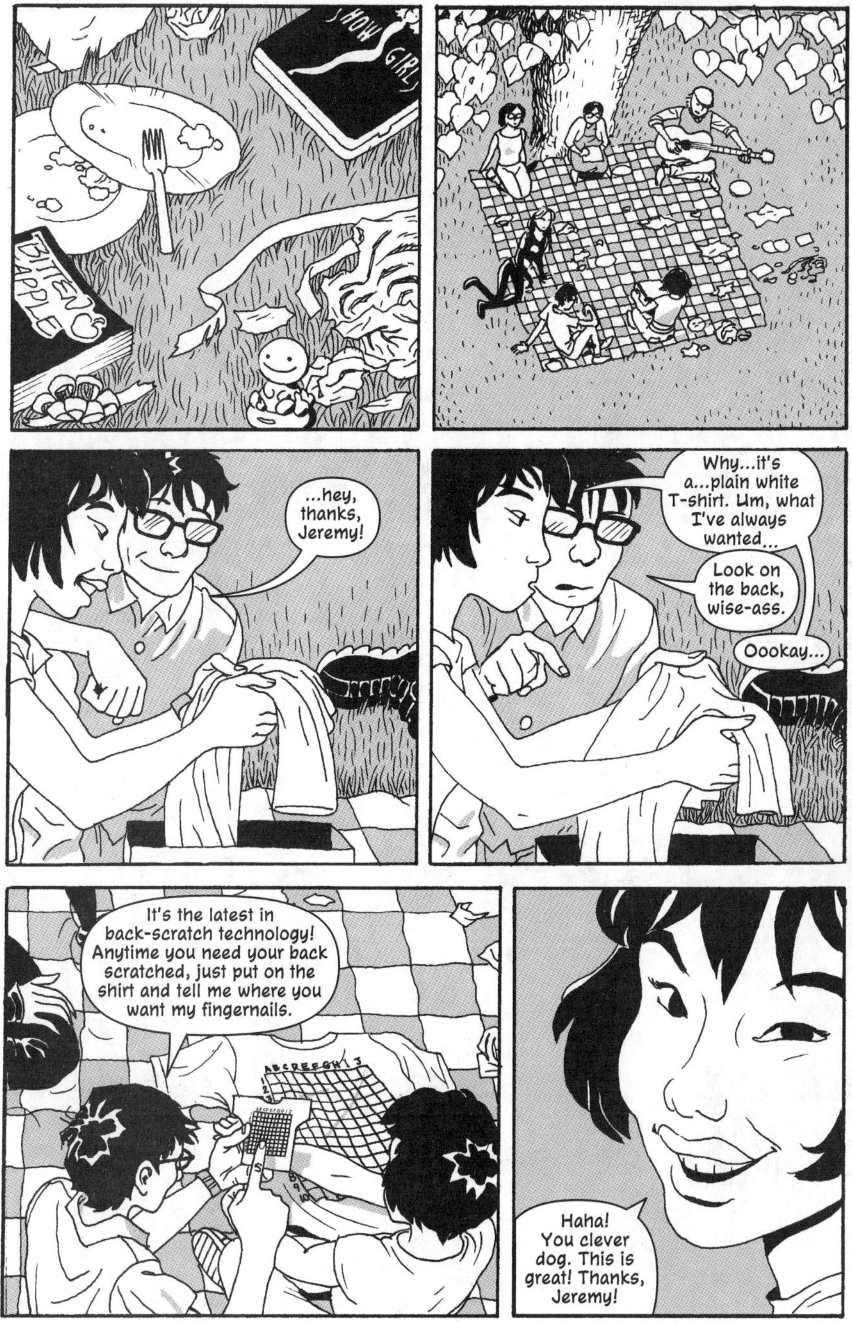
...hey, thanks, Jeremy!
Why...it's a...plain white T-shirt. Um, what I've always wanted...
Look on the back, wise-ass.
Oookay...
It's the latest in back-scratch technology! Anytime you need your back scratched, just put on the shirt and tell me where you want my fingernails.
Haha! You clever dog. This is great! Thanks, Jeremy!

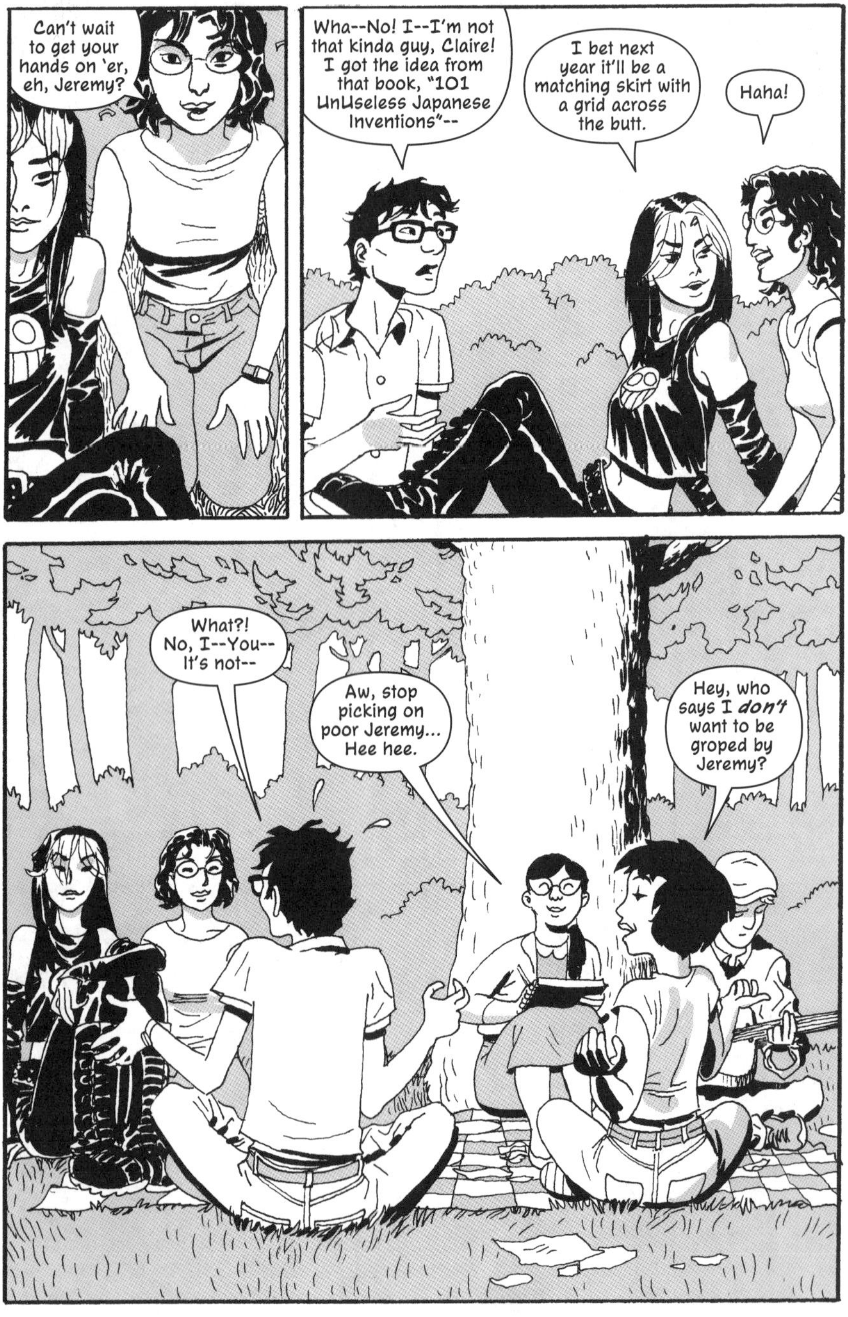

Can't wait to get your hands on 'er, eh, Jeremy?
Wha--No! I--I'm not that kinda guy, Claire! I got the idea from that book, "101 UnUseless Japanese Inventions"--
I bet next year it'll be a matching skirt with a grid across the butt.
Haha!
What?! No, I--You-- It's not--
Aw, stop picking on poor Jeremy... Hee hee.
Hey, who says I *don't* want to be groped by Jeremy?

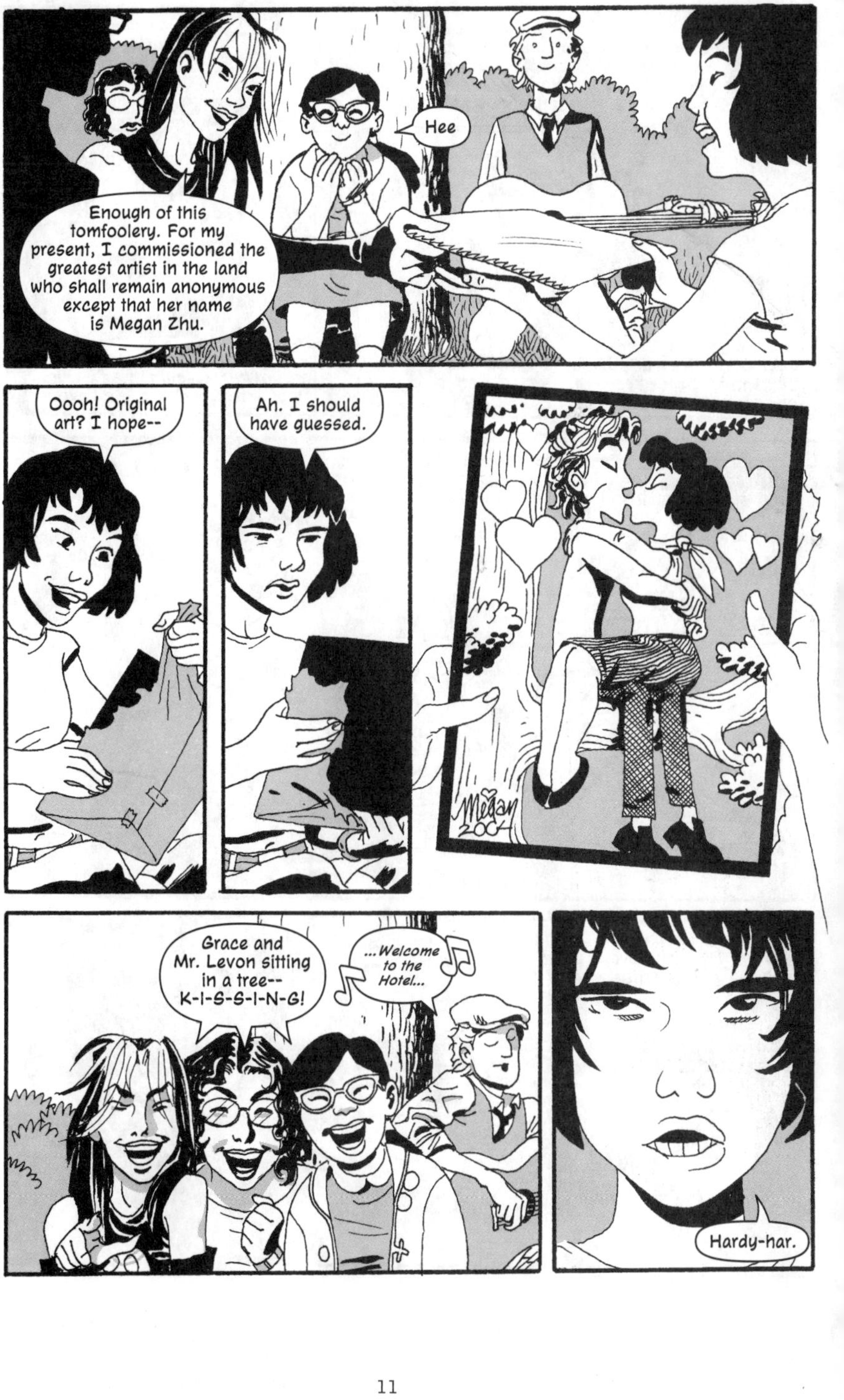
Hee
Enough of this tomfoolery. For my present, I commissioned the greatest artist in the land who shall remain anonymous except that her name is Megan Zhu.
Oooh! Original art? I hope--
Ah. I should have guessed.
Megan 200-
Grace and Mr. Levon sitting in a tree-- K-I-S-S-I-N-G!
...Welcome to the Hotel...
Hardy-har.

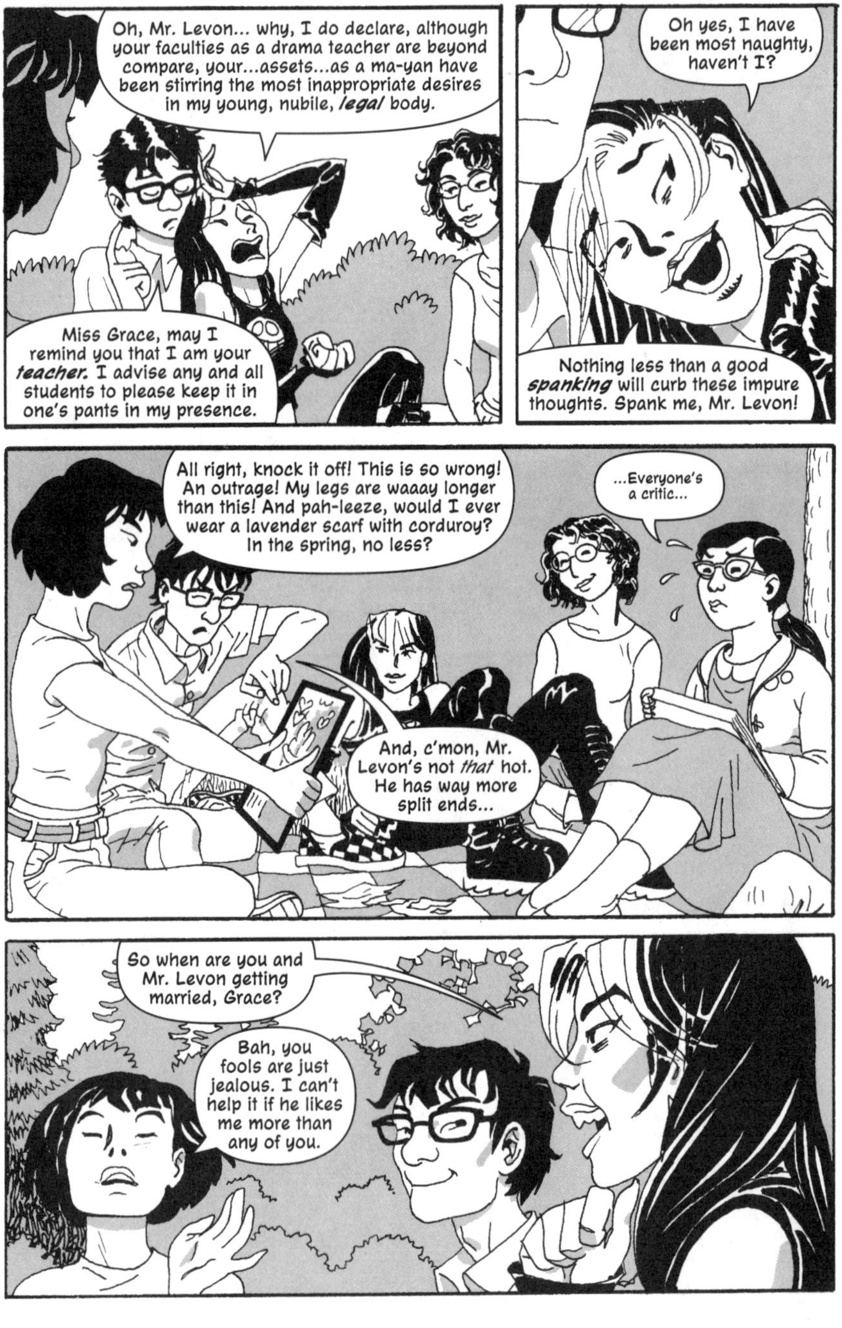

Oh, Mr. Levon... why, I do declare, although your faculties as a drama teacher are beyond compare, your...assets...as a ma-yan have been stirring the most inappropriate desires in my young, nubile, *legal* body.
Miss Grace, may I remind you that I am your ***teacher.*** I advise any and all students to please keep it in one's pants in my presence.
Oh yes, I have been most naughty, haven't I?
Nothing less than a good ***spanking*** will curb these impure thoughts. Spank me, Mr. Levon!
All right, knock it off! This is so wrong! An outrage! My legs are waaay longer than this! And pah-leeze, would I ever wear a lavender scarf with corduroy? In the spring, no less?
...Everyone's a critic...
And, c'mon, Mr. Levon's not *that* hot. He has way more split ends...
So when are you and Mr. Levon getting married, Grace?
Bah, you fools are just jealous. I can't help it if he likes me more than any of you.

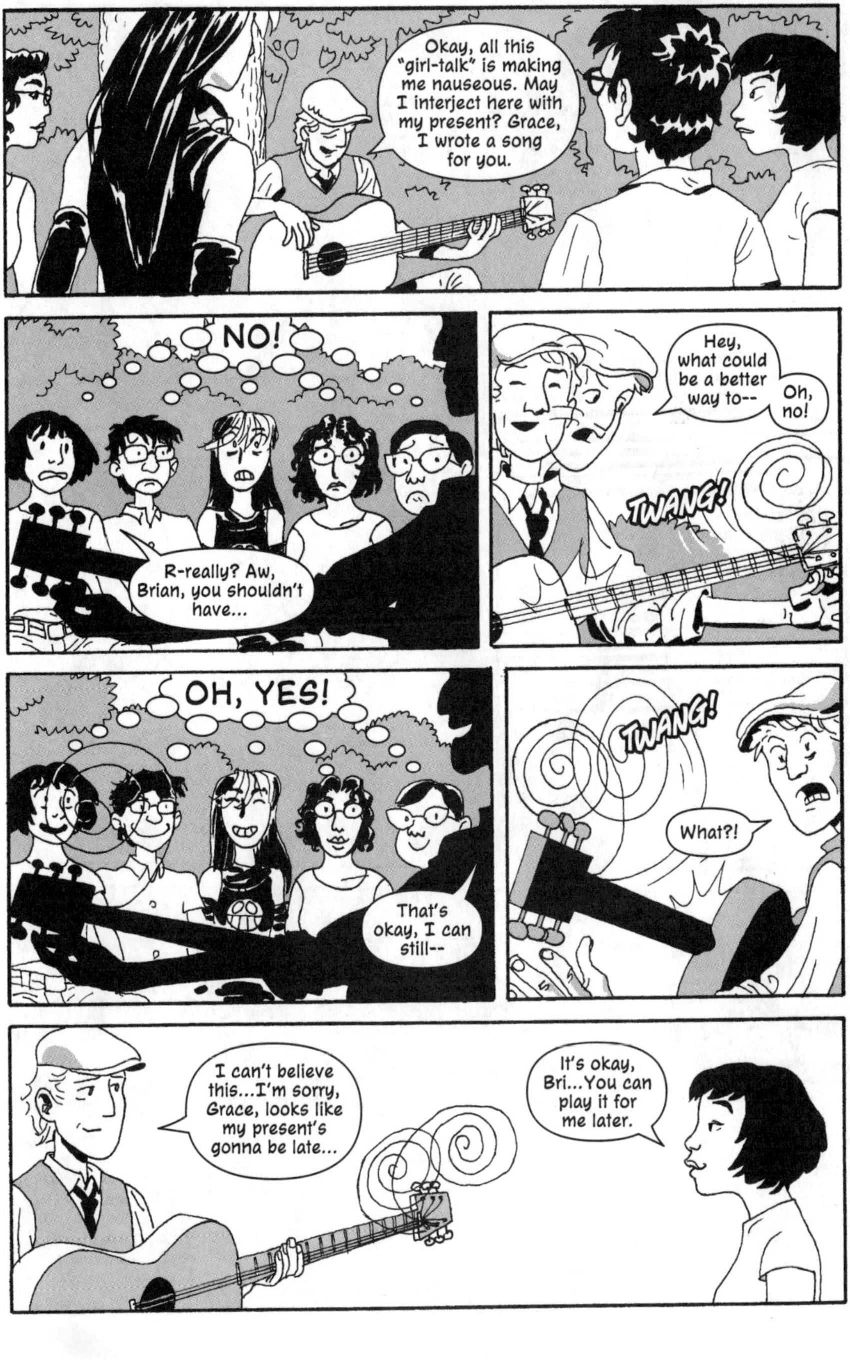

Okay, all this "girl-talk" is making me nauseous. May I interject here with my present? Grace, I wrote a song for you.
NO!
R-really? Aw, Brian, you shouldn't have...
Hey, what could be a better way to--
Oh, no!
TWANG!
OH, YES!
That's okay, I can still--
TWANG!
What?!
I can't believe this...I'm sorry, Grace, looks like my present's gonna be late...
It's okay, Bri...You can play it for me later.

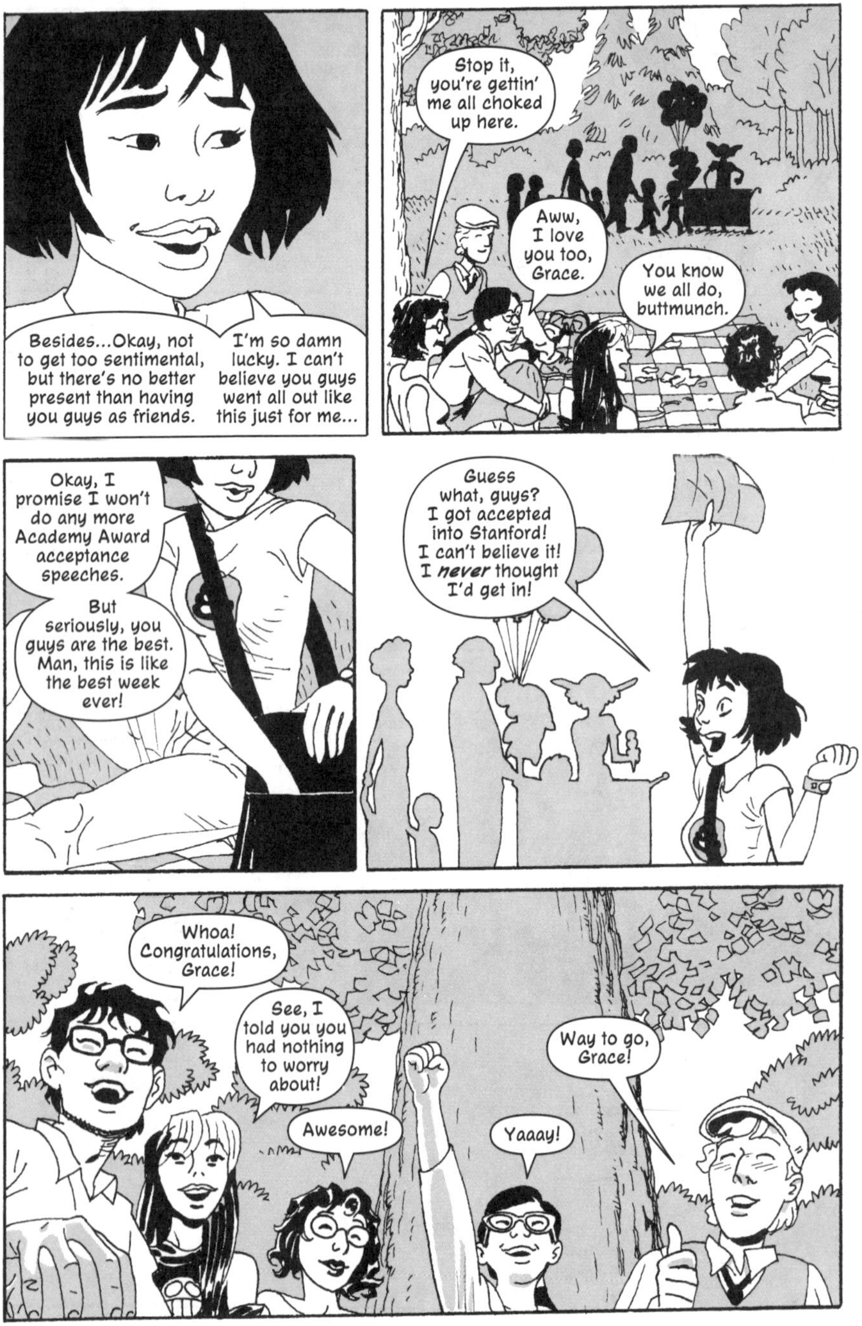

Besides...Okay, not to get too sentimental, but there's no better present than having you guys as friends.
I'm so damn lucky. I can't believe you guys went all out like this just for me...
Stop it, you're gettin' me all choked up here.
Aww, I love you too, Grace.
You know we all do, buttmunch.
Okay, I promise I won't do any more Academy Award acceptance speeches.
But seriously, you guys are the best. Man, this is like the best week ever!
Guess what, guys? I got accepted into Stanford! I can't believe it! I ***never*** thought I'd get in!
Whoa! Congratulations, Grace!
See, I told you you had nothing to worry about!
Awesome!
Yaaay!
Way to go, Grace!

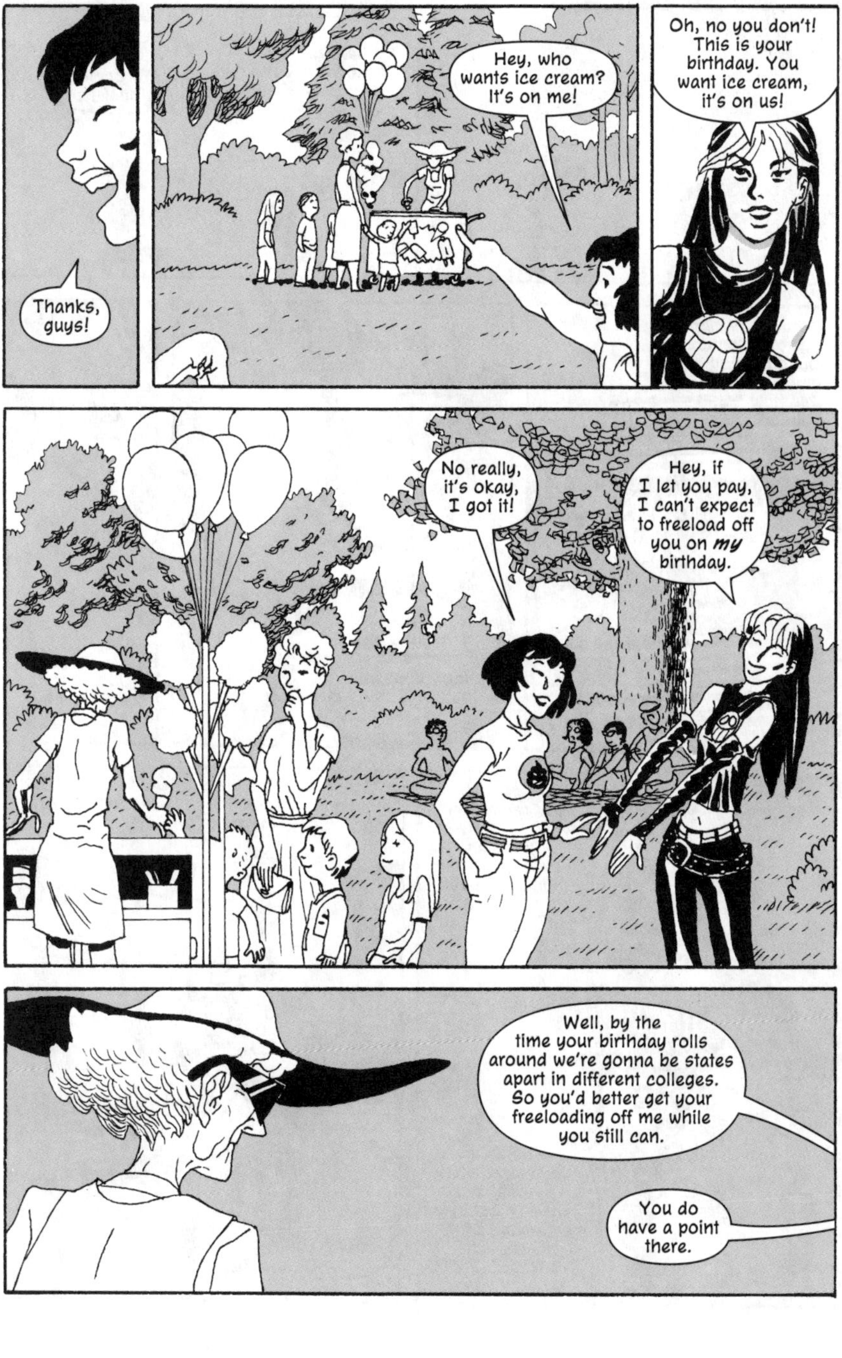

Thanks, guys!
Hey, who wants ice cream? It's on me!
Oh, no you don't! This is your birthday. You want ice cream, it's on us!
No really, it's okay, I got it!
Hey, if I let you pay, I can't expect to freeload off you on *my* birthday.
Well, by the time your birthday rolls around we're gonna be states apart in different colleges. So you'd better get your freeloading off me while you still can.
You do have a point there.

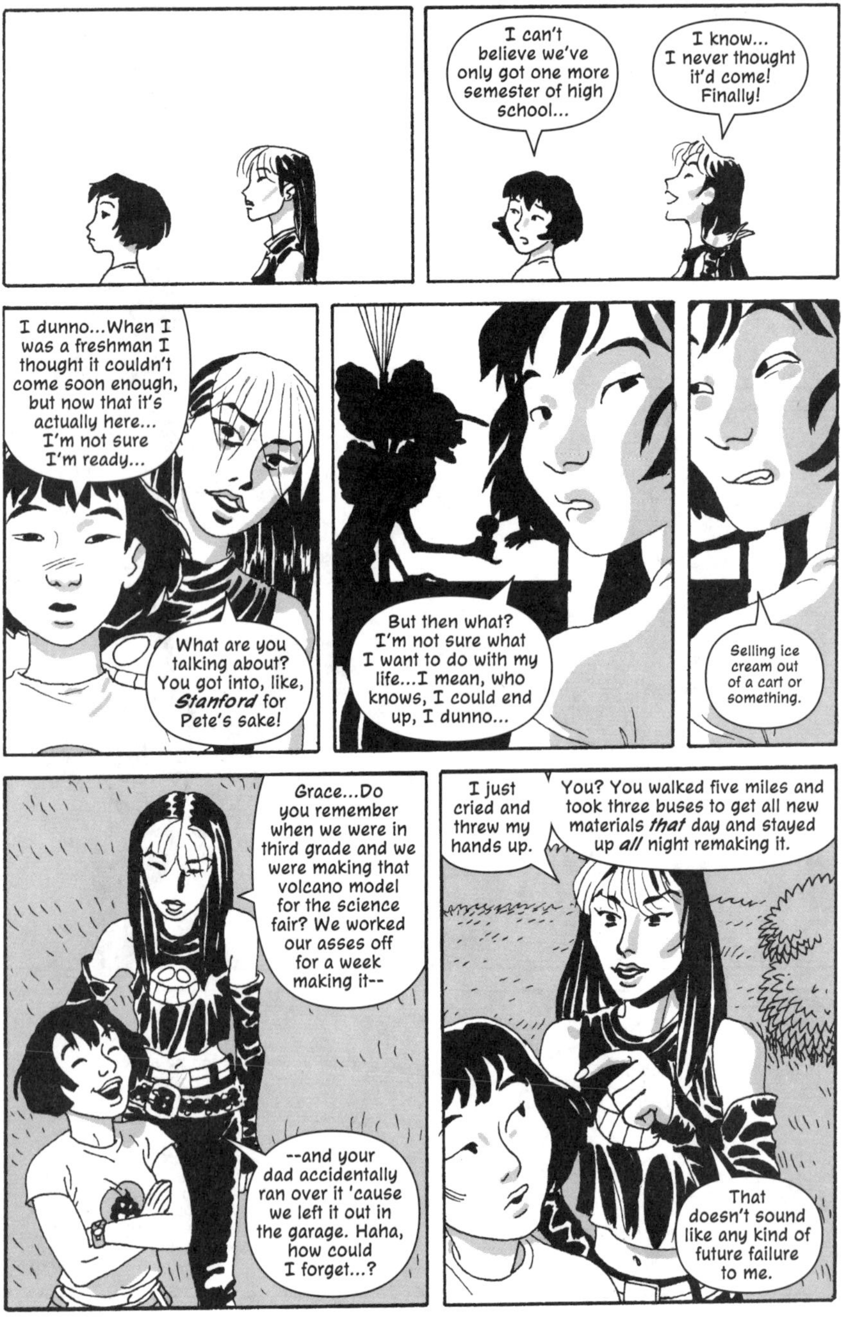

I can't believe we've only got one more semester of high school...
I know... I never thought it'd come! Finally!
I dunno...When I was a freshman I thought it couldn't come soon enough, but now that it's actually here... I'm not sure I'm ready...
What are you talking about? You got into, like, *Stanford* for Pete's sake!
But then what? I'm not sure what I want to do with my life...I mean, who knows, I could end up, I dunno...
Selling ice cream out of a cart or something.
Grace...Do you remember when we were in third grade and we were making that volcano model for the science fair? We worked our asses off for a week making it--
--and your dad accidentally ran over it 'cause we left it out in the garage. Haha, how could I forget...?
I just cried and threw my hands up.
You? You walked five miles and took three buses to get all new materials *that* day and stayed up *all* night remaking it.
That doesn't sound like any kind of future failure to me.

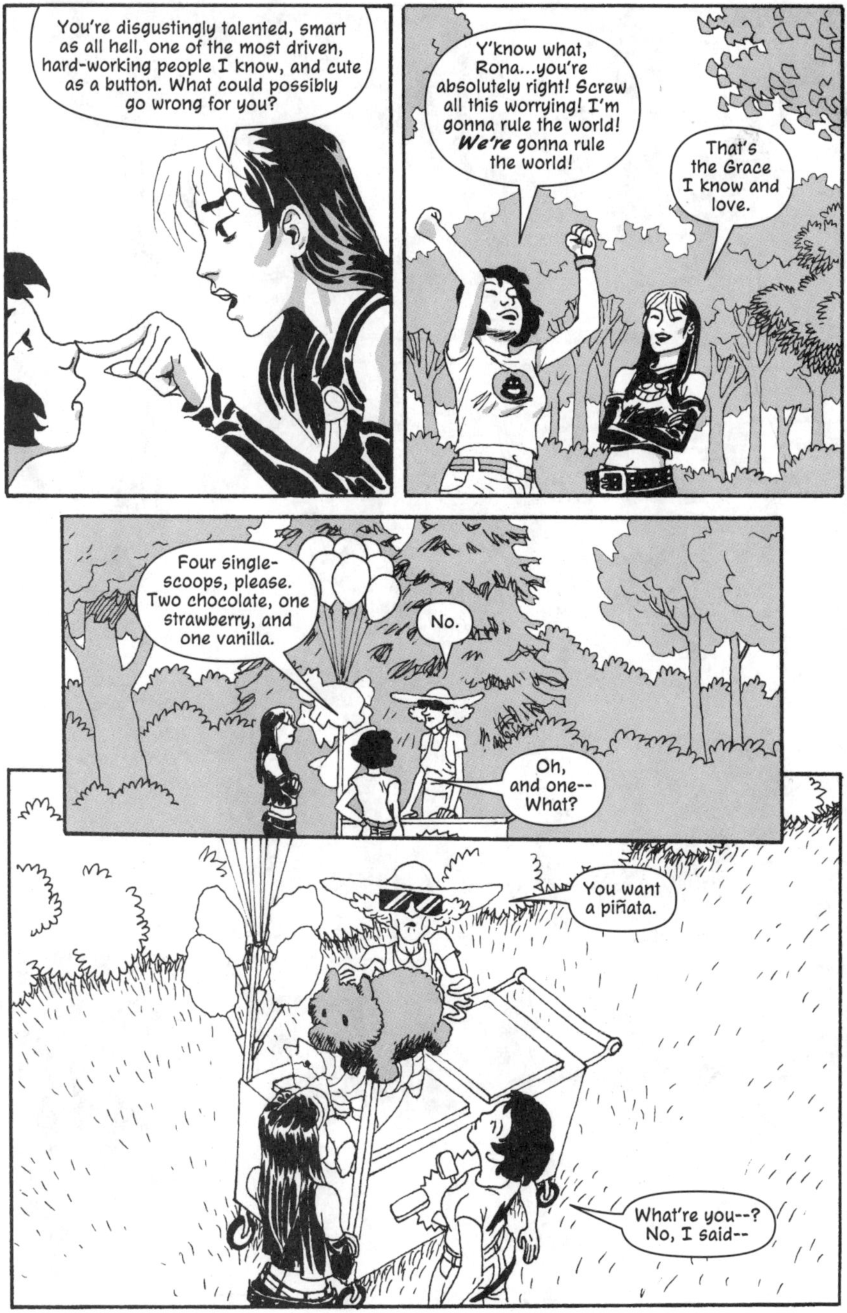
You're disgustingly talented, smart as all hell, one of the most driven, hard-working people I know, and cute as a button. What could possibly go wrong for you?
Y'know what, Rona...you're absolutely right! Screw all this worrying! I'm gonna rule the world! *We're* gonna rule the world!
That's the Grace I know and love.
Four single-scoops, please. Two chocolate, one strawberry, and one vanilla.
No.
Oh, and one-- What?
You want a piñata.
What're you--? No, I said--

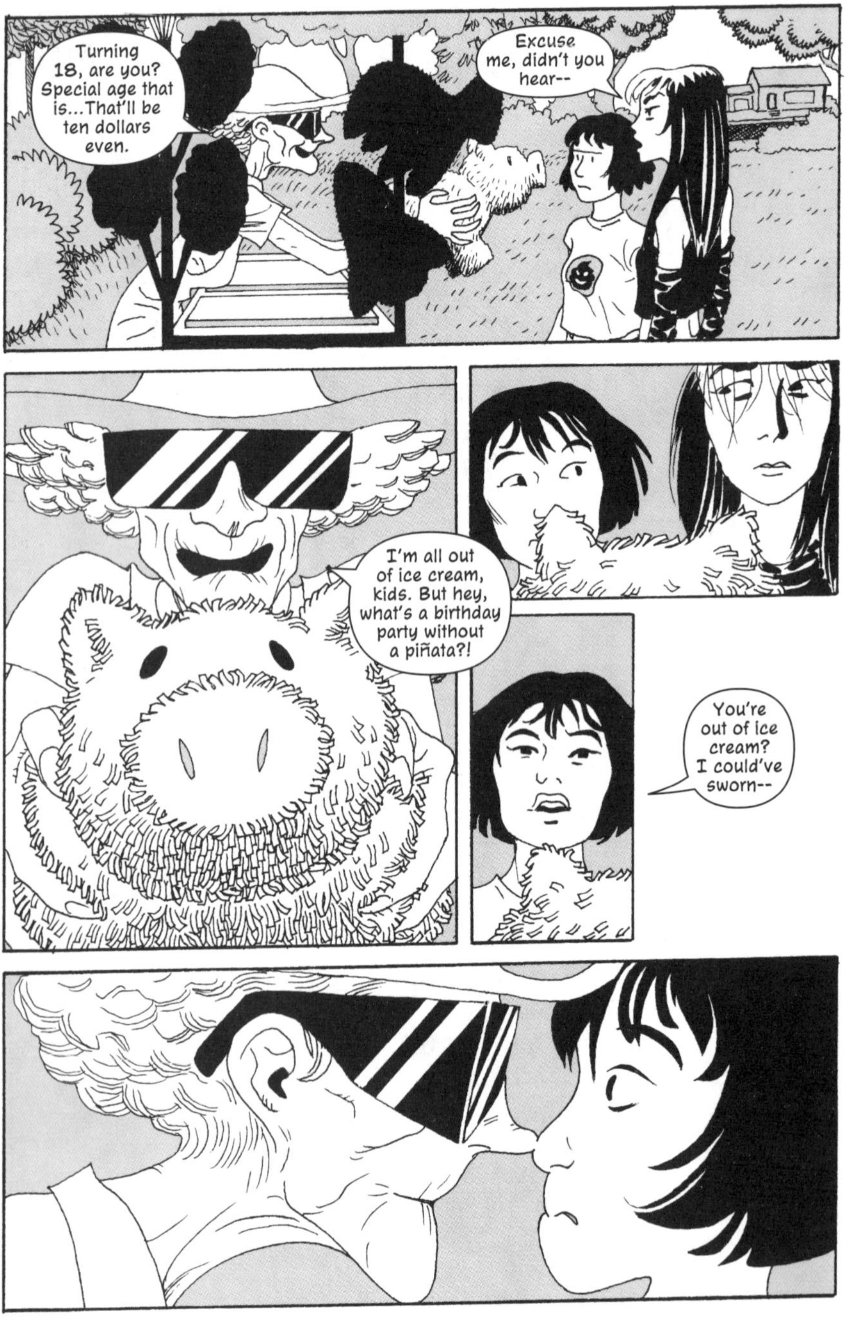
Turning 18, are you? Special age that is...That'll be ten dollars even.
Excuse me, didn't you hear--
I'm all out of ice cream, kids. But hey, what's a birthday party without a piñata?!
You're out of ice cream? I could've sworn--

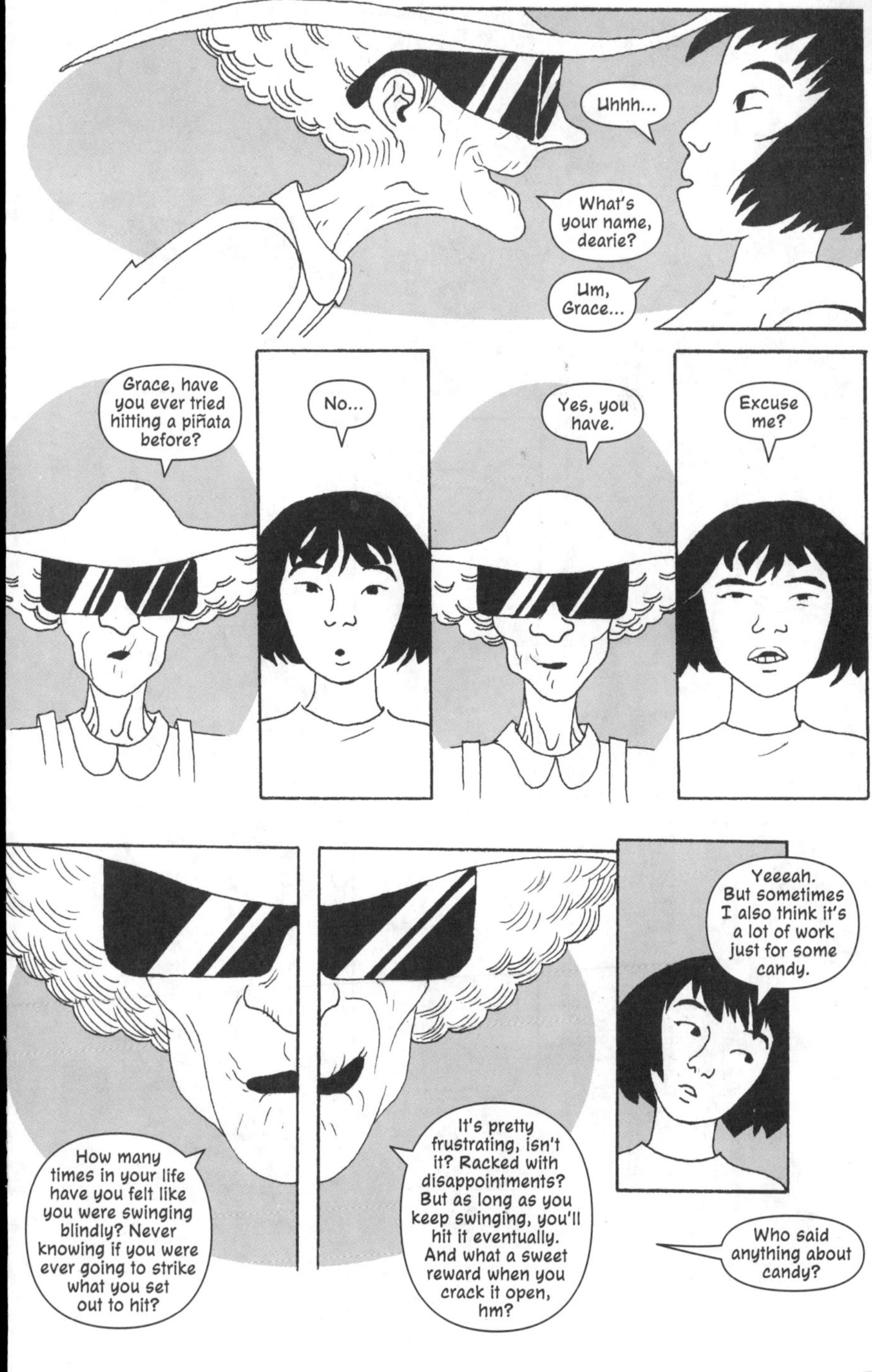
Uhhh...
What's your name, dearie?
Um, Grace...
Grace, have you ever tried hitting a piñata before?
No...
Yes, you have.
Excuse me?
How many times in your life have you felt like you were swinging blindly? Never knowing if you were ever going to strike what you set out to hit?
It's pretty frustrating, isn't it? Racked with disappointments? But as long as you keep swinging, you'll hit it eventually. And what a sweet reward when you crack it open, hm?
Yeeeah. But sometimes I also think it's a lot of work just for some candy.
Who said anything about candy?

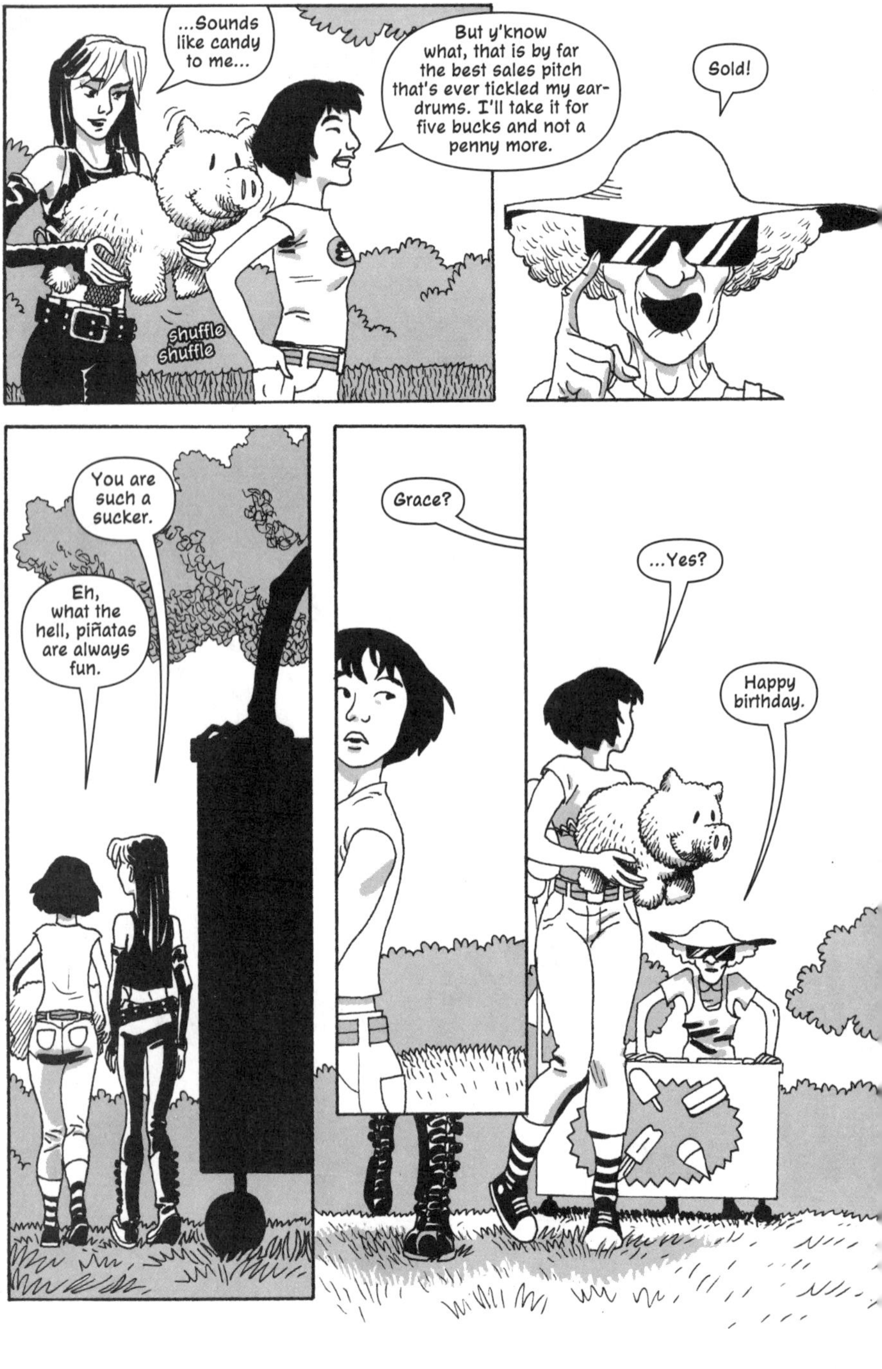
...Sounds like candy to me...
shuffle shuffle
But y'know what, that is by far the best sales pitch that's ever tickled my ear-drums. I'll take it for five bucks and not a penny more.
Sold!
You are such a sucker.
Eh, what the hell, piñatas are always fun.
Grace?
...Yes?
Happy birthday.

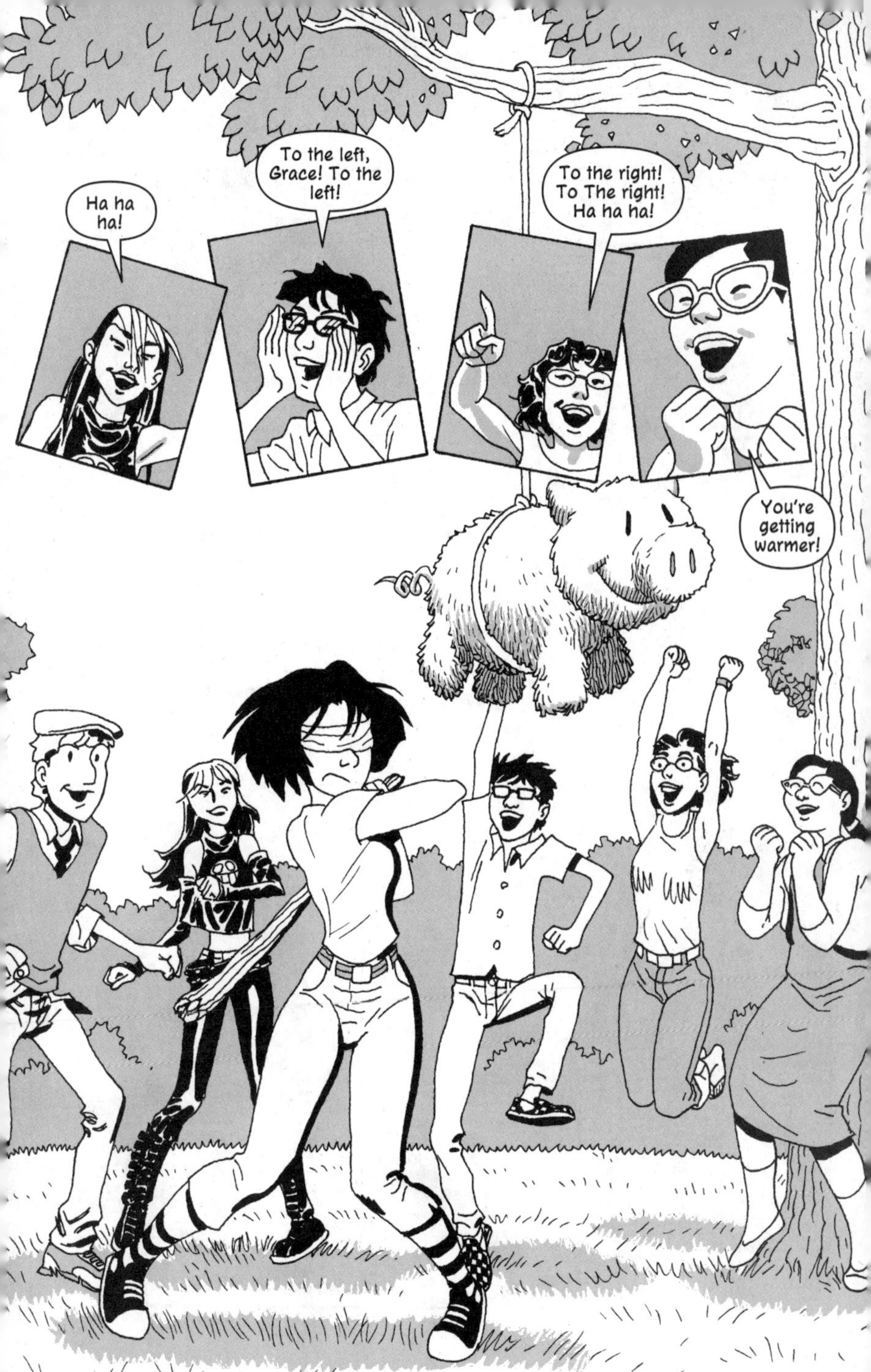
Ha ha ha!
To the left, Grace! To the left!
To the right! To The right! Ha ha ha!
You're getting warmer!

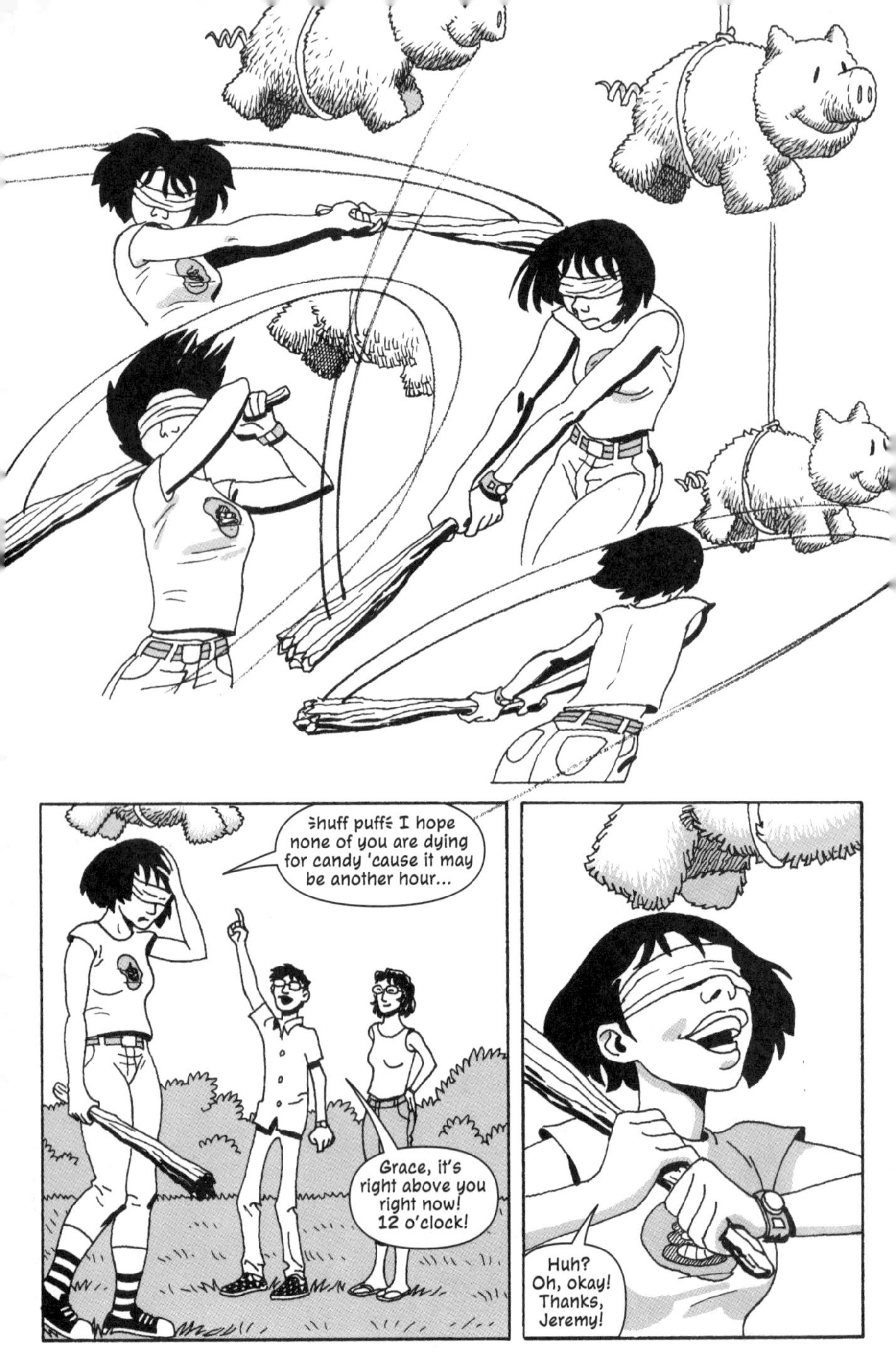

≈huff puff≈ I hope none of you are dying for candy 'cause it may be another hour...
Grace, it's right above you right now! 12 o'clock!
Huh? Oh, okay! Thanks, Jeremy!

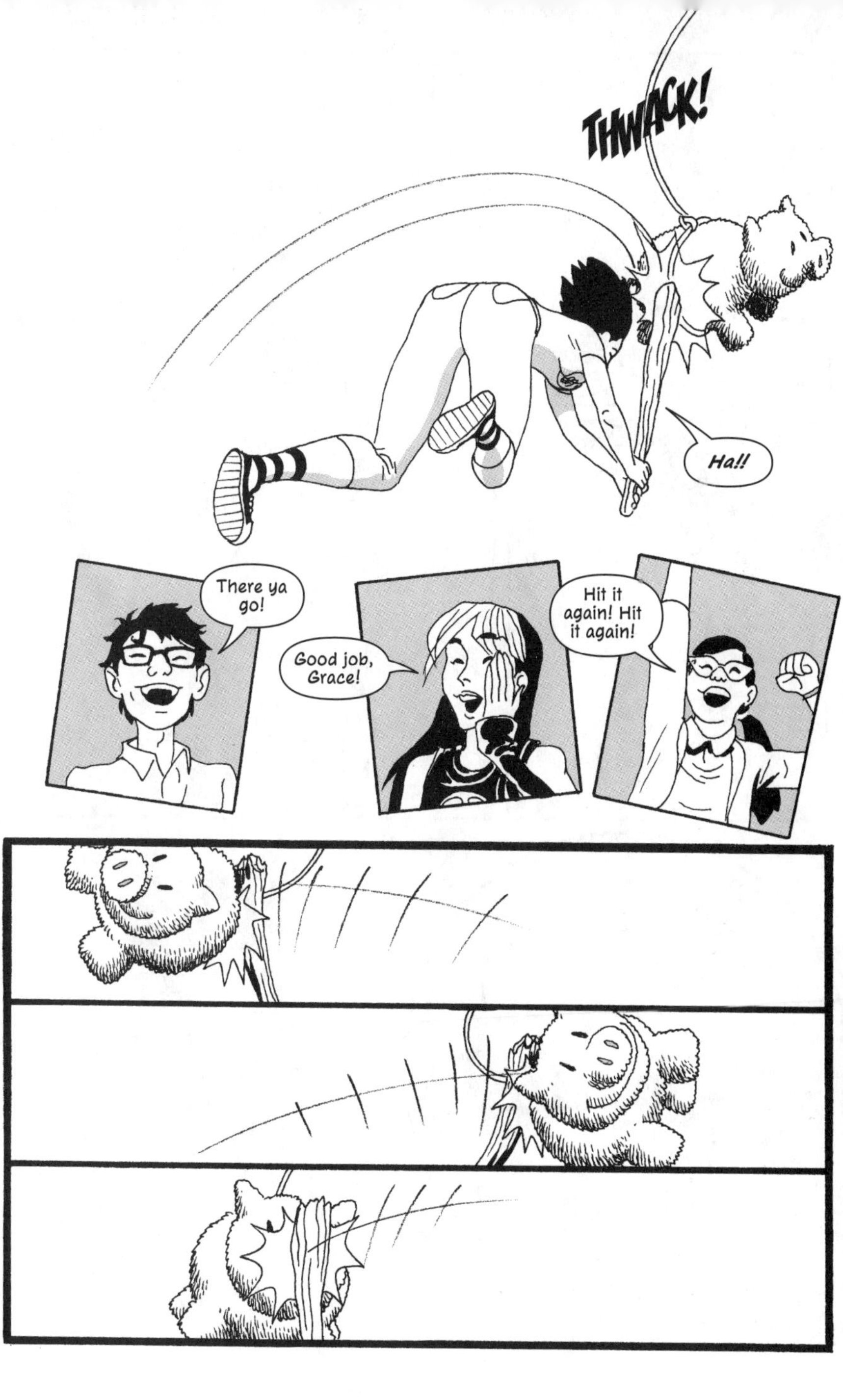
THWACK!
Ha!!
There ya go!
Good job, Grace!
Hit it again! Hit it again!

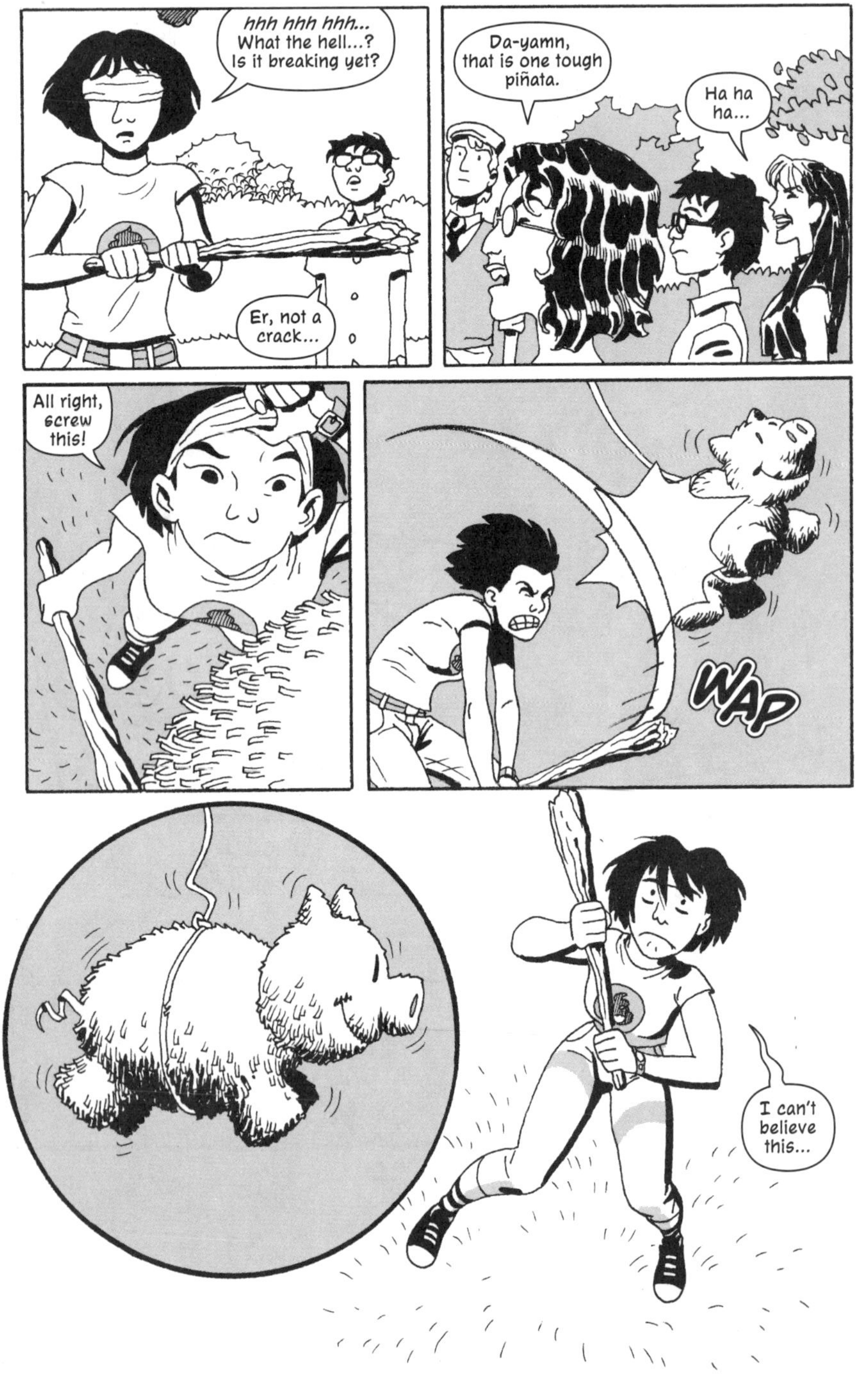
hhh hhh hhh...
What the hell...?
Is it breaking yet?
Er, not a crack...
Da-yamn, that is one tough piñata.
Ha ha ha...
All right, screw this!
WAP
I can't believe this...

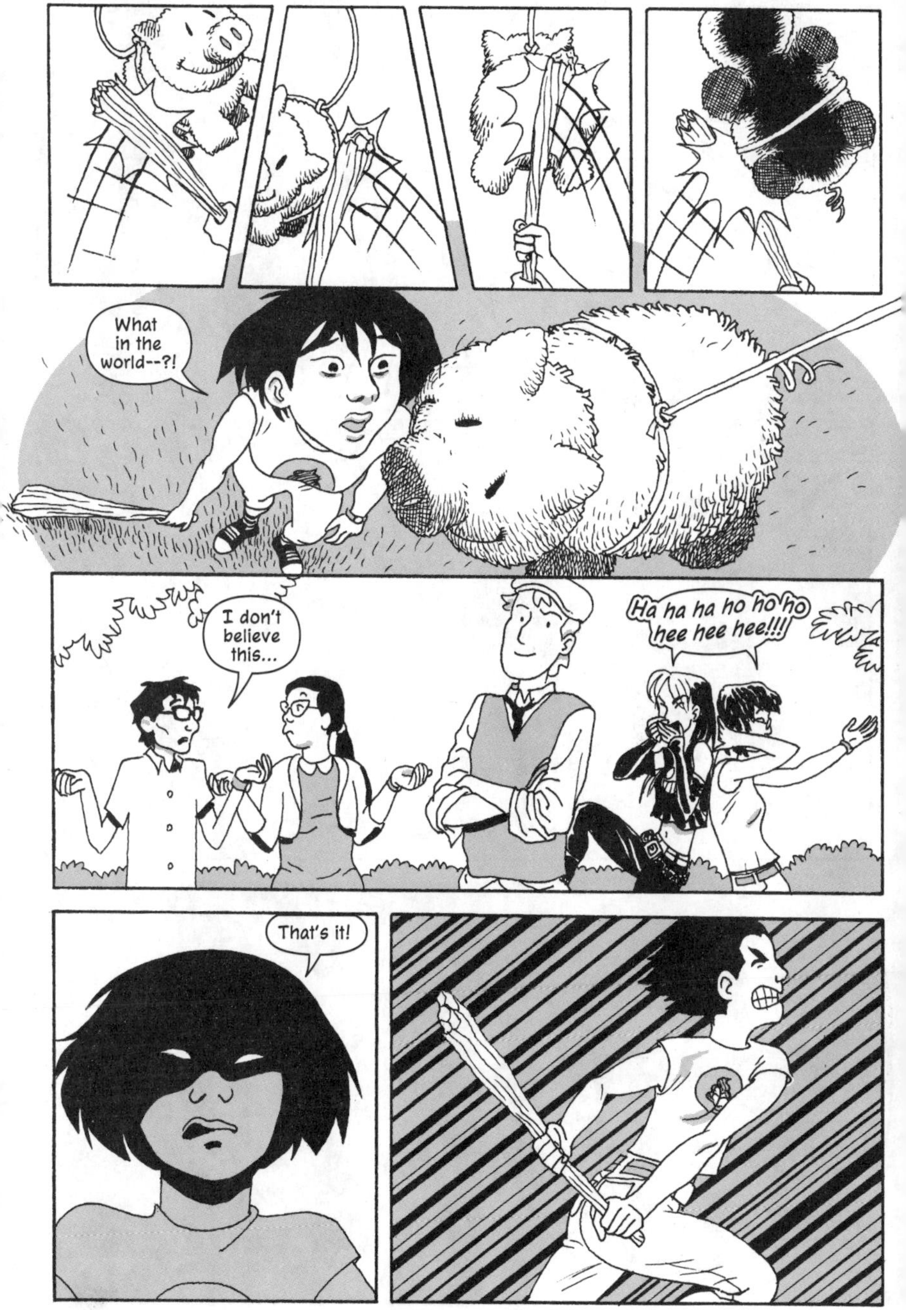
What in the world--?!
I don't believe this...
Ha ha ha ho ho ho hee hee hee!!!
That's it!

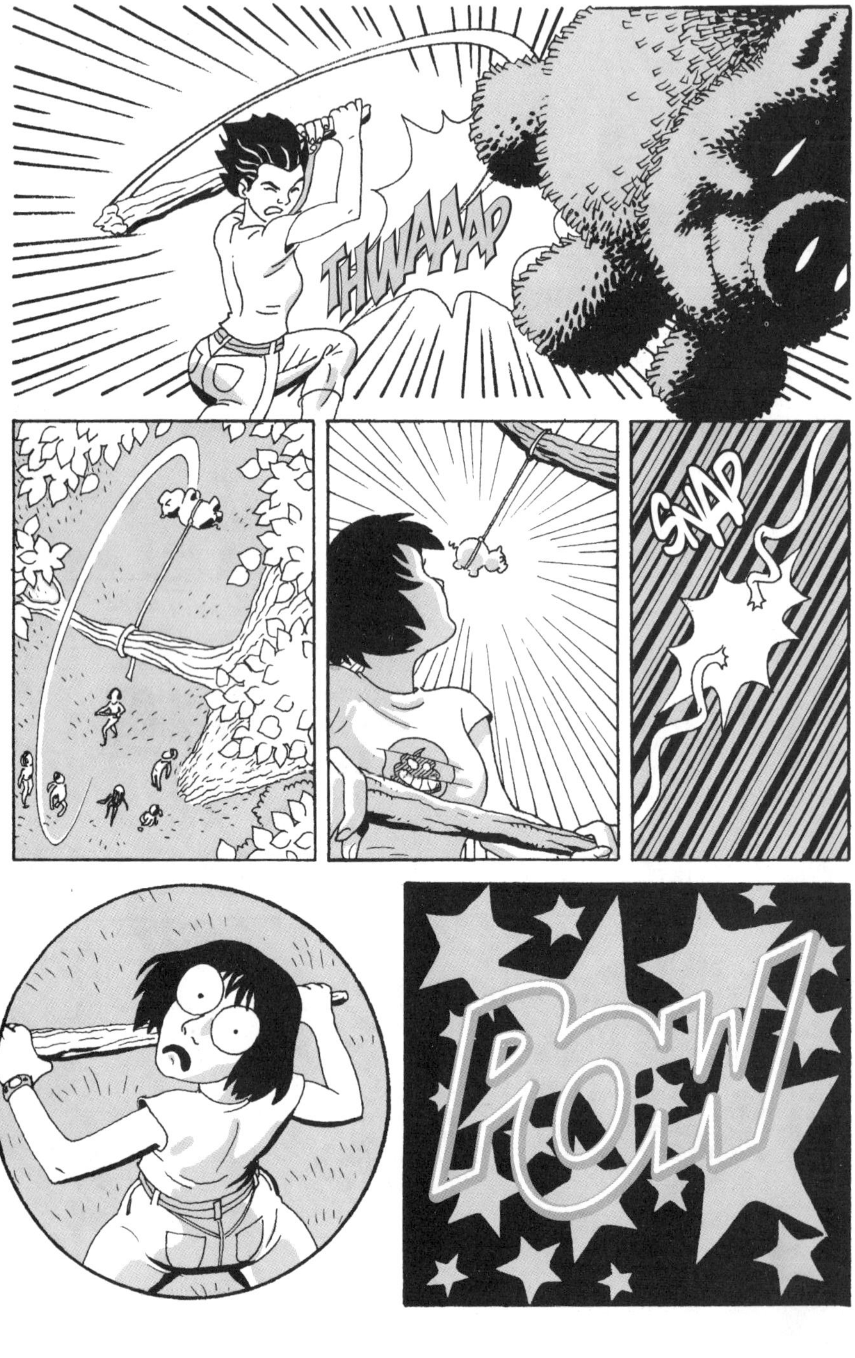

THWAAAP
SNAP
POW

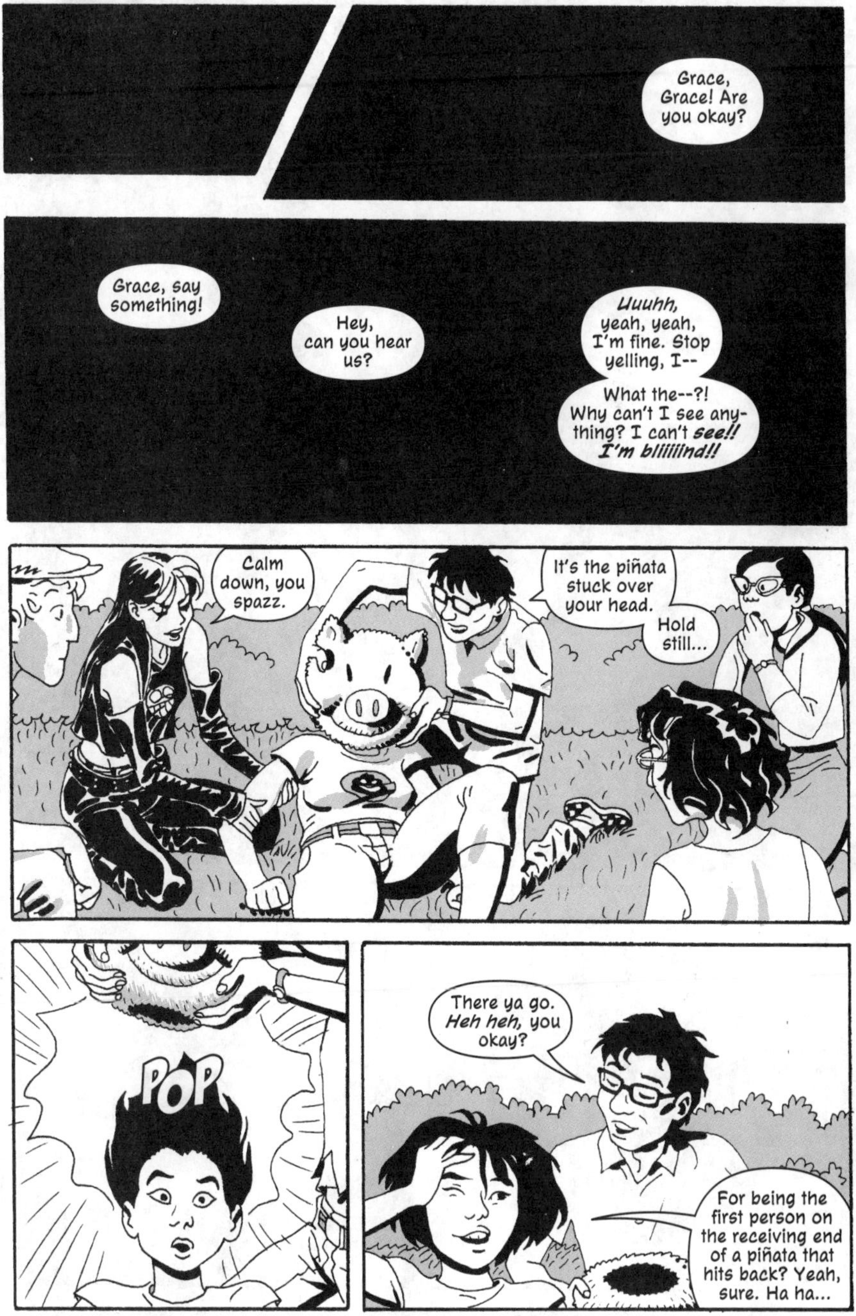
Grace, Grace! Are you okay?
Grace, say something!
Hey, can you hear us?
Uuuhh, yeah, yeah, I'm fine. Stop yelling, I--
What the--?! Why can't I see anything? I can't ***see!! I'm bliiiiind!!***
Calm down, you spazz.
It's the piñata stuck over your head.
Hold still...
POP
There ya go. *Heh heh,* you okay?
For being the first person on the receiving end of a piñata that hits back? Yeah, sure. Ha ha...

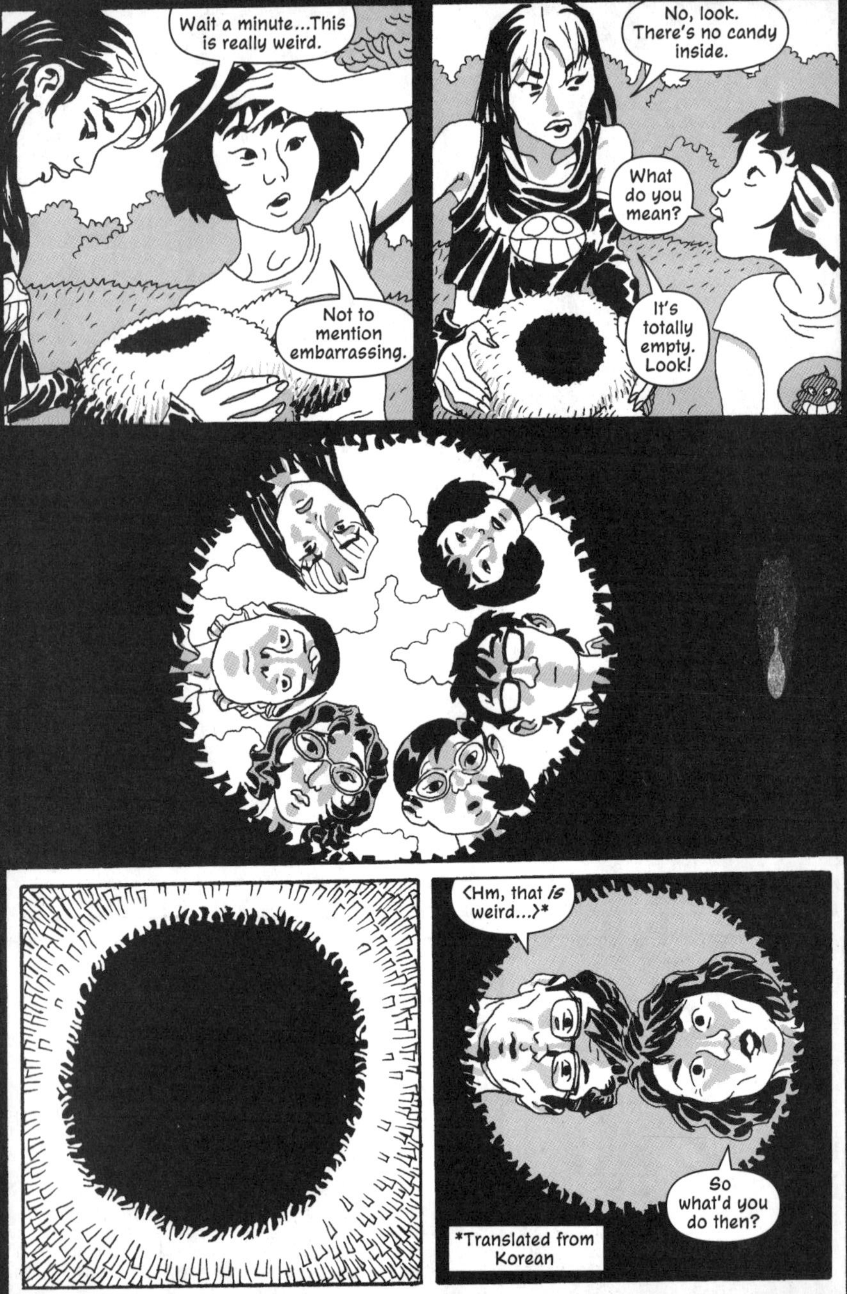
Wait a minute...This is really weird.
Not to mention embarrassing.
No, look. There's no candy inside.
What do you mean?
It's totally empty. Look!
<Hm, that *is* weird...>*
So what'd you do then?
*Translated from Korean

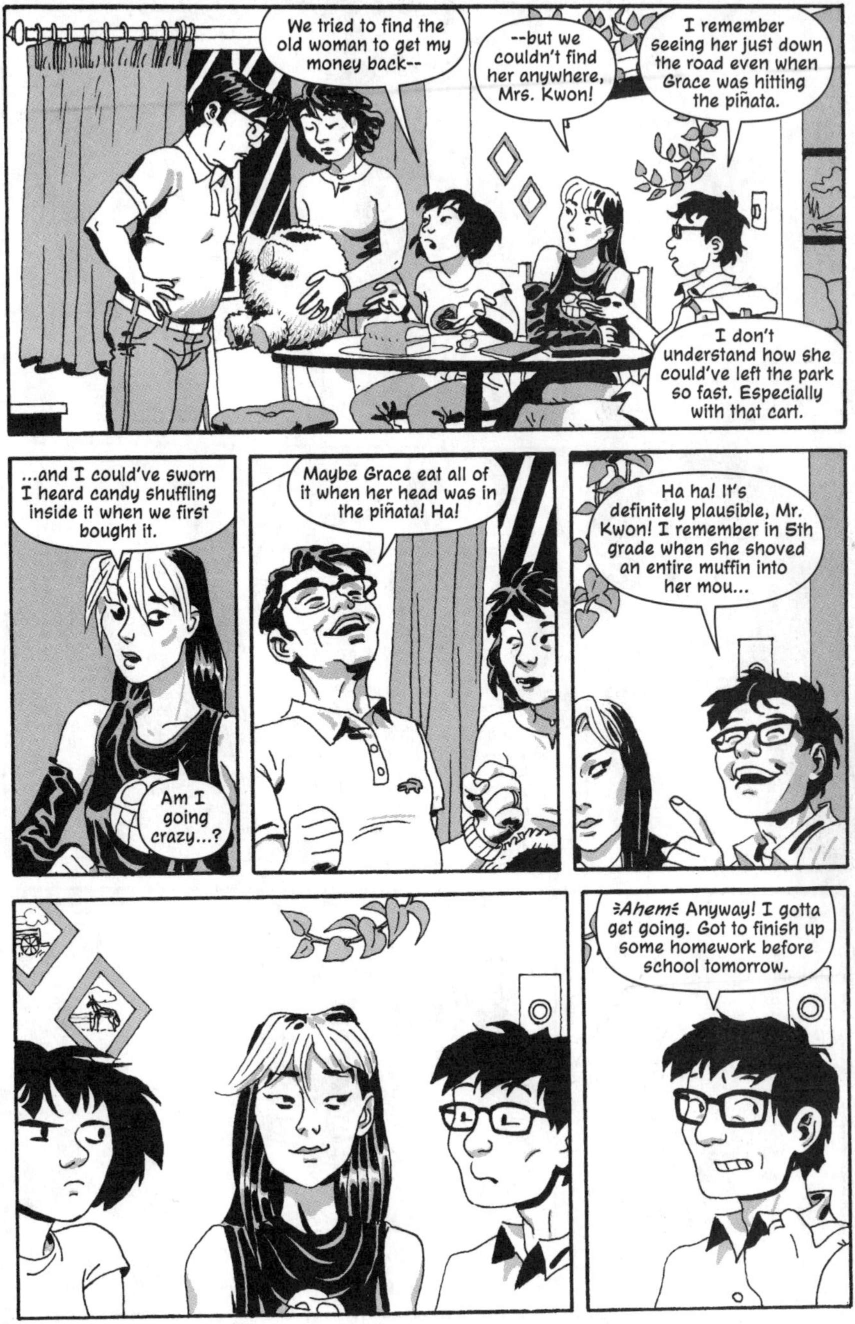
We tried to find the old woman to get my money back--
--but we couldn't find her anywhere, Mrs. Kwon!
I remember seeing her just down the road even when Grace was hitting the piñata.
I don't understand how she could've left the park so fast. Especially with that cart.
...and I could've sworn I heard candy shuffling inside it when we first bought it.
Am I going crazy...?
Maybe Grace eat all of it when her head was in the piñata! Ha!
Ha ha! It's definitely plausible, Mr. Kwon! I remember in 5th grade when she shoved an entire muffin into her mou...
Ahem Anyway! I gotta get going. Got to finish up some homework before school tomorrow.

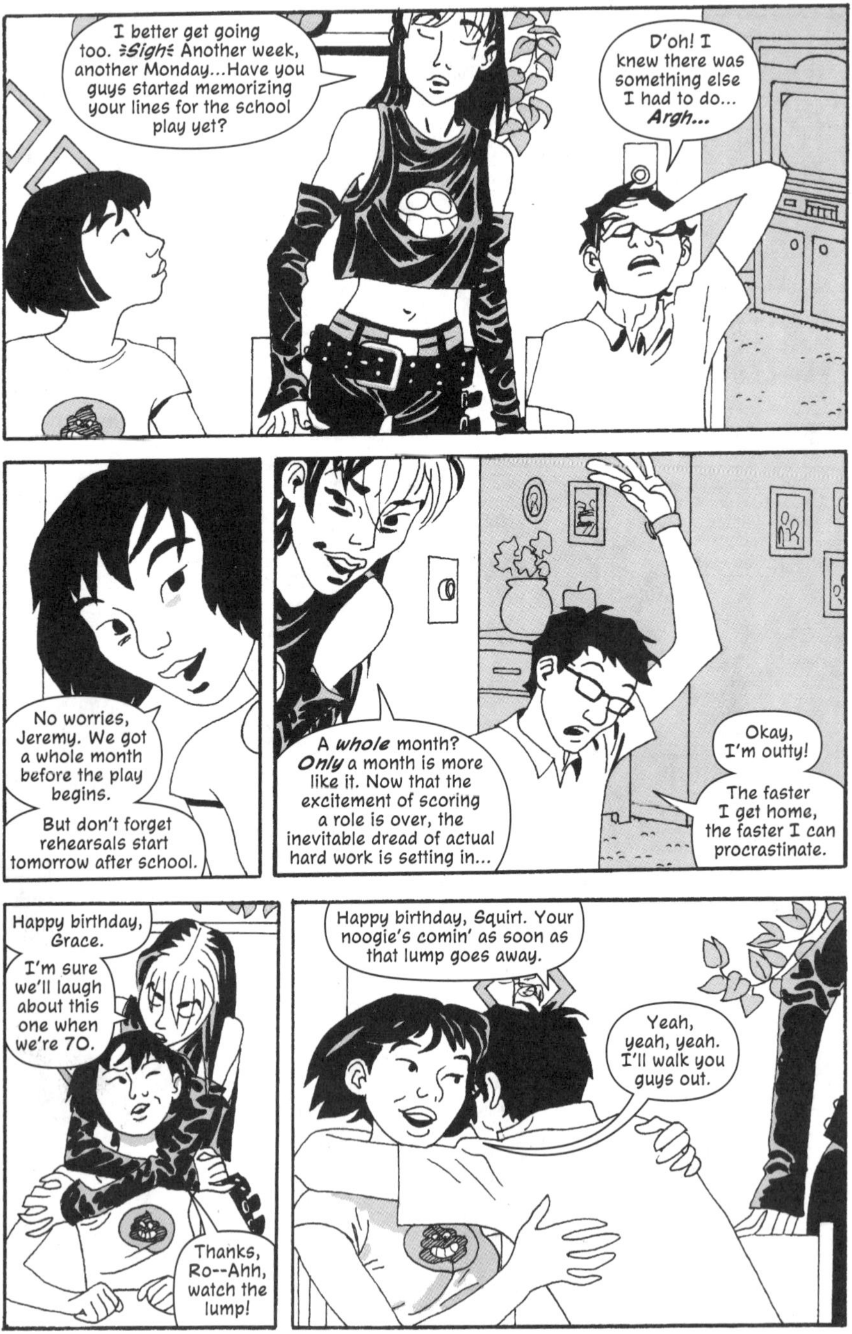
I better get going too. ≶Sigh≶ Another week, another Monday...Have you guys started memorizing your lines for the school play yet?
D'oh! I knew there was something else I had to do... *Argh...*
No worries, Jeremy. We got a whole month before the play begins.
But don't forget rehearsals start tomorrow after school.
A *whole* month? *Only* a month is more like it. Now that the excitement of scoring a role is over, the inevitable dread of actual hard work is setting in...
Okay, I'm outty!
The faster I get home, the faster I can procrastinate.
Happy birthday, Grace.
I'm sure we'll laugh about this one when we're 70.
Thanks, Ro--Ahh, watch the lump!
Happy birthday, Squirt. Your noogie's comin' as soon as that lump goes away.
Yeah, yeah, yeah. I'll walk you guys out.

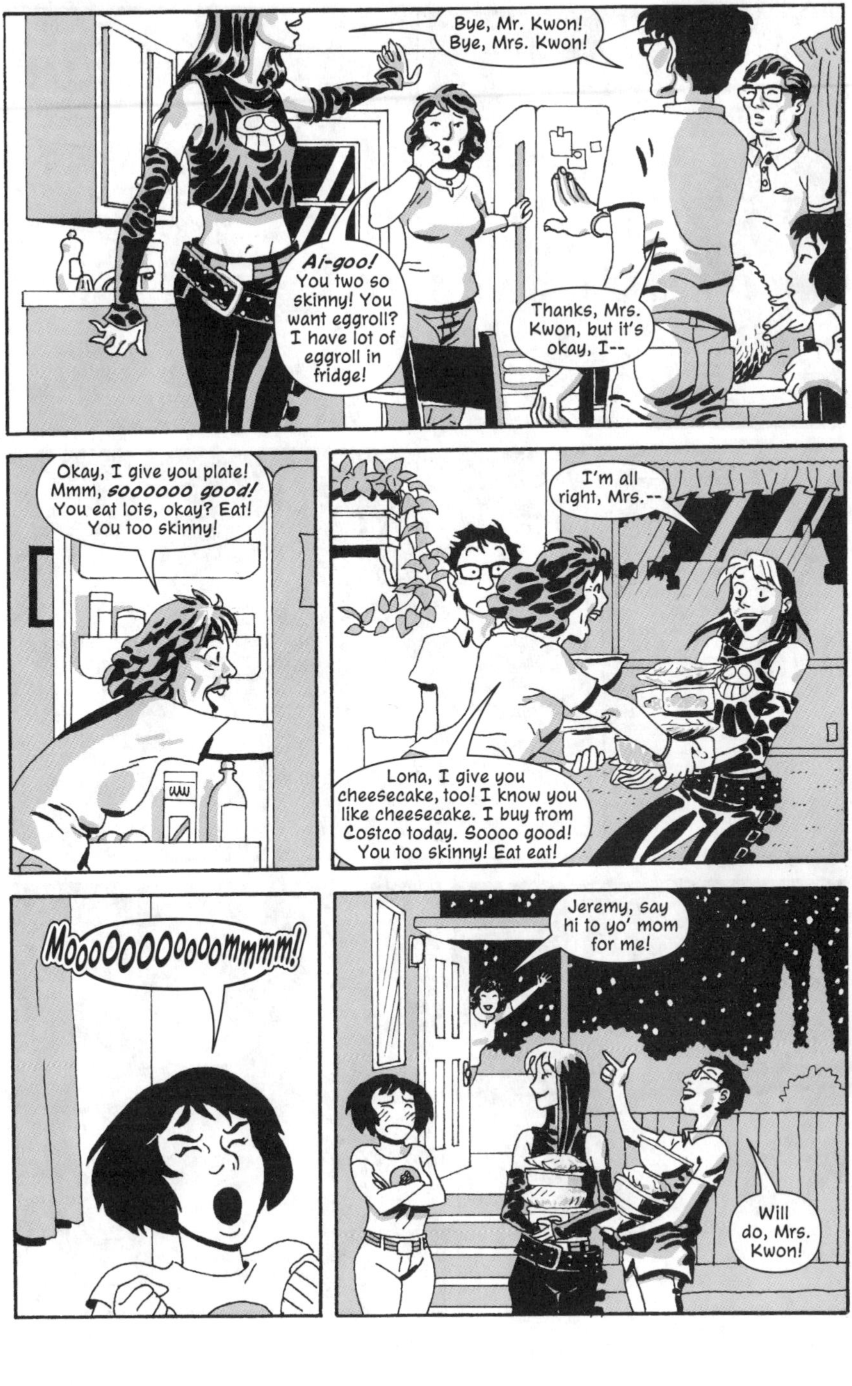
Bye, Mr. Kwon!
Bye, Mrs. Kwon!
Ai-goo! You two so skinny! You want eggroll? I have lot of eggroll in fridge!
Thanks, Mrs. Kwon, but it's okay, I--
Okay, I give you plate! Mmm, soooooo good! You eat lots, okay? Eat! You too skinny!
I'm all right, Mrs.--
Lona, I give you cheesecake, too! I know you like cheesecake. I buy from Costco today. Soooo good! You too skinny! Eat eat!
MoooOOOOoooommmm!
Jeremy, say hi to yo' mom for me!
Will do, Mrs. Kwon!

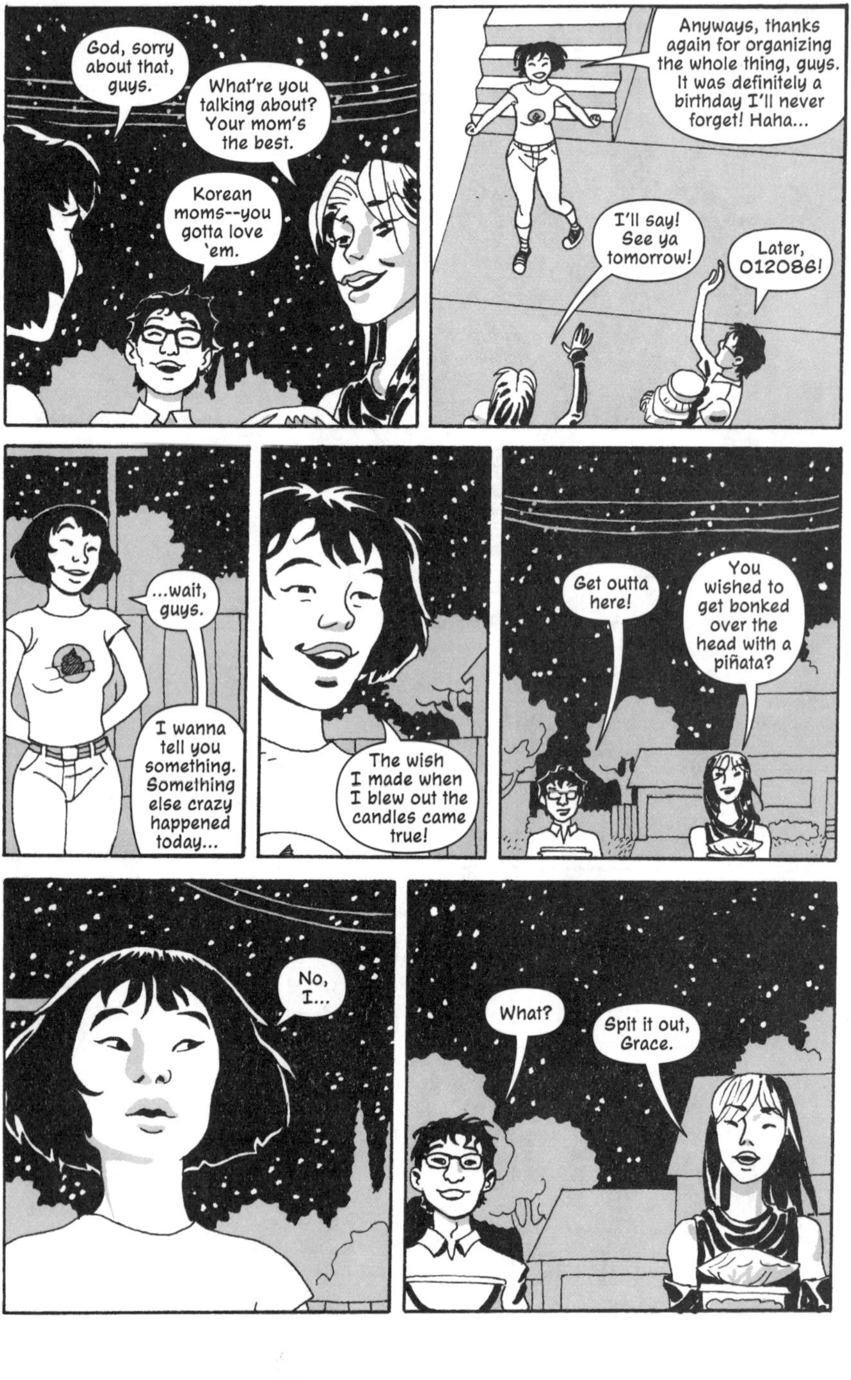
God, sorry about that, guys.
What're you talking about? Your mom's the best.
Korean moms--you gotta love 'em.
Anyways, thanks again for organizing the whole thing, guys. It was definitely a birthday I'll never forget! Haha...
I'll say! See ya tomorrow!
Later, 012086!
...wait, guys.
I wanna tell you something. Something else crazy happened today...
The wish I made when I blew out the candles came true!
Get outta here!
You wished to get bonked over the head with a piñata?
No, I...
What?
Spit it out, Grace.

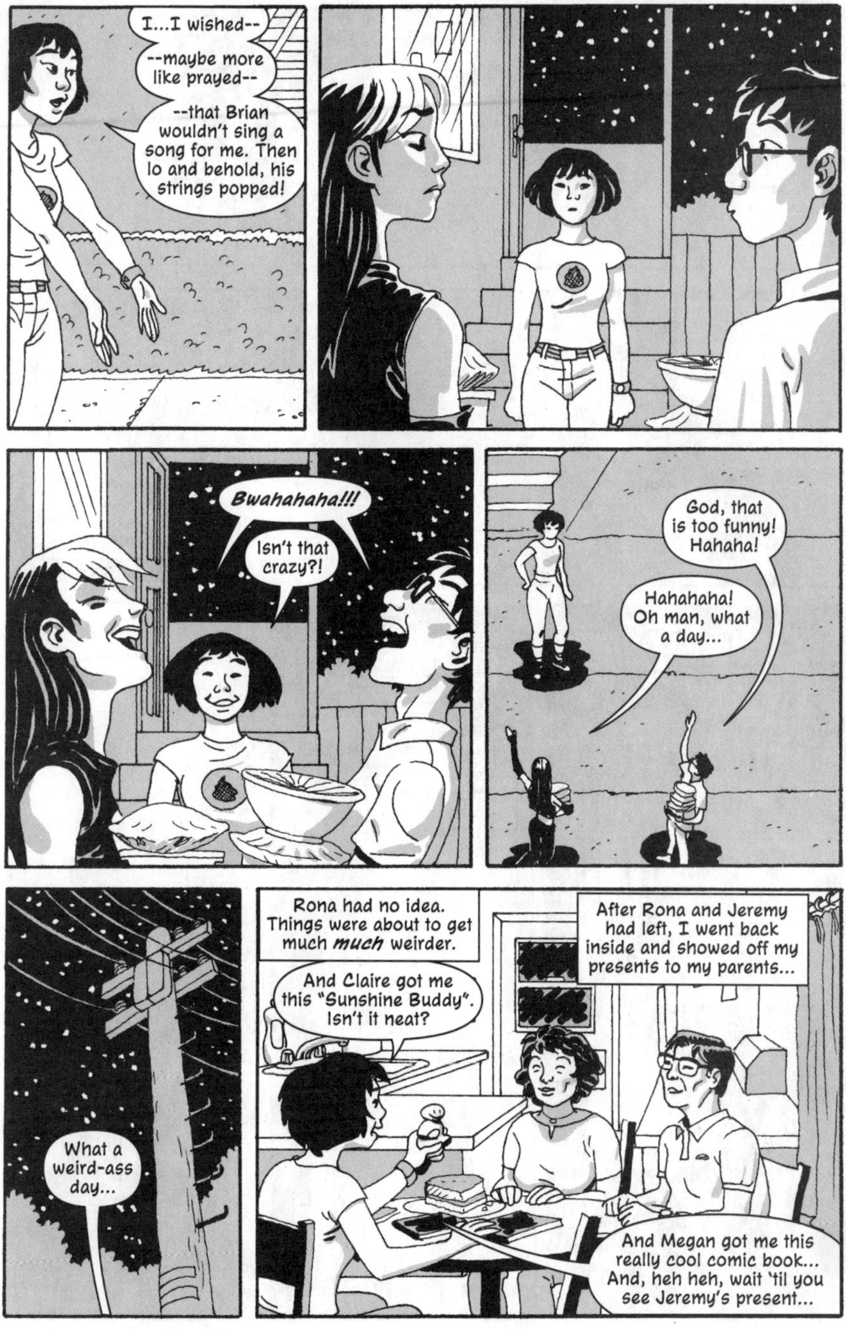
I...I wished--
--maybe more like prayed--
--that Brian wouldn't sing a song for me. Then lo and behold, his strings popped!
Bwahahaha!!!
Isn't that crazy?!
God, that is too funny! Hahaha!
Hahahaha! Oh man, what a day...
What a weird-ass day...
Rona had no idea. Things were about to get much *much* weirder.
After Rona and Jeremy had left, I went back inside and showed off my presents to my parents...
And Claire got me this "Sunshine Buddy". Isn't it neat?
And Megan got me this really cool comic book... And, heh heh, wait 'til you see Jeremy's present...

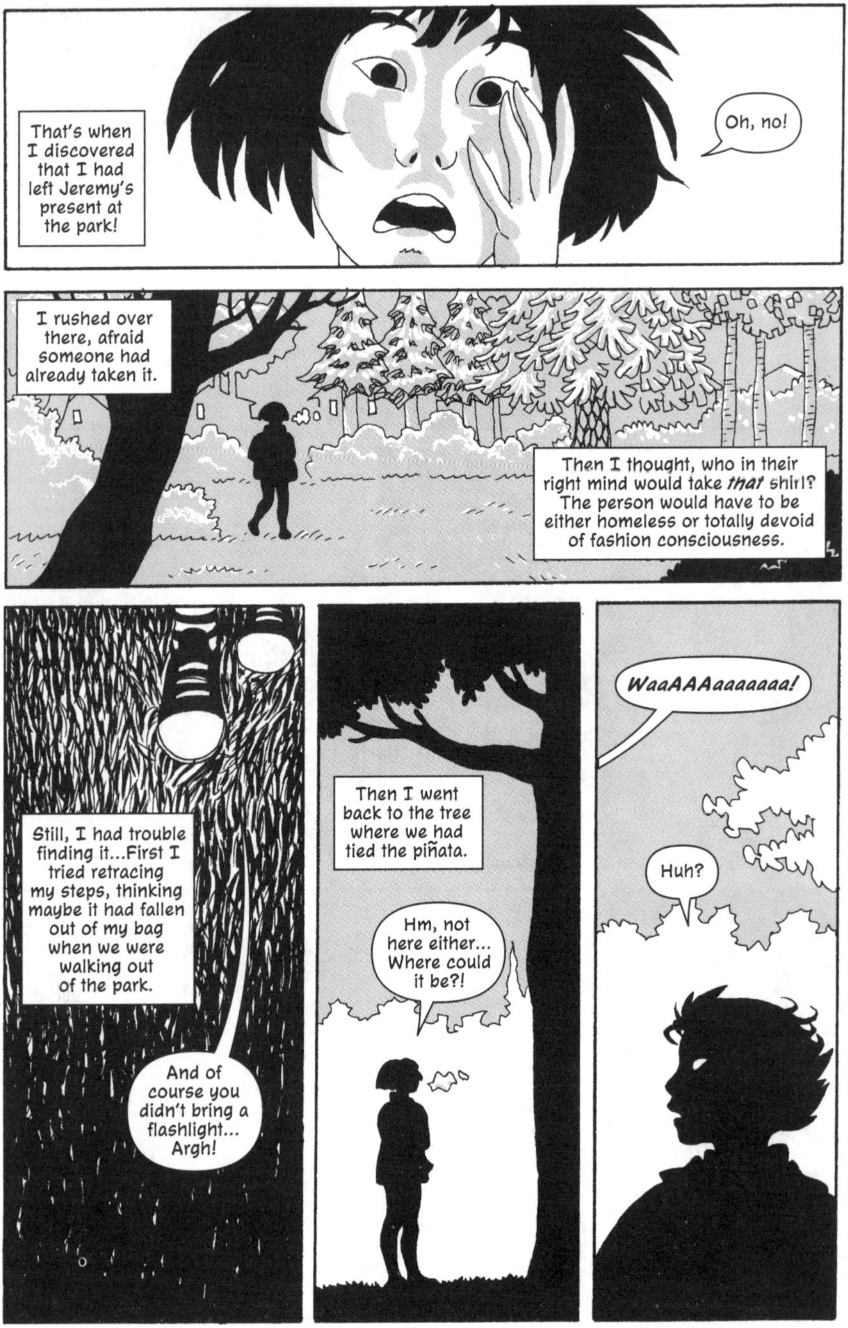
That's when I discovered that I had left Jeremy's present at the park!
Oh, no!
I rushed over there, afraid someone had already taken it.
Then I thought, who in their right mind would take *that* shirt? The person would have to be either homeless or totally devoid of fashion consciousness.
Still, I had trouble finding it...First I tried retracing my steps, thinking maybe it had fallen out of my bag when we were walking out of the park.
And of course you didn't bring a flashlight... Argh!
Then I went back to the tree where we had tied the piñata.
Hm, not here either... Where could it be?!
WaaAAAaaaaaaa!
Huh?

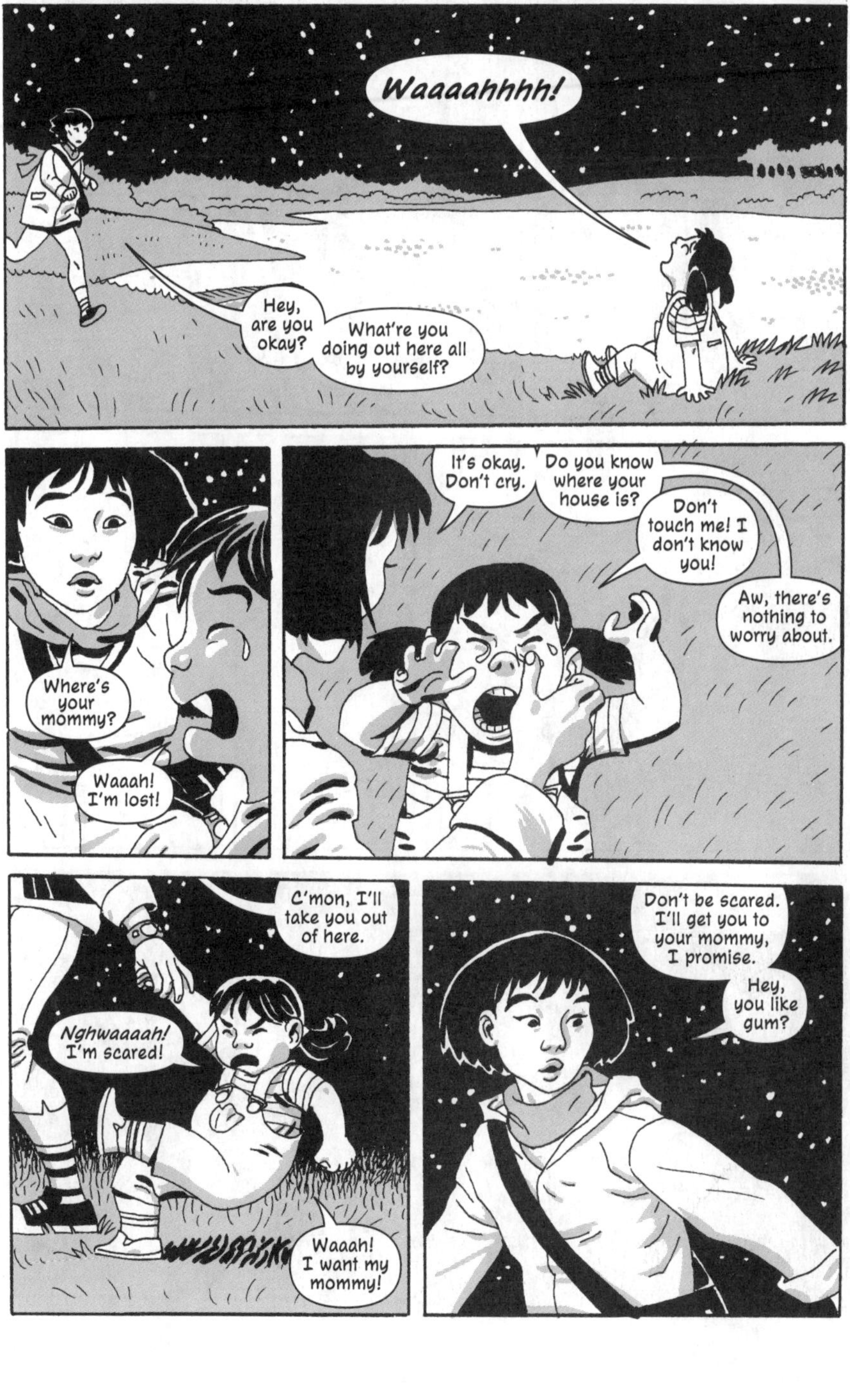
Waaaahhhh!
Hey, are you okay?
What're you doing out here all by yourself?
Where's your mommy?
Waaah! I'm lost!
It's okay. Don't cry.
Do you know where your house is?
Don't touch me! I don't know you!
Aw, there's nothing to worry about.
C'mon, I'll take you out of here.
Nghwaaaah! I'm scared!
Waaah! I want my mommy!
Don't be scared. I'll get you to your mommy, I promise.
Hey, you like gum?

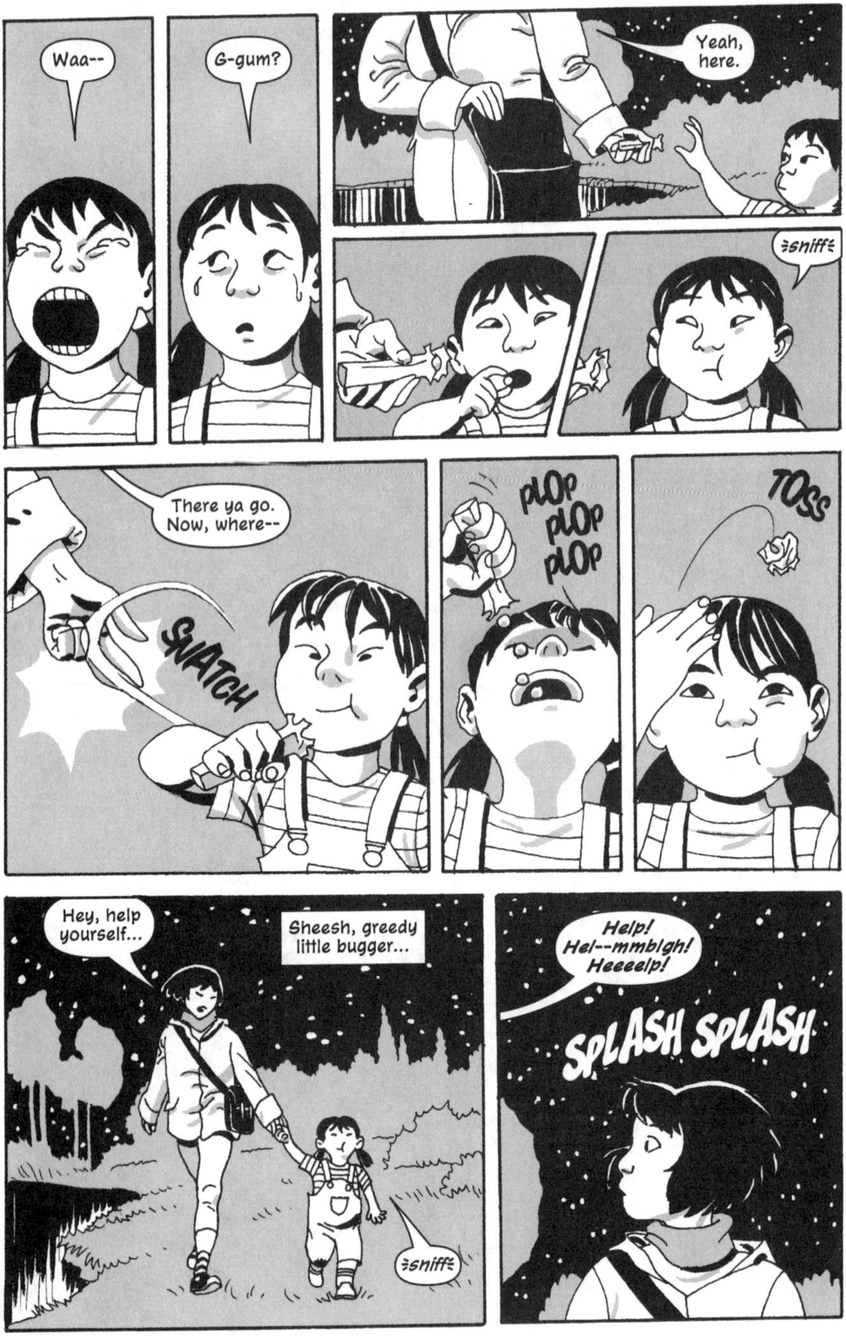

Waa--
G-gum?
Yeah, here.
sniff
There ya go. Now, where--
SWATCH
PLOP PLOP PLOP
TOSS
Hey, help yourself...
Sheesh, greedy little bugger...
sniff
Help! Hel--mmblgh! Heeeelp!
SPLASH SPLASH

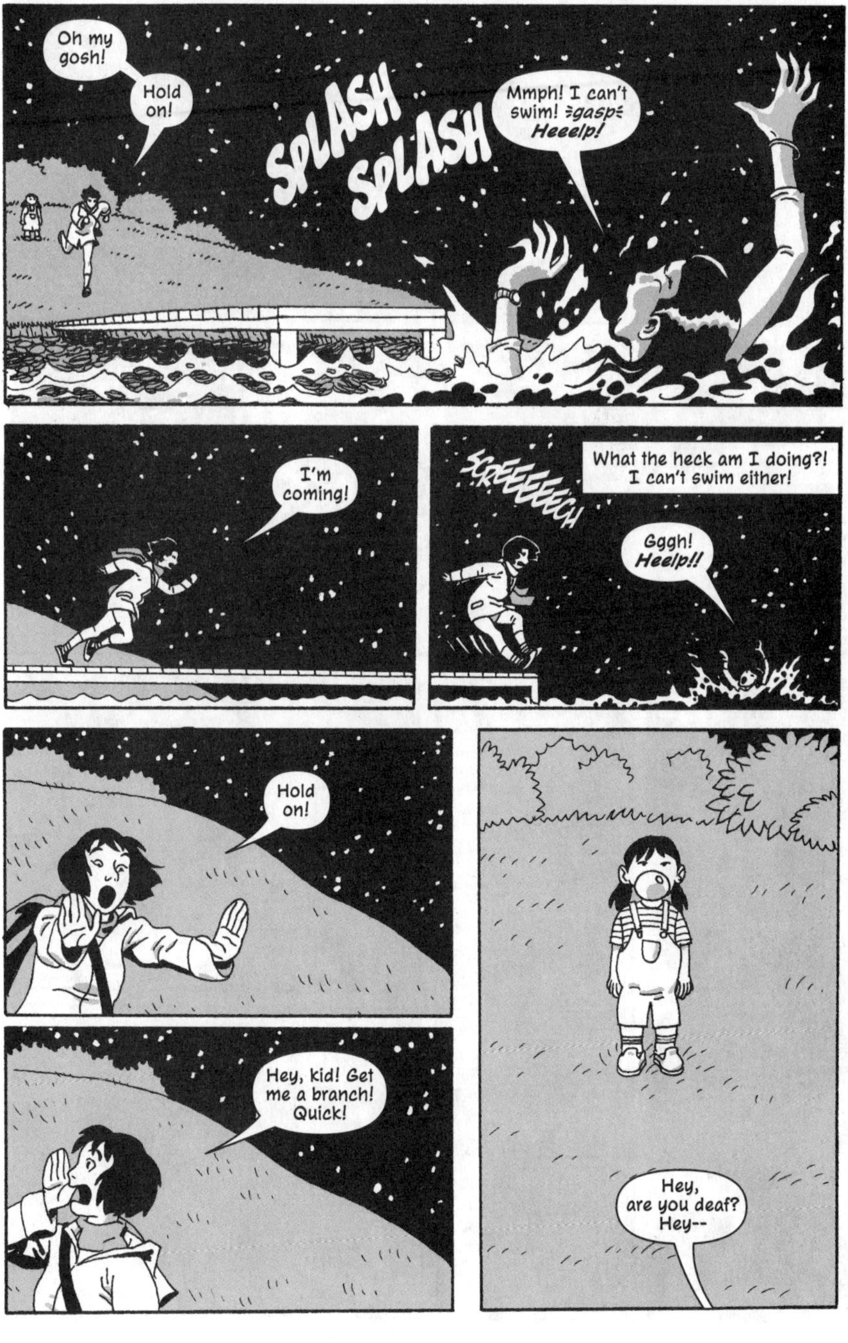
Oh my gosh!
Hold on!
SPLASH
SPLASH
Mmph! I can't swim! gasp Heeelp!
I'm coming!
SCREEEEEECH
What the heck am I doing?! I can't swim either!
Gggh! Heelp!!
Hold on!
Hey, kid! Get me a branch! Quick!
Hey, are you deaf? Hey--

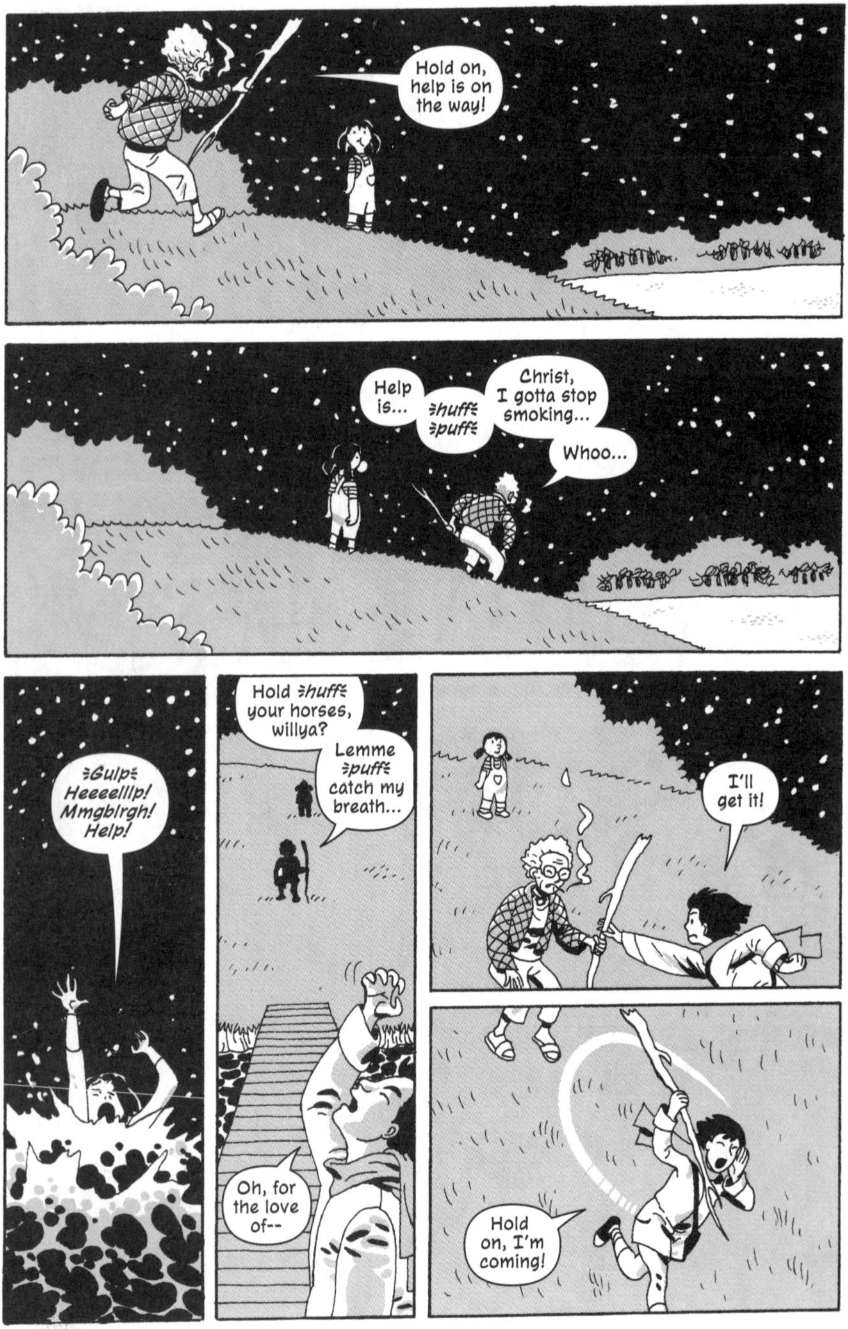

Hold on, help is on the way!
Help is...
≡huff≡ ≡puff≡
Christ, I gotta stop smoking...
Whoo...
≡Gulp≡ Heeeelllp! Mmgblrgh! Help!
Hold ≡huff≡ your horses, willya?
Lemme ≡puff≡ catch my breath...
Oh, for the love of--
I'll get it!
Hold on, I'm coming!

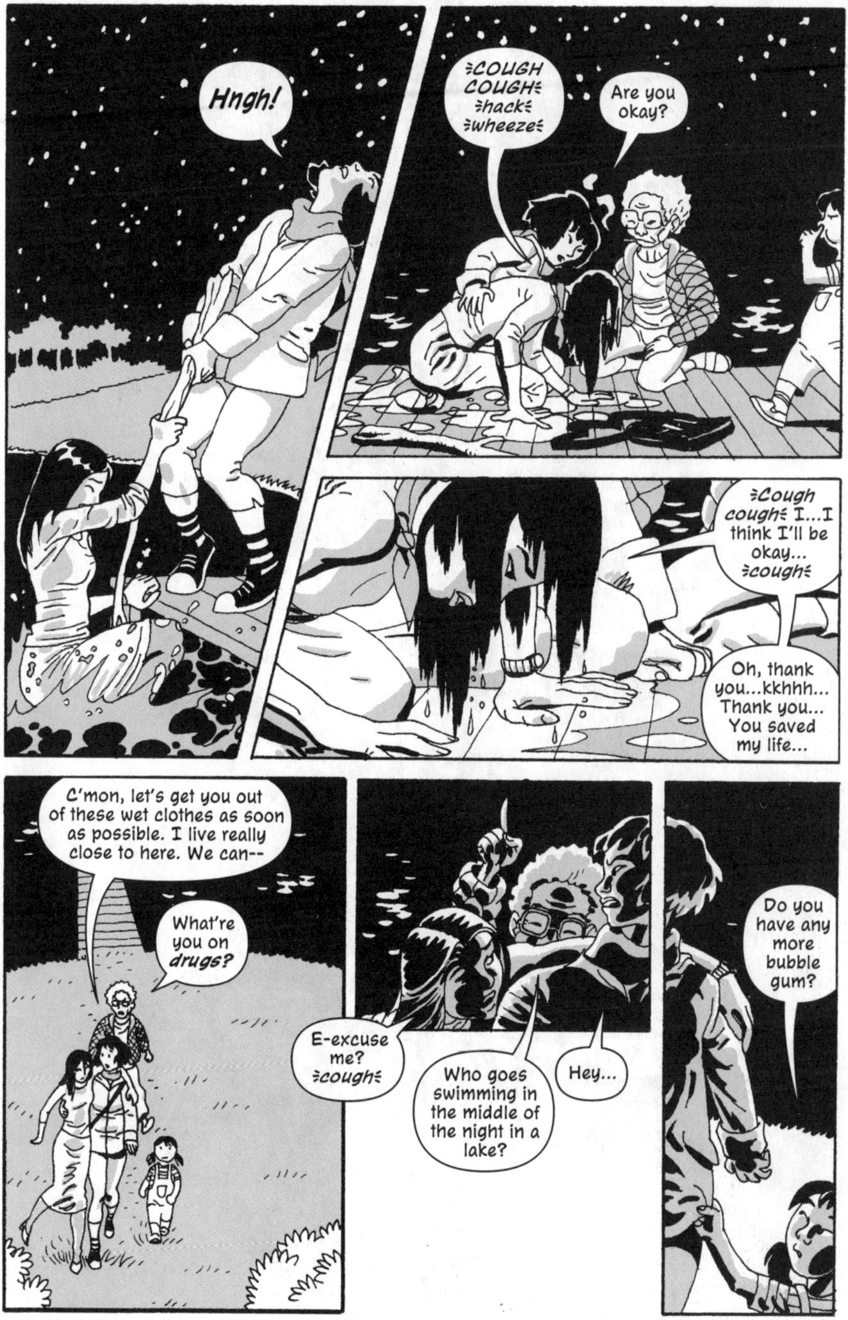

Hngh!
COUGH COUGH hack wheeze
Are you okay?
Cough cough I...I think I'll be okay... cough
Oh, thank you...kkhhh... Thank you... You saved my life...
C'mon, let's get you out of these wet clothes as soon as possible. I live really close to here. We can--
What're you on *drugs?*
E-excuse me? cough
Who goes swimming in the middle of the night in a lake?
Hey...
Do you have any more bubble gum?

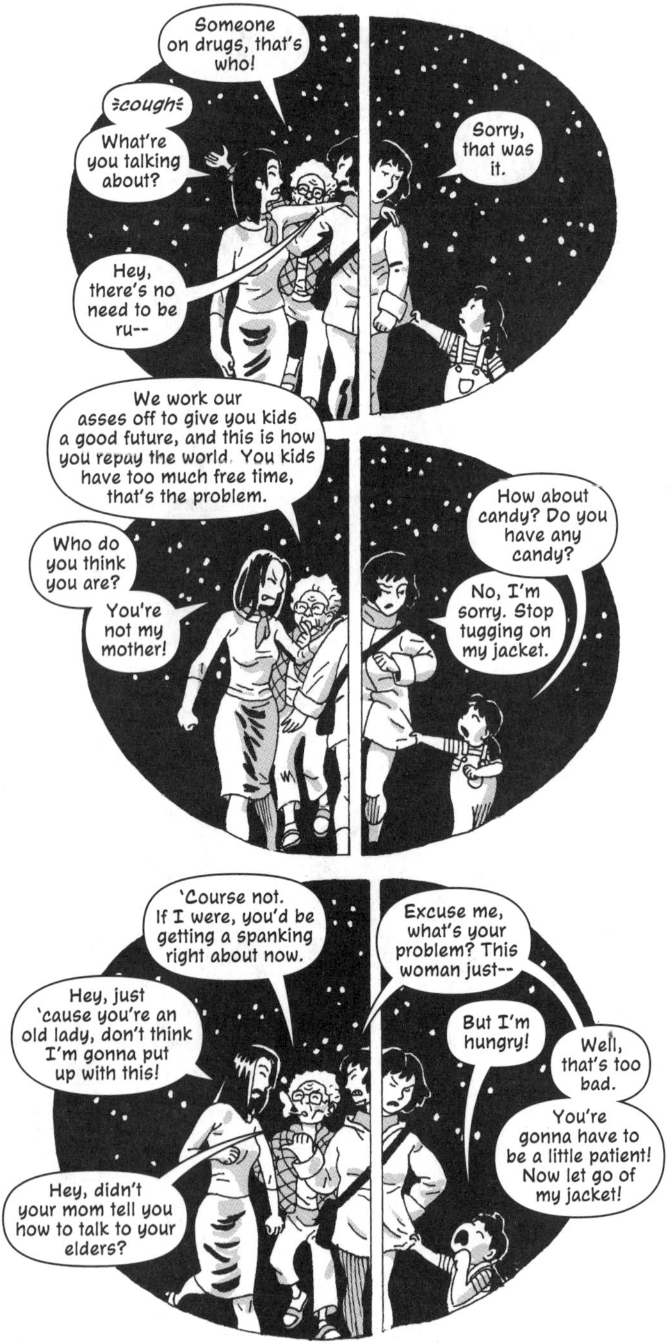
Someone on drugs, that's who!
≡cough≡
What're you talking about?
Hey, there's no need to be ru--
Sorry, that was it.
We work our asses off to give you kids a good future, and this is how you repay the world. You kids have too much free time, that's the problem.
Who do you think you are?
You're not my mother!
How about candy? Do you have any candy?
No, I'm sorry. Stop tugging on my jacket.
'Course not. If I were, you'd be getting a spanking right about now.
Hey, just 'cause you're an old lady, don't think I'm gonna put up with this!
Hey, didn't your mom tell you how to talk to your elders?
Excuse me, what's your problem? This woman just--
But I'm hungry!
Well, that's too bad.
You're gonna have to be a little patient! Now let go of my jacket!

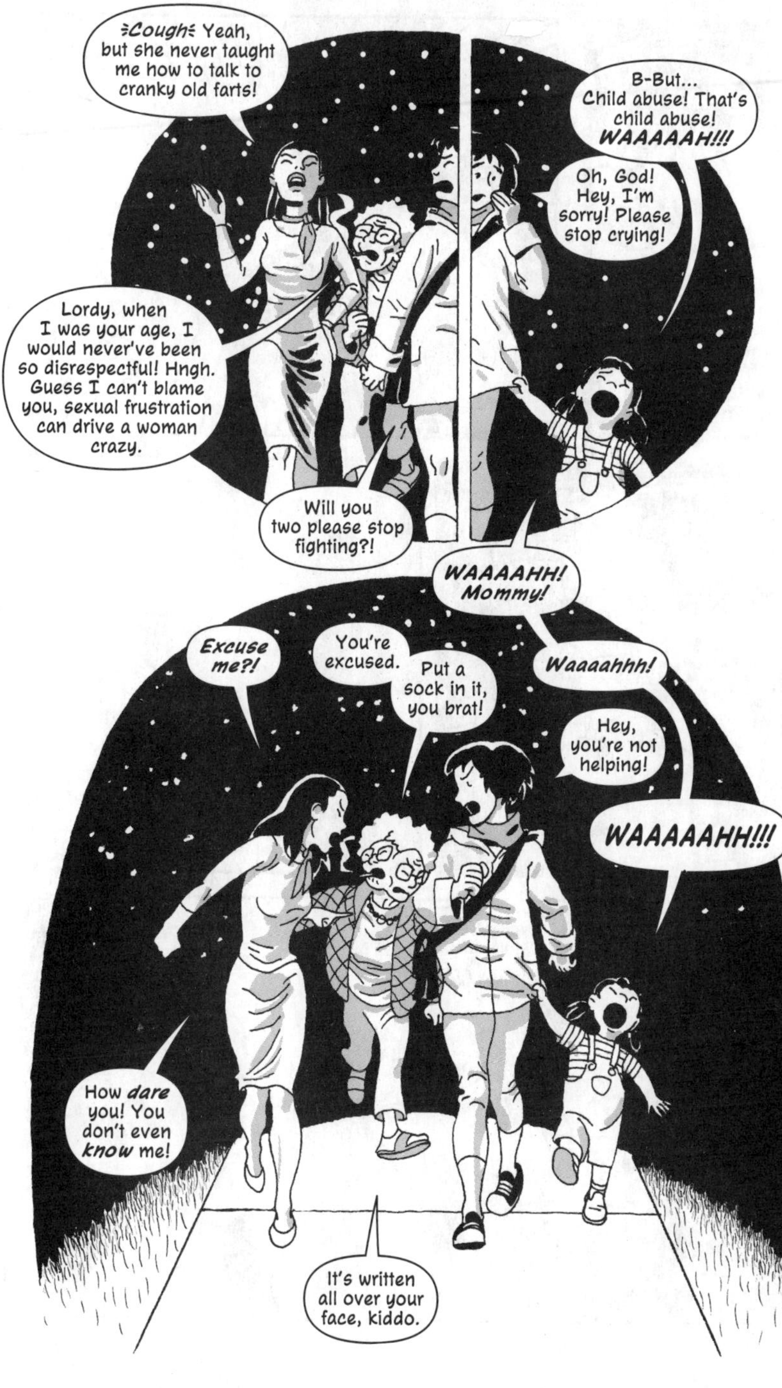

≋Cough≋ Yeah, but she never taught me how to talk to cranky old farts!
B-But... Child abuse! That's child abuse! WAAAAAH!!!
Oh, God! Hey, I'm sorry! Please stop crying!
Lordy, when I was your age, I would never've been so disrespectful! Hngh. Guess I can't blame you, sexual frustration can drive a woman crazy.
Will you two please stop fighting?!
WAAAAHH! Mommy!
Excuse me?!
You're excused.
Put a sock in it, you brat!
Waaaahhh!
Hey, you're not helping!
WAAAAAHH!!!
How dare you! You don't even know me!
It's written all over your face, kiddo.

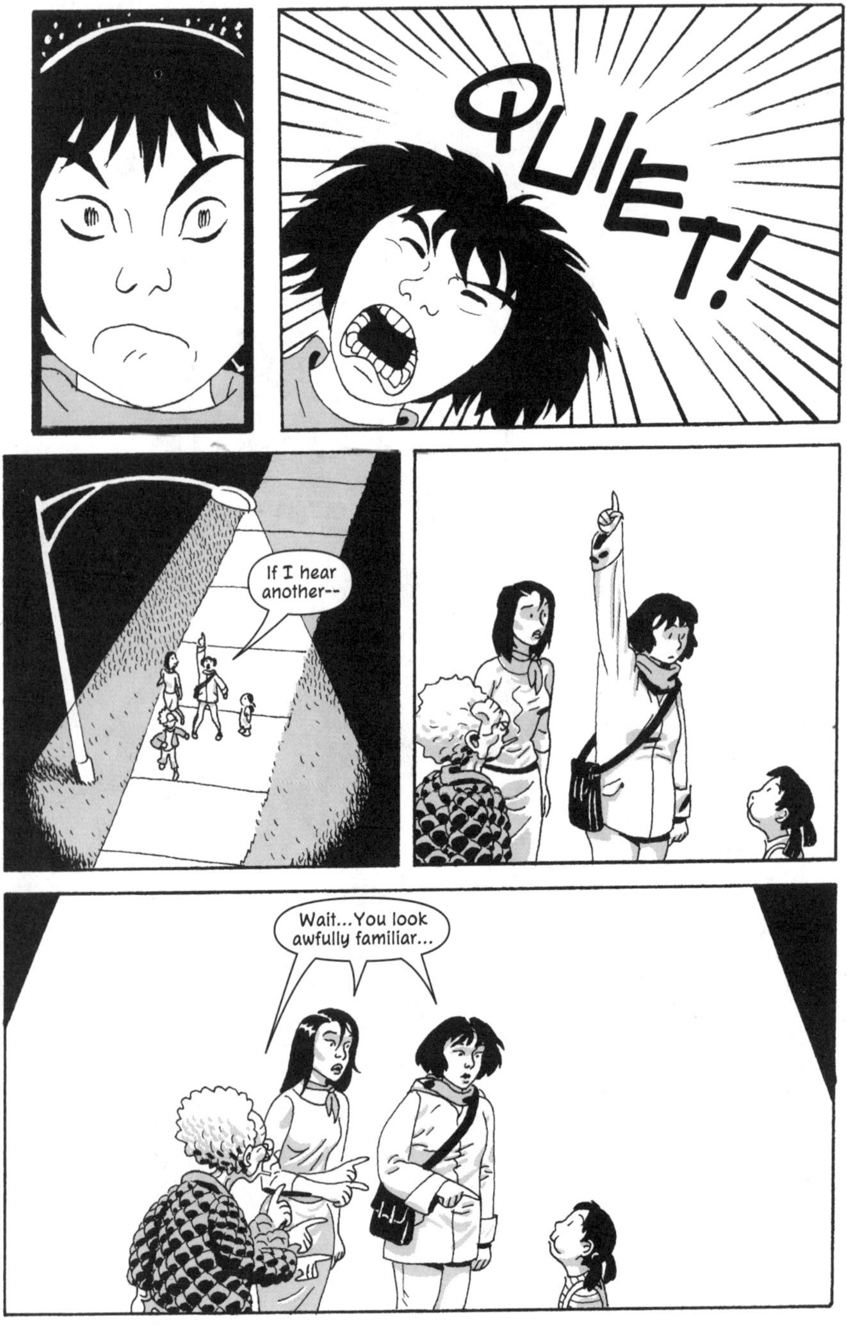
QUIET!
If I hear another--
Wait...You look awfully familiar...

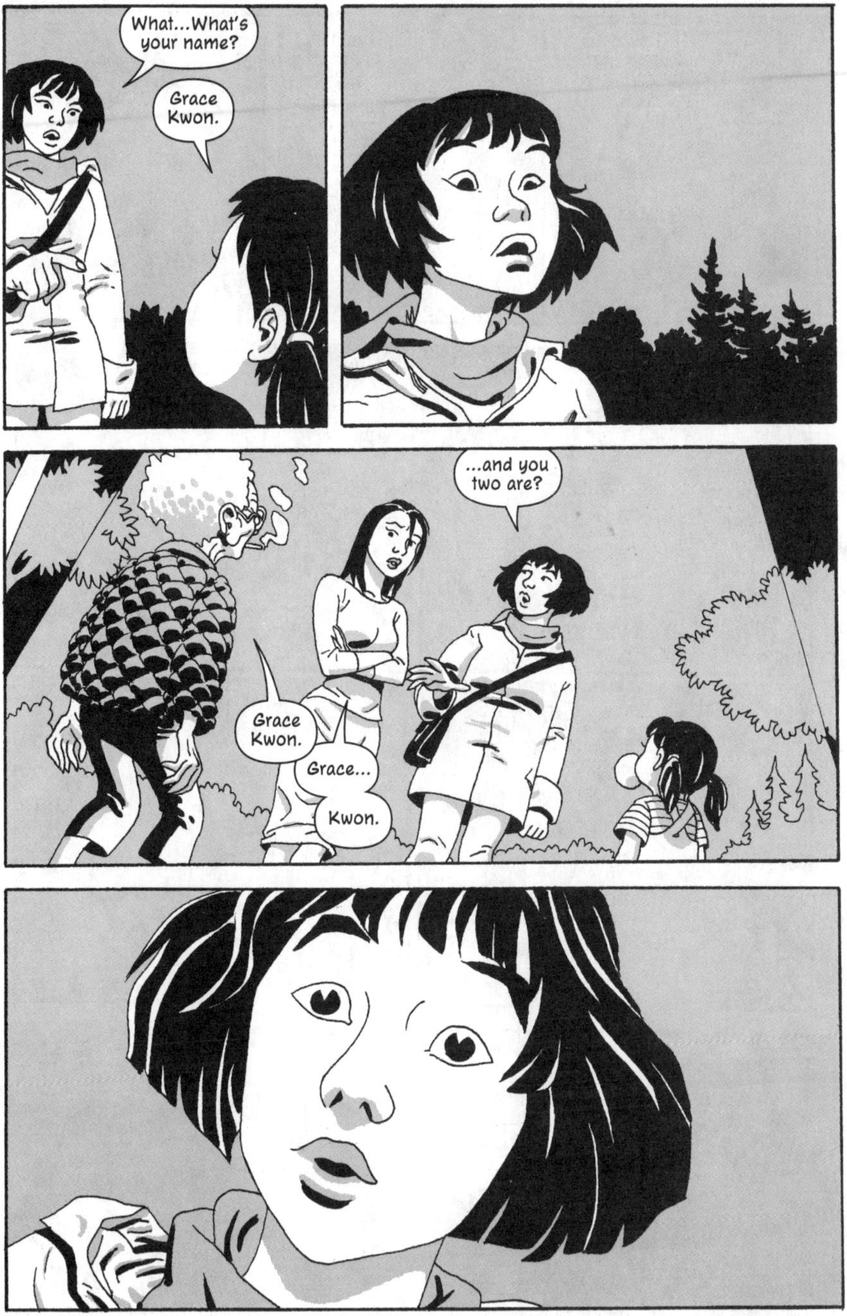
What...What's your name?
Grace Kwon.
...and you two are?
Grace Kwon.
Grace...
Kwon.

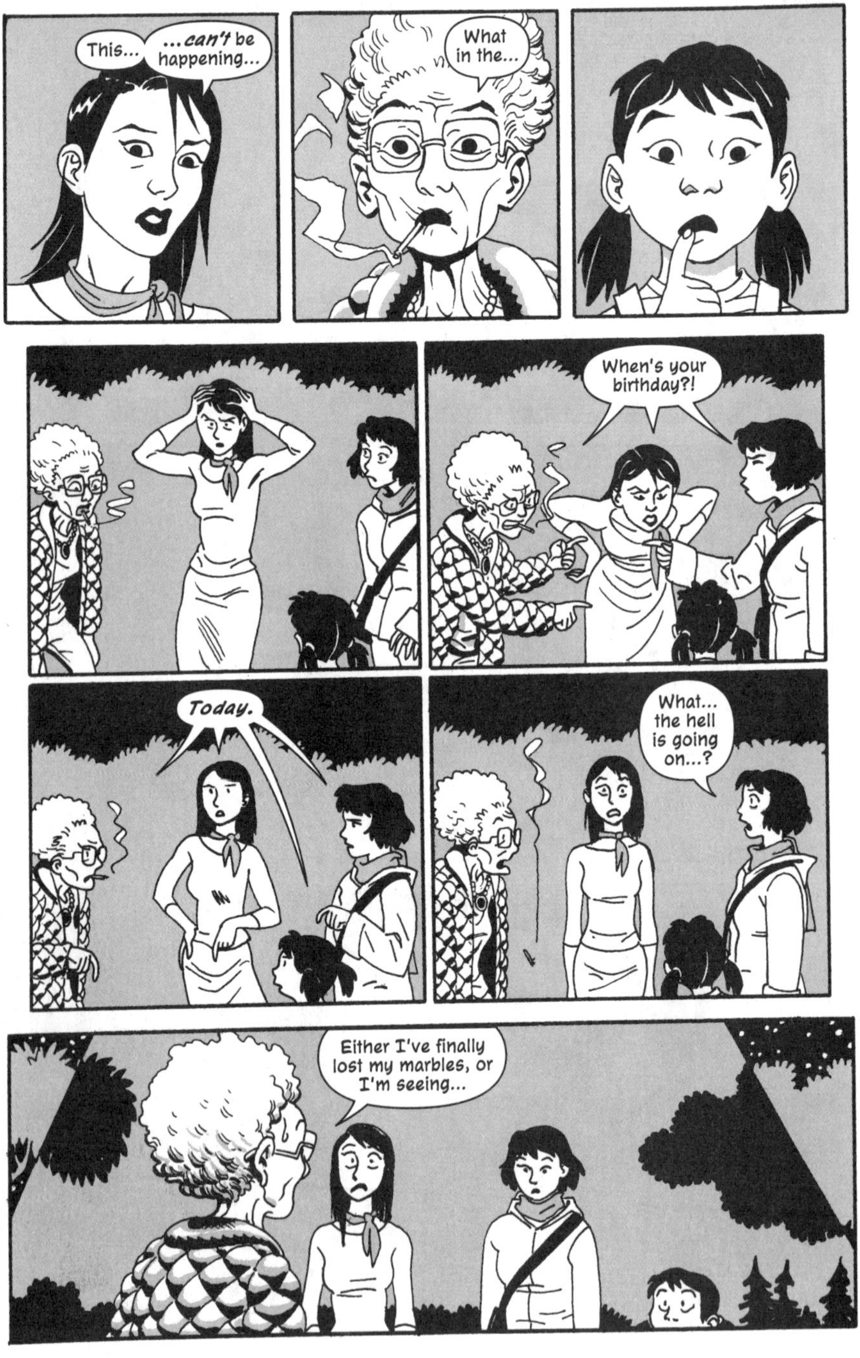
This...
...can't be happening...
What in the...
When's your birthday?!
Today.
What... the hell is going on...?
Either I've finally lost my marbles, or I'm seeing...

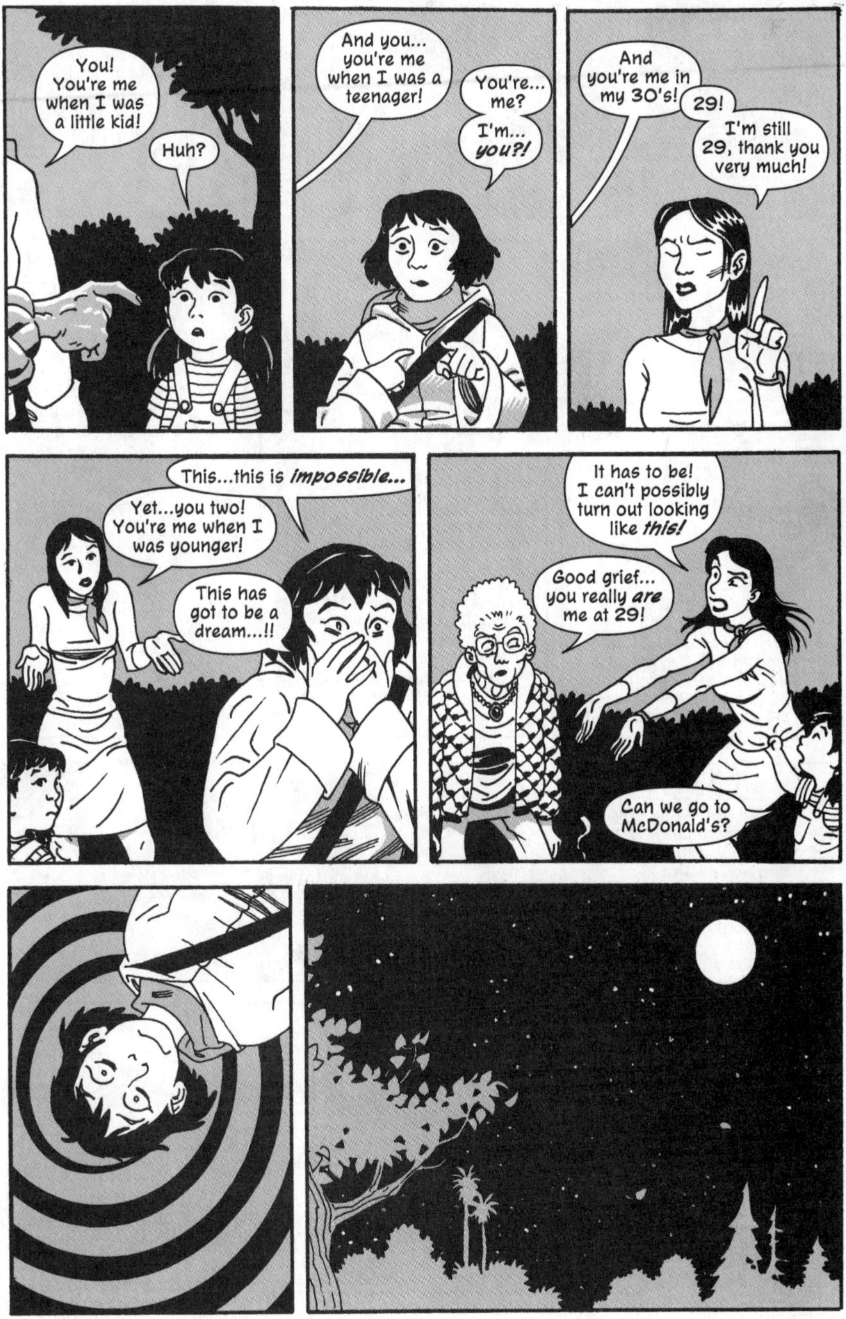

You! You're me when I was a little kid!
Huh?
And you... you're me when I was a teenager!
You're... me?
I'm... *you?!*
And you're me in my 30's!
29!
I'm still 29, thank you very much!
This...this is *impossible...*
Yet...you two! You're me when I was younger!
This has got to be a dream...!!
It has to be! I can't possibly turn out looking like *this!*
Good grief... you really *are* me at 29!
Can we go to McDonald's?

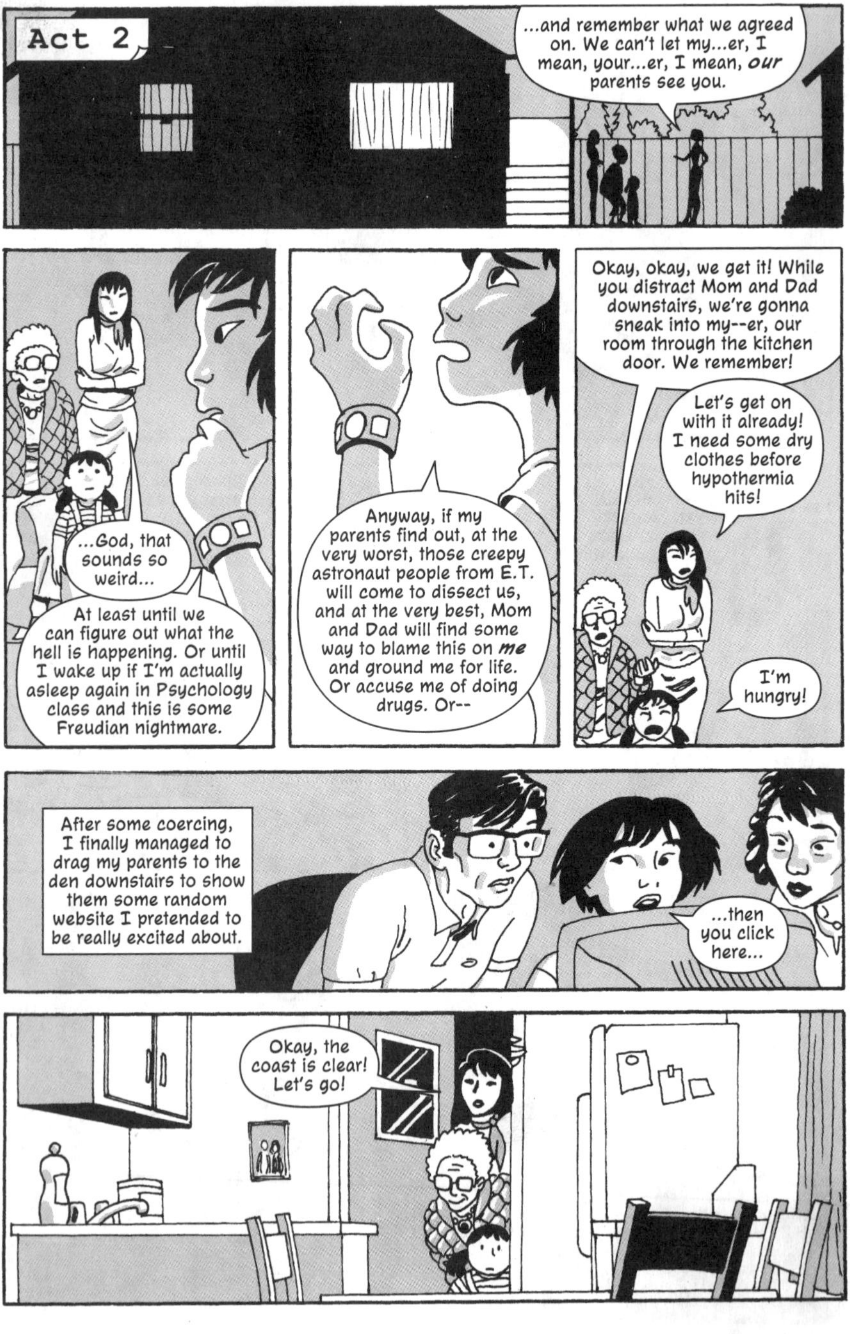

Act 2
...and remember what we agreed on. We can't let my...er, I mean, your...er, I mean, *our* parents see you.
...God, that sounds so weird...
At least until we can figure out what the hell is happening. Or until I wake up if I'm actually asleep again in Psychology class and this is some Freudian nightmare.
Anyway, if my parents find out, at the very worst, those creepy astronaut people from E.T. will come to dissect us, and at the very best, Mom and Dad will find some way to blame this on *me* and ground me for life. Or accuse me of doing drugs. Or--
Okay, okay, we get it! While you distract Mom and Dad downstairs, we're gonna sneak into my--er, our room through the kitchen door. We remember!
Let's get on with it already! I need some dry clothes before hypothermia hits!
I'm hungry!
After some coercing, I finally managed to drag my parents to the den downstairs to show them some random website I pretended to be really excited about.
...then you click here...
Okay, the coast is clear! Let's go!

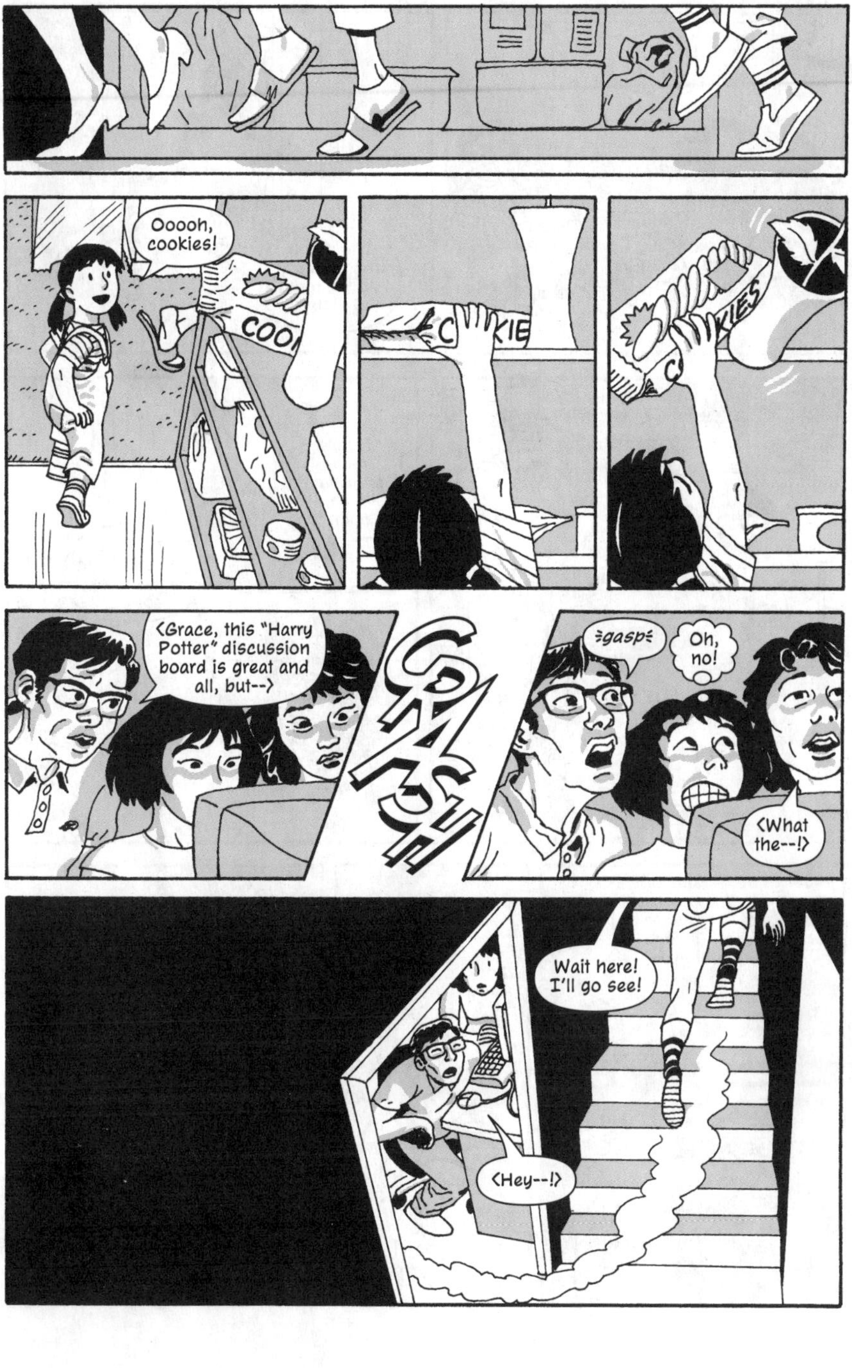
Ooooh, cookies!
COO
C KIE
C KIES
<Grace, this "Harry Potter" discussion board is great and all, but-->
CRASH
gasp
Oh, no!
<What the--!>
Wait here! I'll go see!
<Hey--!>

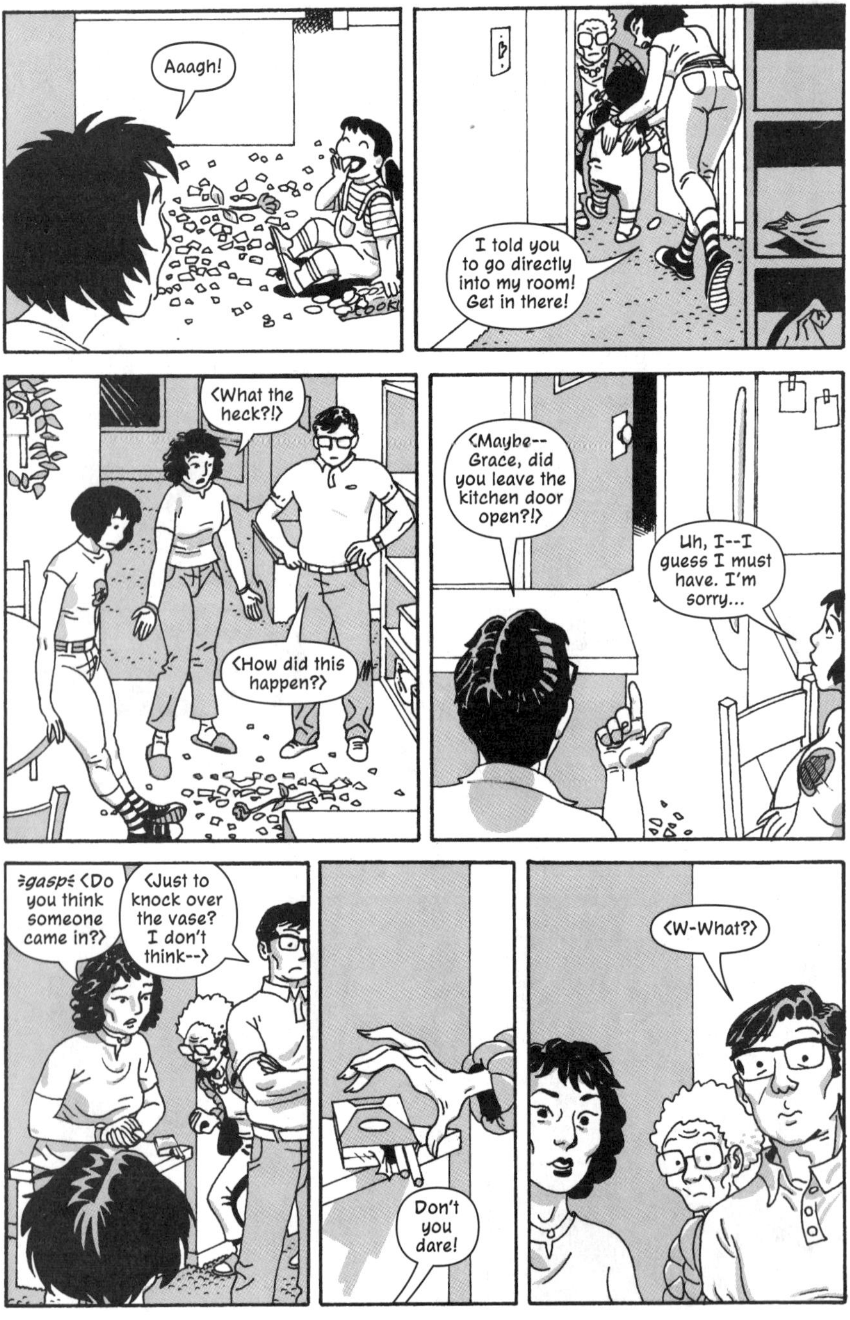

Aaagh!
I told you to go directly into my room! Get in there!
<What the heck?!>
<How did this happen?>
<Maybe-- Grace, did you leave the kitchen door open?!>
Uh, I--I guess I must have. I'm sorry...
gasp <Do you think someone came in?>
<Just to knock over the vase? I don't think-->
Don't you dare!
<W-What?>

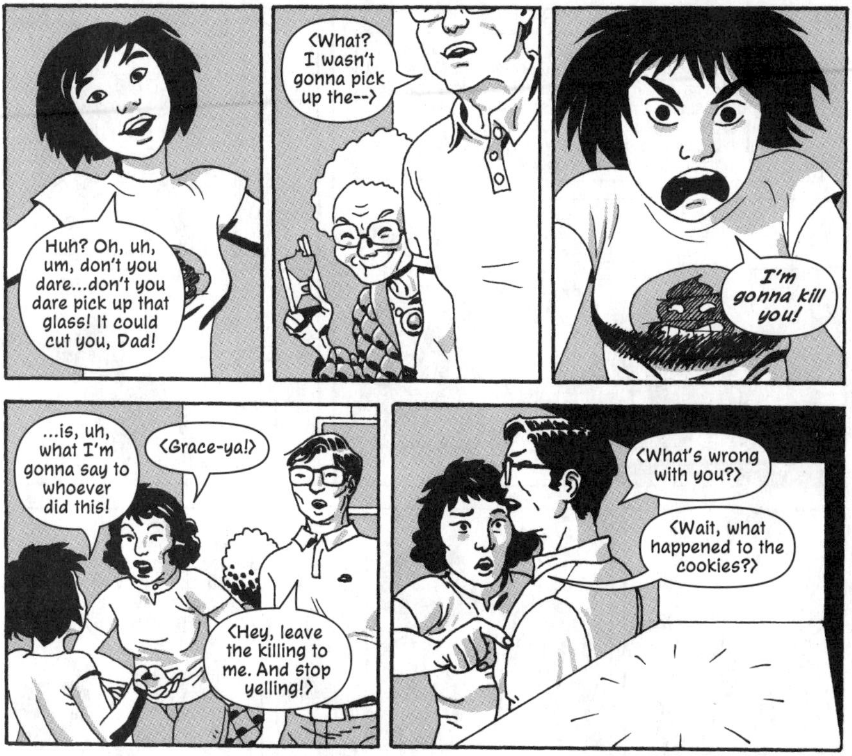
Huh? Oh, uh, um, don't you dare...don't you dare pick up that glass! It could cut you, Dad!
<What? I wasn't gonna pick up the-->
I'm gonna kill you!
...is, uh, what I'm gonna say to whoever did this!
<Grace-ya!>
<Hey, leave the killing to me. And stop yelling!>
<What's wrong with you?>
<Wait, what happened to the cookies?>

After my parents realized that both the cookies and my dad's cigarettes were gone, they searched through all the rooms in the house with a bat and roller in hand. I had my "other selves" hide in my closet while I pretended to look through my room. They were finally satisfied after bolting all the doors.

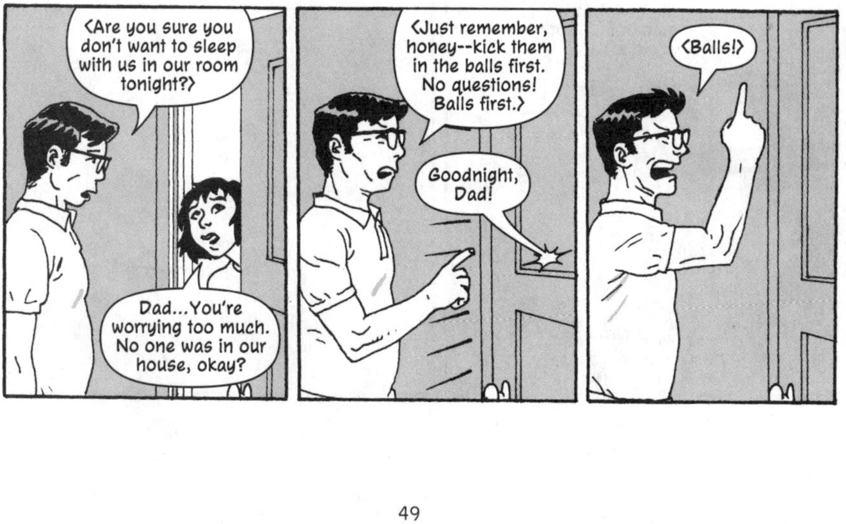
<Are you sure you don't want to sleep with us in our room tonight?>
Dad...You're worrying too much. No one was in our house, okay?
<Just remember, honey--kick them in the balls first. No questions! Balls first.>
Goodnight, Dad!
<Balls!>

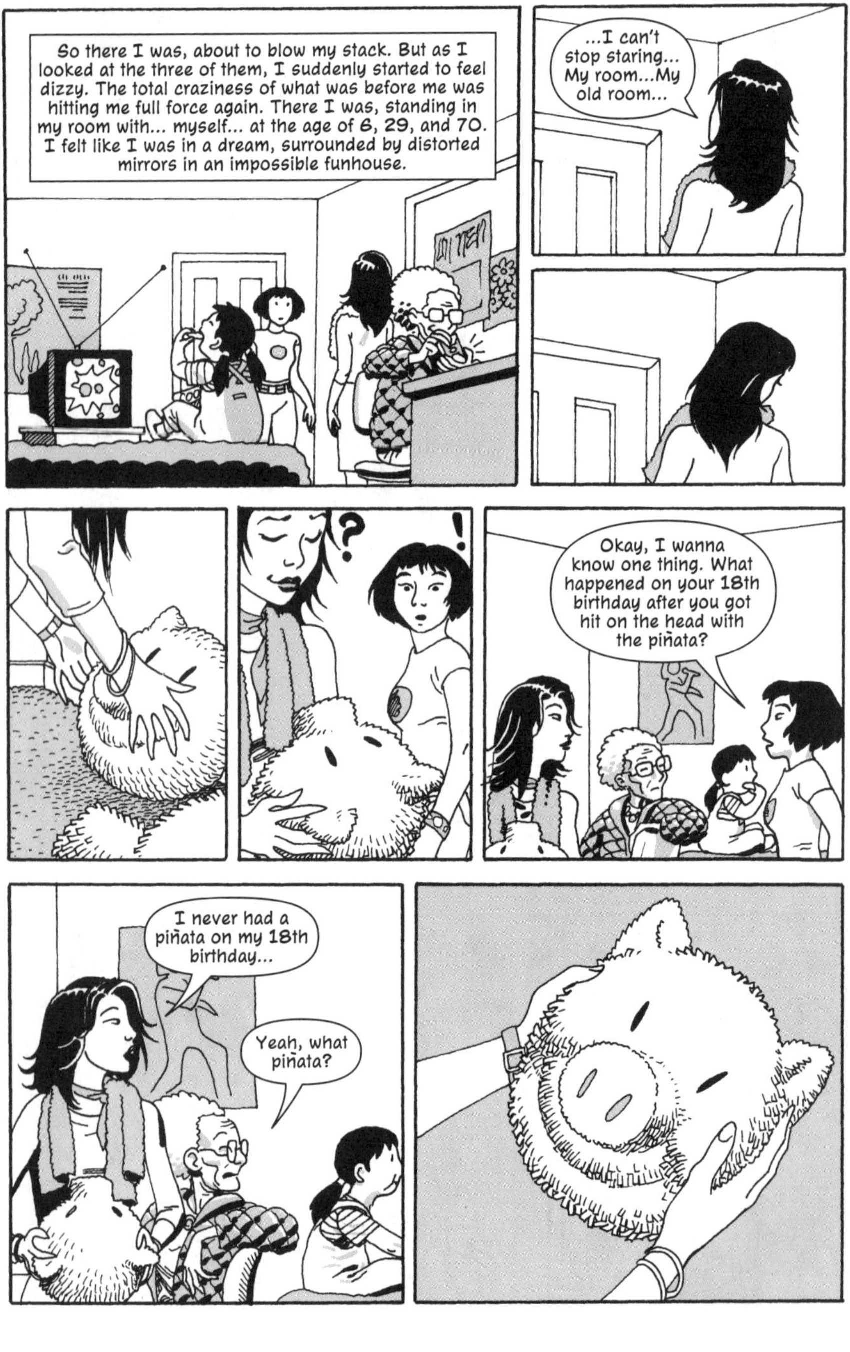
So there I was, about to blow my stack. But as I looked at the three of them, I suddenly started to feel dizzy. The total craziness of what was before me was hitting me full force again. There I was, standing in my room with... myself... at the age of 6, 29, and 70. I felt like I was in a dream, surrounded by distorted mirrors in an impossible funhouse.
...I can't stop staring... My room...My old room...
?
!
Okay, I wanna know one thing. What happened on your 18th birthday after you got hit on the head with the piñata?
I never had a piñata on my 18th birthday...
Yeah, what piñata?

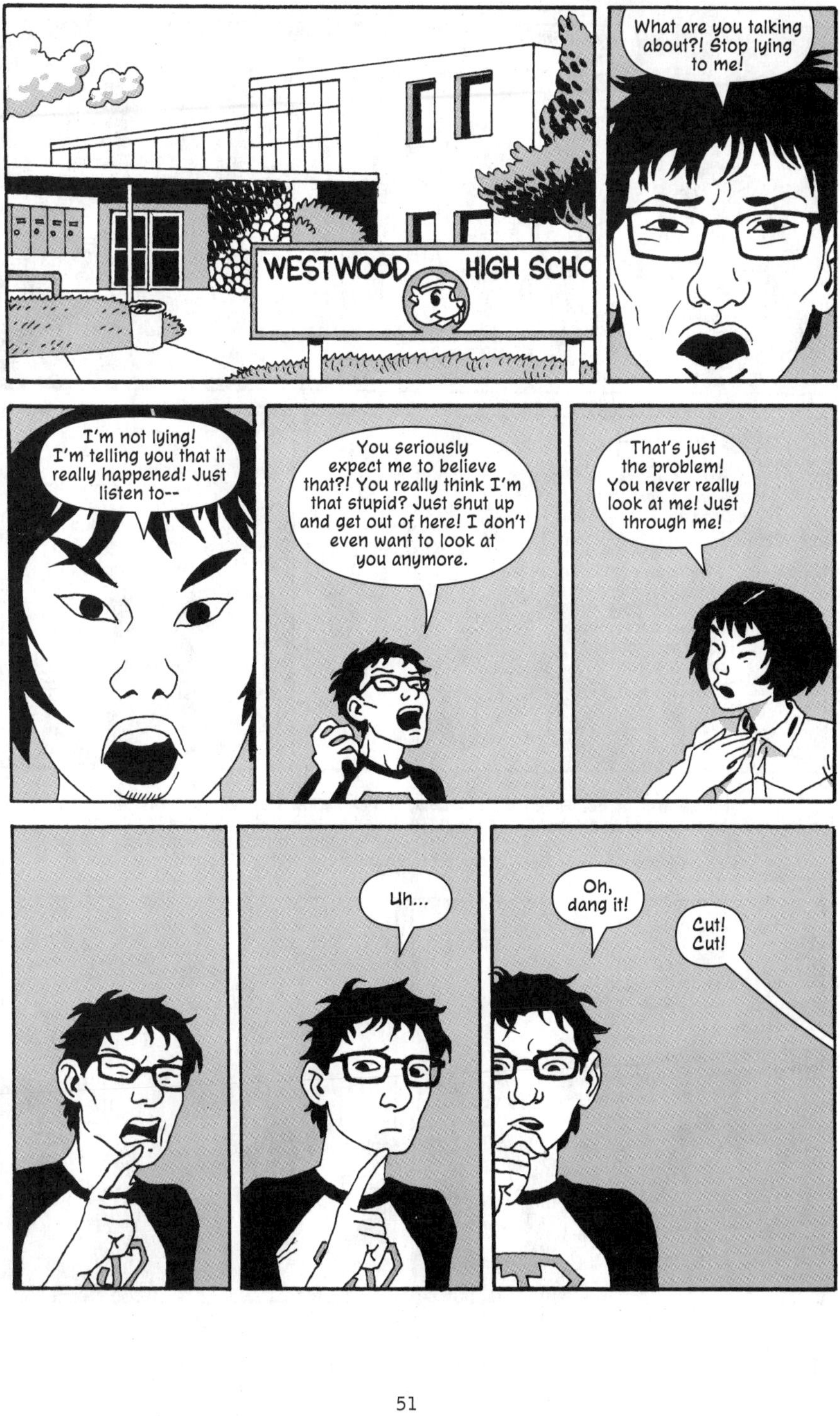

WESTWOOD HIGH SCHO
What are you talking about?! Stop lying to me!
I'm not lying! I'm telling you that it really happened! Just listen to--
You seriously expect me to believe that?! You really think I'm that stupid? Just shut up and get out of here! I don't even want to look at you anymore.
That's just the problem! You never really look at me! Just through me!
Uh...
Oh, dang it!
Cut! Cut!

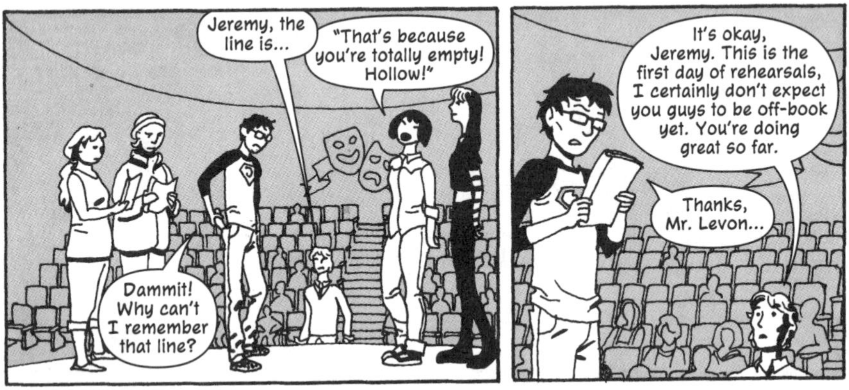
Jeremy, the line is...
"That's because you're totally empty! Hollow!"
Dammit! Why can't I remember that line?
It's okay, Jeremy. This is the first day of rehearsals, I certainly don't expect you guys to be off-book yet. You're doing great so far.
Thanks, Mr. Levon...

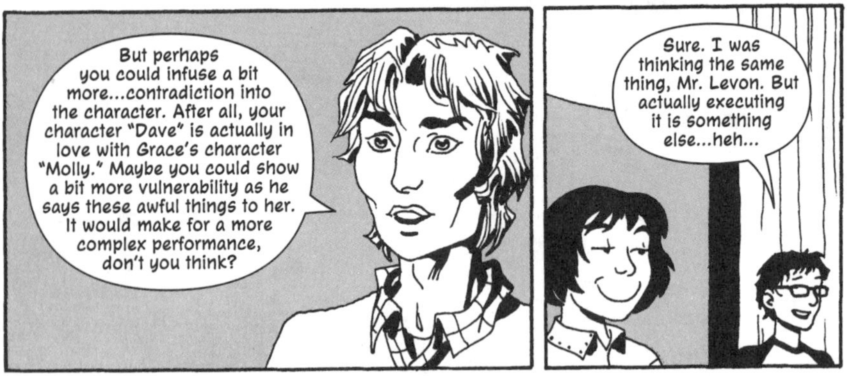
But perhaps you could infuse a bit more...contradiction into the character. After all, your character "Dave" is actually in love with Grace's character "Molly." Maybe you could show a bit more vulnerability as he says these awful things to her. It would make for a more complex performance, don't you think?
Sure. I was thinking the same thing, Mr. Levon. But actually executing it is something else...heh...

Mr. Levon teaches English and Drama, and somehow I ended up having him for both classes this semester. At only 24, he's the youngest teacher in the school. He's fresh out of college and this is his first year teaching. It took me a few after-school "study-sessions" and a Google search to find that out, but that's beside the point.

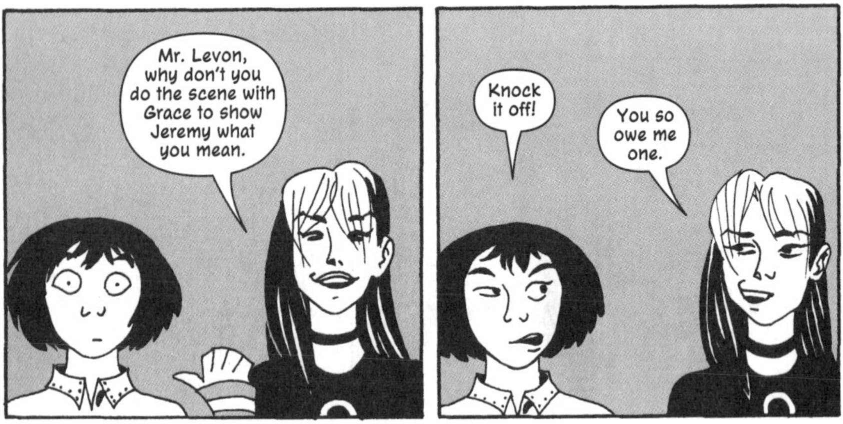
Mr. Levon, why don't you do the scene with Grace to show Jeremy what you mean.
Knock it off!
You so owe me one.

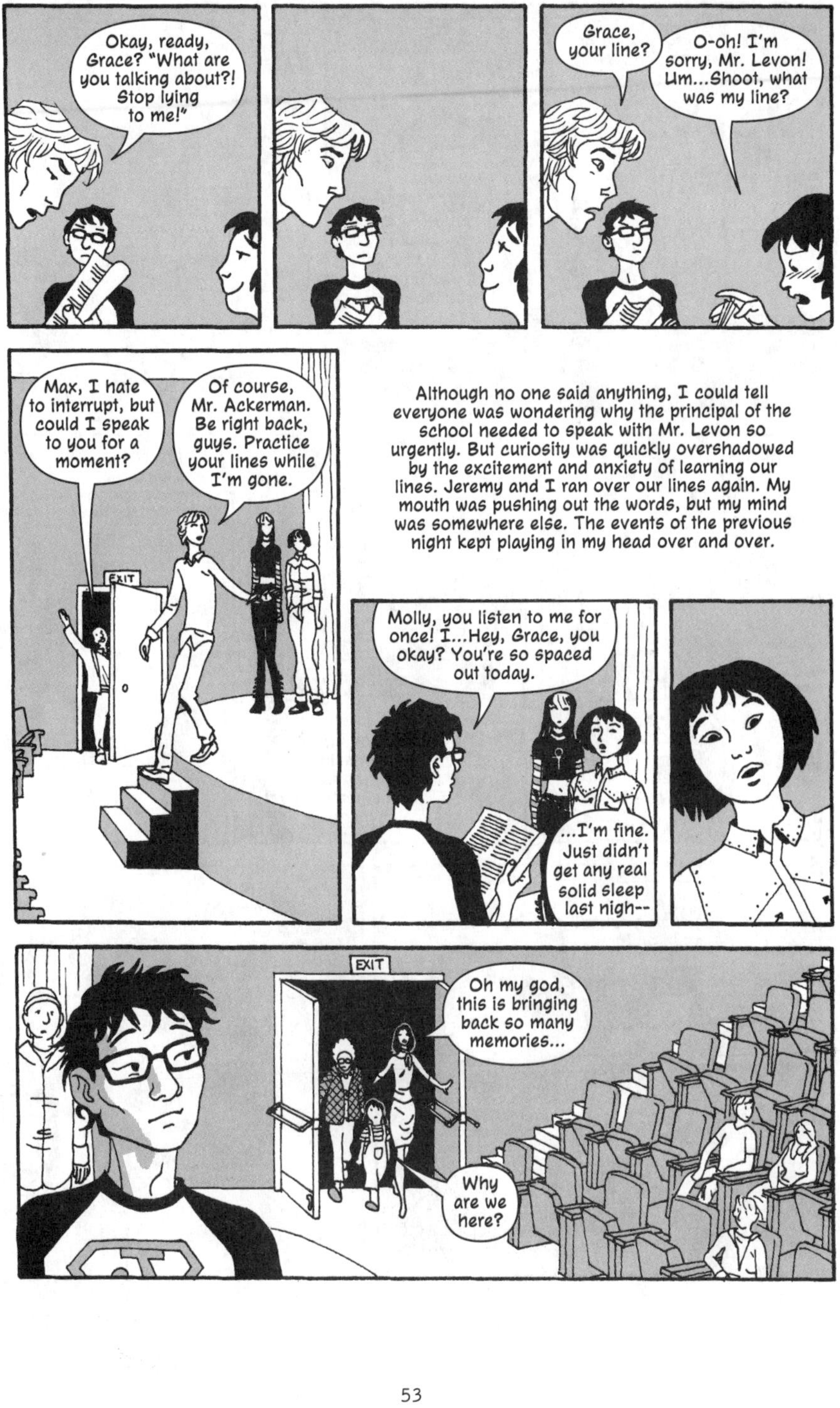
Okay, ready, Grace? "What are you talking about?! Stop lying to me!"
Grace, your line?
O-oh! I'm sorry, Mr. Levon! Um...Shoot, what was my line?
Max, I hate to interrupt, but could I speak to you for a moment?
Of course, Mr. Ackerman. Be right back, guys. Practice your lines while I'm gone.
EXIT
Although no one said anything, I could tell everyone was wondering why the principal of the school needed to speak with Mr. Levon so urgently. But curiosity was quickly overshadowed by the excitement and anxiety of learning our lines. Jeremy and I ran over our lines again. My mouth was pushing out the words, but my mind was somewhere else. The events of the previous night kept playing in my head over and over.
Molly, you listen to me for once! I...Hey, Grace, you okay? You're so spaced out today.
...I'm fine. Just didn't get any real solid sleep last nigh--
EXIT
Oh my god, this is bringing back so many memories...
Why are we here?

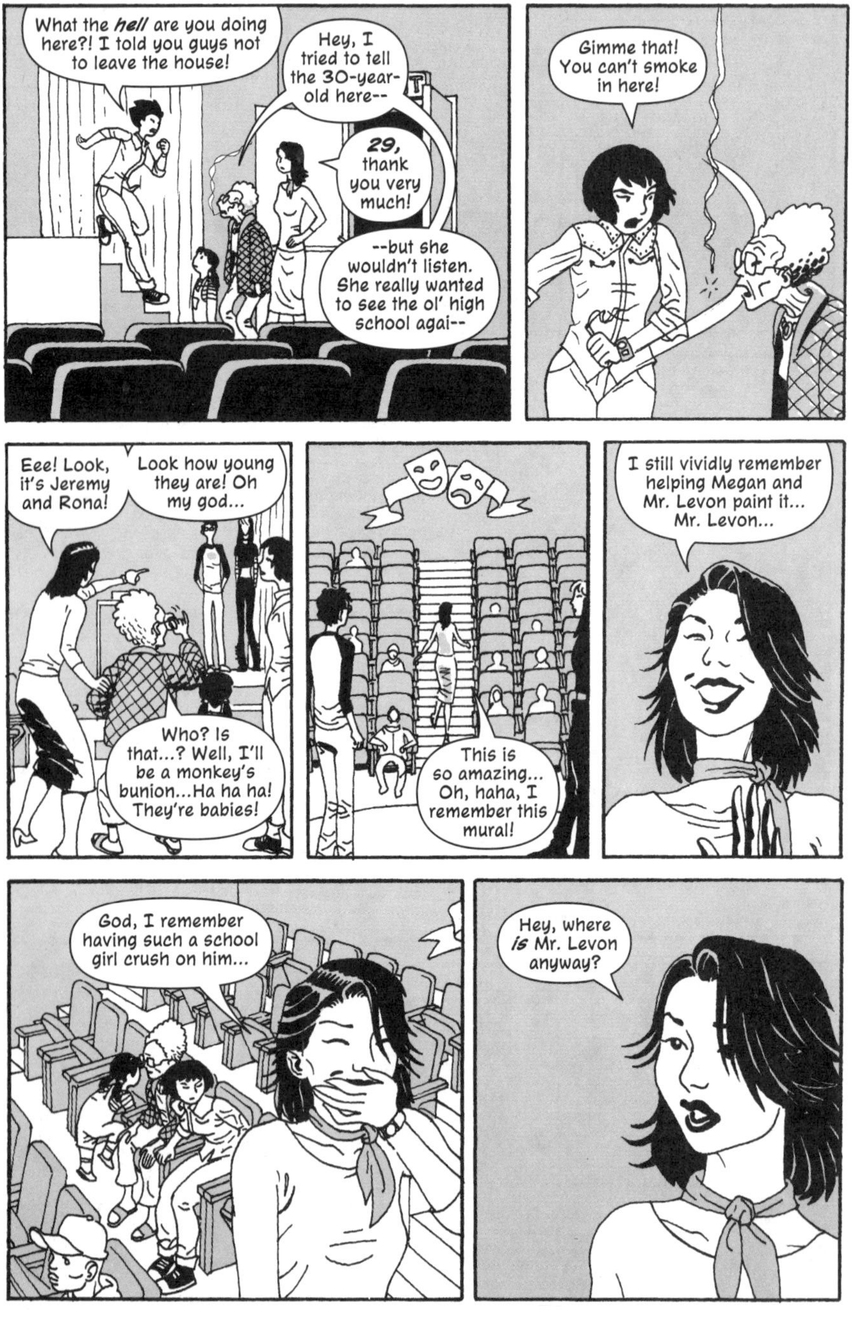
What the *hell* are you doing here?! I told you guys not to leave the house!
Hey, I tried to tell the 30-year-old here--
29, thank you very much!
--but she wouldn't listen. She really wanted to see the ol' high school agai--
Gimme that! You can't smoke in here!
Eee! Look, it's Jeremy and Rona!
Look how young they are! Oh my god...
Who? Is that...? Well, I'll be a monkey's bunion...Ha ha ha! They're babies!
This is so amazing... Oh, haha, I remember this mural!
I still vividly remember helping Megan and Mr. Levon paint it... Mr. Levon...
God, I remember having such a school girl crush on him...
Hey, where *is* Mr. Levon anyway?

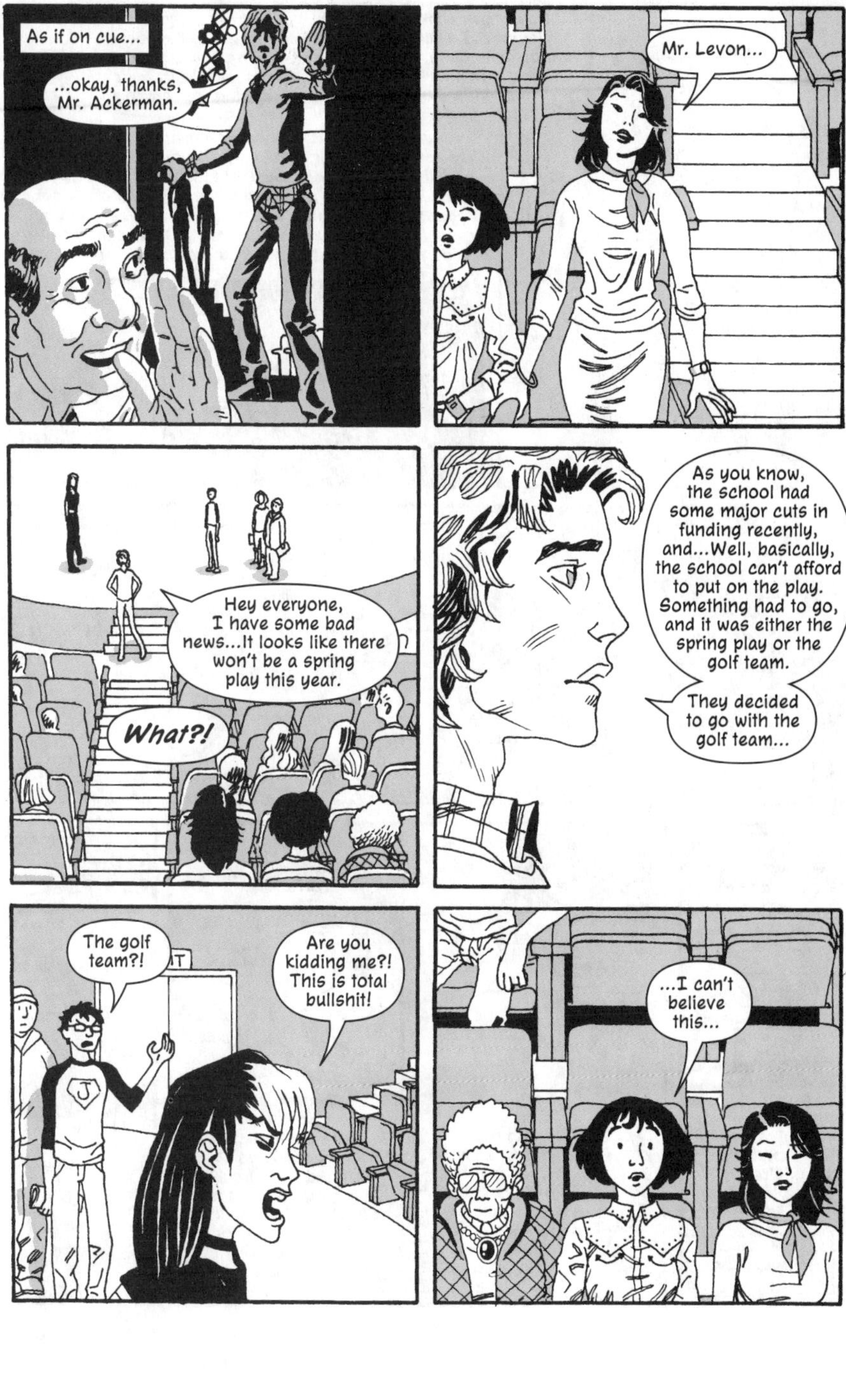
As if on cue...
...okay, thanks, Mr. Ackerman.
Mr. Levon...
Hey everyone, I have some bad news...It looks like there won't be a spring play this year.
What?!
As you know, the school had some major cuts in funding recently, and...Well, basically, the school can't afford to put on the play. Something had to go, and it was either the spring play or the golf team.
They decided to go with the golf team...
The golf team?!
Are you kidding me?! This is total bullshit!
...I can't believe this...

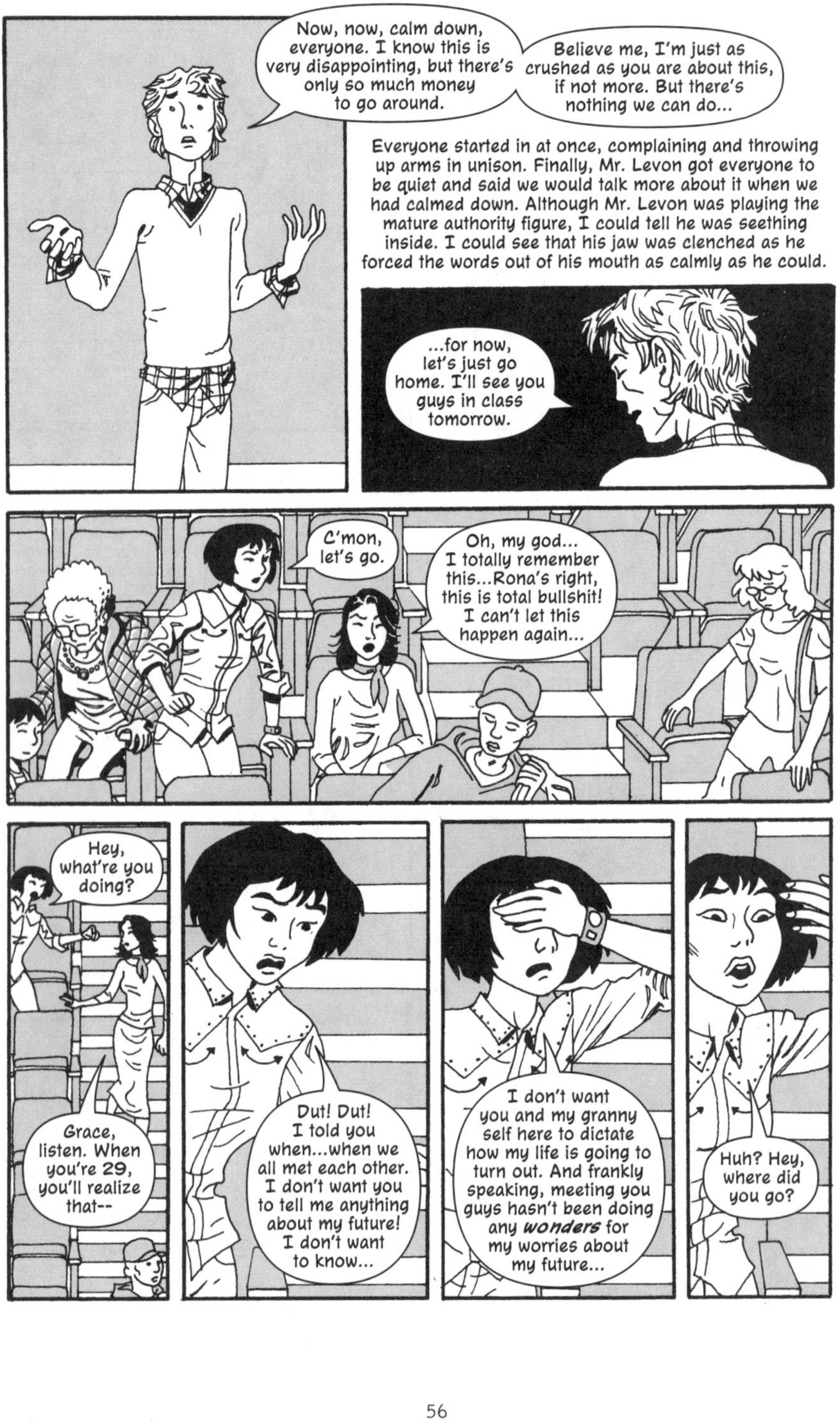
Now, now, calm down, everyone. I know this is very disappointing, but there's only so much money to go around.
Believe me, I'm just as crushed as you are about this, if not more. But there's nothing we can do...
Everyone started in at once, complaining and throwing up arms in unison. Finally, Mr. Levon got everyone to be quiet and said we would talk more about it when we had calmed down. Although Mr. Levon was playing the mature authority figure, I could tell he was seething inside. I could see that his jaw was clenched as he forced the words out of his mouth as calmly as he could.
...for now, let's just go home. I'll see you guys in class tomorrow.
C'mon, let's go.
Oh, my god... I totally remember this...Rona's right, this is total bullshit! I can't let this happen again...
Hey, what're you doing?
Grace, listen. When you're 29, you'll realize that--
Dut! Dut! I told you when...when we all met each other. I don't want you to tell me anything about my future! I don't want to know...
I don't want you and my granny self here to dictate how my life is going to turn out. And frankly speaking, meeting you guys hasn't been doing any *wonders* for my worries about my future...
Huh? Hey, where did you go?

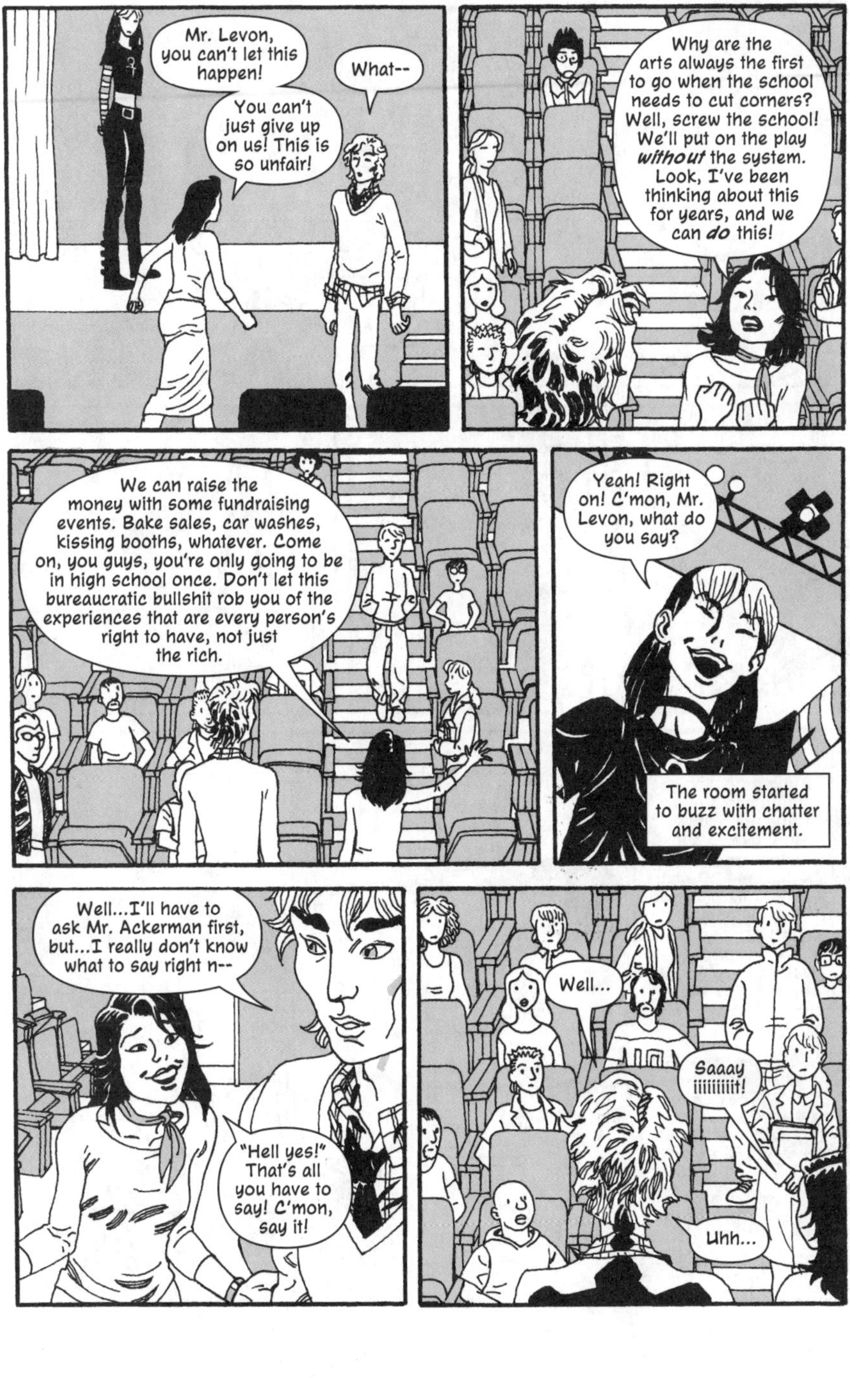

Mr. Levon, you can't let this happen!
You can't just give up on us! This is so unfair!
What--
Why are the arts always the first to go when the school needs to cut corners? Well, screw the school! We'll put on the play *without* the system. Look, I've been thinking about this for years, and we can *do* this!
We can raise the money with some fundraising events. Bake sales, car washes, kissing booths, whatever. Come on, you guys, you're only going to be in high school once. Don't let this bureaucratic bullshit rob you of the experiences that are every person's right to have, not just the rich.
Yeah! Right on! C'mon, Mr. Levon, what do you say?
The room started to buzz with chatter and excitement.
Well...I'll have to ask Mr. Ackerman first, but...I really don't know what to say right n--
"Hell yes!" That's all you have to say! C'mon, say it!
Well...
Saaay iiiiiiiiit!
Uhh...

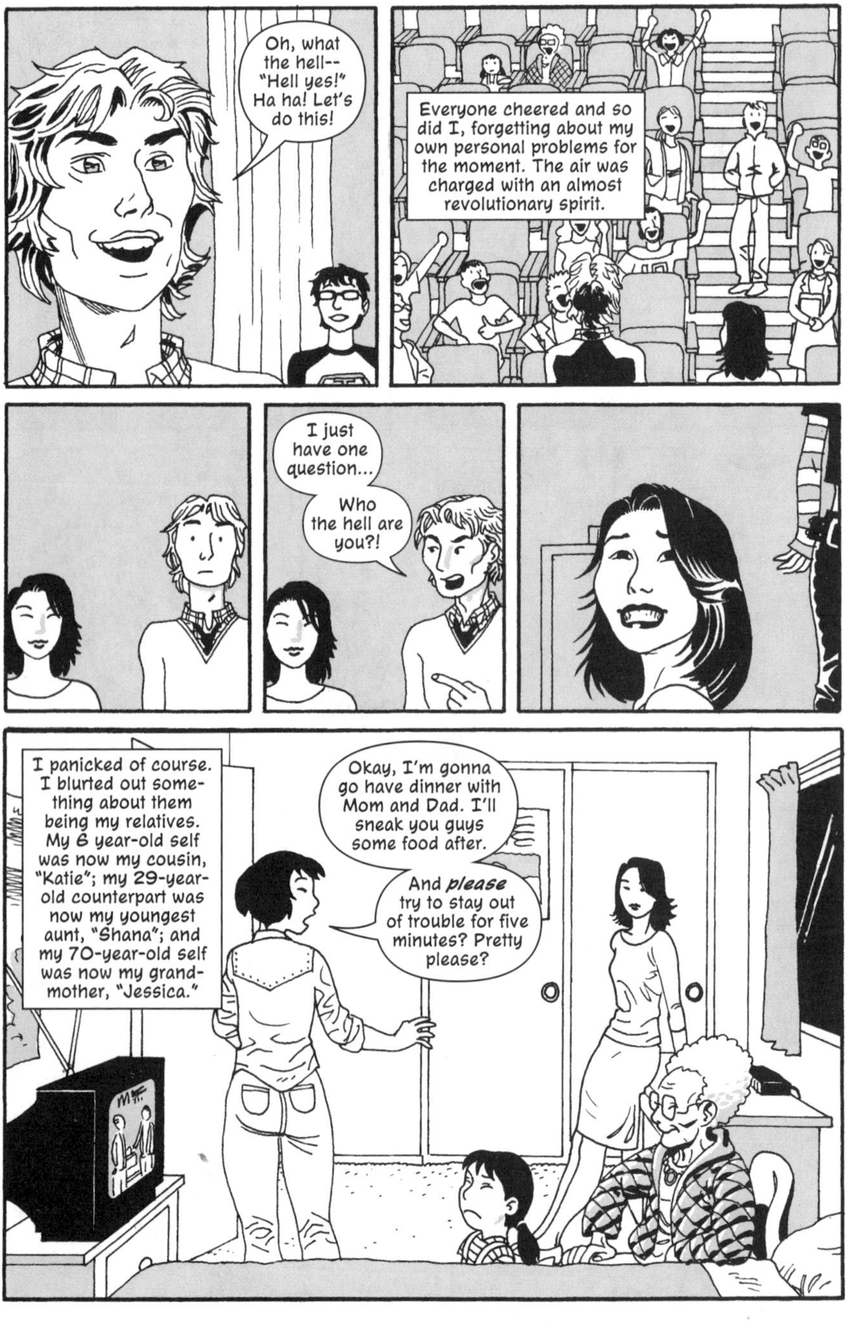

Oh, what the hell-- "Hell yes!" Ha ha! Let's do this!
Everyone cheered and so did I, forgetting about my own personal problems for the moment. The air was charged with an almost revolutionary spirit.
I just have one question...
Who the hell are you?!
I panicked of course. I blurted out something about them being my relatives. My 6 year-old self was now my cousin, "Katie"; my 29-year-old counterpart was now my youngest aunt, "Shana"; and my 70-year-old self was now my grandmother, "Jessica."
Okay, I'm gonna go have dinner with Mom and Dad. I'll sneak you guys some food after.
And *please* try to stay out of trouble for five minutes? Pretty please?

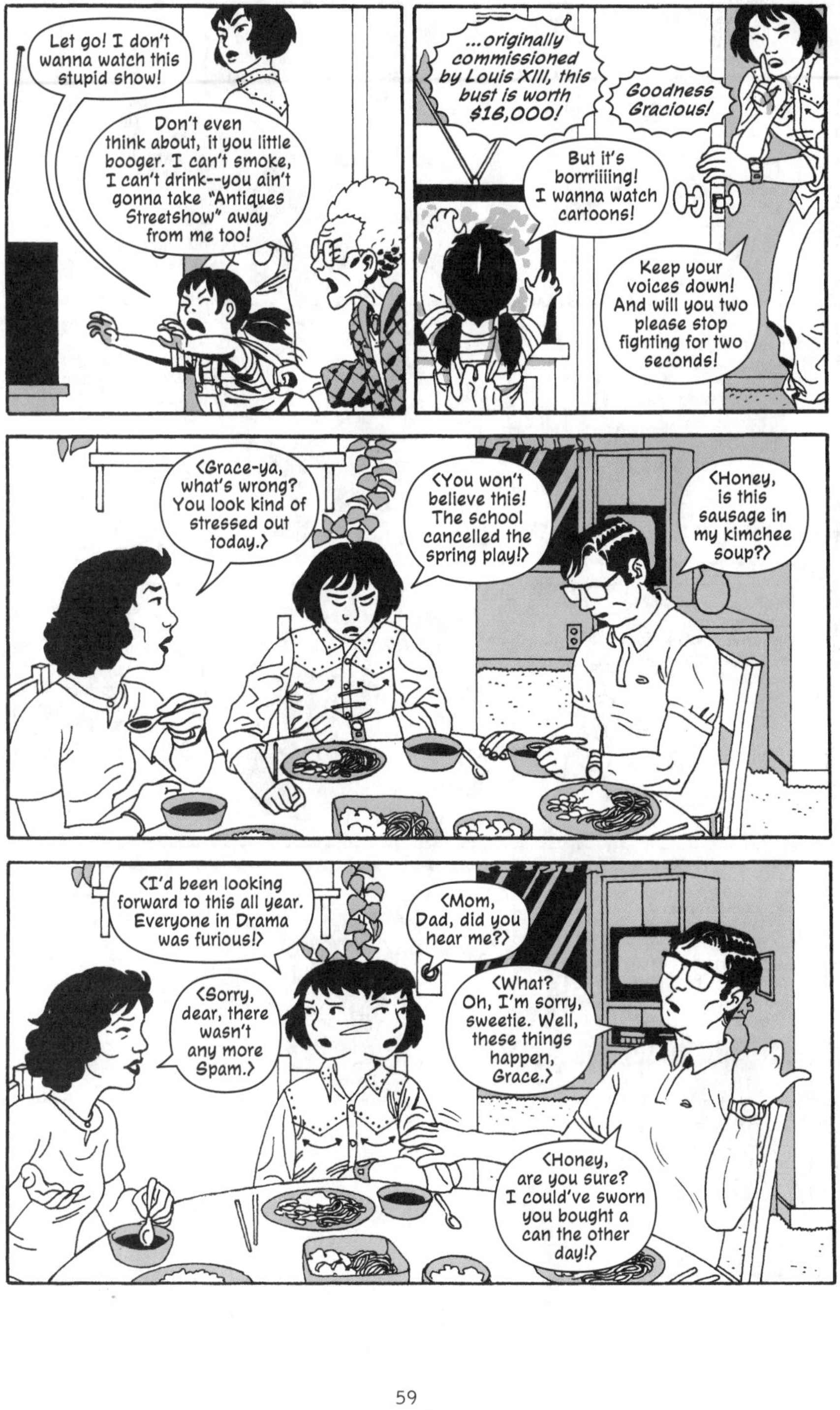
Let go! I don't wanna watch this stupid show!
Don't even think about, it you little booger. I can't smoke, I can't drink--you ain't gonna take "Antiques Streetshow" away from me too!
...originally commissioned by Louis XIII, this bust is worth $16,000!
Goodness Gracious!
But it's borrriiiing! I wanna watch cartoons!
Keep your voices down! And will you two please stop fighting for two seconds!
<Grace-ya, what's wrong? You look kind of stressed out today.>
<You won't believe this! The school cancelled the spring play!>
<Honey, is this sausage in my kimchee soup?>
<I'd been looking forward to this all year. Everyone in Drama was furious!>
<Mom, Dad, did you hear me?>
<Sorry, dear, there wasn't any more Spam.>
<What? Oh, I'm sorry, sweetie. Well, these things happen, Grace.>
<Honey, are you sure? I could've sworn you bought a can the other day!>

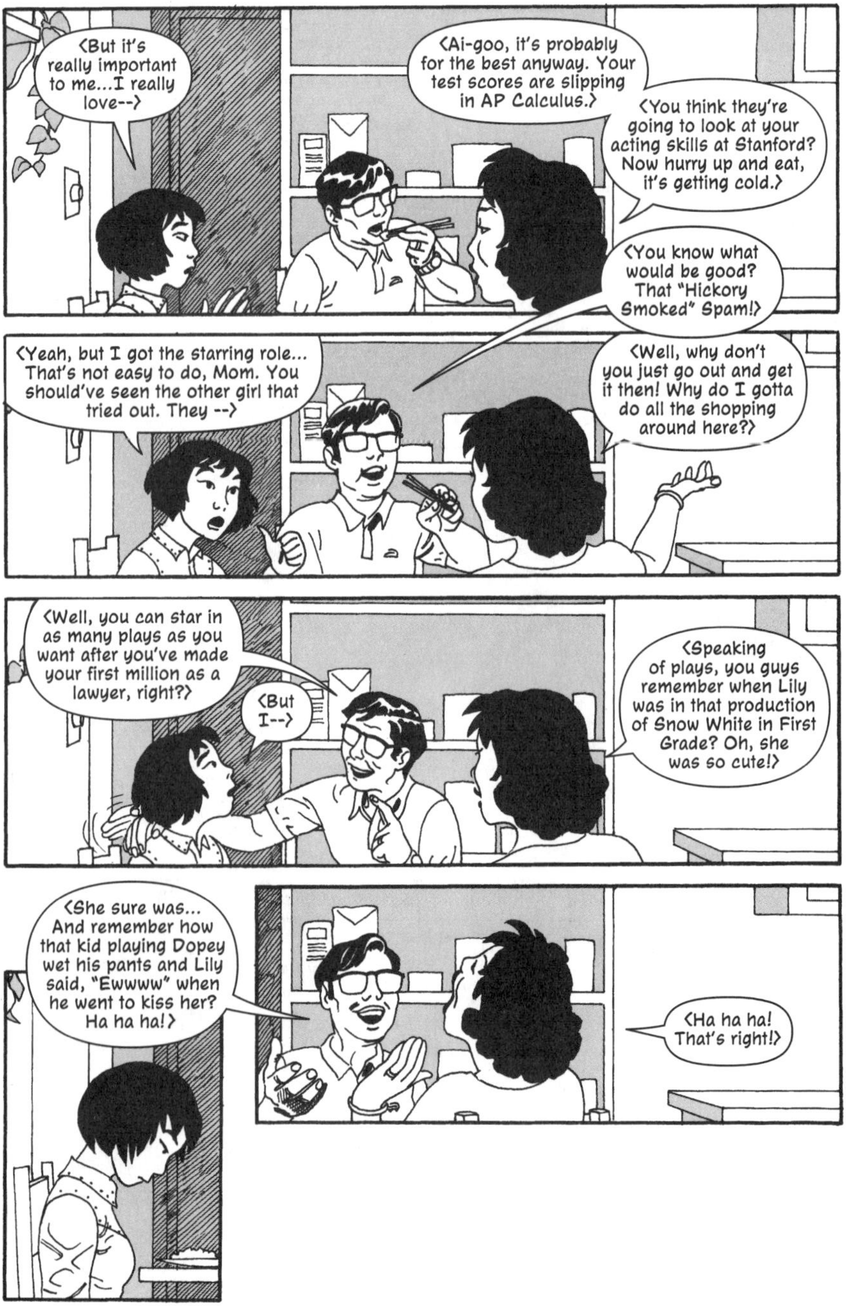

<But it's really important to me...I really love-->
<Ai-goo, it's probably for the best anyway. Your test scores are slipping in AP Calculus.>
<You think they're going to look at your acting skills at Stanford? Now hurry up and eat, it's getting cold.>
<You know what would be good? That "Hickory Smoked" Spam!>
<Yeah, but I got the starring role... That's not easy to do, Mom. You should've seen the other girl that tried out. They -->
<Well, why don't you just go out and get it then! Why do I gotta do all the shopping around here?>
<Well, you can star in as many plays as you want after you've made your first million as a lawyer, right?>
<But I-->
<Speaking of plays, you guys remember when Lily was in that production of Snow White in First Grade? Oh, she was so cute!>
<She sure was... And remember how that kid playing Dopey wet his pants and Lily said, "Ewwww" when he went to kiss her? Ha ha ha!>
<Ha ha ha! That's right!>

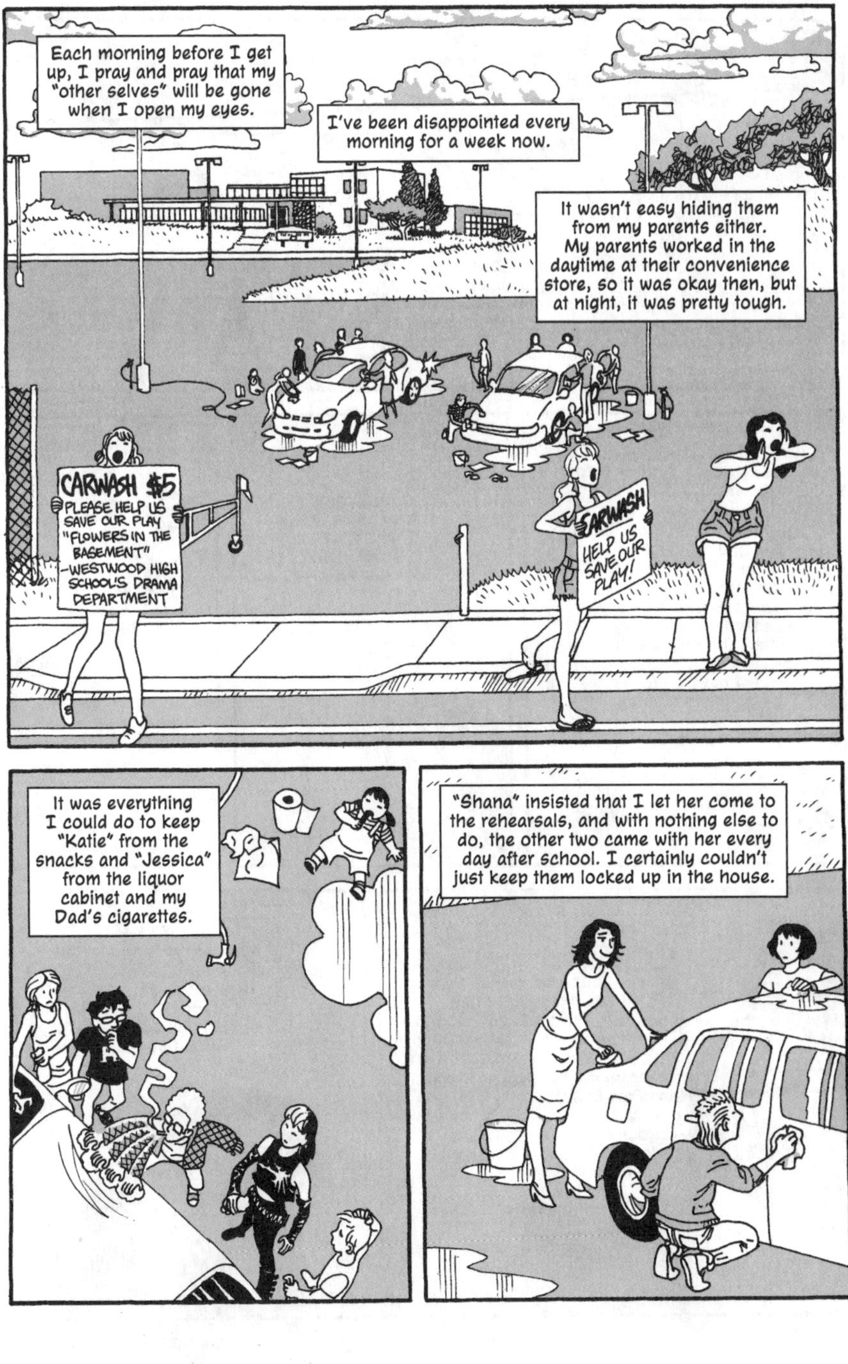

Each morning before I get up, I pray and pray that my "other selves" will be gone when I open my eyes.
I've been disappointed every morning for a week now.
It wasn't easy hiding them from my parents either. My parents worked in the daytime at their convenience store, so it was okay then, but at night, it was pretty tough.
CARWASH $5
PLEASE HELP US SAVE OUR PLAY "FLOWERS IN THE BASEMENT" —WESTWOOD HIGH SCHOOL'S DRAMA DEPARTMENT
CARWASH
HELP US SAVE OUR PLAY!
It was everything I could do to keep "Katie" from the snacks and "Jessica" from the liquor cabinet and my Dad's cigarettes.
"Shana" insisted that I let her come to the rehearsals, and with nothing else to do, the other two came with her every day after school. I certainly couldn't just keep them locked up in the house.

Geez, could you be any more blatant?

I can't stop looking at him... God, I remember what a crush I had on him back in high school, and here he is again. It's so unreal.

I don't know if I'd use the word "crush"--I just think he's a really great teacher. And he's so mature and--

Grace. Knock it off. I'm you, remember! You can't lie to yourself. And you know you shouldn't be embarrassed. I mean, he's young, talented, incredibly cute... Why wouldn't I--er, you, uh, *we* have a crush? It's perfectly natural.

God, I forgot how immature I was at 18... Never even kissed a boy...

Ha ha ha!

Hey, who're you calling immature?!

Hey, if I can't call *myself* immature, to whom can I?

Grace, let me tell you something. When you "grow up" and get into the "real world," you're gonna find that guys like Mr. Levon are rarer than a Packers jersey at a Star Trek convention. When you're young, there's always a great guy around the corner just waiting for you. So if you miss one, no big whoop, there'll be another one in ten minutes, right?

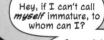

Wrong.

I don't know what you're trying to say, but the bottom line is he's my *teacher.* He can't date his students. I'm in high school, for Christ's sake! He'd be fired!

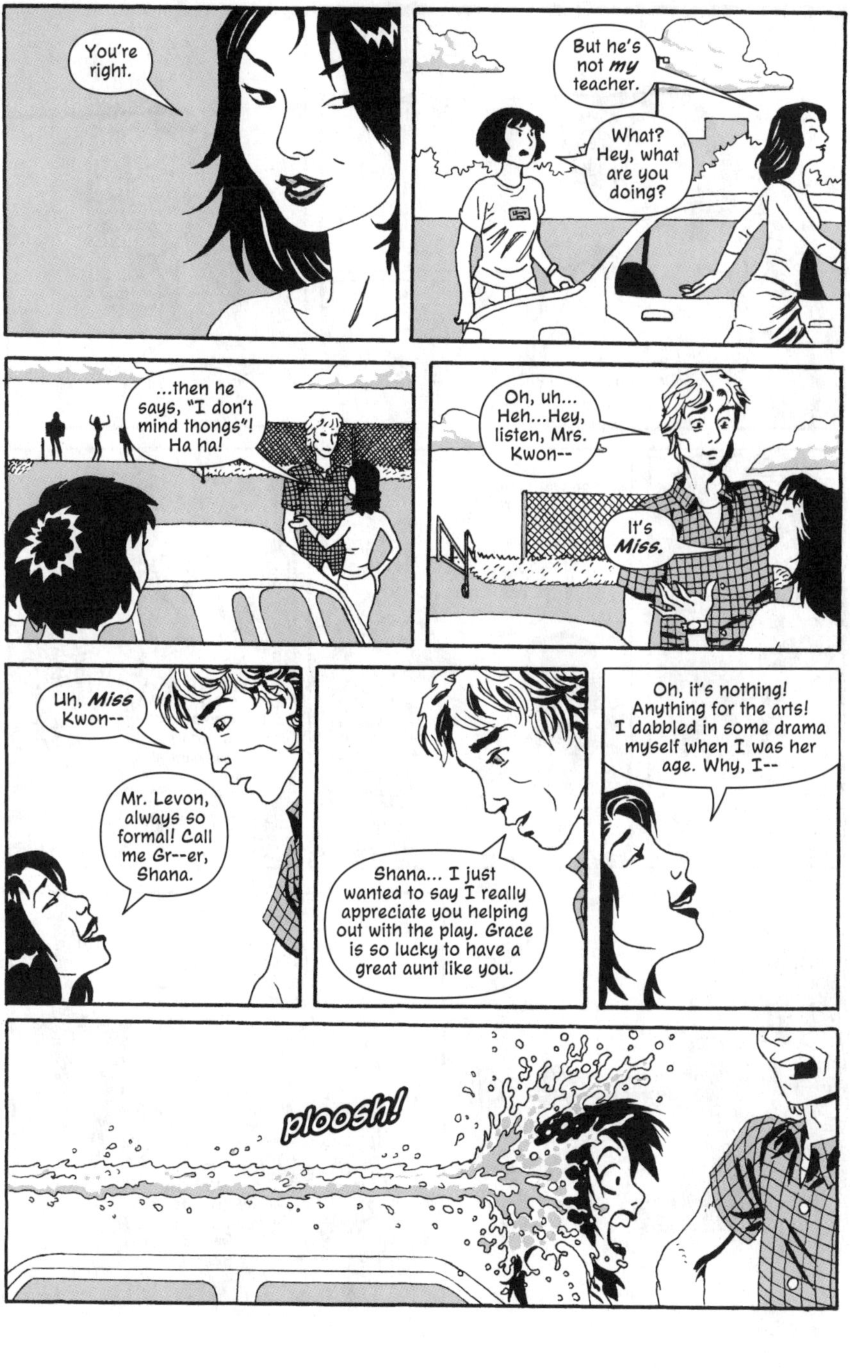
You're right.
But he's not my teacher.
What? Hey, what are you doing?
...then he says, "I don't mind thongs"! Ha ha!
Oh, uh... Heh...Hey, listen, Mrs. Kwon--
It's Miss.
Uh, Miss Kwon--
Mr. Levon, always so formal! Call me Gr--er, Shana.
Shana... I just wanted to say I really appreciate you helping out with the play. Grace is so lucky to have a great aunt like you.
Oh, it's nothing! Anything for the arts! I dabbled in some drama myself when I was her age. Why, I--
ploosh!

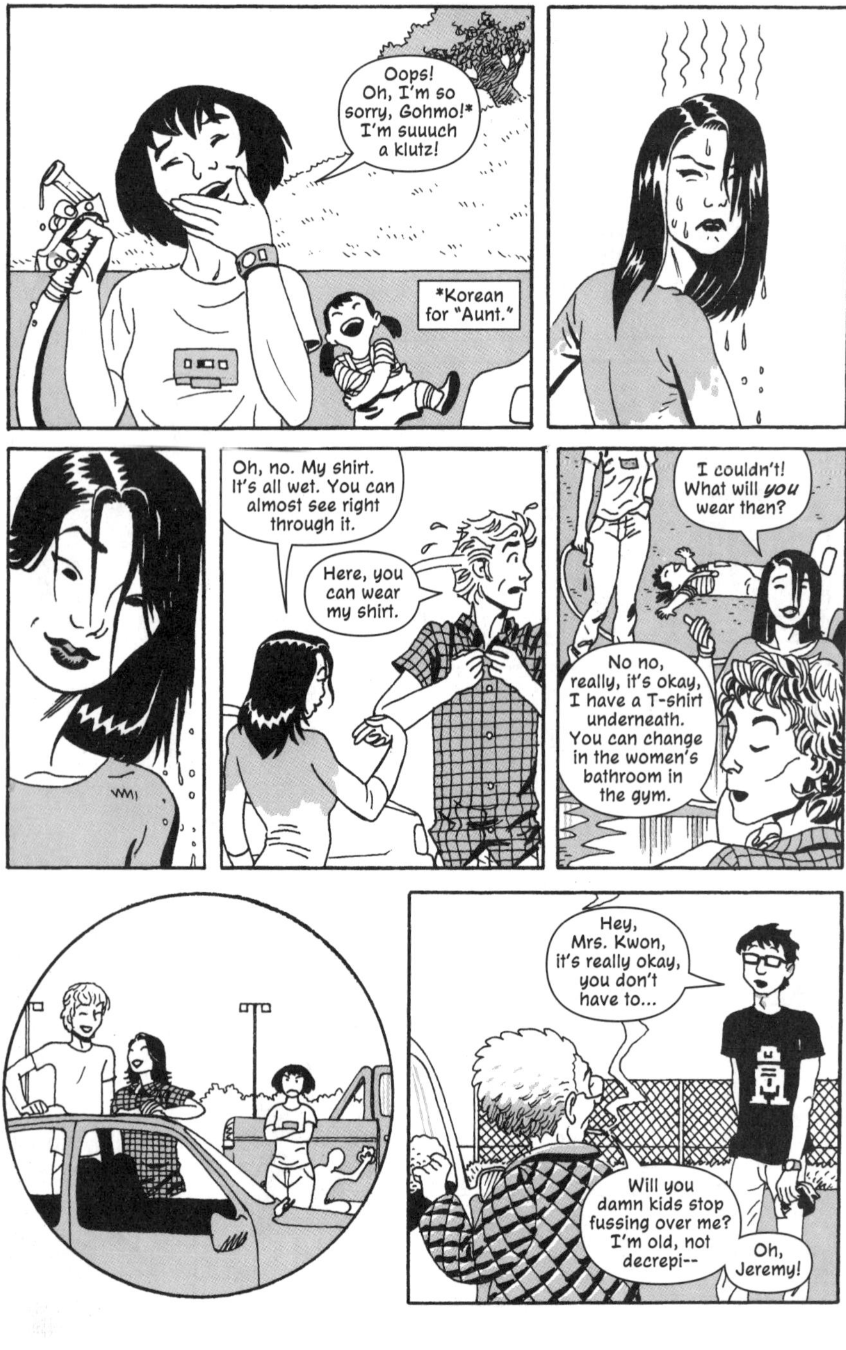
Oops! Oh, I'm so sorry, Gohmo!* I'm suuuch a klutz!
*Korean for "Aunt."
Oh, no. My shirt. It's all wet. You can almost see right through it.
Here, you can wear my shirt.
I couldn't! What will *you* wear then?
No no, really, it's okay, I have a T-shirt underneath. You can change in the women's bathroom in the gym.
Hey, Mrs. Kwon, it's really okay, you don't have to...
Will you damn kids stop fussing over me? I'm old, not decrepi--
Oh, Jeremy!

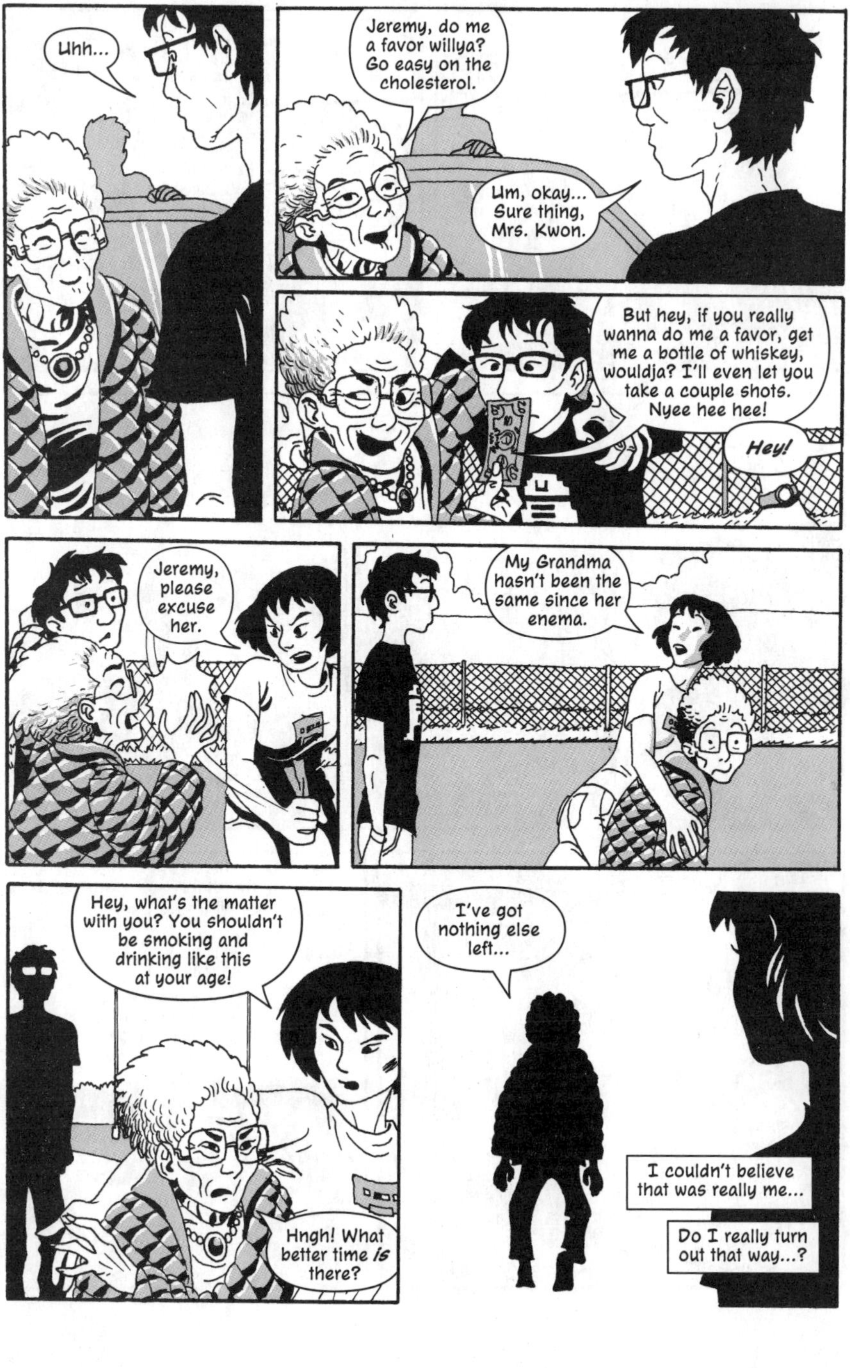
Uhh...
Jeremy, do me a favor willya? Go easy on the cholesterol.
Um, okay... Sure thing, Mrs. Kwon.
But hey, if you really wanna do me a favor, get me a bottle of whiskey, wouldja? I'll even let you take a couple shots. Nyee hee hee!
Hey!
Jeremy, please excuse her.
My Grandma hasn't been the same since her enema.
Hey, what's the matter with you? You shouldn't be smoking and drinking like this at your age!
Hngh! What better time *is* there?
I've got nothing else left...
I couldn't believe that was really me...
Do I really turn out that way...?

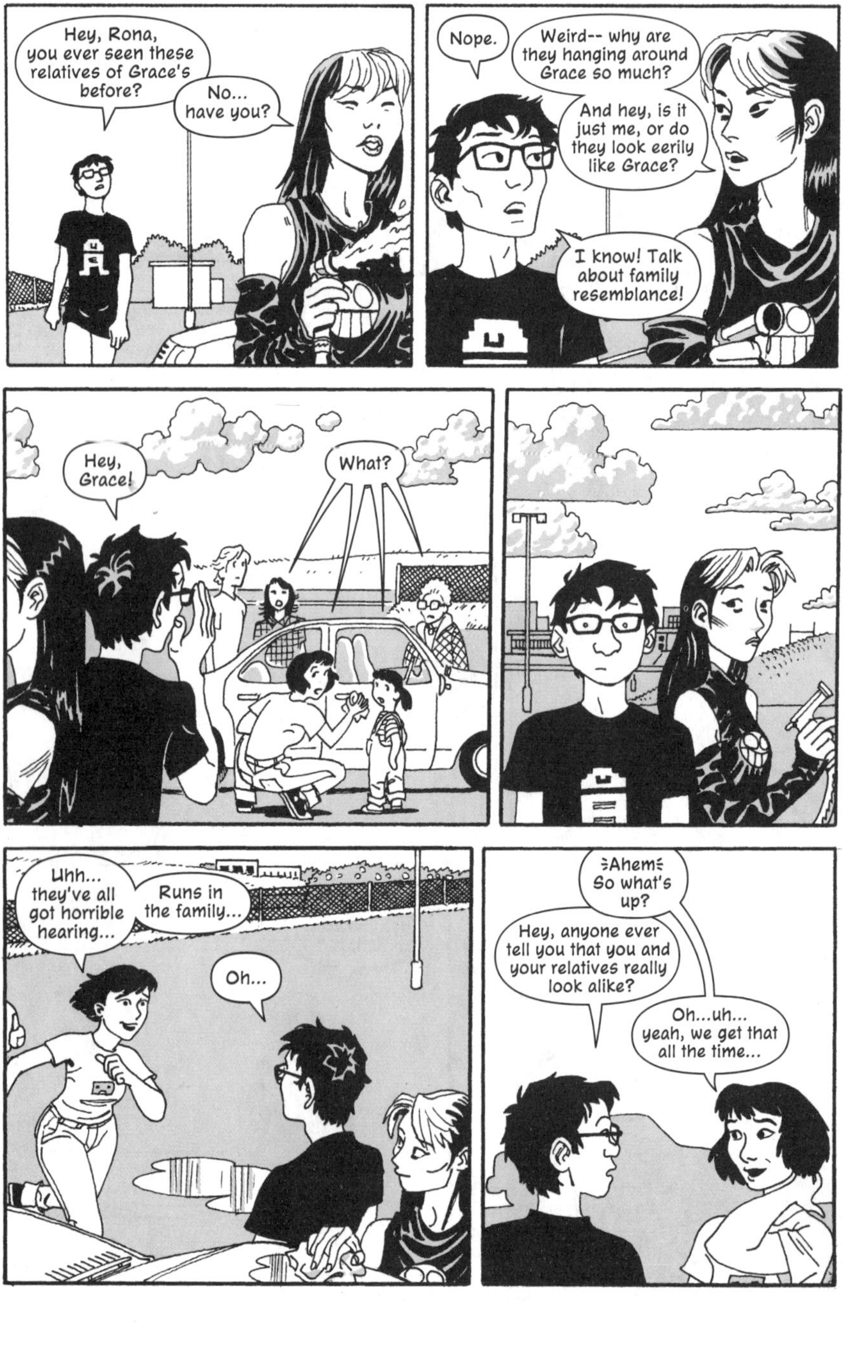
Hey, Rona, you ever seen these relatives of Grace's before?
No... have you?
Nope.
Weird-- why are they hanging around Grace so much?
And hey, is it just me, or do they look eerily like Grace?
I know! Talk about family resemblance!
Hey, Grace!
What?
Uhh... they've all got horrible hearing...
Runs in the family...
Oh...
Ahem So what's up?
Hey, anyone ever tell you that you and your relatives really look alike?
Oh...uh... yeah, we get that all the time...

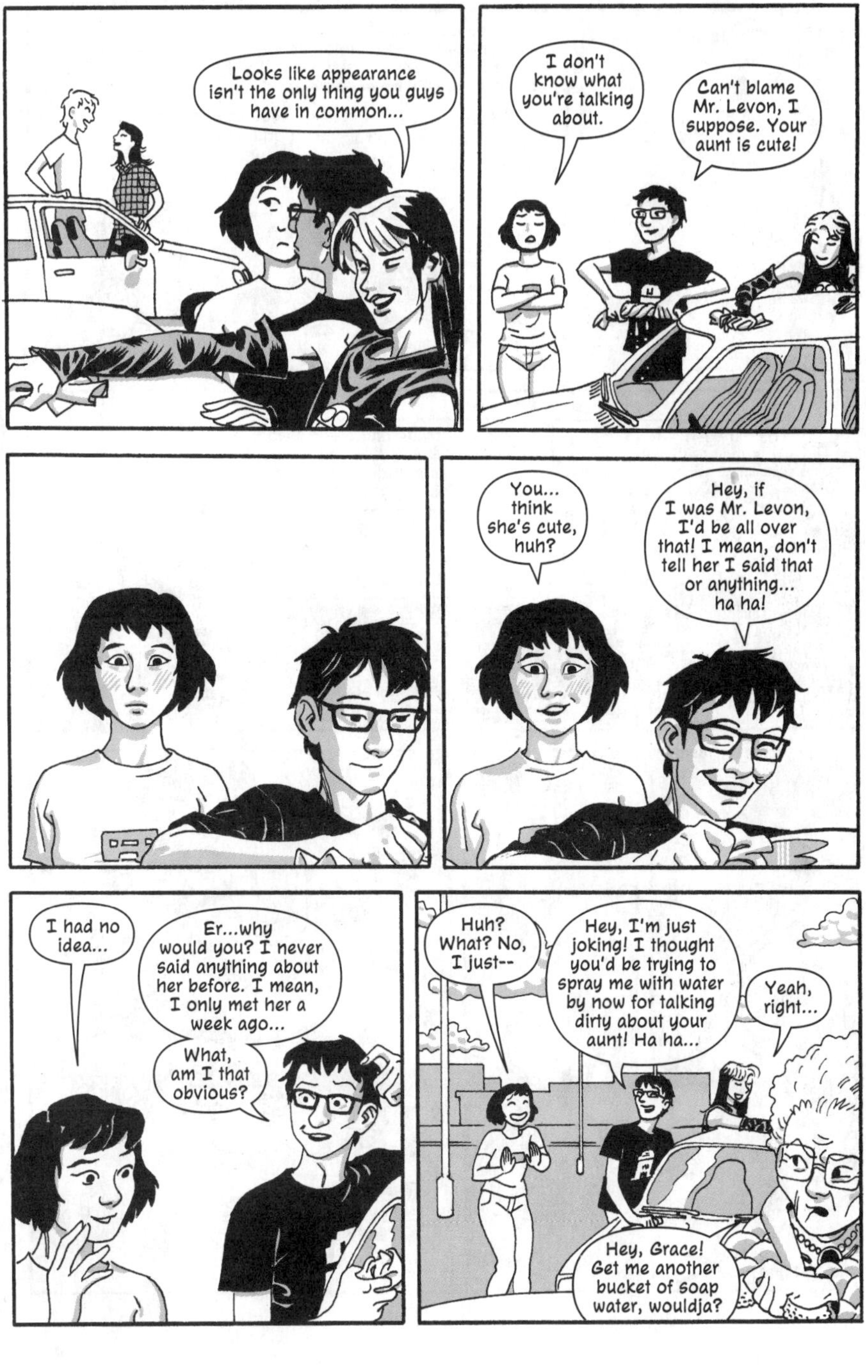
Looks like appearance isn't the only thing you guys have in common...
I don't know what you're talking about.
Can't blame Mr. Levon, I suppose. Your aunt is cute!
You... think she's cute, huh?
Hey, if I was Mr. Levon, I'd be all over that! I mean, don't tell her I said that or anything... ha ha!
I had no idea...
Er...why would you? I never said anything about her before. I mean, I only met her a week ago...
What, am I that obvious?
Huh? What? No, I just--
Hey, I'm just joking! I thought you'd be trying to spray me with water by now for talking dirty about your aunt! Ha ha...
Yeah, right...
Hey, Grace! Get me another bucket of soap water, wouldja?

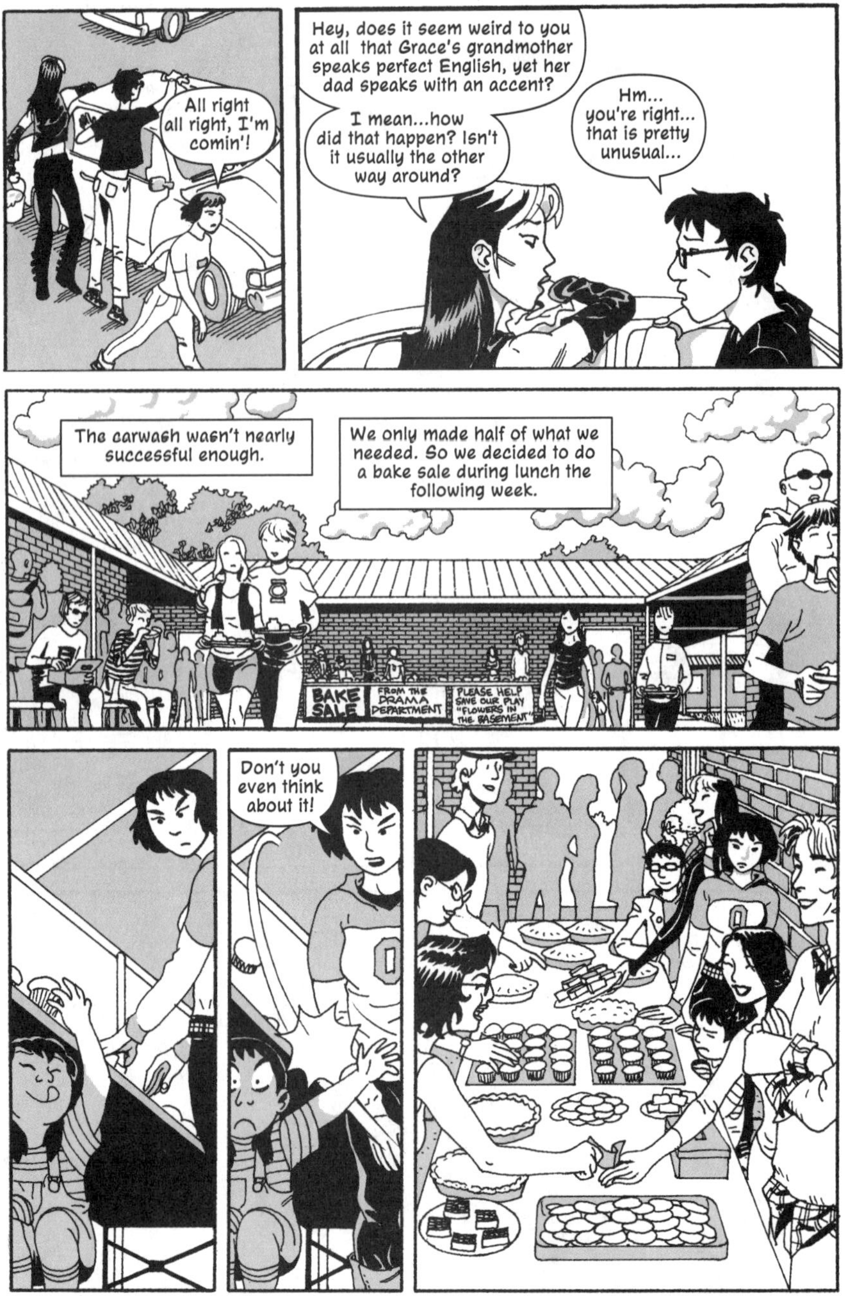
All right all right, I'm comin'!
Hey, does it seem weird to you at all that Grace's grandmother speaks perfect English, yet her dad speaks with an accent?
I mean...how did that happen? Isn't it usually the other way around?
Hm... you're right... that is pretty unusual...
The carwash wasn't nearly successful enough.
We only made half of what we needed. So we decided to do a bake sale during lunch the following week.
BAKE SALE
FROM THE DRAMA DEPARTMENT
PLEASE HELP SAVE OUR PLAY "FLOWERS IN THE BASEMENT"
Don't you even think about it!

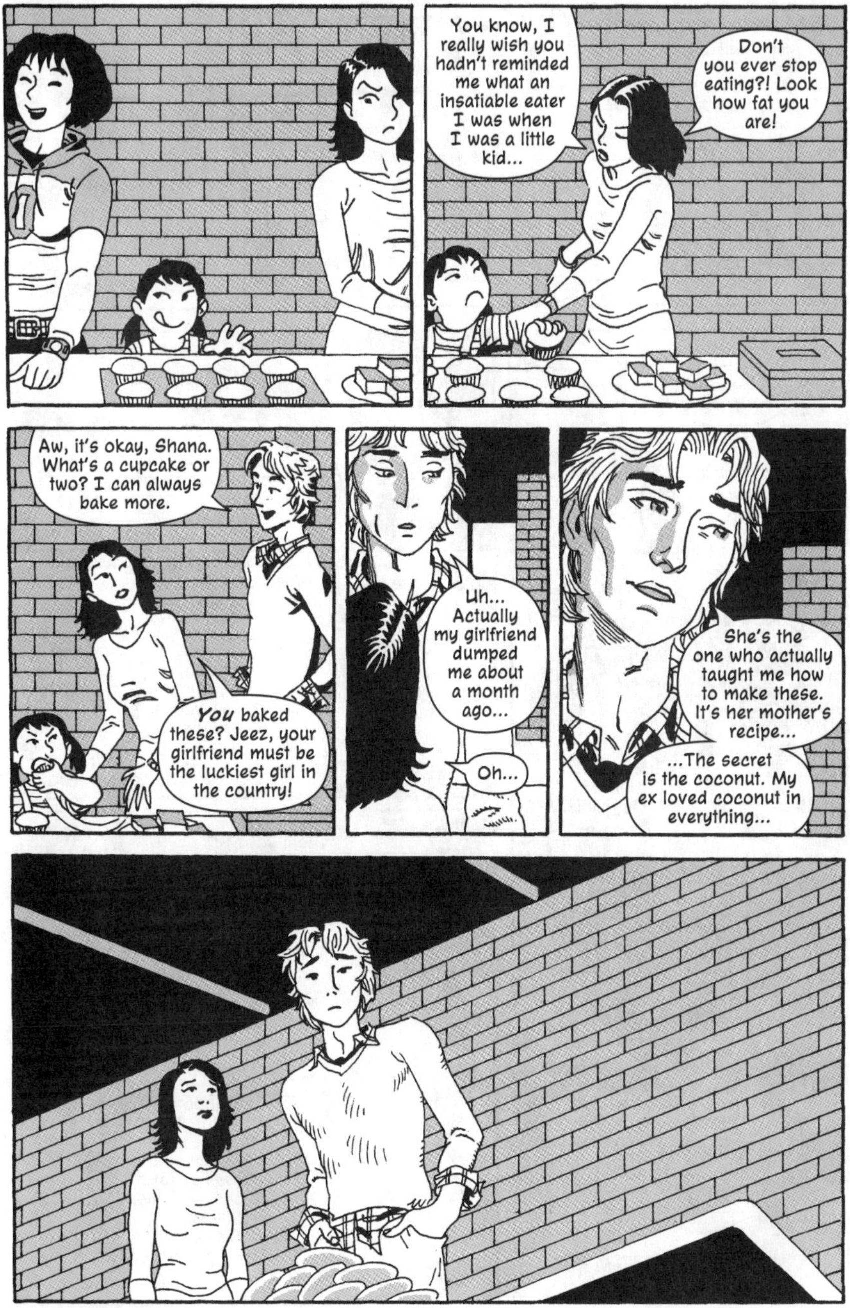
You know, I really wish you hadn't reminded me what an insatiable eater I was when I was a little kid...
Don't you ever stop eating?! Look how fat you are!
Aw, it's okay, Shana. What's a cupcake or two? I can always bake more.
You baked these? Jeez, your girlfriend must be the luckiest girl in the country!
Uh... Actually my girlfriend dumped me about a month ago...
Oh...
She's the one who actually taught me how to make these. It's her mother's recipe...
...The secret is the coconut. My ex loved coconut in everything...

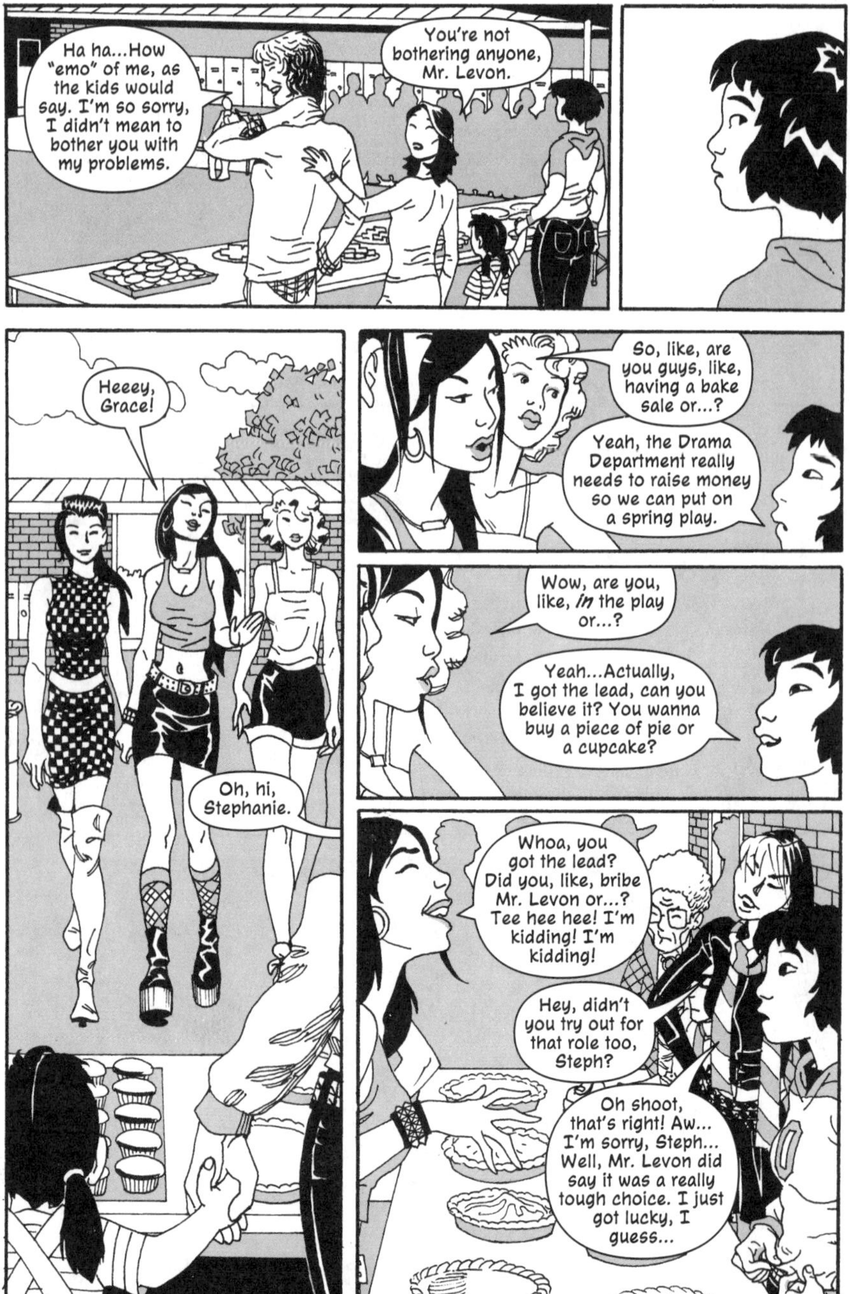
Ha ha...How "emo" of me, as the kids would say. I'm so sorry, I didn't mean to bother you with my problems.
You're not bothering anyone, Mr. Levon.
Heeey, Grace!
Oh, hi, Stephanie.
So, like, are you guys, like, having a bake sale or...?
Yeah, the Drama Department really needs to raise money so we can put on a spring play.
Wow, are you, like, *in* the play or...?
Yeah...Actually, I got the lead, can you believe it? You wanna buy a piece of pie or a cupcake?
Whoa, you got the lead? Did you, like, bribe Mr. Levon or...? Tee hee hee! I'm kidding! I'm kidding!
Hey, didn't you try out for that role too, Steph?
Oh shoot, that's right! Aw... I'm sorry, Steph... Well, Mr. Levon did say it was a really tough choice. I just got lucky, I guess...

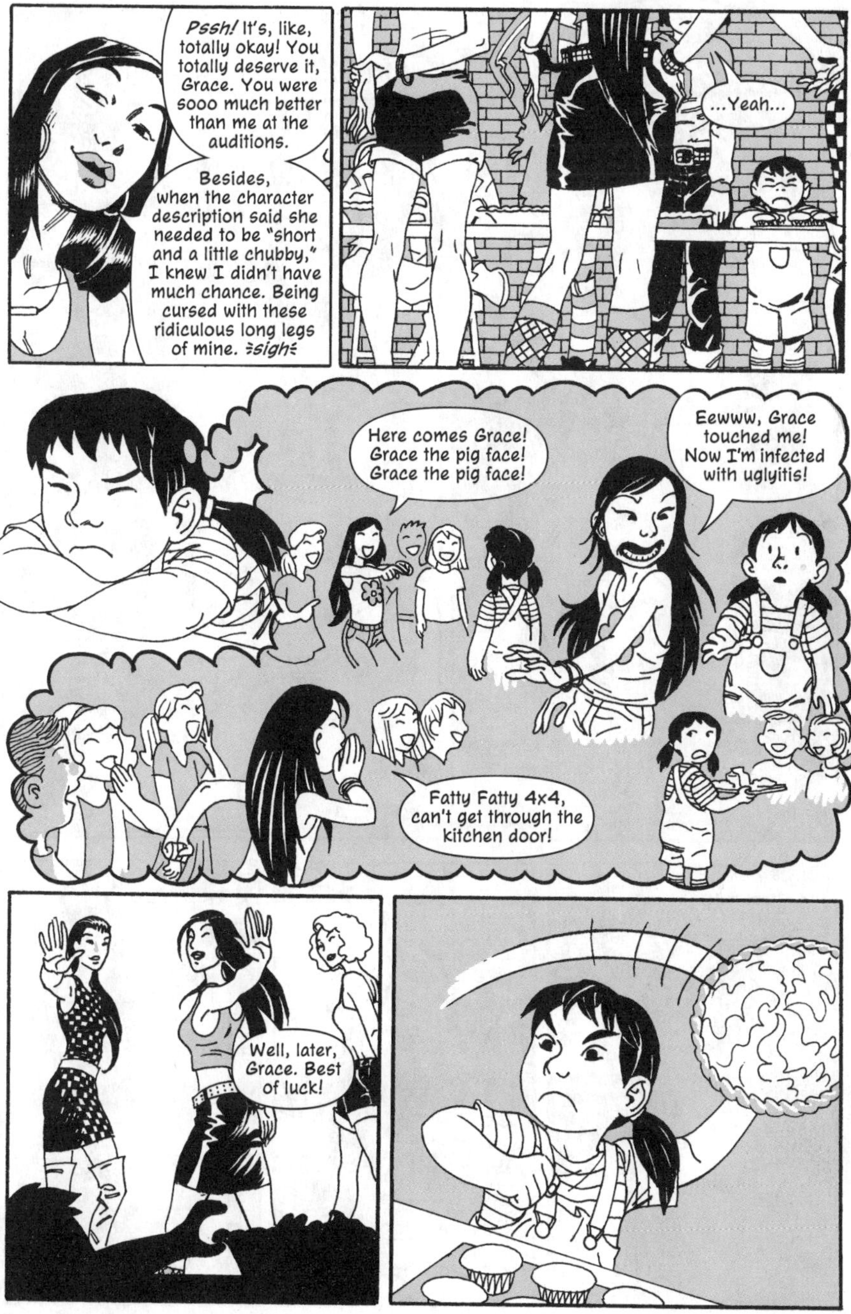
Pssh! It's, like, totally okay! You totally deserve it, Grace. You were sooo much better than me at the auditions.
Besides, when the character description said she needed to be "short and a little chubby," I knew I didn't have much chance. Being cursed with these ridiculous long legs of mine. ≷sigh≶
...Yeah...
Here comes Grace! Grace the pig face! Grace the pig face!
Eewww, Grace touched me! Now I'm infected with uglyitis!
Fatty Fatty 4x4, can't get through the kitchen door!
Well, later, Grace. Best of luck!

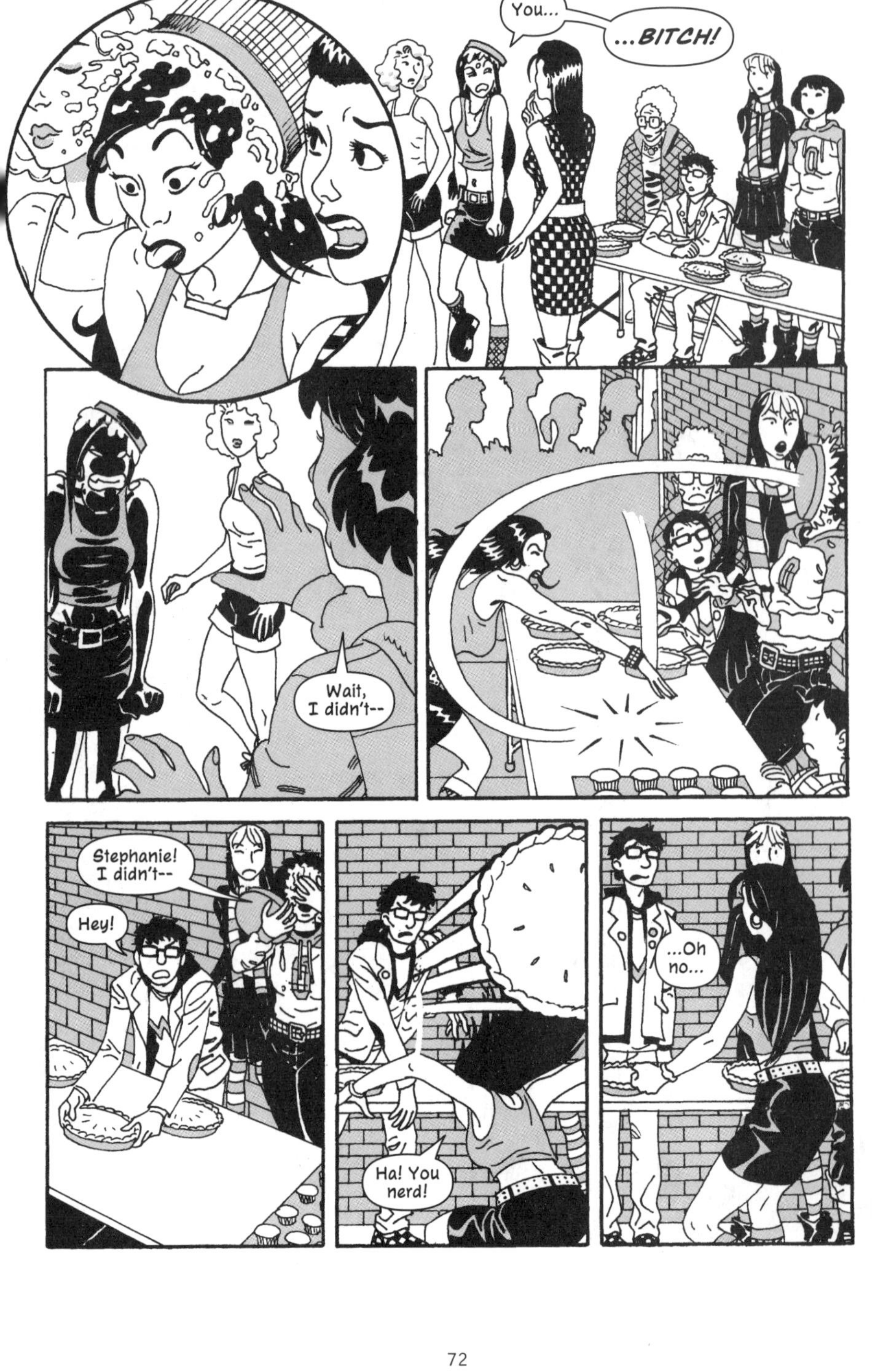
You...
...BITCH!
Wait, I didn't--
Stephanie! I didn't--
Hey!
Ha! You nerd!
...Oh no...

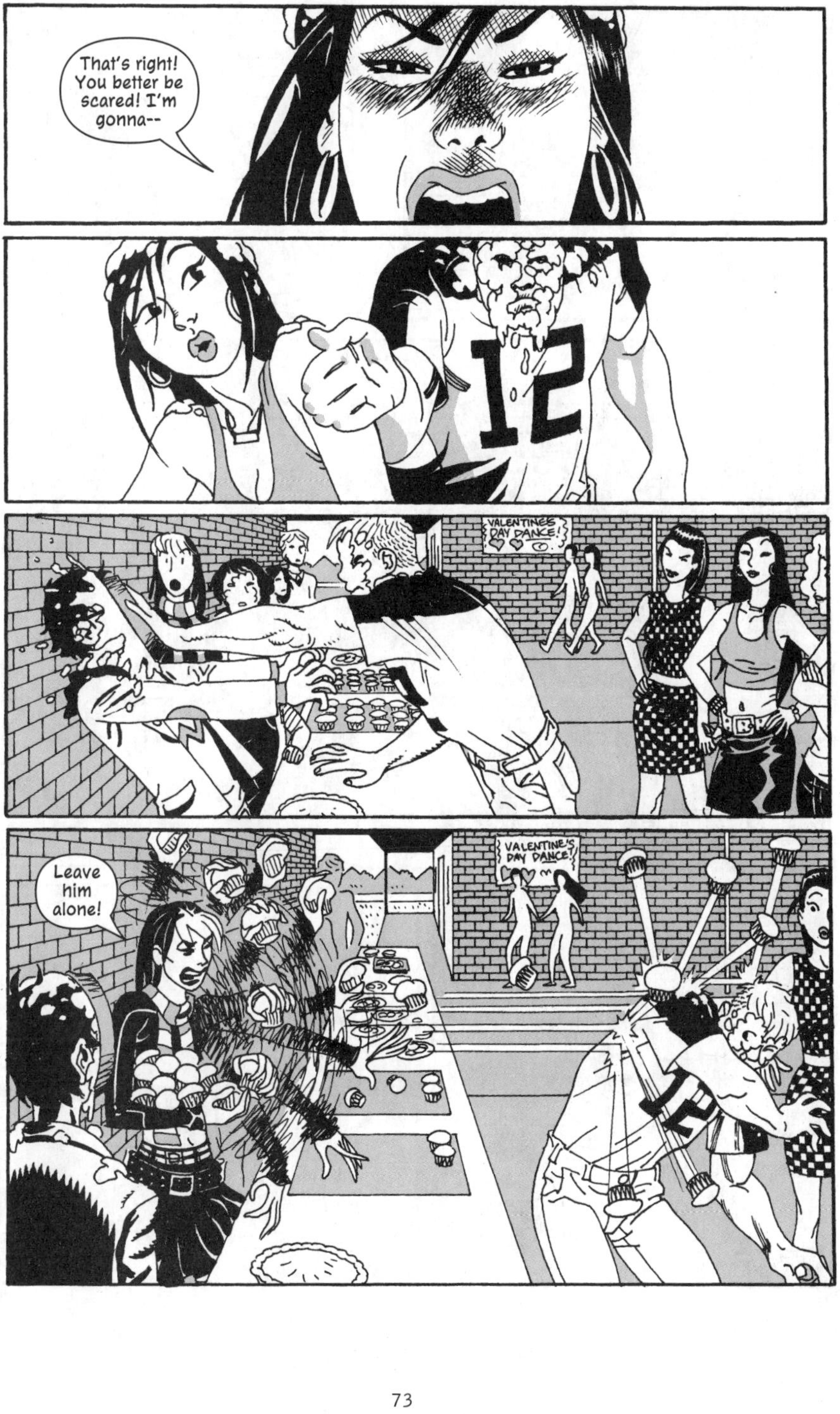
That's right! You better be scared! I'm gonna--
VALENTINE'S DAY DANCE!
Leave him alone!
VALENTINE'S DAY DANCE

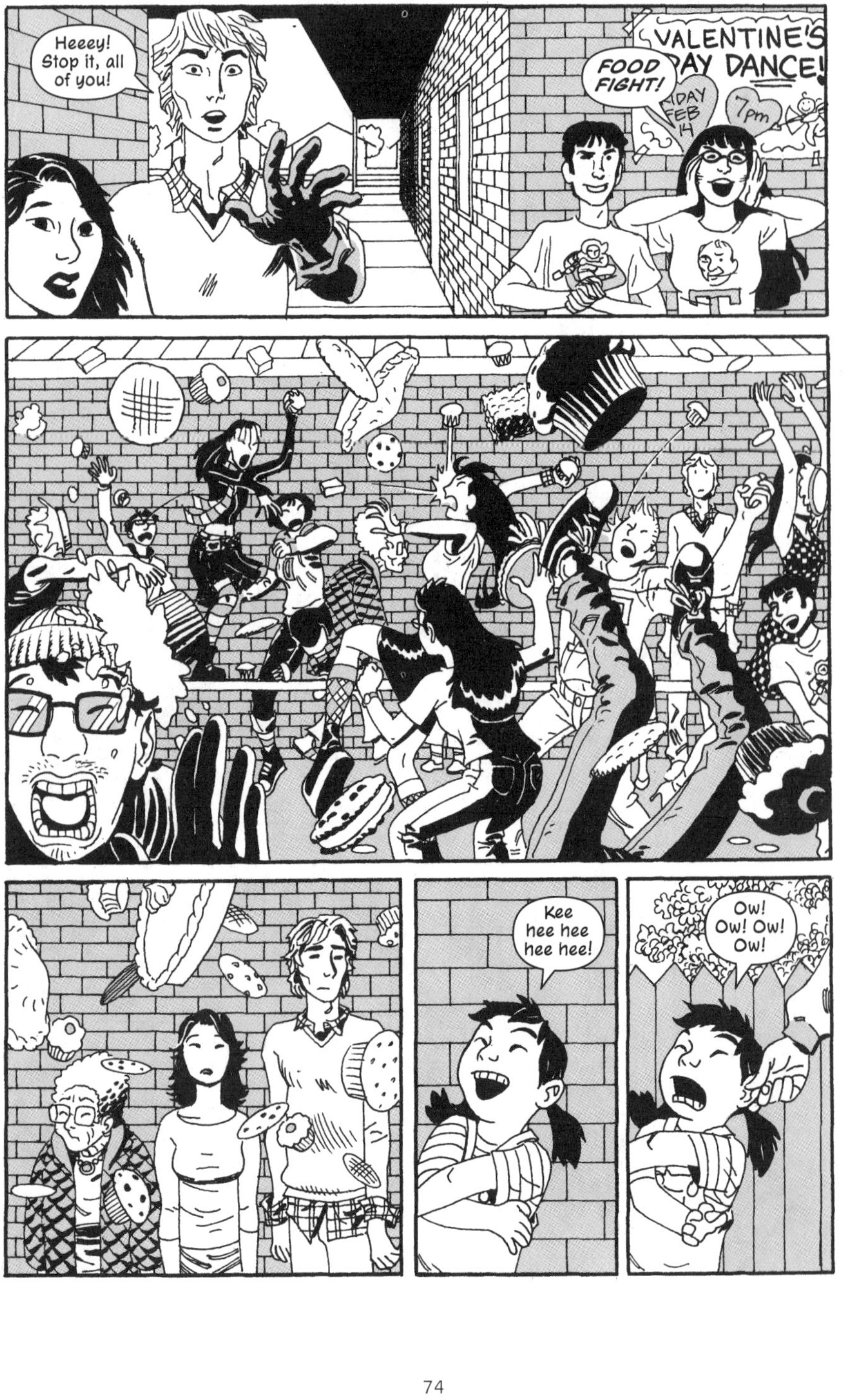
Heeey! Stop it, all of you!
FOOD FIGHT!
VALENTINE'S
AY DANCE!
IDAY FEB 14
7pm
Kee hee hee hee hee!
Ow! Ow! Ow! Ow!

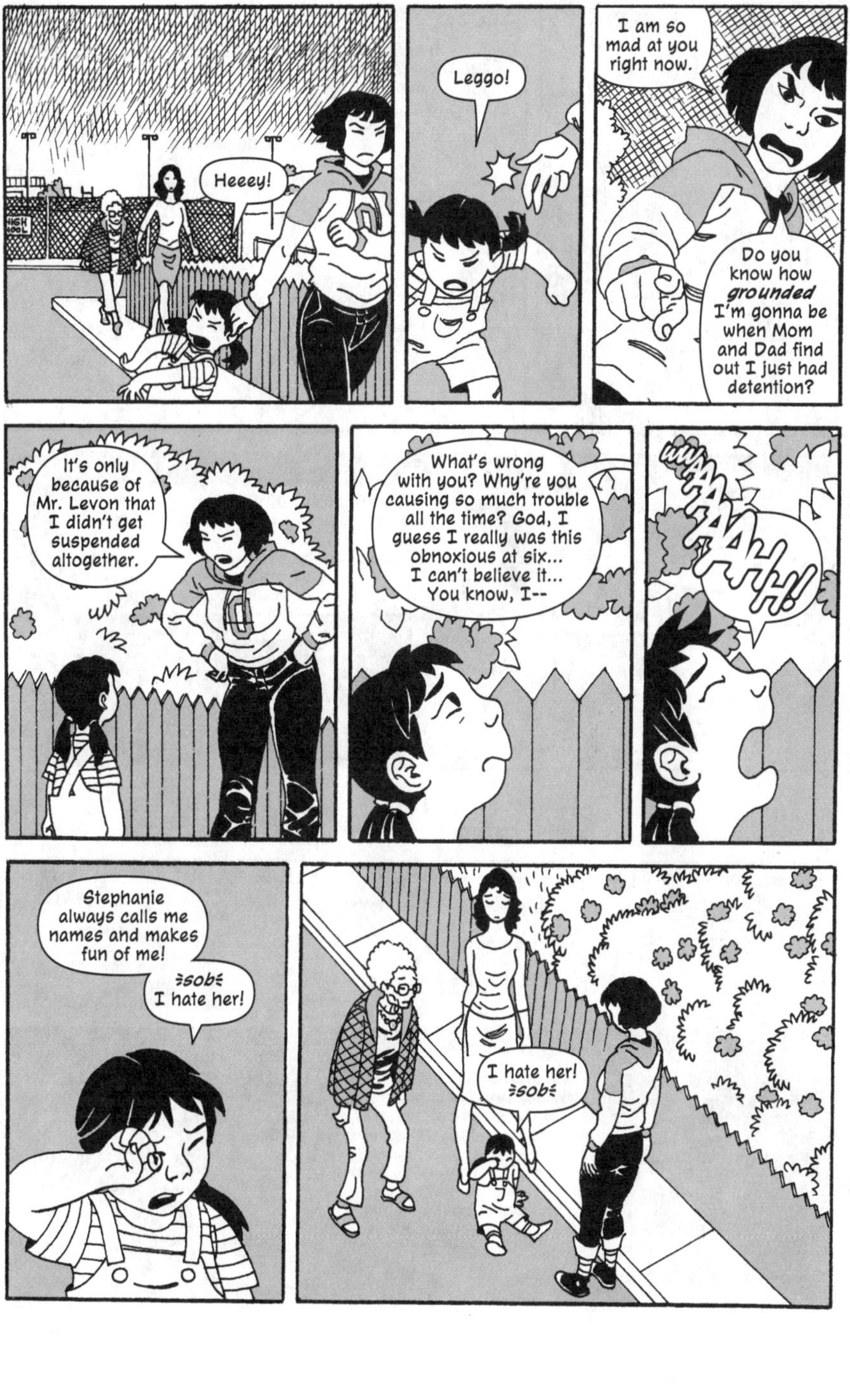
HIGH SCHOOL
Heeey!
Leggo!
I am so mad at you right now.
Do you know how ***grounded*** I'm gonna be when Mom and Dad find out I just had detention?
It's only because of Mr. Levon that I didn't get suspended altogether.
What's wrong with you? Why're you causing so much trouble all the time? God, I guess I really was this obnoxious at six... I can't believe it... You know, I--
WWAAAAAHH!
Stephanie always calls me names and makes fun of me!
sob I hate her!
I hate her! *sob*

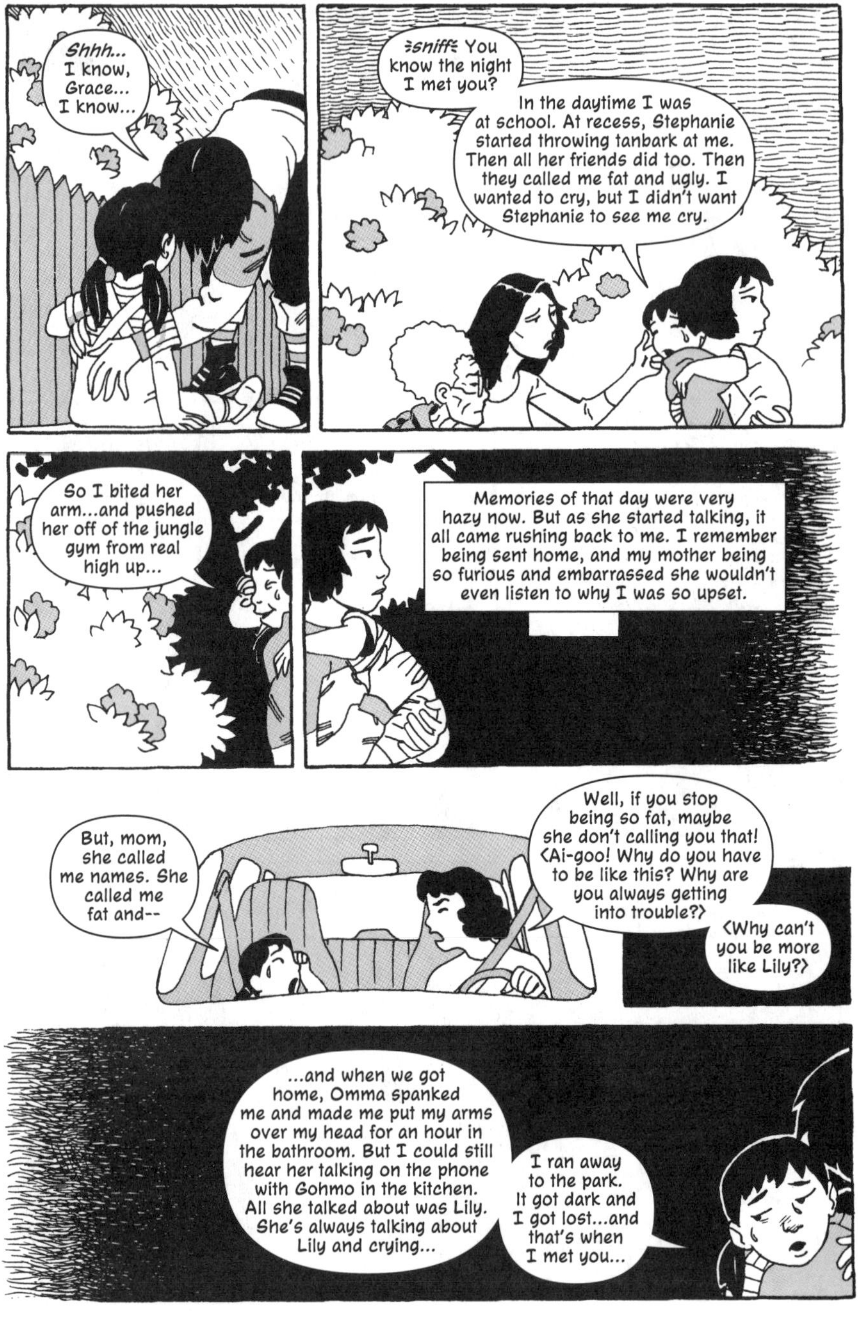
Shhh... I know, Grace... I know...
≡sniff≡ You know the night I met you?
In the daytime I was at school. At recess, Stephanie started throwing tanbark at me. Then all her friends did too. Then they called me fat and ugly. I wanted to cry, but I didn't want Stephanie to see me cry.
So I bited her arm...and pushed her off of the jungle gym from real high up...
Memories of that day were very hazy now. But as she started talking, it all came rushing back to me. I remember being sent home, and my mother being so furious and embarrassed she wouldn't even listen to why I was so upset.
But, mom, she called me names. She called me fat and--
Well, if you stop being so fat, maybe she don't calling you that! <Ai-goo! Why do you have to be like this? Why are you always getting into trouble?>
<Why can't you be more like Lily?>
...and when we got home, Omma spanked me and made me put my arms over my head for an hour in the bathroom. But I could still hear her talking on the phone with Gohmo in the kitchen. All she talked about was Lily. She's always talking about Lily and crying...
I ran away to the park. It got dark and I got lost...and that's when I met you...

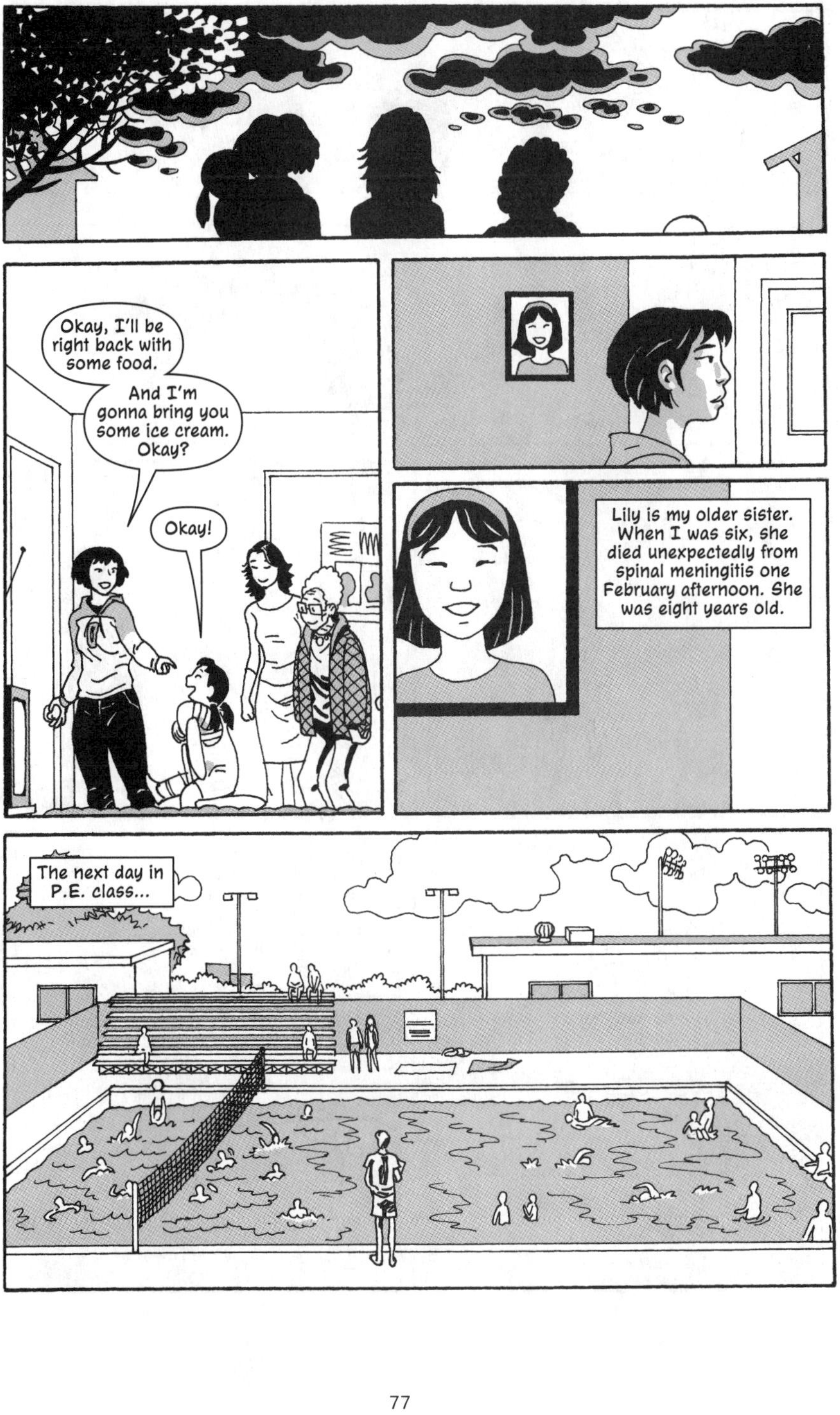
Okay, I'll be right back with some food.
And I'm gonna bring you some ice cream. Okay?
Okay!
Lily is my older sister. When I was six, she died unexpectedly from spinal meningitis one February afternoon. She was eight years old.
The next day in P.E. class...

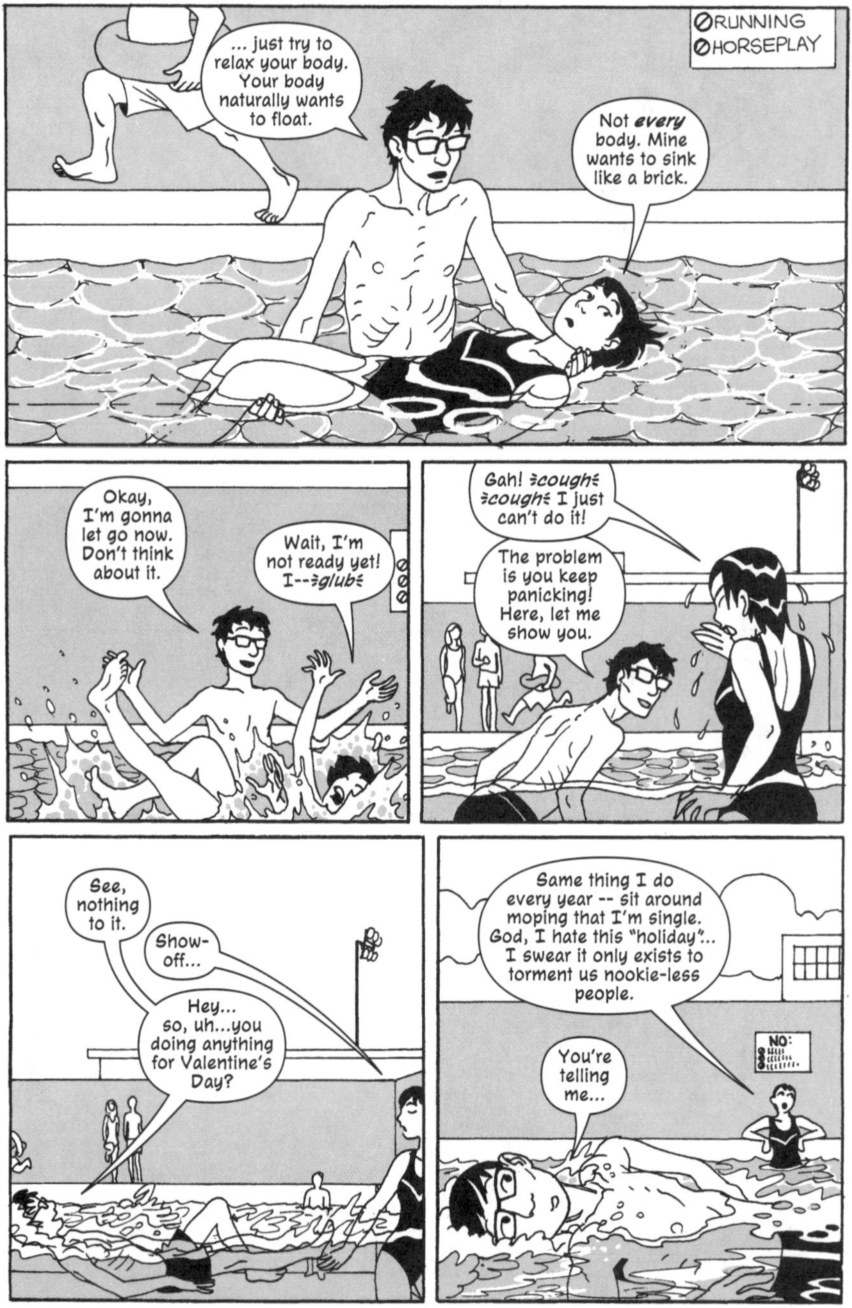
RUNNING
HORSEPLAY
... just try to relax your body. Your body naturally wants to float.
Not *every* body. Mine wants to sink like a brick.
Okay, I'm gonna let go now. Don't think about it.
Wait, I'm not ready yet! I-- *glub*
Gah! ≷*cough*≶ ≷*cough*≶ I just can't do it!
The problem is you keep panicking! Here, let me show you.
See, nothing to it.
Show-off...
Hey... so, uh...you doing anything for Valentine's Day?
Same thing I do every year -- sit around moping that I'm single. God, I hate this "holiday"... I swear it only exists to torment us nookie-less people.
NO:
You're telling me...

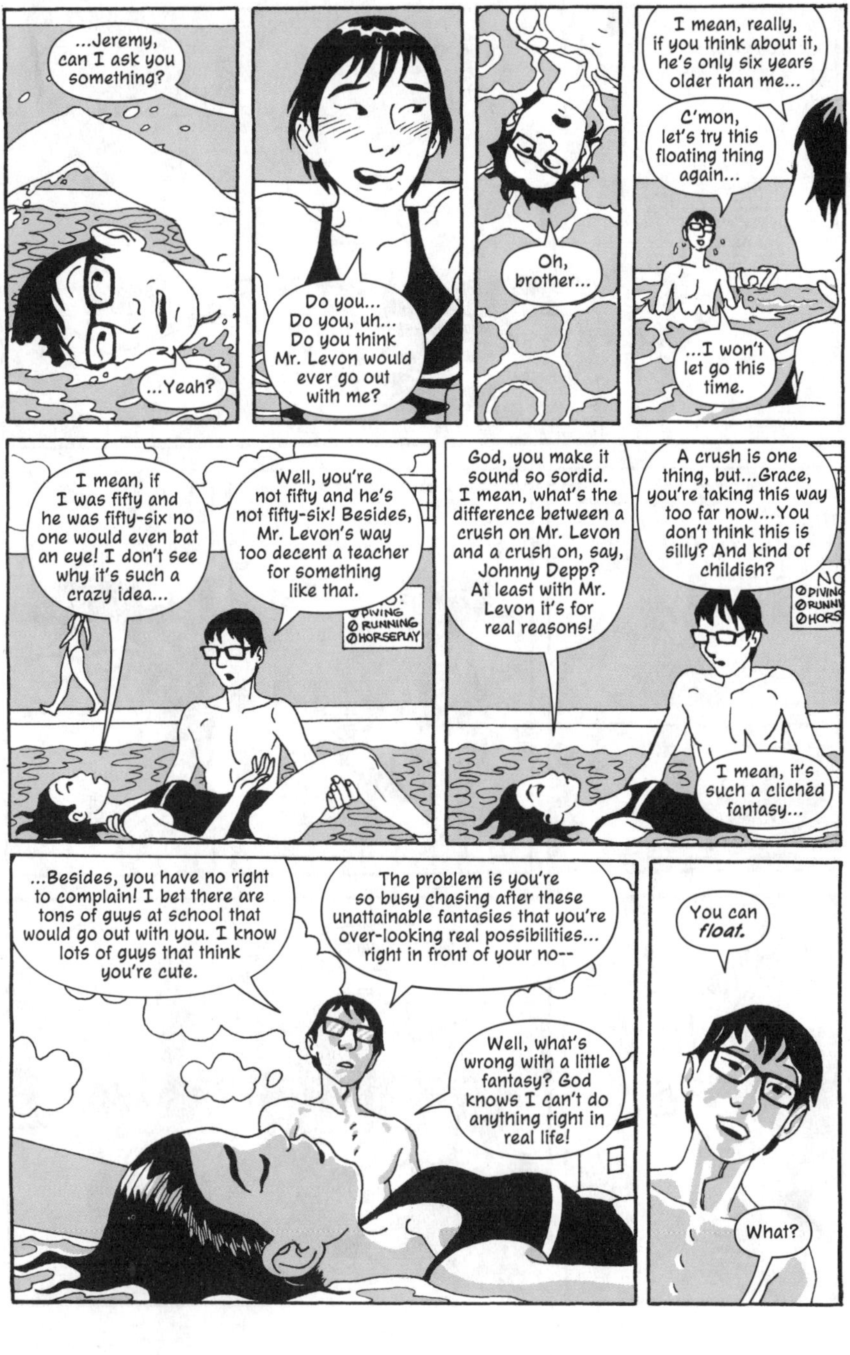
...Jeremy, can I ask you something?
...Yeah?
Do you... Do you, uh... Do you think Mr. Levon would ever go out with me?
Oh, brother...
I mean, really, if you think about it, he's only six years older than me...
C'mon, let's try this floating thing again...
...I won't let go this time.
I mean, if I was fifty and he was fifty-six no one would even bat an eye! I don't see why it's such a crazy idea...
Well, you're not fifty and he's not fifty-six! Besides, Mr. Levon's way too decent a teacher for something like that.
NO: DIVING RUNNING HORSEPLAY
God, you make it sound so sordid. I mean, what's the difference between a crush on Mr. Levon and a crush on, say, Johnny Depp? At least with Mr. Levon it's for real reasons!
A crush is one thing, but...Grace, you're taking this way too far now...You don't think this is silly? And kind of childish?
I mean, it's such a clichéd fantasy...
...Besides, you have no right to complain! I bet there are tons of guys at school that would go out with you. I know lots of guys that think you're cute.
The problem is you're so busy chasing after these unattainable fantasies that you're over-looking real possibilities... right in front of your no--
Well, what's wrong with a little fantasy? God knows I can't do anything right in real life!
You can *float.*
What?

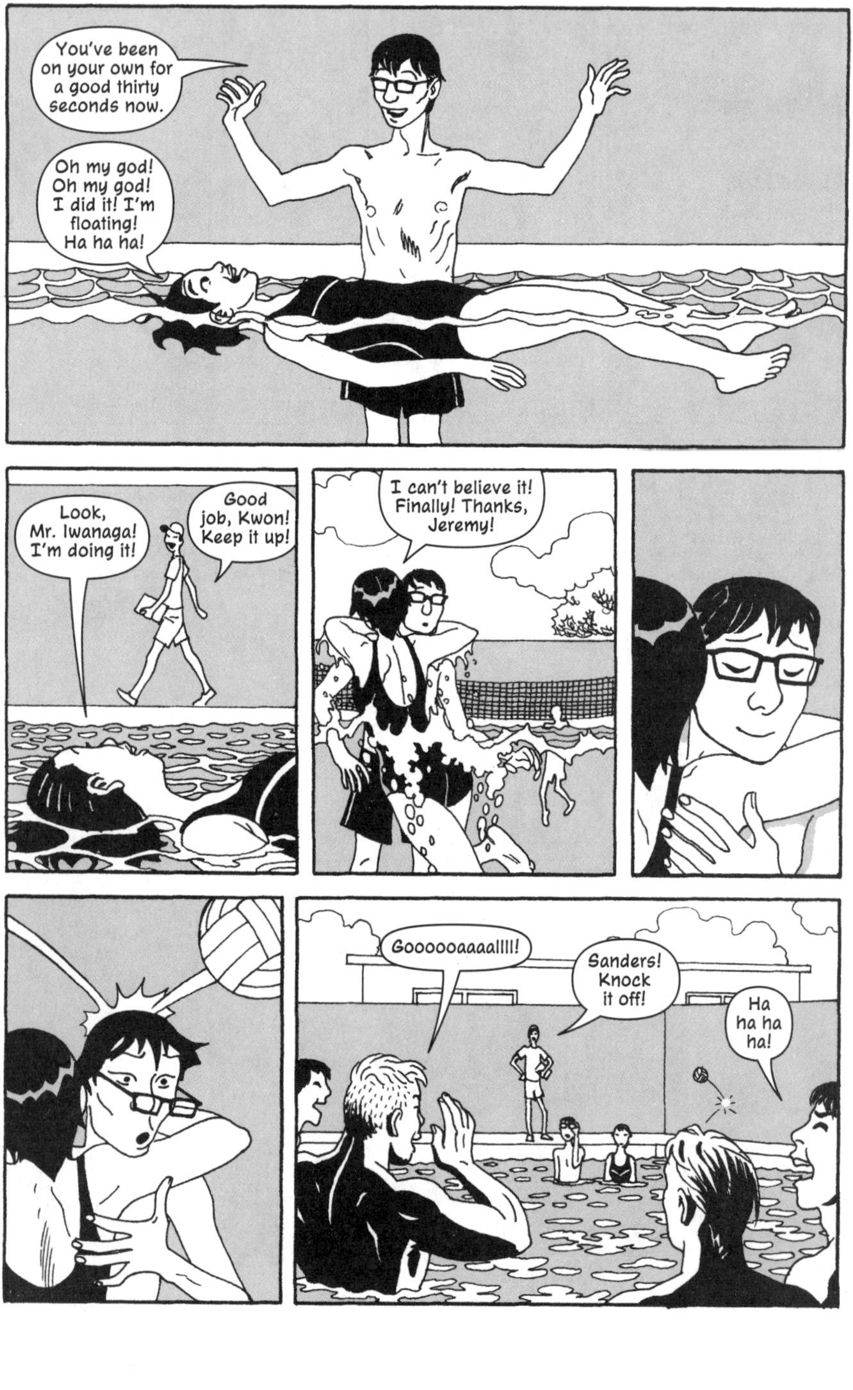

You've been on your own for a good thirty seconds now.
Oh my god! Oh my god! I did it! I'm floating! Ha ha ha!
Look, Mr. Iwanaga! I'm doing it!
Good job, Kwon! Keep it up!
I can't believe it! Finally! Thanks, Jeremy!
Gooooaaaallll!
Sanders! Knock it off!
Ha ha ha ha!

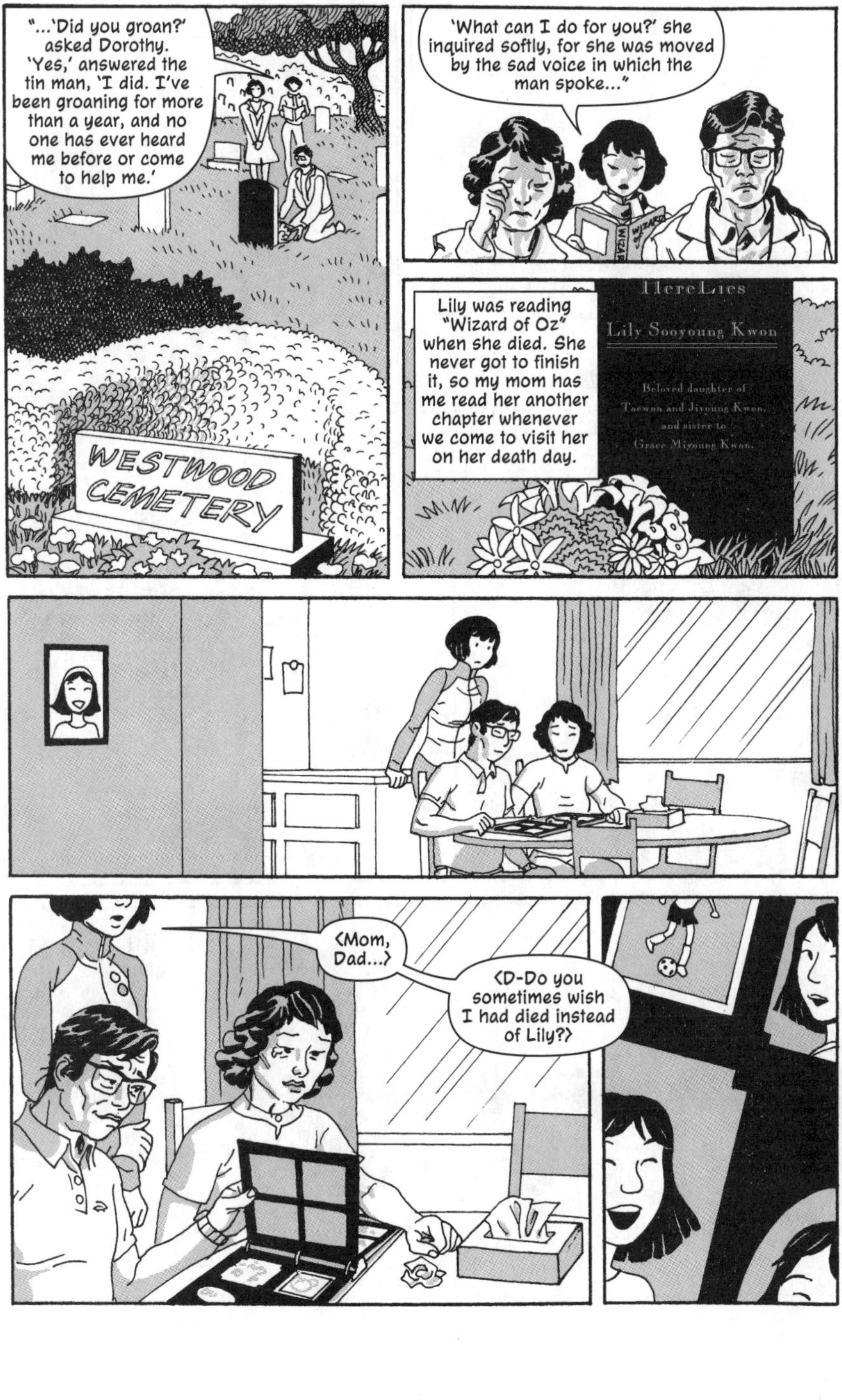
"...'Did you groan?' asked Dorothy. 'Yes,' answered the tin man, 'I did. I've been groaning for more than a year, and no one has ever heard me before or come to help me.'
WESTWOOD CEMETERY
'What can I do for you?' she inquired softly, for she was moved by the sad voice in which the man spoke..."
Lily was reading "Wizard of Oz" when she died. She never got to finish it, so my mom has me read her another chapter whenever we come to visit her on her death day.
Here Lies
Lily Sooyoung Kwon
Beloved daughter of Taewon and Jiyoung Kwon, and sister to Grace Miyoung Kwon.
<Mom, Dad...>
<D-Do you sometimes wish I had died instead of Lily?>

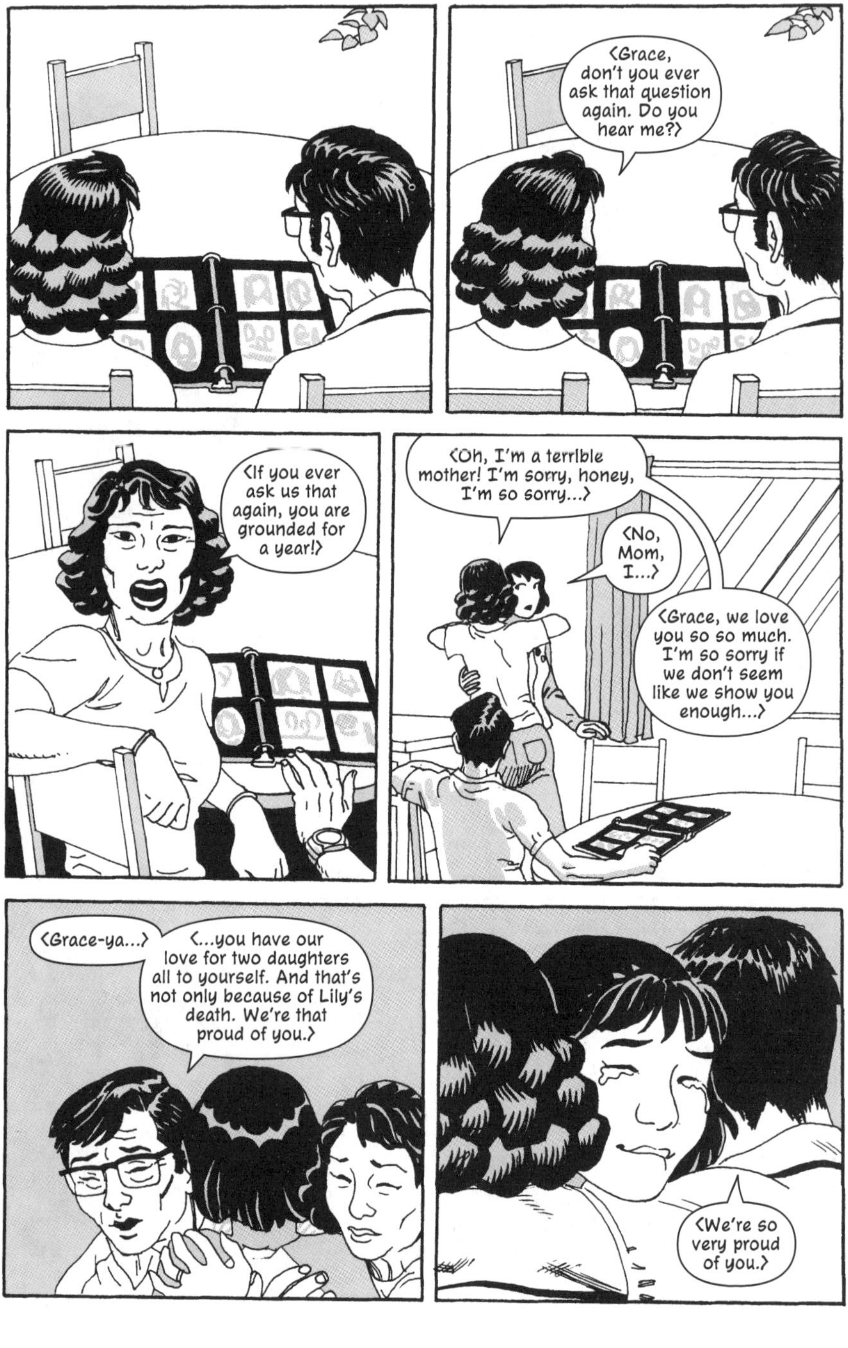

<Grace, don't you ever ask that question again. Do you hear me?>
<If you ever ask us that again, you are grounded for a year!>
<Oh, I'm a terrible mother! I'm sorry, honey, I'm so sorry...>
<No, Mom, I...>
<Grace, we love you so so much. I'm so sorry if we don't seem like we show you enough...>
<Grace-ya...>
<...you have our love for two daughters all to yourself. And that's not only because of Lily's death. We're that proud of you.>
<We're so very proud of you.>

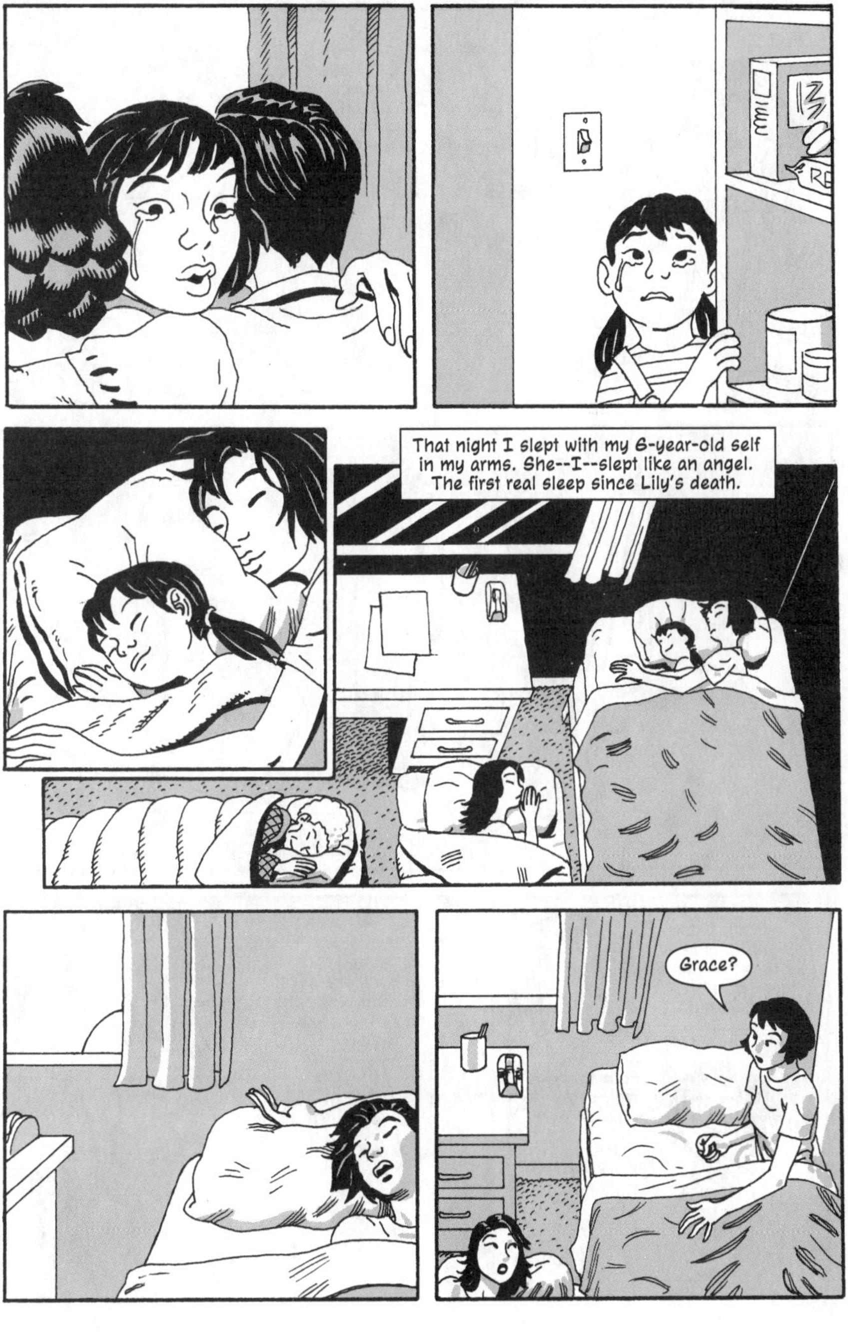
That night I slept with my 6-year-old self in my arms. She--I--slept like an angel. The first real sleep since Lily's death.
Grace?

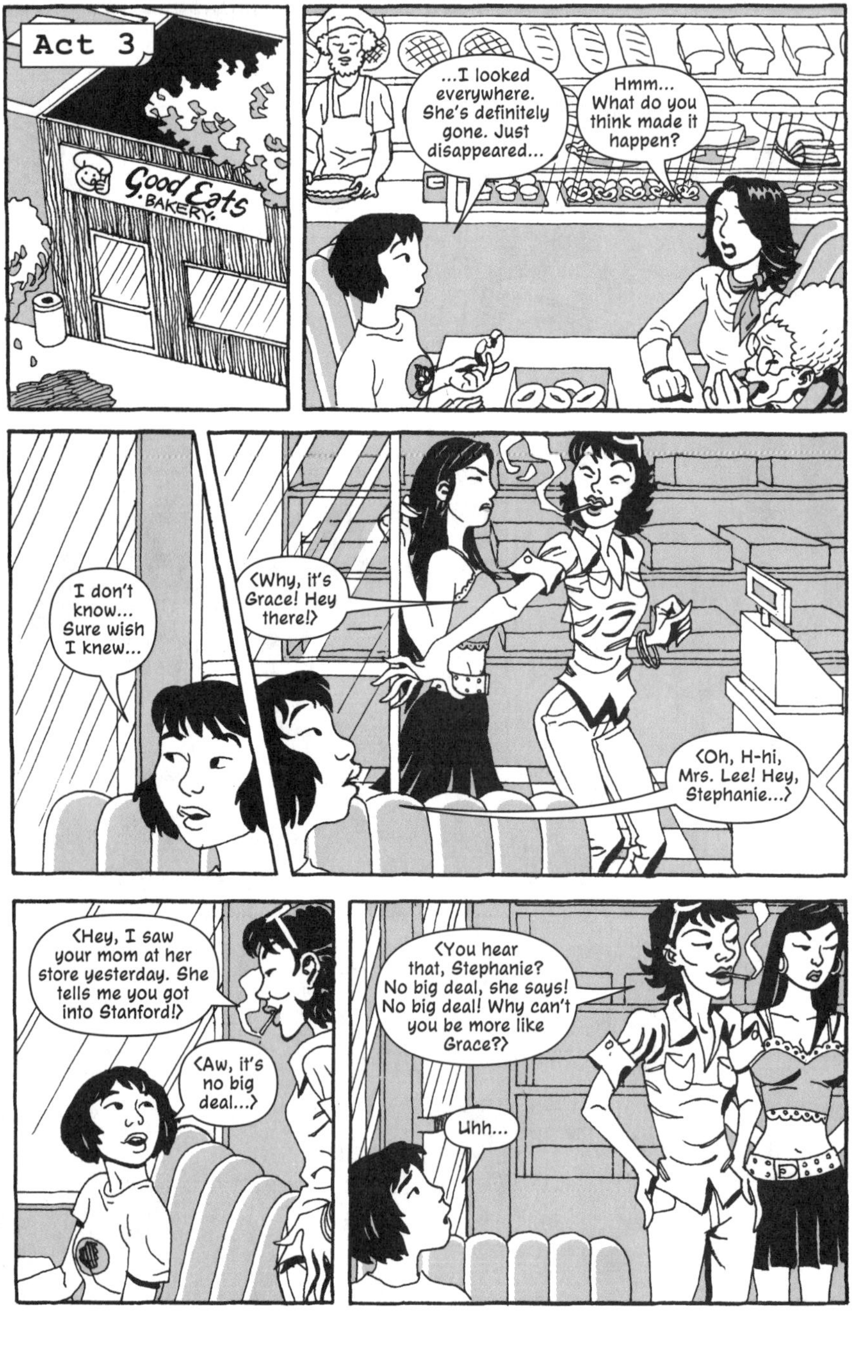
Act 3
Good Eats BAKERY
...I looked everywhere. She's definitely gone. Just disappeared...
Hmm... What do you think made it happen?
I don't know... Sure wish I knew...
<Why, it's Grace! Hey there!>
<Oh, H-hi, Mrs. Lee! Hey, Stephanie...>
<Hey, I saw your mom at her store yesterday. She tells me you got into Stanford!>
<Aw, it's no big deal...>
<You hear that, Stephanie? No big deal, she says! No big deal! Why can't you be more like Grace?>
Uhh...

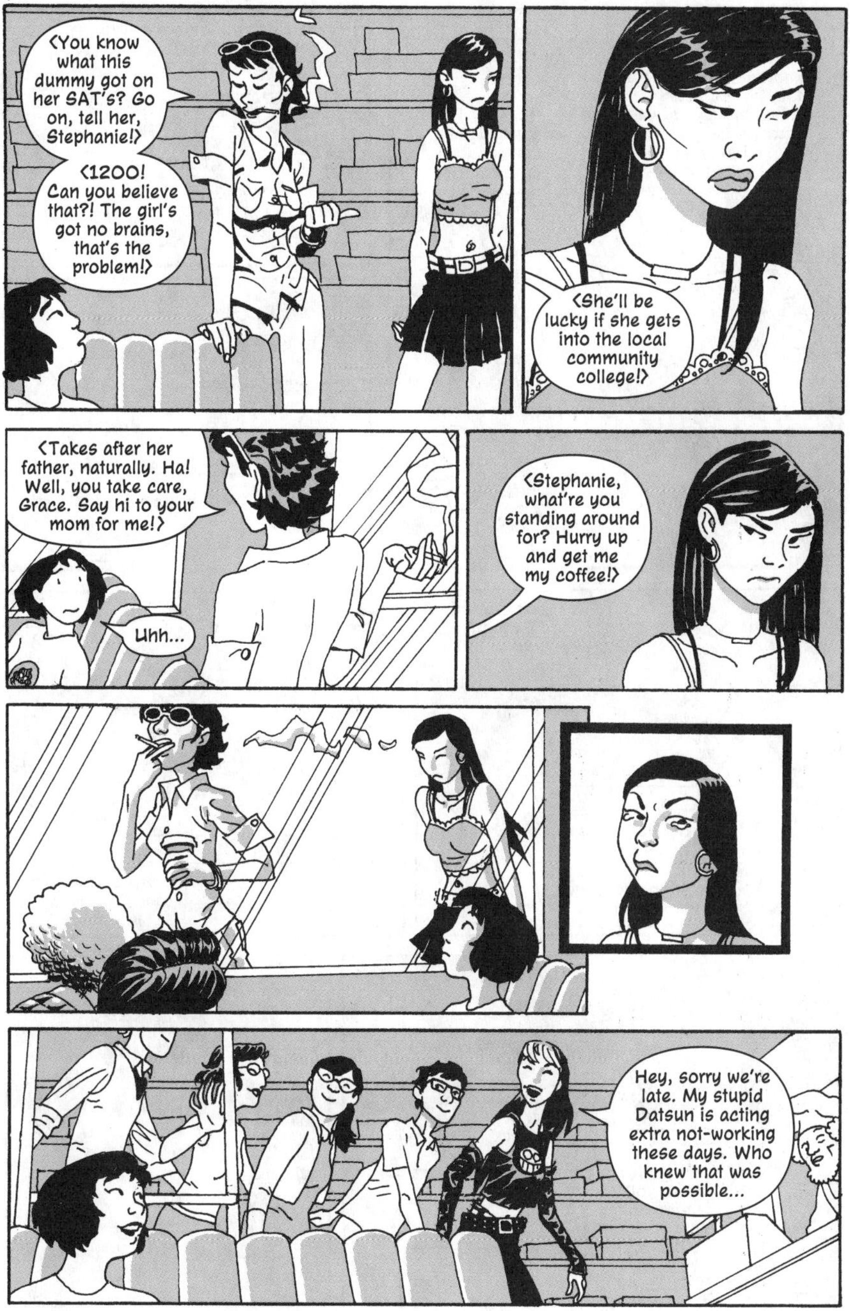
<You know what this dummy got on her SAT's? Go on, tell her, Stephanie!>
<1200! Can you believe that?! The girl's got no brains, that's the problem!>
<She'll be lucky if she gets into the local community college!>
<Takes after her father, naturally. Ha! Well, you take care, Grace. Say hi to your mom for me!>
Uhh...
<Stephanie, what're you standing around for? Hurry up and get me my coffee!>
Hey, sorry we're late. My stupid Datsun is acting extra not-working these days. Who knew that was possible...

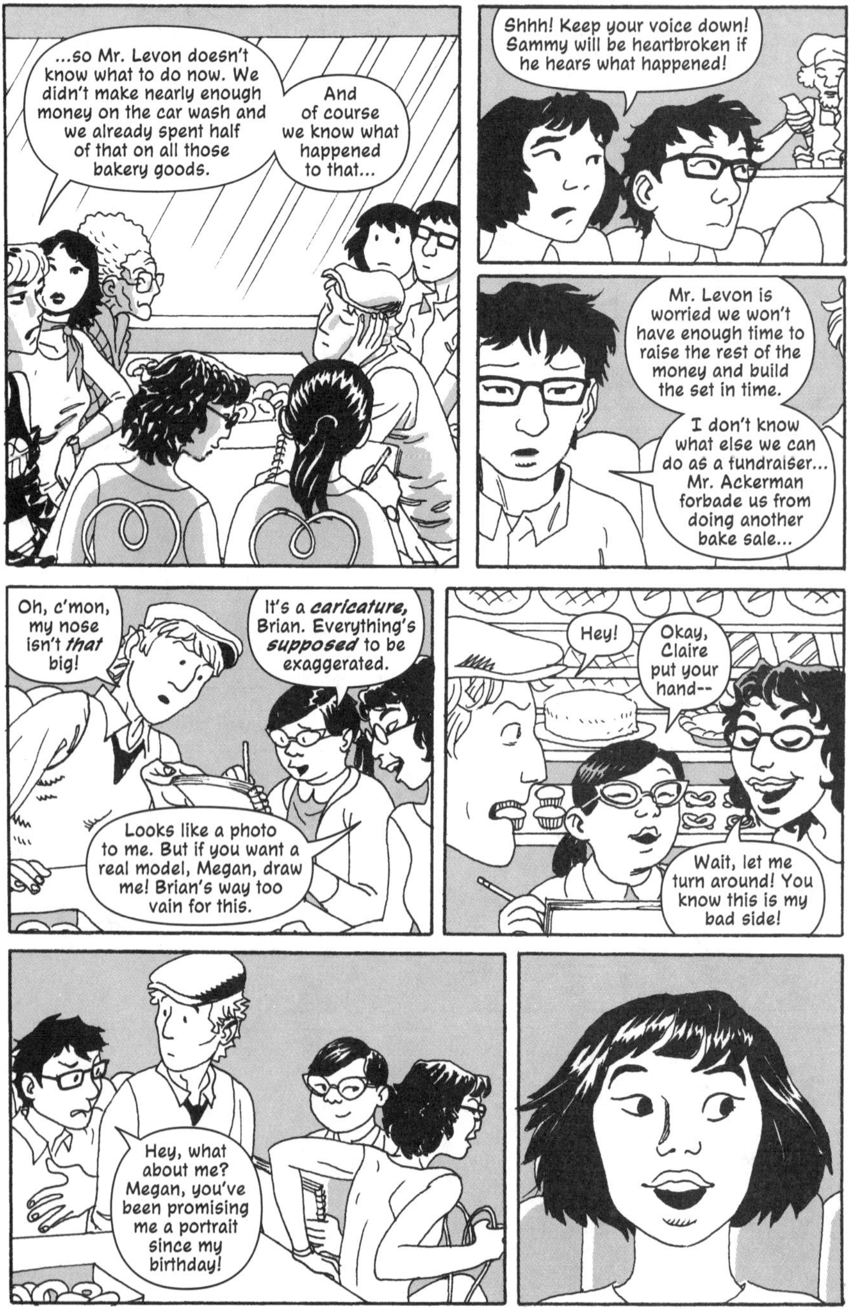
...so Mr. Levon doesn't know what to do now. We didn't make nearly enough money on the car wash and we already spent half of that on all those bakery goods.
And of course we know what happened to that...
Shhh! Keep your voice down! Sammy will be heartbroken if he hears what happened!
Mr. Levon is worried we won't have enough time to raise the rest of the money and build the set in time.
I don't know what else we can do as a fundraiser... Mr. Ackerman forbade us from doing another bake sale...
Oh, c'mon, my nose isn't *that* big!
It's a ***caricature,*** Brian. Everything's ***supposed*** to be exaggerated.
Looks like a photo to me. But if you want a real model, Megan, draw me! Brian's way too vain for this.
Hey!
Okay, Claire put your hand--
Wait, let me turn around! You know this is my bad side!
Hey, what about me? Megan, you've been promising me a portrait since my birthday!

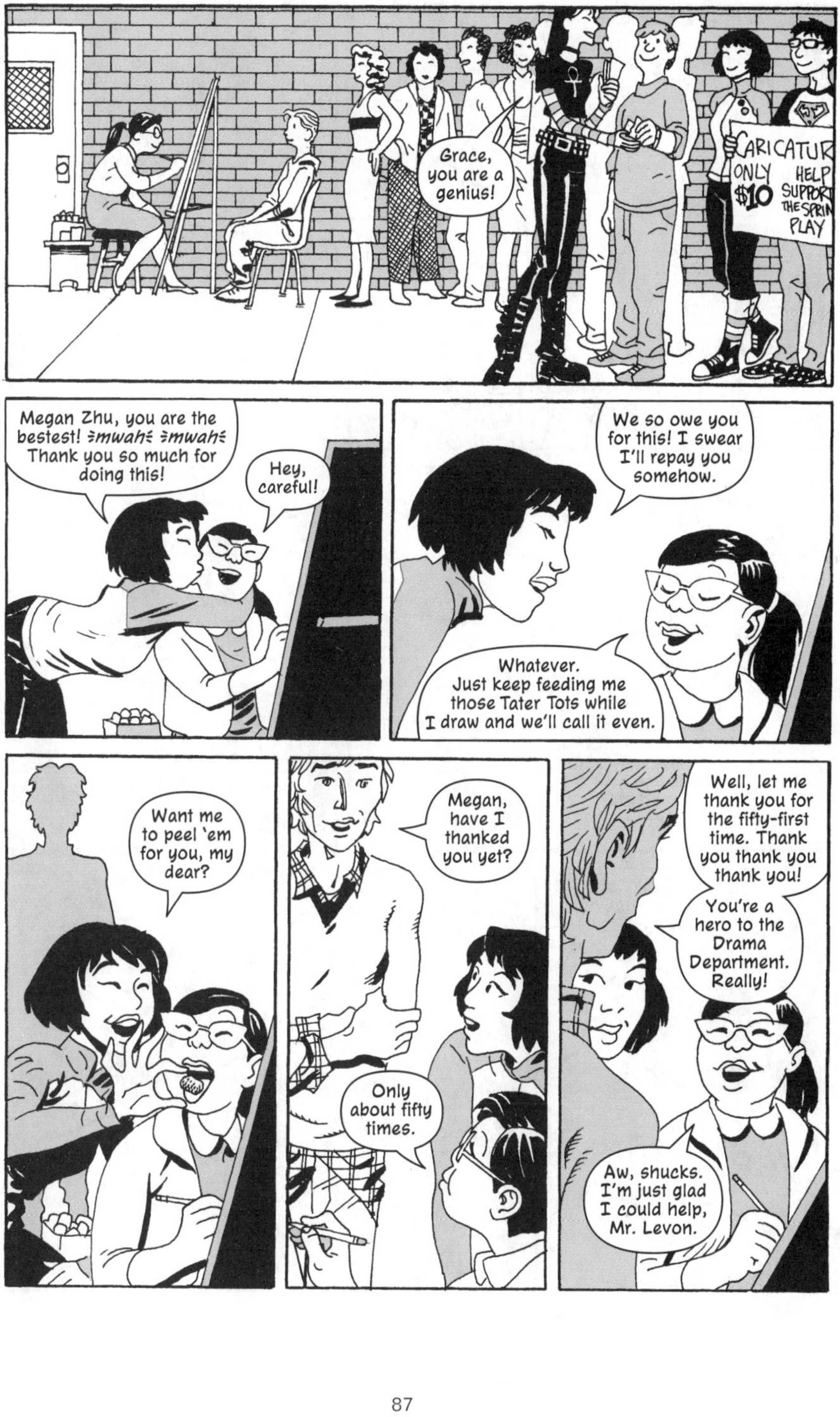
Grace, you are a genius!
CARICATURES ONLY $10 HELP SUPPORT THE SPRING PLAY
Megan Zhu, you are the bestest! ≡mwah≡ ≡mwah≡ Thank you so much for doing this!
Hey, careful!
We so owe you for this! I swear I'll repay you somehow.
Whatever. Just keep feeding me those Tater Tots while I draw and we'll call it even.
Want me to peel 'em for you, my dear?
Megan, have I thanked you yet?
Only about fifty times.
Well, let me thank you for the fifty-first time. Thank you thank you thank you!
You're a hero to the Drama Department. Really!
Aw, shucks. I'm just glad I could help, Mr. Levon.

Panel 1:

Grace, this was a fantastic idea! You and Megan just saved the play.

Well, I don't know if I...I mean, Megan's actually doing all the...Anyone could've...

Panel 2:

Grace, I also had a question for you...

Yes...?

Panel 3:

Uh, well, I was just wondering if your Aunt Shana was coming to the play. Since she's helped us out so much, I thought I should at least give her and her boyfriend free tickets.

Or her husband, if she's married of course... Ha ha, I mean, I'm pretty sure she's not married...but I guess, I shouldn't...I mean... So...is she married?...or does she have a boyfriend?

Panel 4:

No, she's single.

Panel 5:

Oh...I see. Well, I'll just reserve one ticket for her then.

Boy, is she ever single.

Panel 6:

Pardon?

Yup, poor Aunt Shana. She just seems to have the worst luck with men. Her last boyfriend left her without warning on their wedding day!

Panel 7:

Oh, that's horrible!

I talked to him shortly before he left her. I couldn't believe how shallow he was!

He kept telling me that he just couldn't stand the pus anymore.

Poor Sha--

Pus?

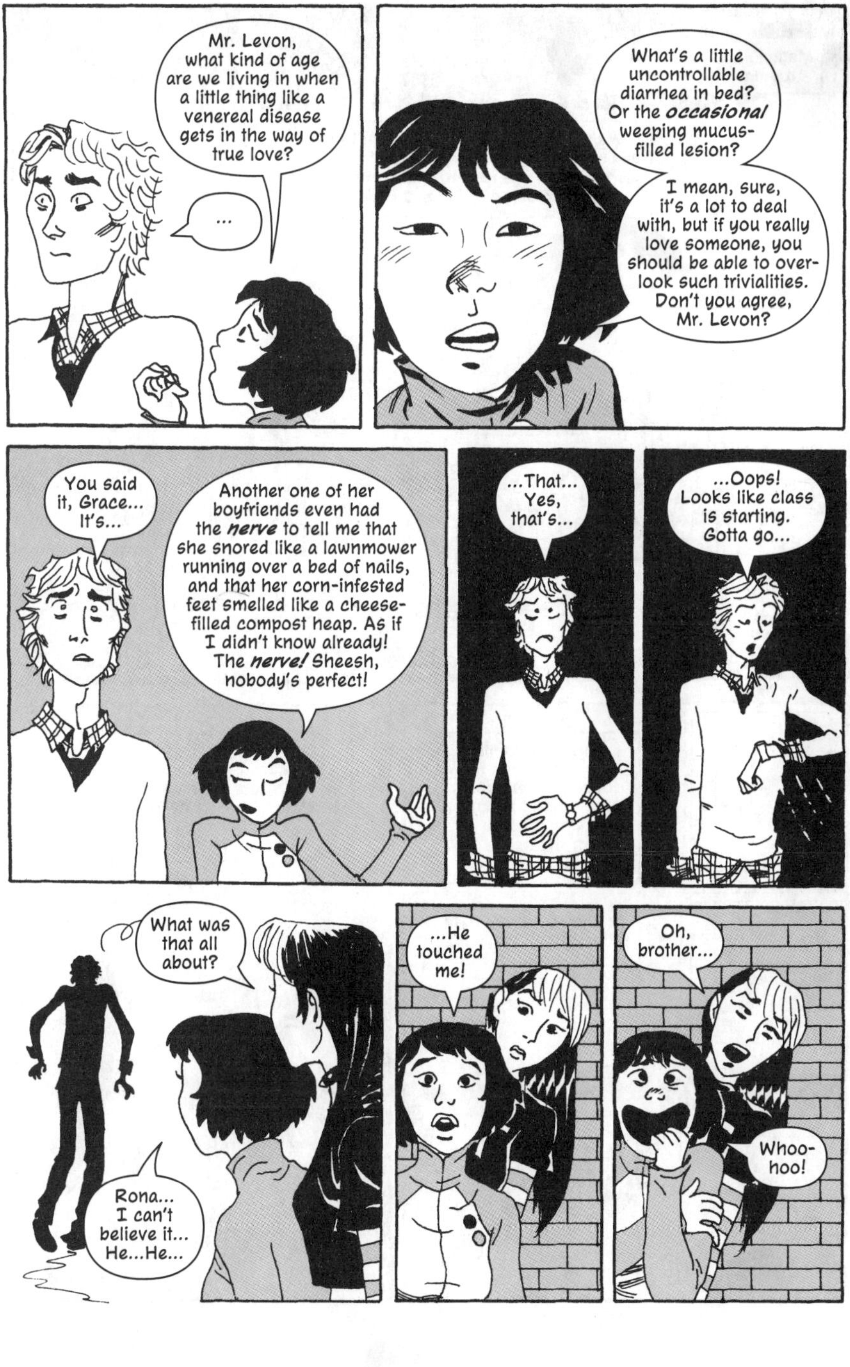
Mr. Levon, what kind of age are we living in when a little thing like a venereal disease gets in the way of true love?
...
What's a little uncontrollable diarrhea in bed? Or the *occasional* weeping mucus-filled lesion?
I mean, sure, it's a lot to deal with, but if you really love someone, you should be able to overlook such trivialities. Don't you agree, Mr. Levon?
You said it, Grace... It's...
Another one of her boyfriends even had the *nerve* to tell me that she snored like a lawnmower running over a bed of nails, and that her corn-infested feet smelled like a cheese-filled compost heap. As if I didn't know already! The *nerve!* Sheesh, nobody's perfect!
...That... Yes, that's...
...Oops! Looks like class is starting. Gotta go...
What was that all about?
Rona... I can't believe it... He...He...
...He touched me!
Oh, brother...
Whoo-hoo!

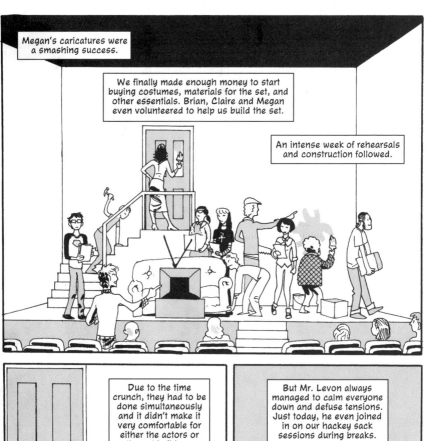

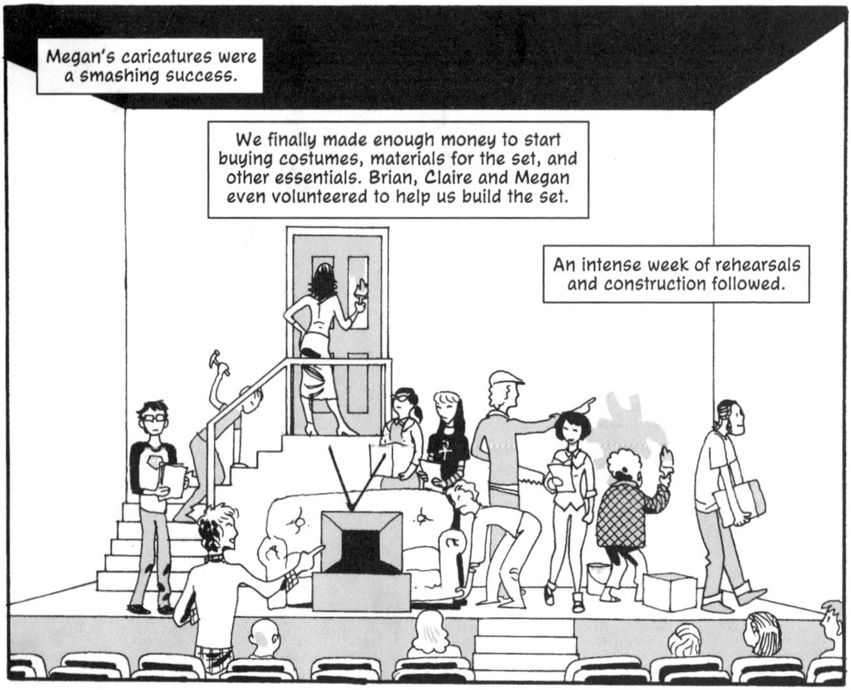
Megan's caricatures were a smashing success.
We finally made enough money to start buying costumes, materials for the set, and other essentials. Brian, Claire and Megan even volunteered to help us build the set.
An intense week of rehearsals and construction followed.

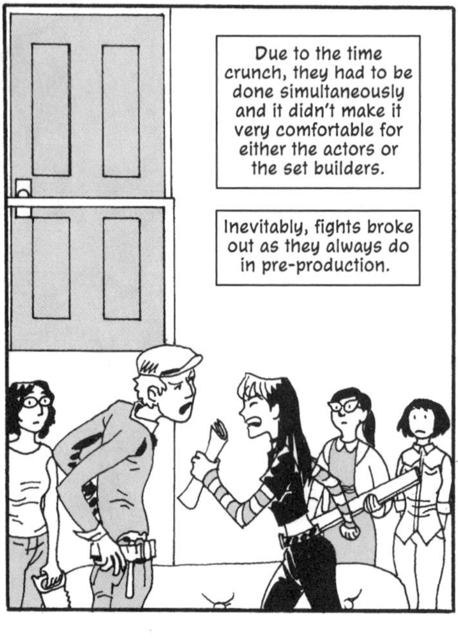
Due to the time crunch, they had to be done simultaneously and it didn't make it very comfortable for either the actors or the set builders.
Inevitably, fights broke out as they always do in pre-production.

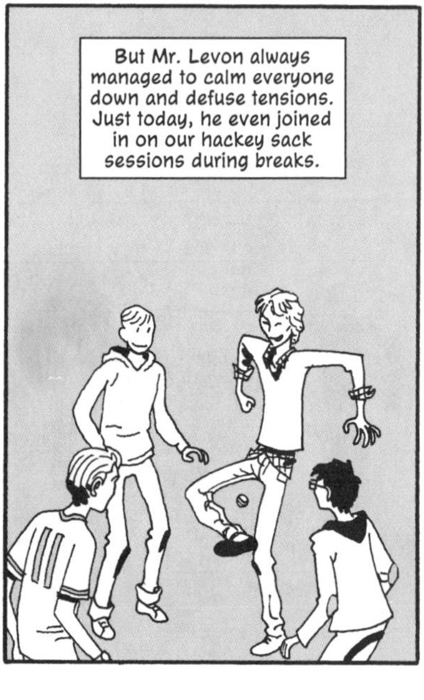
But Mr. Levon always managed to calm everyone down and defuse tensions. Just today, he even joined in on our hackey sack sessions during breaks.

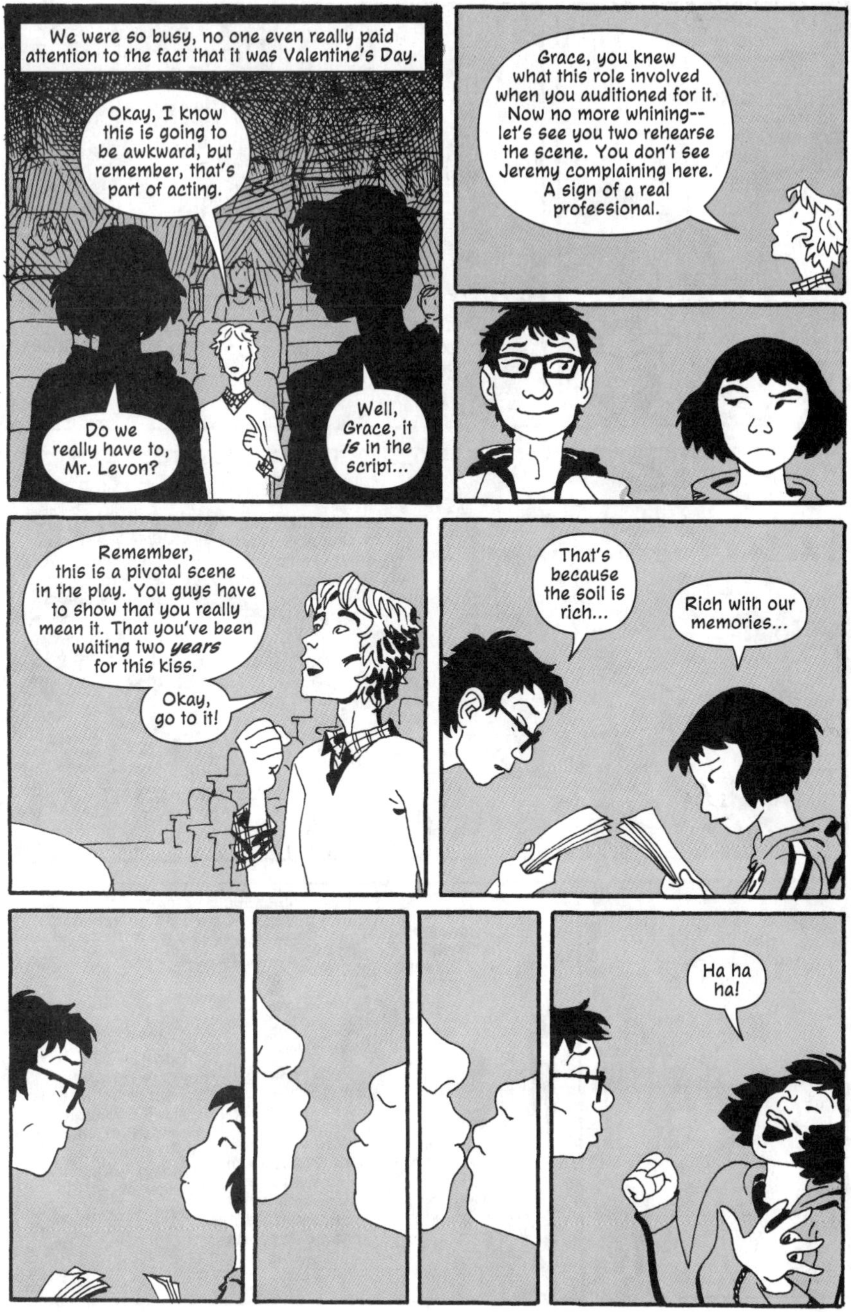
We were so busy, no one even really paid attention to the fact that it was Valentine's Day.
Okay, I know this is going to be awkward, but remember, that's part of acting.
Do we really have to, Mr. Levon?
Well, Grace, it *is* in the script...
Grace, you knew what this role involved when you auditioned for it. Now no more whining-- let's see you two rehearse the scene. You don't see Jeremy complaining here. A sign of a real professional.
Remember, this is a pivotal scene in the play. You guys have to show that you really mean it. That you've been waiting two *years* for this kiss.
Okay, go to it!
That's because the soil is rich...
Rich with our memories...
Ha ha ha!

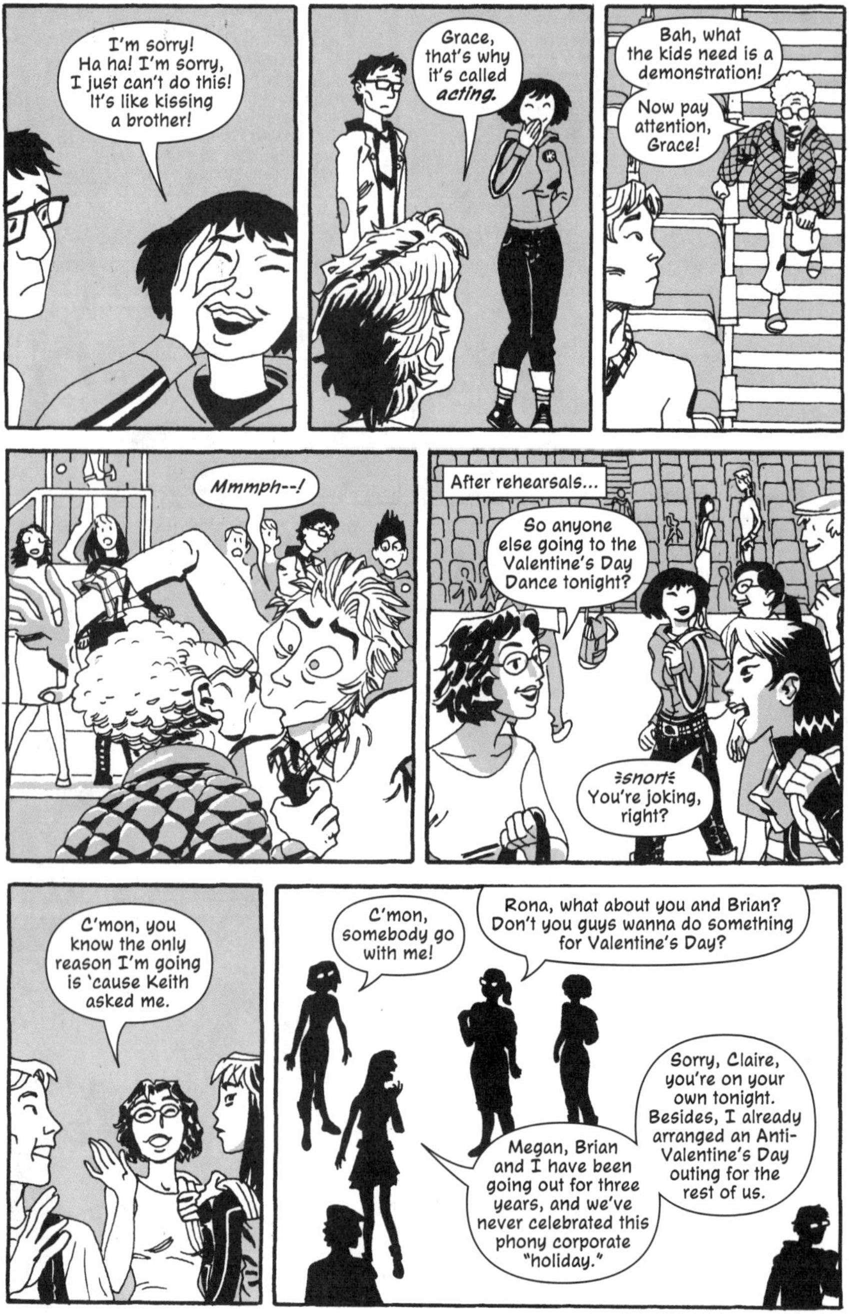
I'm sorry!
Ha ha! I'm sorry,
I just can't do this!
It's like kissing
a brother!
Grace,
that's why
it's called
acting.
Bah, what
the kids need is a
demonstration!
Now pay
attention,
Grace!
Mmmph--!
After rehearsals...
So anyone
else going to the
Valentine's Day
Dance tonight?
snort
You're joking,
right?
C'mon, you
know the only
reason I'm going
is 'cause Keith
asked me.
C'mon,
somebody go
with me!
Rona, what about you and Brian?
Don't you guys wanna do something
for Valentine's Day?
Megan, Brian
and I have been
going out for three
years, and we've
never celebrated this
phony corporate
"holiday."
Sorry, Claire,
you're on your
own tonight.
Besides, I already
arranged an Anti-
Valentine's Day
outing for the
rest of us.

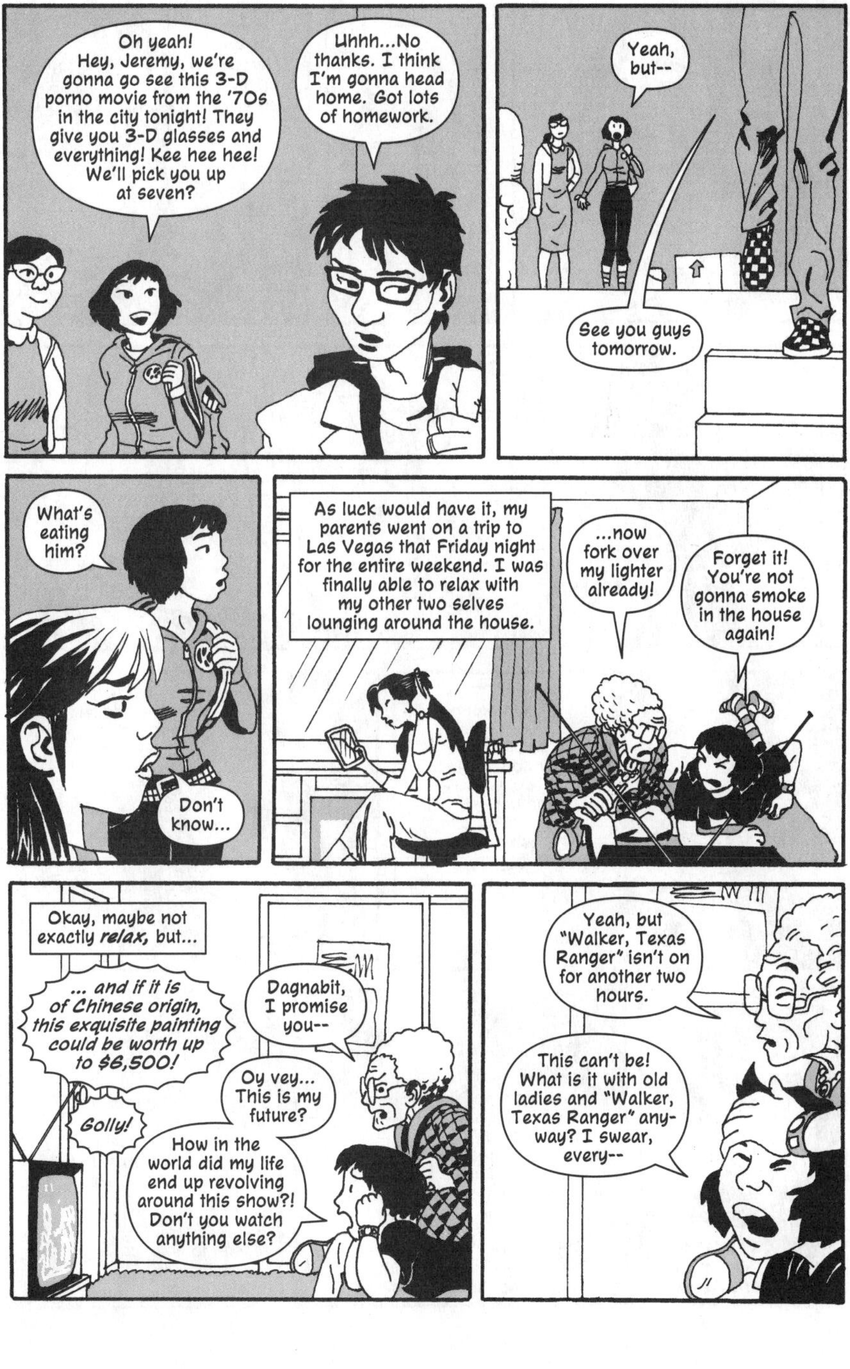
Oh yeah! Hey, Jeremy, we're gonna go see this 3-D porno movie from the '70s in the city tonight! They give you 3-D glasses and everything! Kee hee hee! We'll pick you up at seven?
Uhhh...No thanks. I think I'm gonna head home. Got lots of homework.
Yeah, but--
See you guys tomorrow.
What's eating him?
Don't know...
As luck would have it, my parents went on a trip to Las Vegas that Friday night for the entire weekend. I was finally able to relax with my other two selves lounging around the house.
...now fork over my lighter already!
Forget it! You're not gonna smoke in the house again!
Okay, maybe not exactly *relax*, but...
... and if it is of Chinese origin, this exquisite painting could be worth up to $6,500!
Golly!
Dagnabit, I promise you--
Oy vey... This is my future?
How in the world did my life end up revolving around this show?! Don't you watch anything else?
Yeah, but "Walker, Texas Ranger" isn't on for another two hours.
This can't be! What is it with old ladies and "Walker, Texas Ranger" any-way? I swear, every--

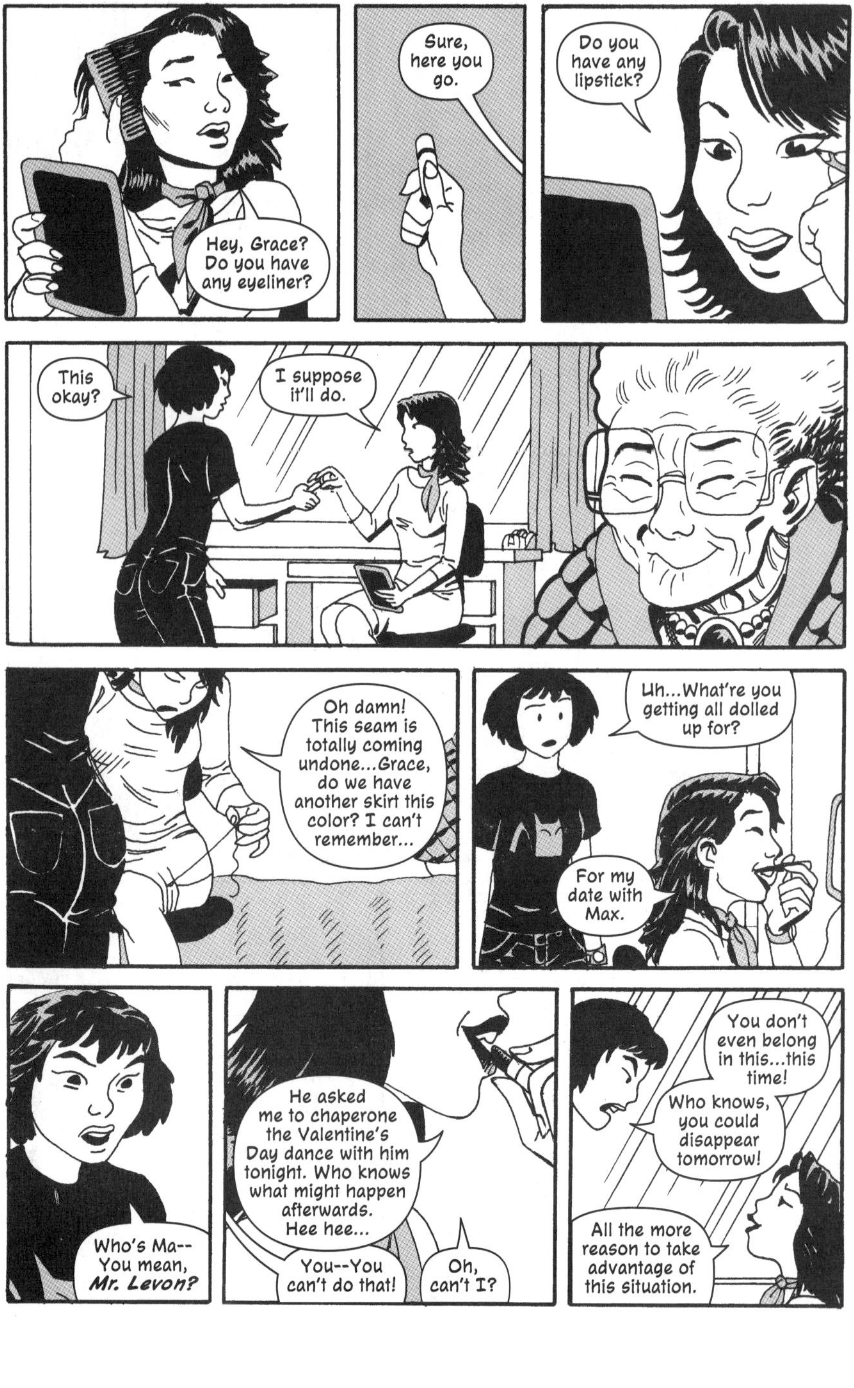

Hey, Grace? Do you have any eyeliner?
Sure, here you go.
Do you have any lipstick?
This okay?
I suppose it'll do.
Oh damn! This seam is totally coming undone...Grace, do we have another skirt this color? I can't remember...
Uh...What're you getting all dolled up for?
For my date with Max.
Who's Ma-- You mean, ***Mr. Levon?***
He asked me to chaperone the Valentine's Day dance with him tonight. Who knows what might happen afterwards. Hee hee...
You--You can't do that!
Oh, can't I?
You don't even belong in this...this time!
Who knows, you could disappear tomorrow!
All the more reason to take advantage of this situation.

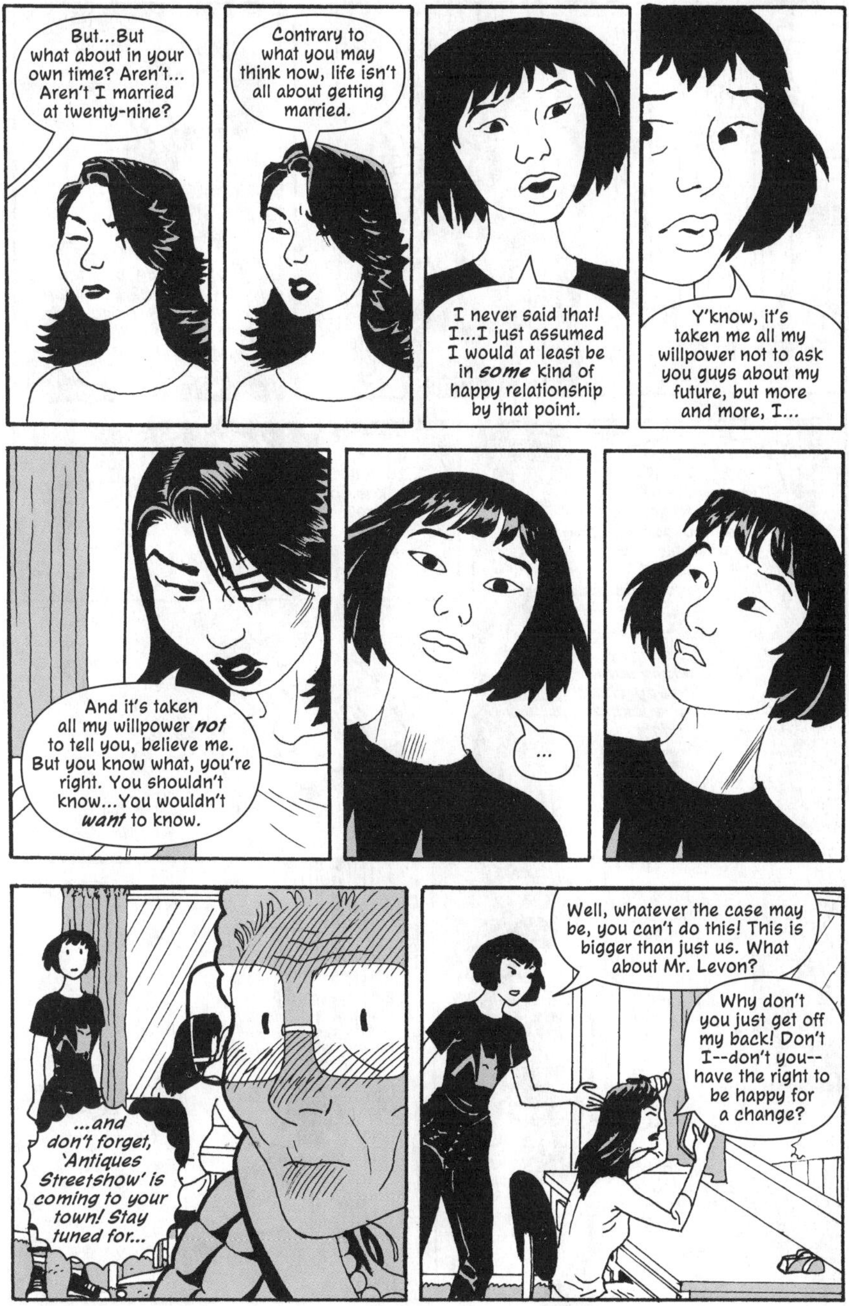

But...But what about in your own time? Aren't... Aren't I married at twenty-nine?
Contrary to what you may think now, life isn't all about getting married.
I never said that! I...I just assumed I would at least be in *some* kind of happy relationship by that point.
Y'know, it's taken me all my willpower not to ask you guys about my future, but more and more, I...
And it's taken all my willpower *not* to tell you, believe me. But you know what, you're right. You shouldn't know...You wouldn't *want* to know.
...
...and don't forget, 'Antiques Streetshow' is coming to your town! Stay tuned for...
Well, whatever the case may be, you can't do this! This is bigger than just us. What about Mr. Levon?
Why don't you just get off my back! Don't I--don't you--have the right to be happy for a change?

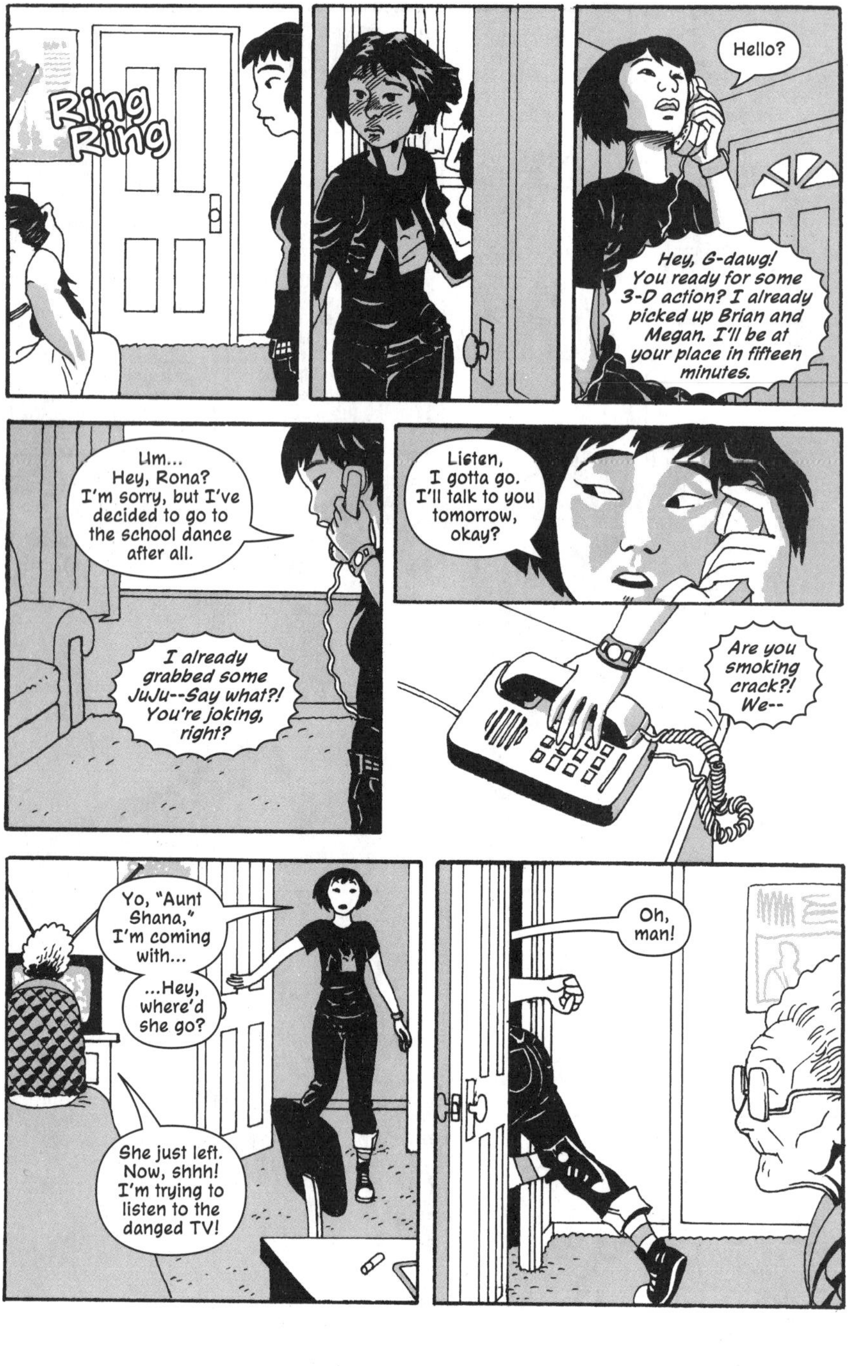
Ring Ring
Hello?
Hey, G-dawg! You ready for some 3-D action? I already picked up Brian and Megan. I'll be at your place in fifteen minutes.
Um... Hey, Rona? I'm sorry, but I've decided to go to the school dance after all.
I already grabbed some JuJu--Say what?! You're joking, right?
Listen, I gotta go. I'll talk to you tomorrow, okay?
Are you smoking crack?! We--
Yo, "Aunt Shana," I'm coming with...
...Hey, where'd she go?
She just left. Now, shhh! I'm trying to listen to the danged TV!
Oh, man!

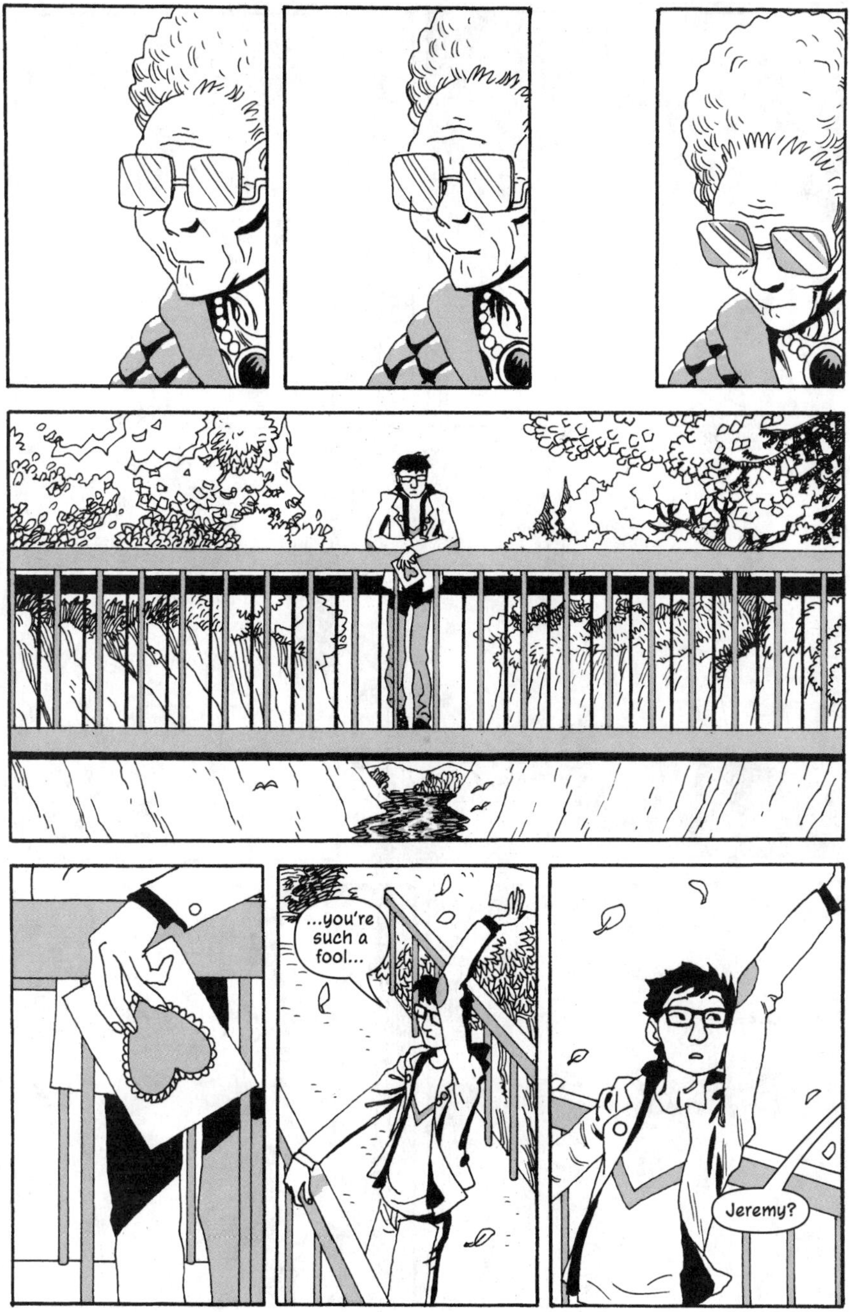
...you're such a fool...
Jeremy?

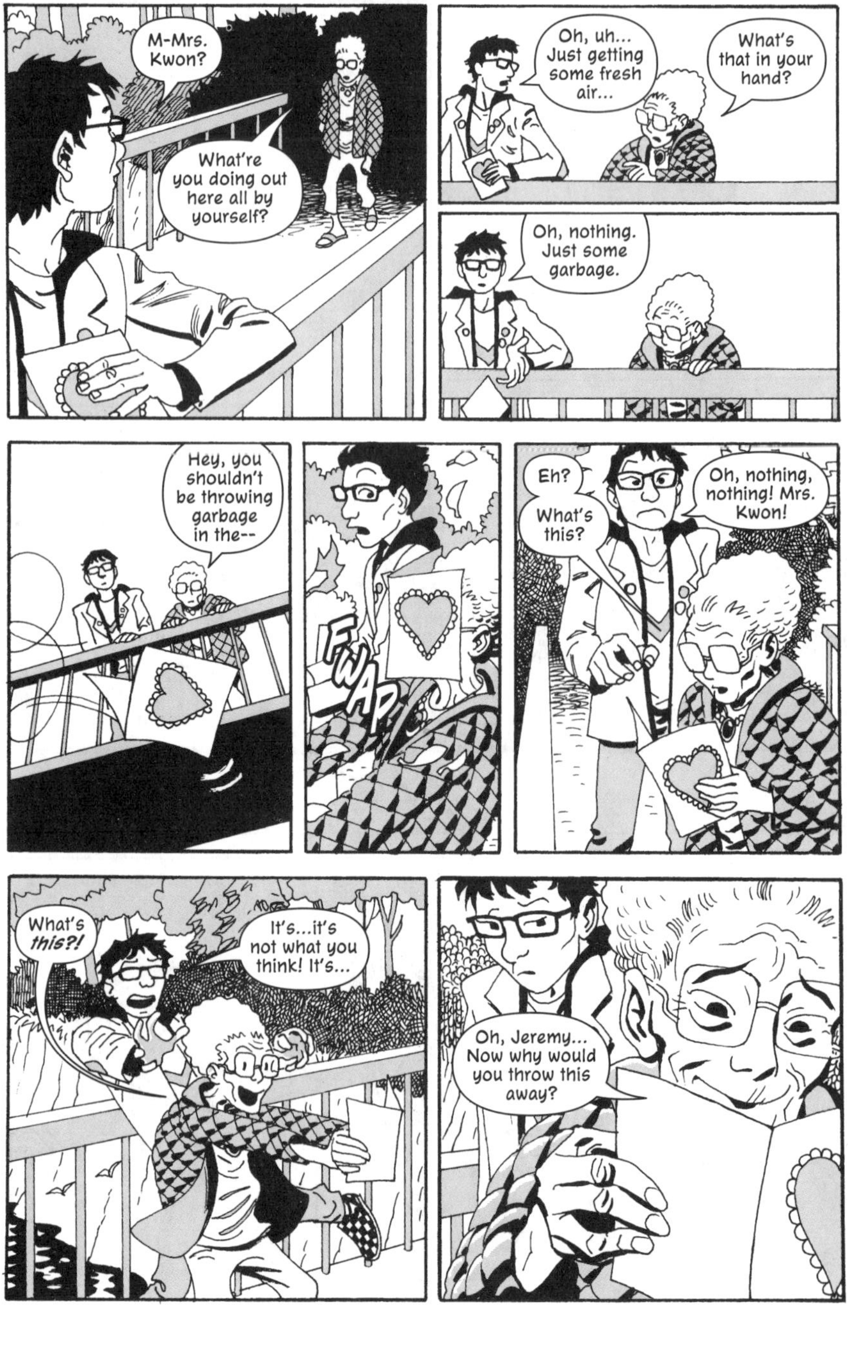
M-Mrs. Kwon?
What're you doing out here all by yourself?
Oh, uh... Just getting some fresh air...
What's that in your hand?
Oh, nothing. Just some garbage.
Hey, you shouldn't be throwing garbage in the--
FWAP
Eh?
What's this?
Oh, nothing, nothing! Mrs. Kwon!
What's *this?!*
It's...it's not what you think! It's...
Oh, Jeremy... Now why would you throw this away?

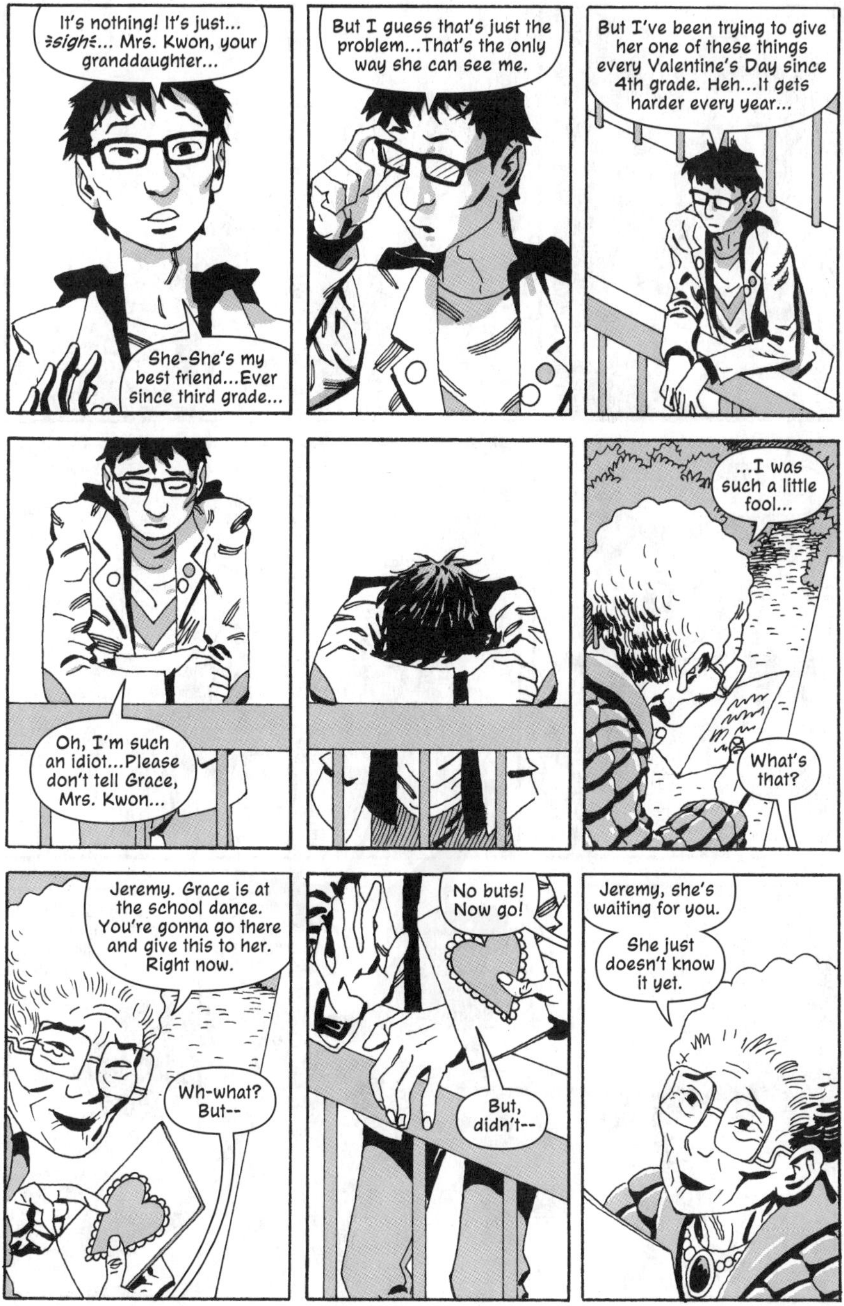

It's nothing! It's just... ≈sigh≈... Mrs. Kwon, your granddaughter...
She-She's my best friend...Ever since third grade...
But I guess that's just the problem...That's the only way she can see me.
But I've been trying to give her one of these things every Valentine's Day since 4th grade. Heh...It gets harder every year...
Oh, I'm such an idiot...Please don't tell Grace, Mrs. Kwon...
...I was such a little fool...
What's that?
Jeremy. Grace is at the school dance. You're gonna go there and give this to her. Right now.
Wh-what? But--
No buts! Now go!
But, didn't--
Jeremy, she's waiting for you.
She just doesn't know it yet.

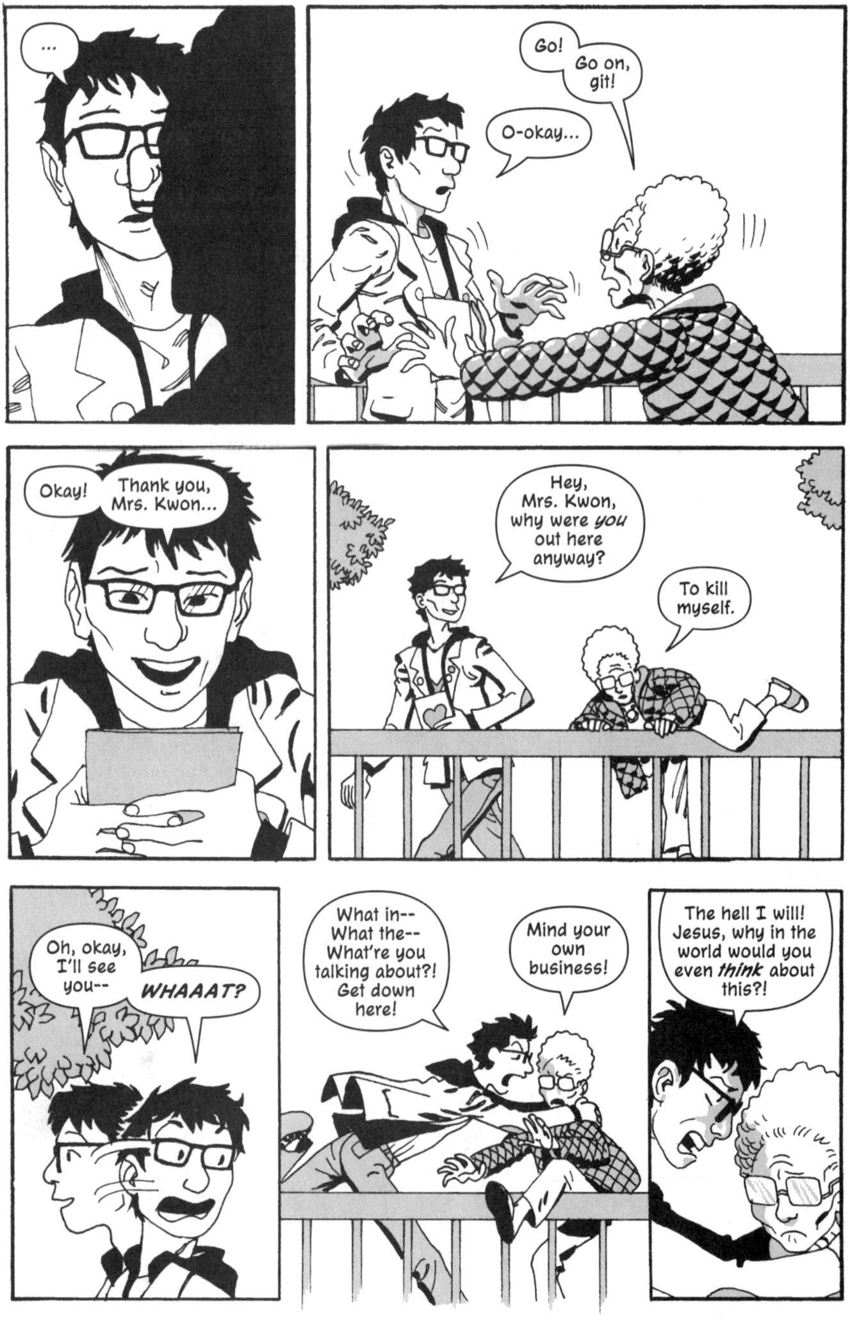
...
Go!
Go on, git!
O-okay...
Okay!
Thank you, Mrs. Kwon...
Hey, Mrs. Kwon, why were *you* out here anyway?
To kill myself.
Oh, okay, I'll see you--
WHAAAT?
What in-- What the-- What're you talking about?! Get down here!
Mind your own business!
The hell I will! Jesus, why in the world would you even *think* about this?!

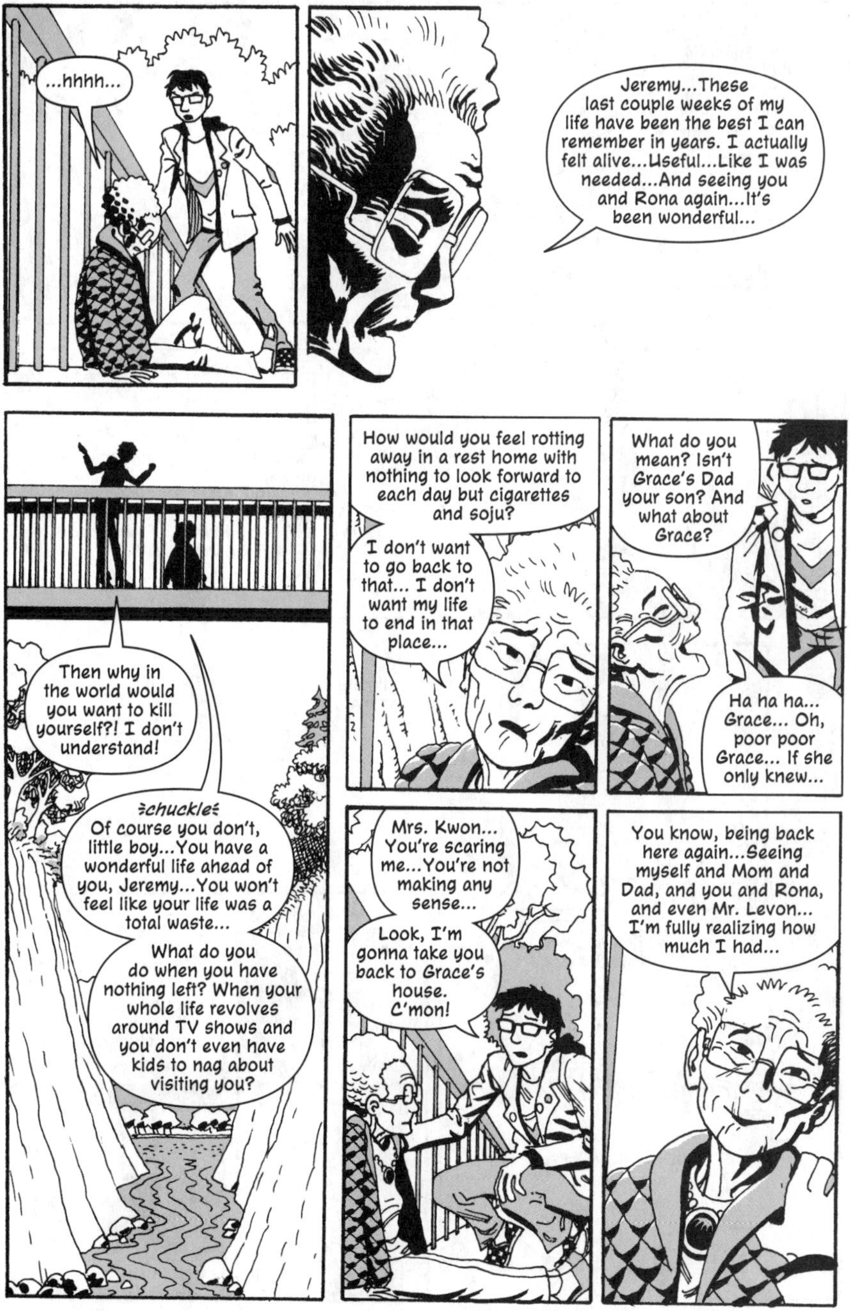

...hhhh...
Jeremy...These last couple weeks of my life have been the best I can remember in years. I actually felt alive...Useful...Like I was needed...And seeing you and Rona again...It's been wonderful...
Then why in the world would you want to kill yourself?! I don't understand!
chuckle
Of course you don't, little boy...You have a wonderful life ahead of you, Jeremy...You won't feel like your life was a total waste...
What do you do when you have nothing left? When your whole life revolves around TV shows and you don't even have kids to nag about visiting you?
How would you feel rotting away in a rest home with nothing to look forward to each day but cigarettes and soju?
I don't want to go back to that... I don't want my life to end in that place...
What do you mean? Isn't Grace's Dad your son? And what about Grace?
Ha ha ha... Grace... Oh, poor poor Grace... If she only knew...
Mrs. Kwon... You're scaring me...You're not making any sense...
Look, I'm gonna take you back to Grace's house. C'mon!
You know, being back here again...Seeing myself and Mom and Dad, and you and Rona, and even Mr. Levon... I'm fully realizing how much I had...

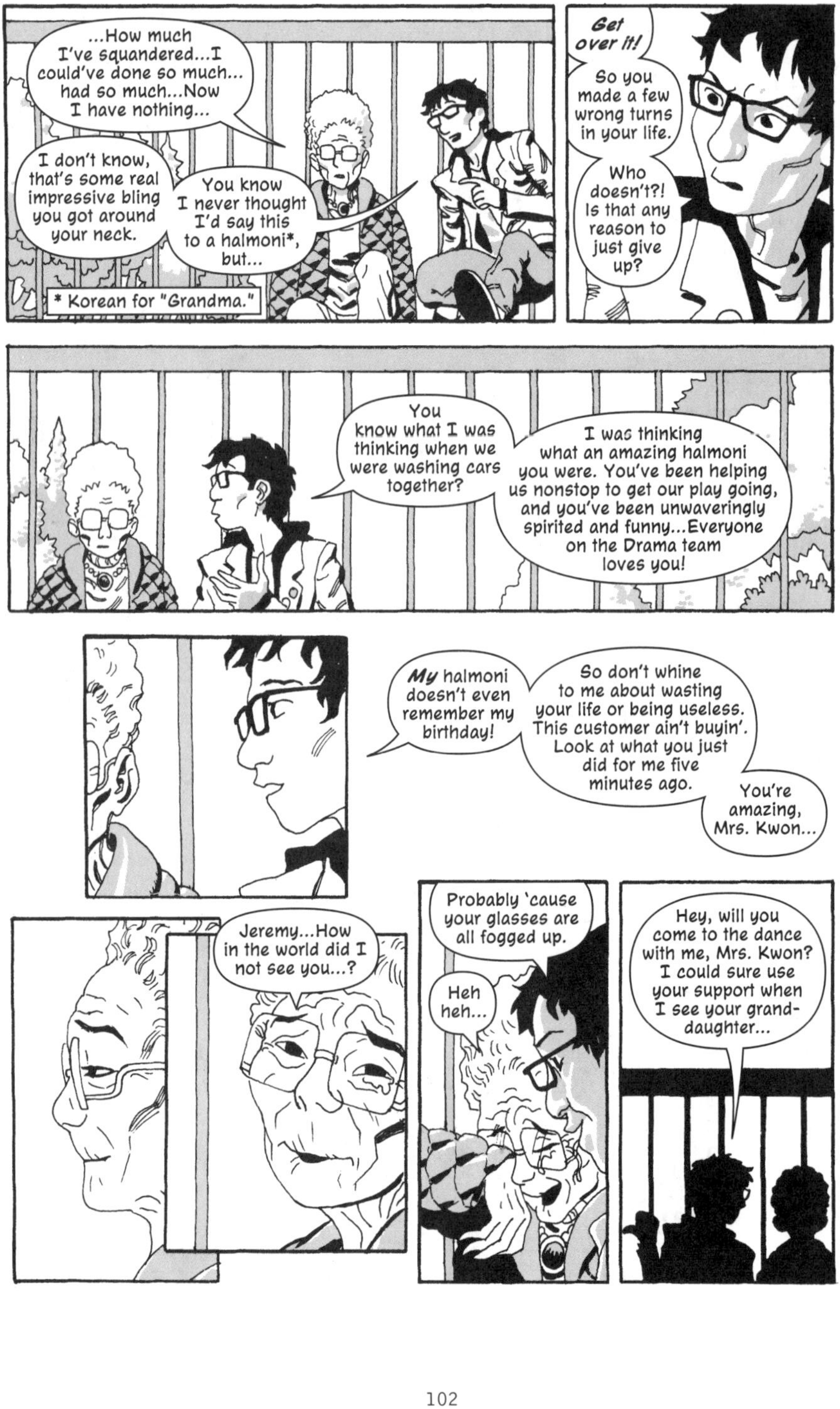
...How much I've squandered...I could've done so much... had so much...Now I have nothing...
I don't know, that's some real impressive bling you got around your neck.
You know I never thought I'd say this to a halmoni*, but...
* Korean for "Grandma."
Get over it!
So you made a few wrong turns in your life.
Who doesn't?! Is that any reason to just give up?
You know what I was thinking when we were washing cars together?
I was thinking what an amazing halmoni you were. You've been helping us nonstop to get our play going, and you've been unwaveringly spirited and funny...Everyone on the Drama team loves you!
My halmoni doesn't even remember my birthday!
So don't whine to me about wasting your life or being useless. This customer ain't buyin'. Look at what you just did for me five minutes ago.
You're amazing, Mrs. Kwon...
Jeremy...How in the world did I not see you...?
Probably 'cause your glasses are all fogged up.
Heh heh...
Hey, will you come to the dance with me, Mrs. Kwon? I could sure use your support when I see your grand-daughter...

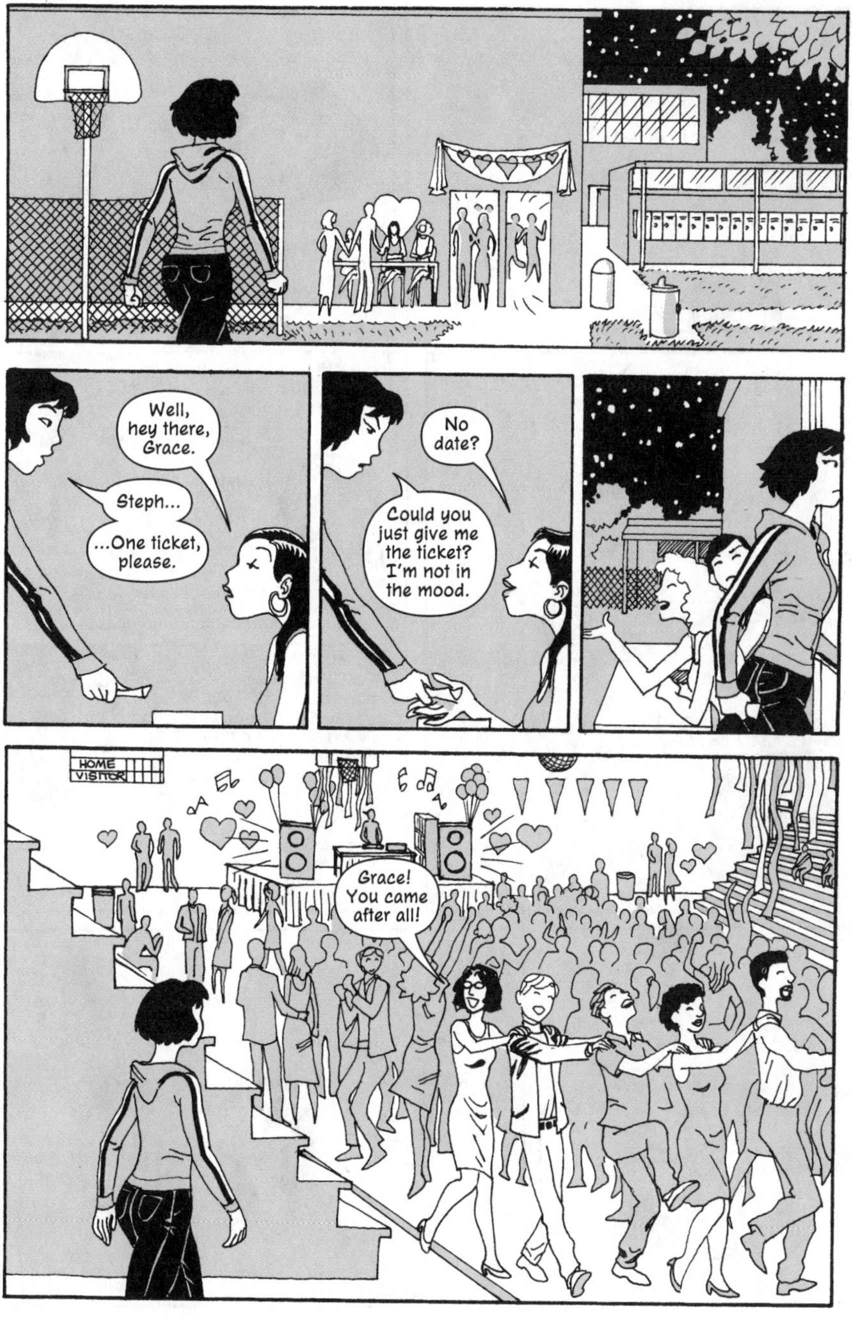
Well, hey there, Grace.
Steph...
...One ticket, please.
No date?
Could you just give me the ticket? I'm not in the mood.
HOME
VISITOR
Grace! You came after all!

Panel 1: Uh, yeah, I thought I'd--

C'mon, dance with us!

Panel 2: ...this song sure takes me back to high school.

You know, Max, when I was in high school, I had a teacher just like you.

RESH--MENTS

Panel: Really? Another teacher that has no clue what he's doing?

He was a first year teacher too. And boy, was he great.

He was patient, and spirited, and he always knew just what to say. I had the biggest crush on him...

Panel: If I had a time machine, I'd go back and tell him how much I appreciated him. How much he taught me. How much he meant to me...

...I'm sure a lot of your students feel the same way about you.

Panel: Naw, I--

In fact, he even looked a lot like you.

Panel: Y-you don't say...

Mm-hmm. Same height... Same dirty blond bed-head hair...

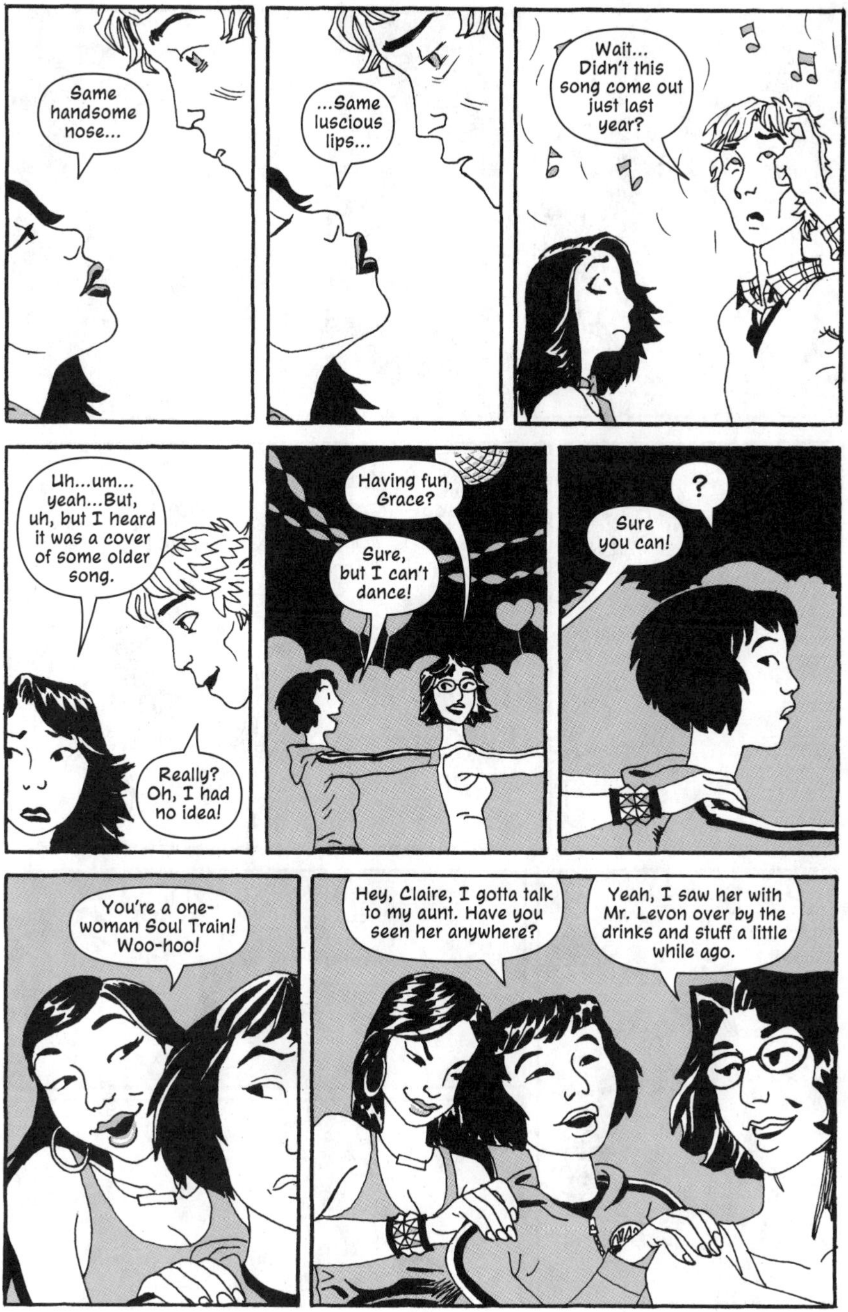
Same handsome nose...
...Same luscious lips...
Wait... Didn't this song come out just last year?
Uh...um... yeah...But, uh, but I heard it was a cover of some older song.
Really? Oh, I had no idea!
Having fun, Grace?
Sure, but I can't dance!
?
Sure you can!
You're a one-woman Soul Train! Woo-hoo!
Hey, Claire, I gotta talk to my aunt. Have you seen her anywhere?
Yeah, I saw her with Mr. Levon over by the drinks and stuff a little while ago.

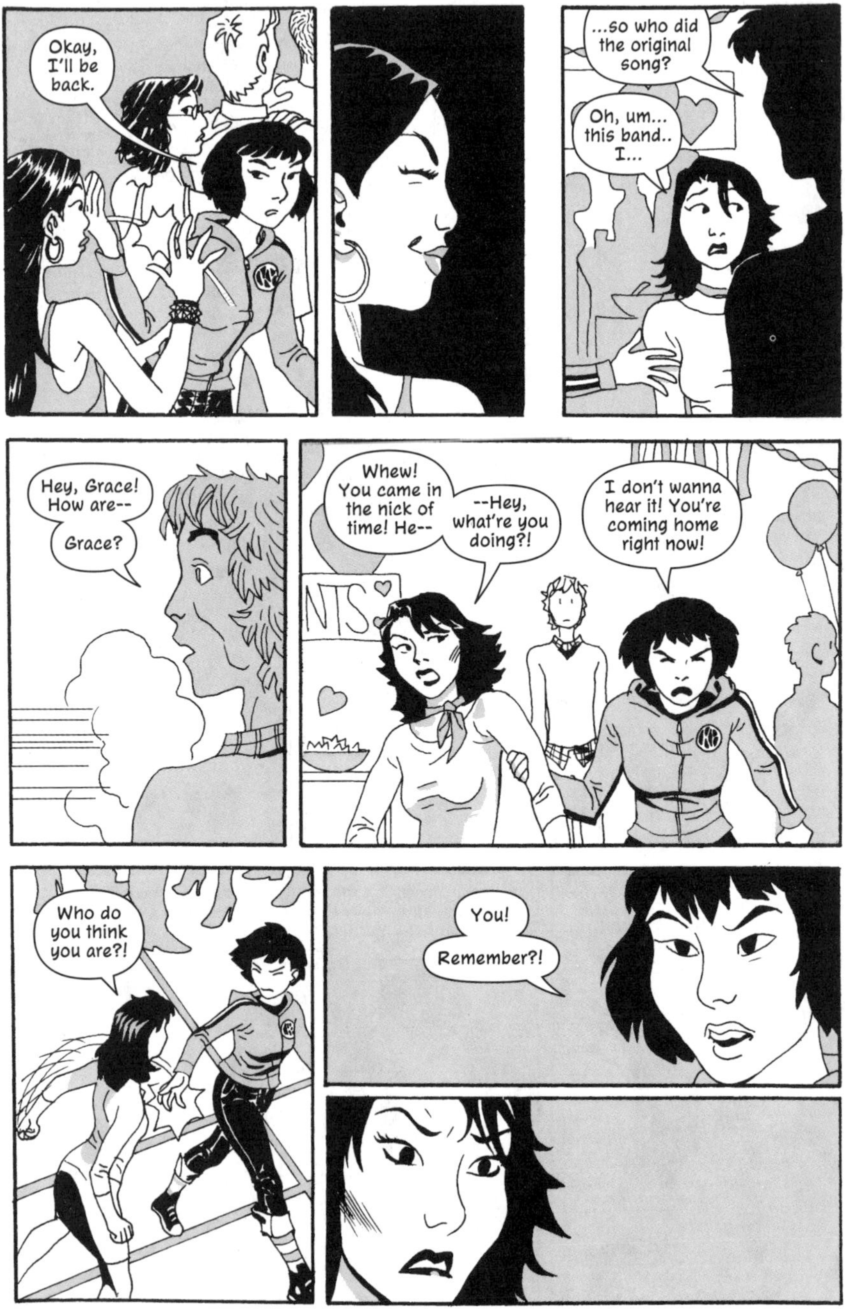

Okay, I'll be back.
...so who did the original song?
Oh, um... this band.. I...
Hey, Grace! How are--
Grace?
Whew! You came in the nick of time! He--
--Hey, what're you doing?!
I don't wanna hear it! You're coming home right now!
Who do you think you are?!
You!
Remember?!

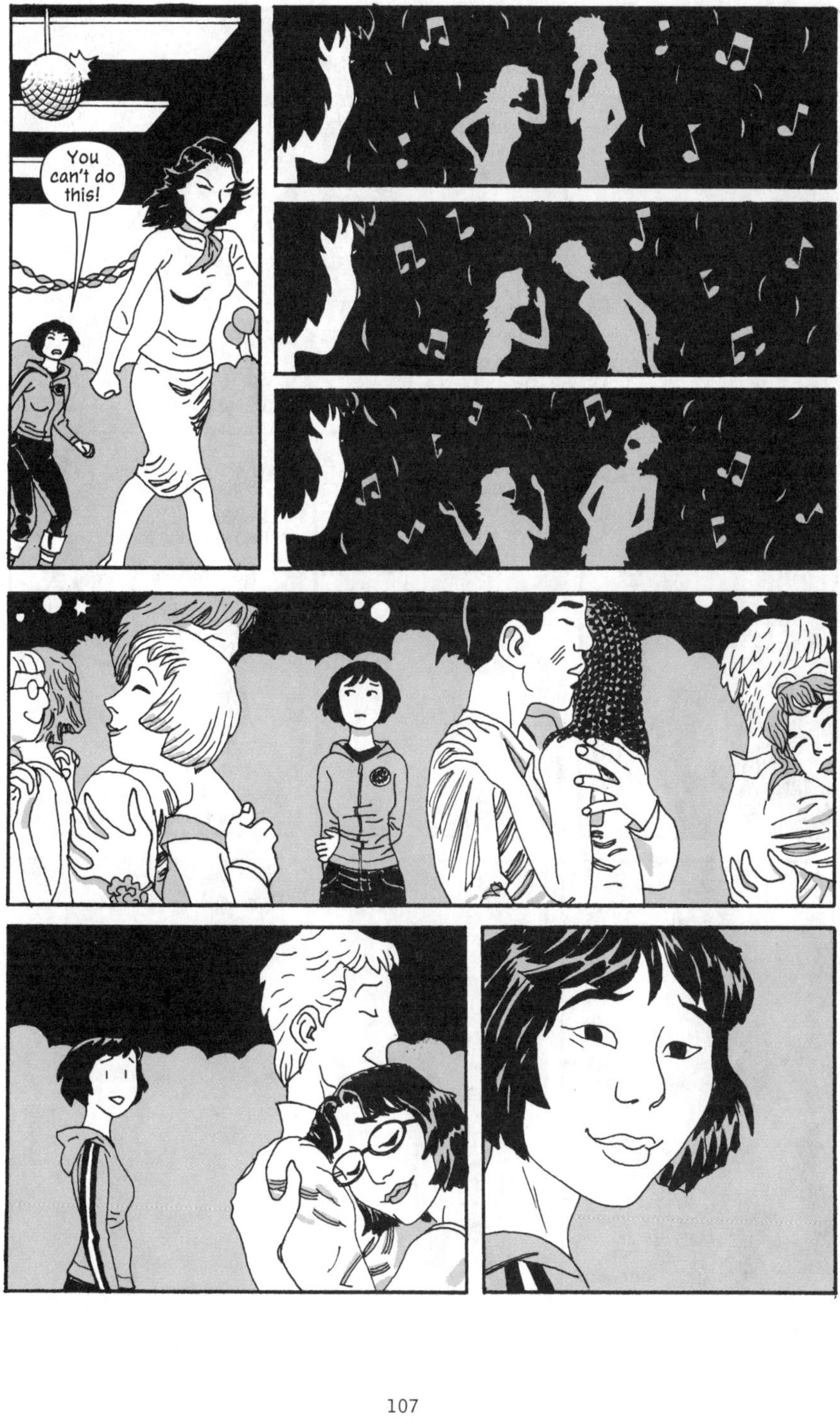
You can't do this!

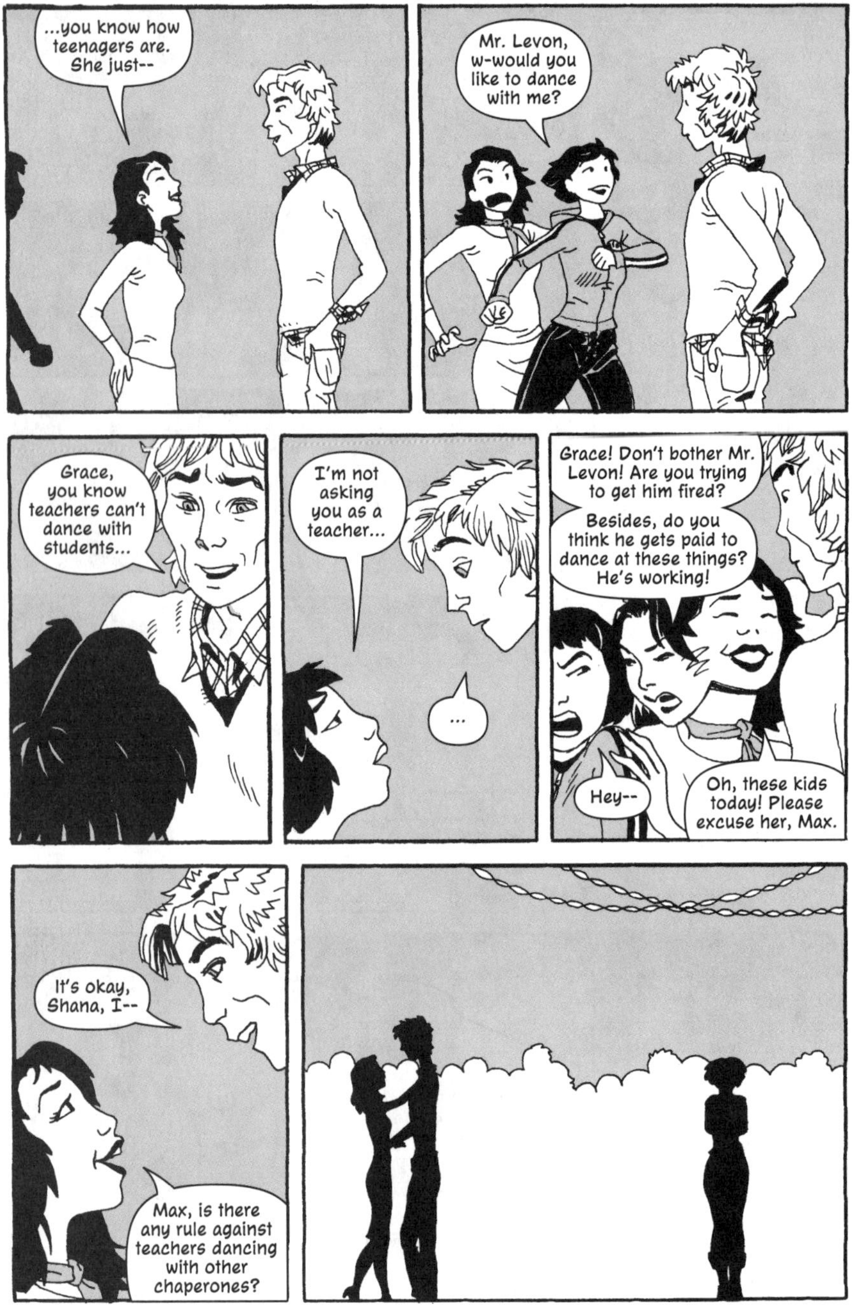
...you know how teenagers are. She just--
Mr. Levon, w-would you like to dance with me?
Grace, you know teachers can't dance with students...
I'm not asking you as a teacher...
...
Grace! Don't bother Mr. Levon! Are you trying to get him fired?
Besides, do you think he gets paid to dance at these things? He's working!
Hey--
Oh, these kids today! Please excuse her, Max.
It's okay, Shana, I--
Max, is there any rule against teachers dancing with other chaperones?

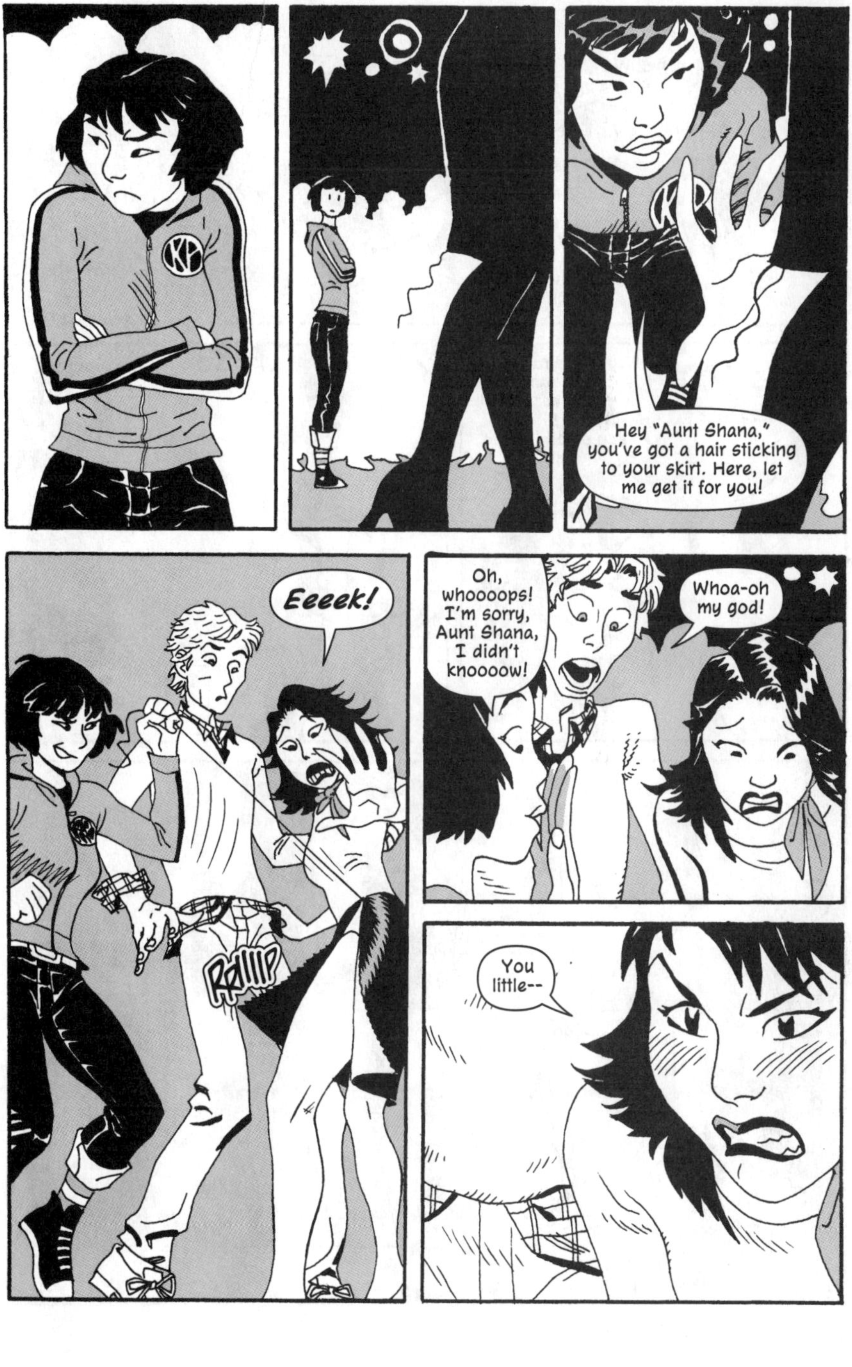
Hey "Aunt Shana," you've got a hair sticking to your skirt. Here, let me get it for you!
Eeeek!
RRIIIIP
Oh, whoooops! I'm sorry, Aunt Shana, I didn't knoooow!
Whoa-oh my god!
You little--

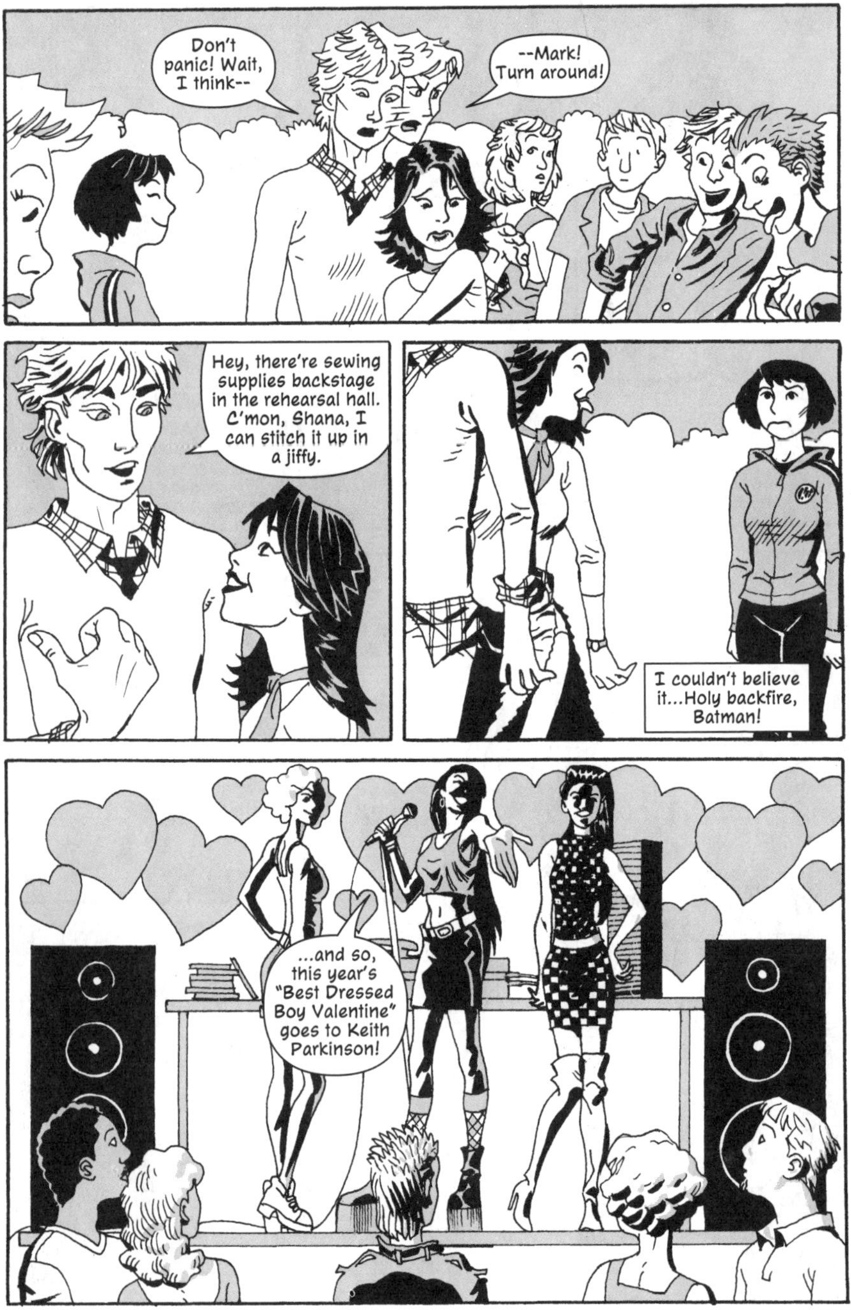

Don't panic! Wait, I think--
--Mark! Turn around!
Hey, there're sewing supplies backstage in the rehearsal hall. C'mon, Shana, I can stitch it up in a jiffy.
I couldn't believe it...Holy backfire, Batman!
...and so, this year's "Best Dressed Boy Valentine" goes to Keith Parkinson!

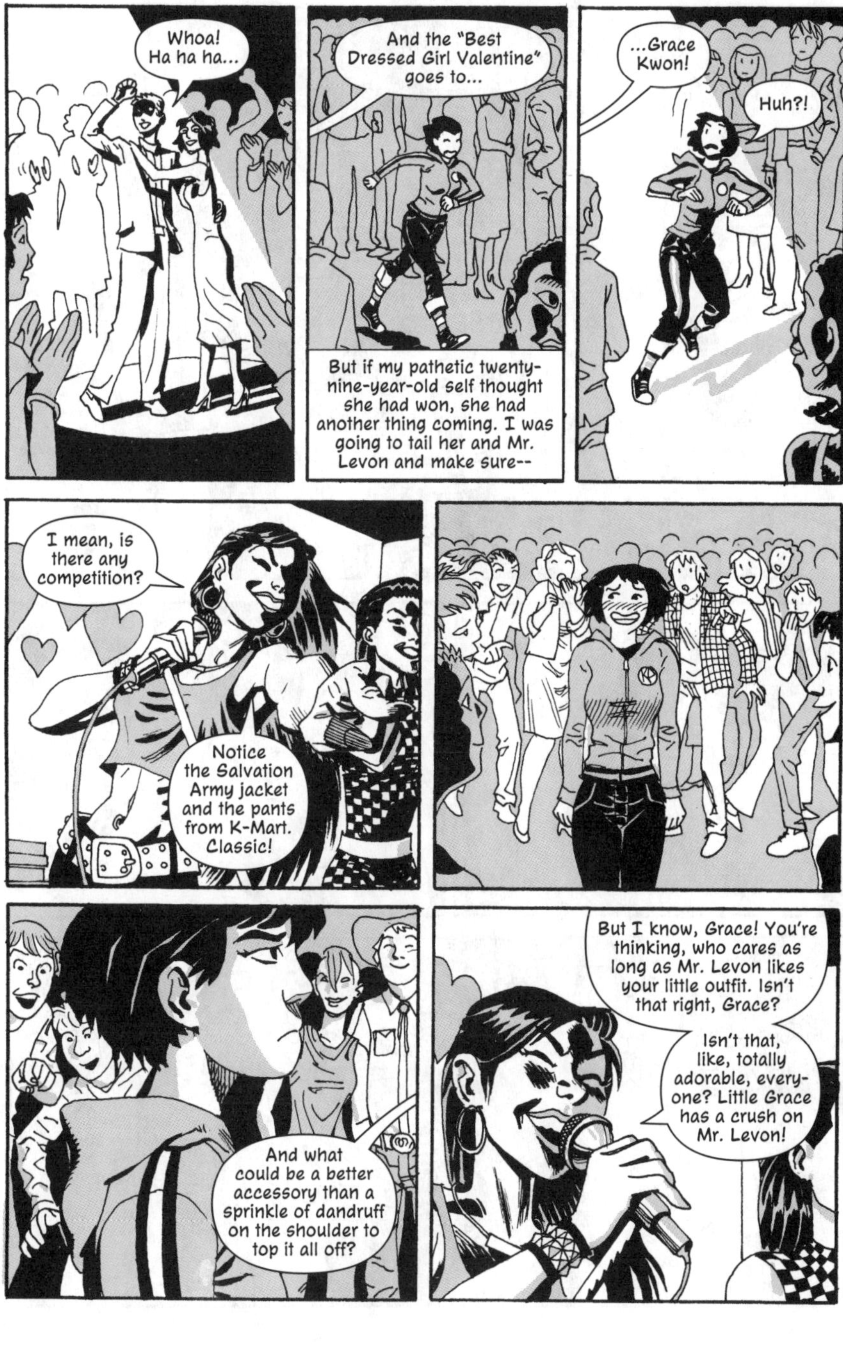
Whoa! Ha ha ha...
And the "Best Dressed Girl Valentine" goes to...
But if my pathetic twenty-nine-year-old self thought she had won, she had another thing coming. I was going to tail her and Mr. Levon and make sure--
...Grace Kwon!
Huh?!
I mean, is there any competition?
Notice the Salvation Army jacket and the pants from K-Mart. Classic!
And what could be a better accessory than a sprinkle of dandruff on the shoulder to top it all off?
But I know, Grace! You're thinking, who cares as long as Mr. Levon likes your little outfit. Isn't that right, Grace?
Isn't that, like, totally adorable, every-one? Little Grace has a crush on Mr. Levon!

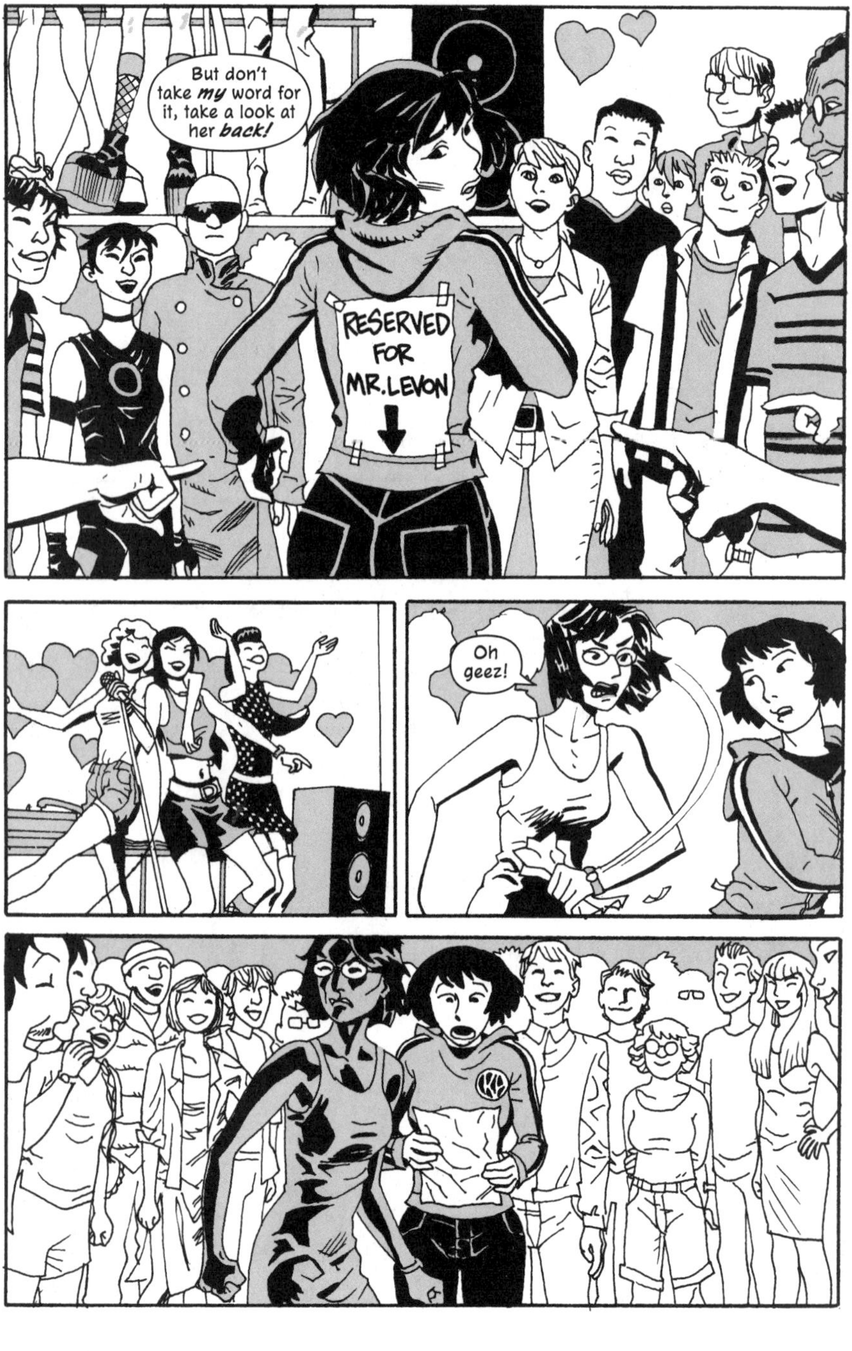

But don't take *my* word for it, take a look at her *back!*
RESERVED FOR MR. LEVON
Oh geez!

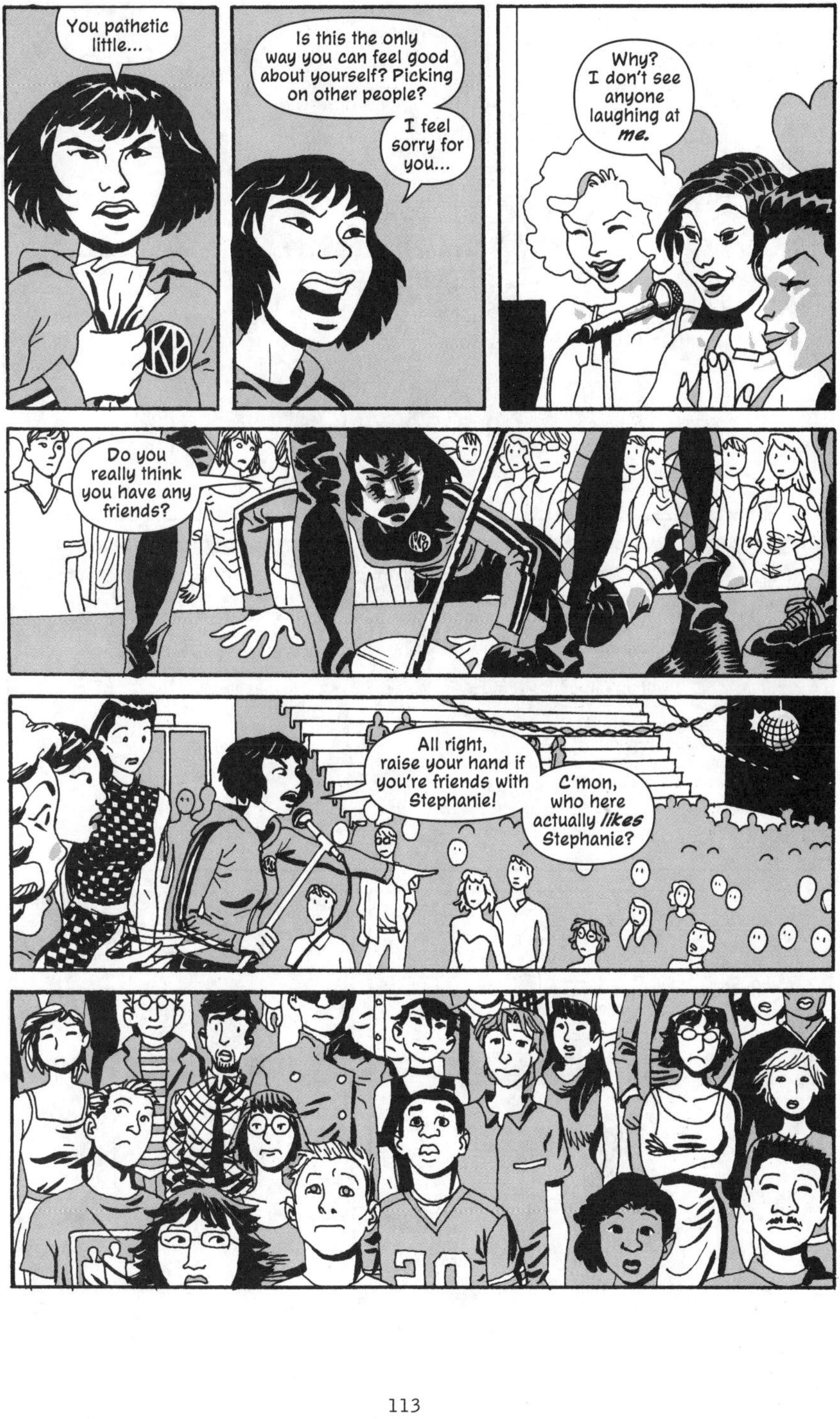
You pathetic little...
Is this the only way you can feel good about yourself? Picking on other people?
I feel sorry for you...
Why? I don't see anyone laughing at *me.*
Do you really think you have any friends?
All right, raise your hand if you're friends with Stephanie!
C'mon, who here actually *likes* Stephanie?

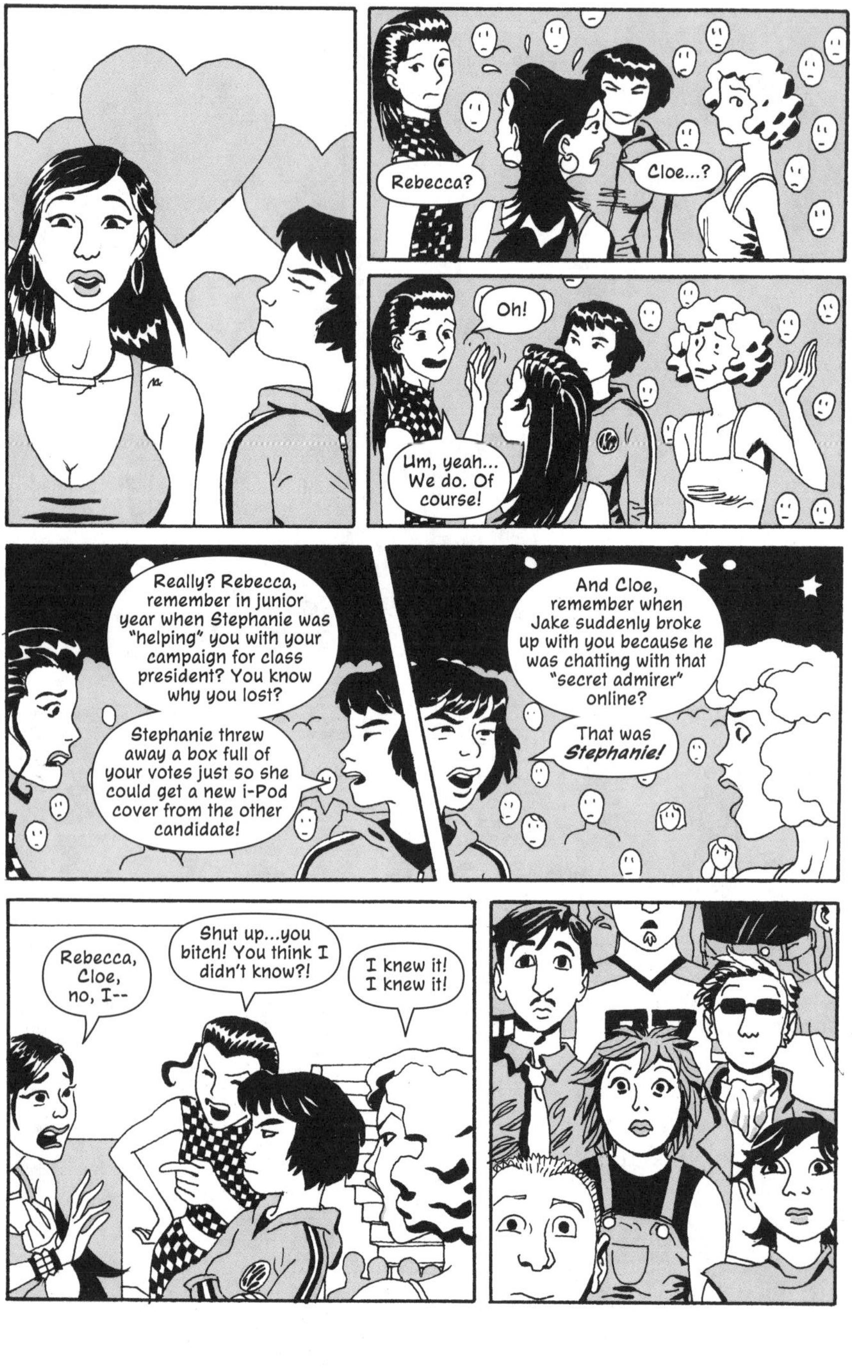
Rebecca?
Cloe...?
Oh!
Um, yeah... We do. Of course!
Really? Rebecca, remember in junior year when Stephanie was "helping" you with your campaign for class president? You know why you lost?
Stephanie threw away a box full of your votes just so she could get a new i-Pod cover from the other candidate!
And Cloe, remember when Jake suddenly broke up with you because he was chatting with that "secret admirer" online?
That was *Stephanie!*
Rebecca, Cloe, no, I--
Shut up...you bitch! You think I didn't know?!
I knew it! I knew it!

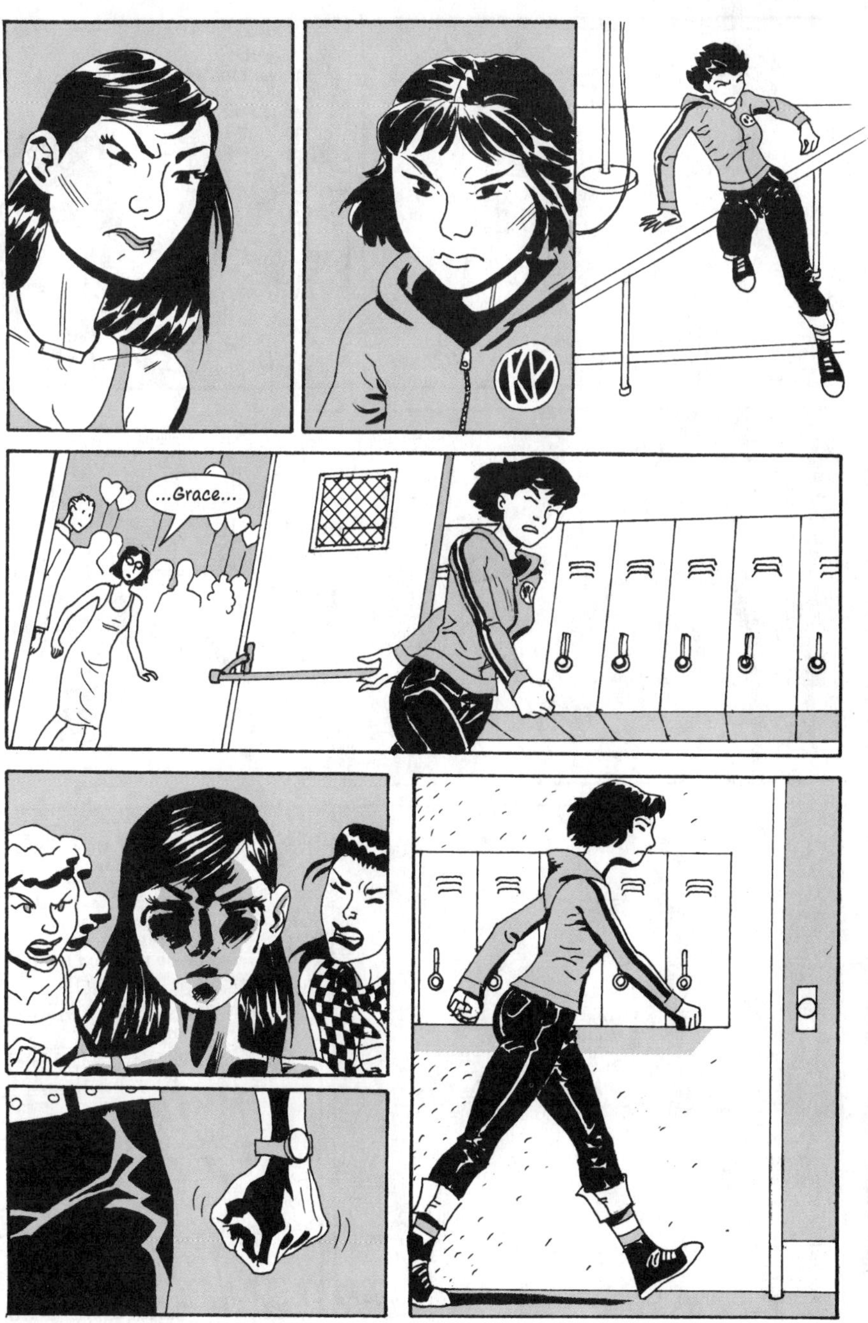
...Grace...

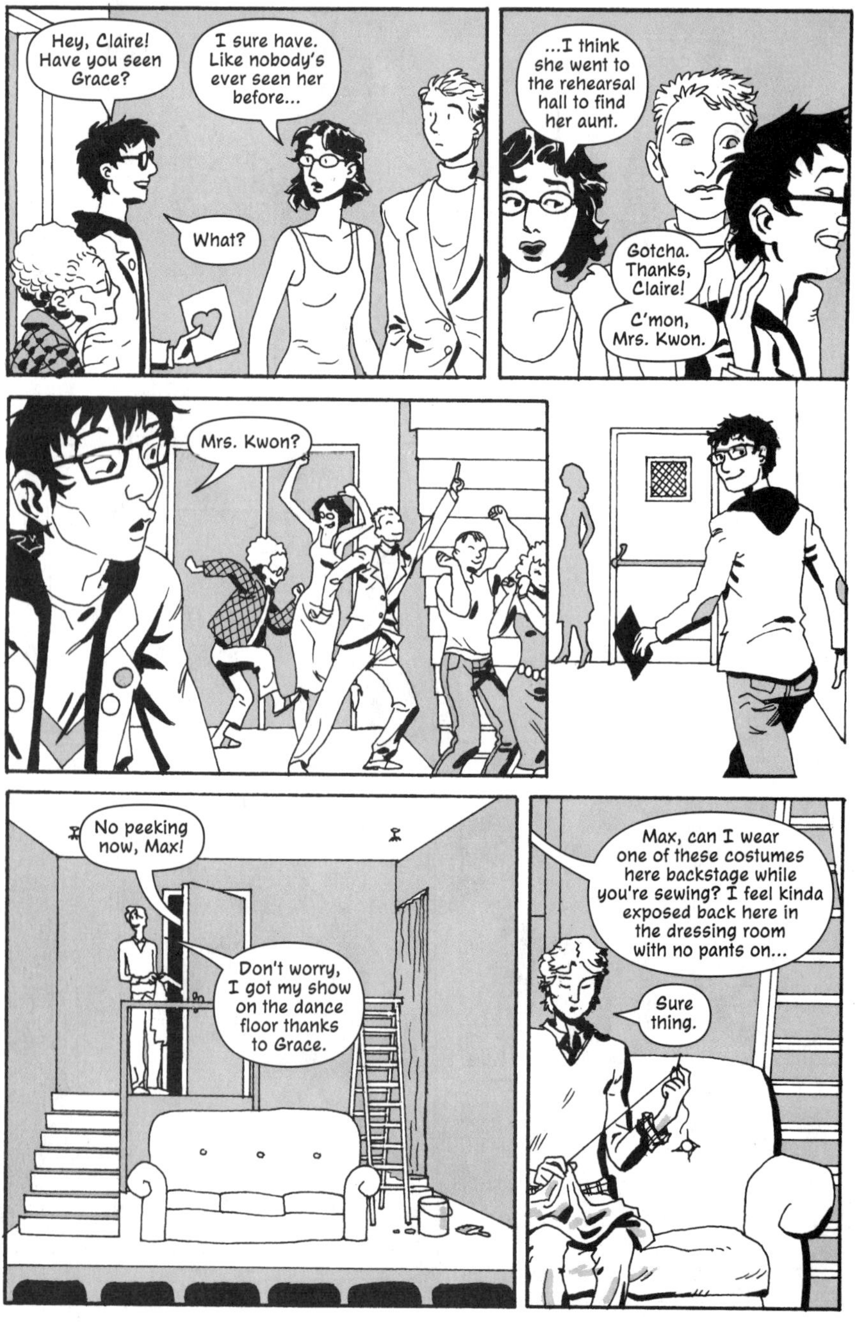
Hey, Claire! Have you seen Grace?
I sure have. Like nobody's ever seen her before...
What?
...I think she went to the rehearsal hall to find her aunt.
Gotcha. Thanks, Claire!
C'mon, Mrs. Kwon.
Mrs. Kwon?
No peeking now, Max!
Don't worry, I got my show on the dance floor thanks to Grace.
Max, can I wear one of these costumes here backstage while you're sewing? I feel kinda exposed back here in the dressing room with no pants on...
Sure thing.

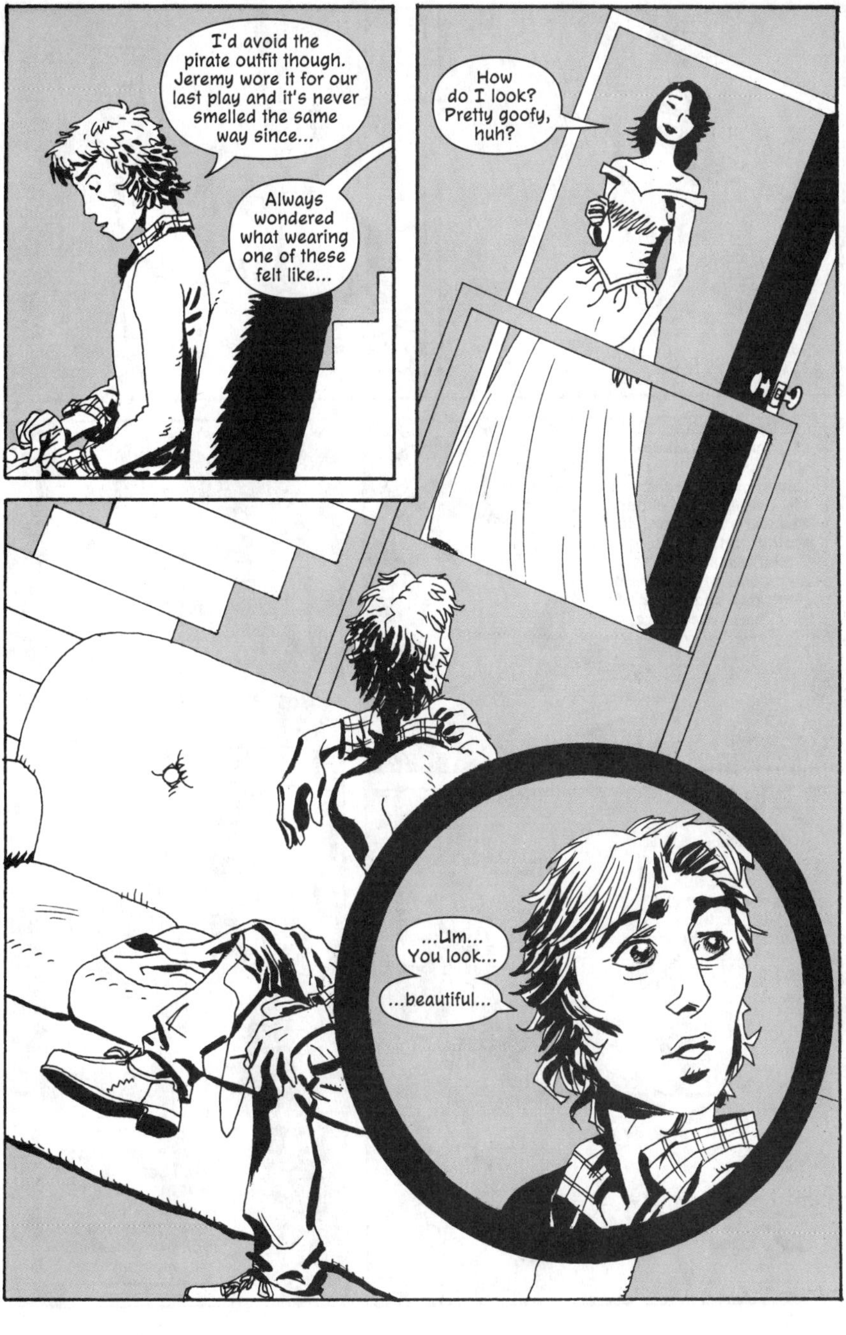
I'd avoid the pirate outfit though. Jeremy wore it for our last play and it's never smelled the same way since...
Always wondered what wearing one of these felt like...
How do I look? Pretty goofy, huh?
...Um... You look...
...beautiful...

By the time I caught up with my twenty-nine-year-old self, she already had Mr. Levon in her clutches. They were whispering to one another, and not being able to overhear what "I" was saying was making me more irritated and desperate than ever before.

I had to stop her before things went out of hand any further.

That does it!

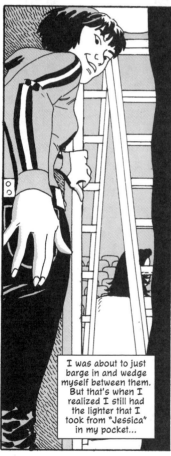

I was about to just barge in and wedge myself between them. But that's when I realized I still had the lighter that I took from "Jessica" in my pocket...

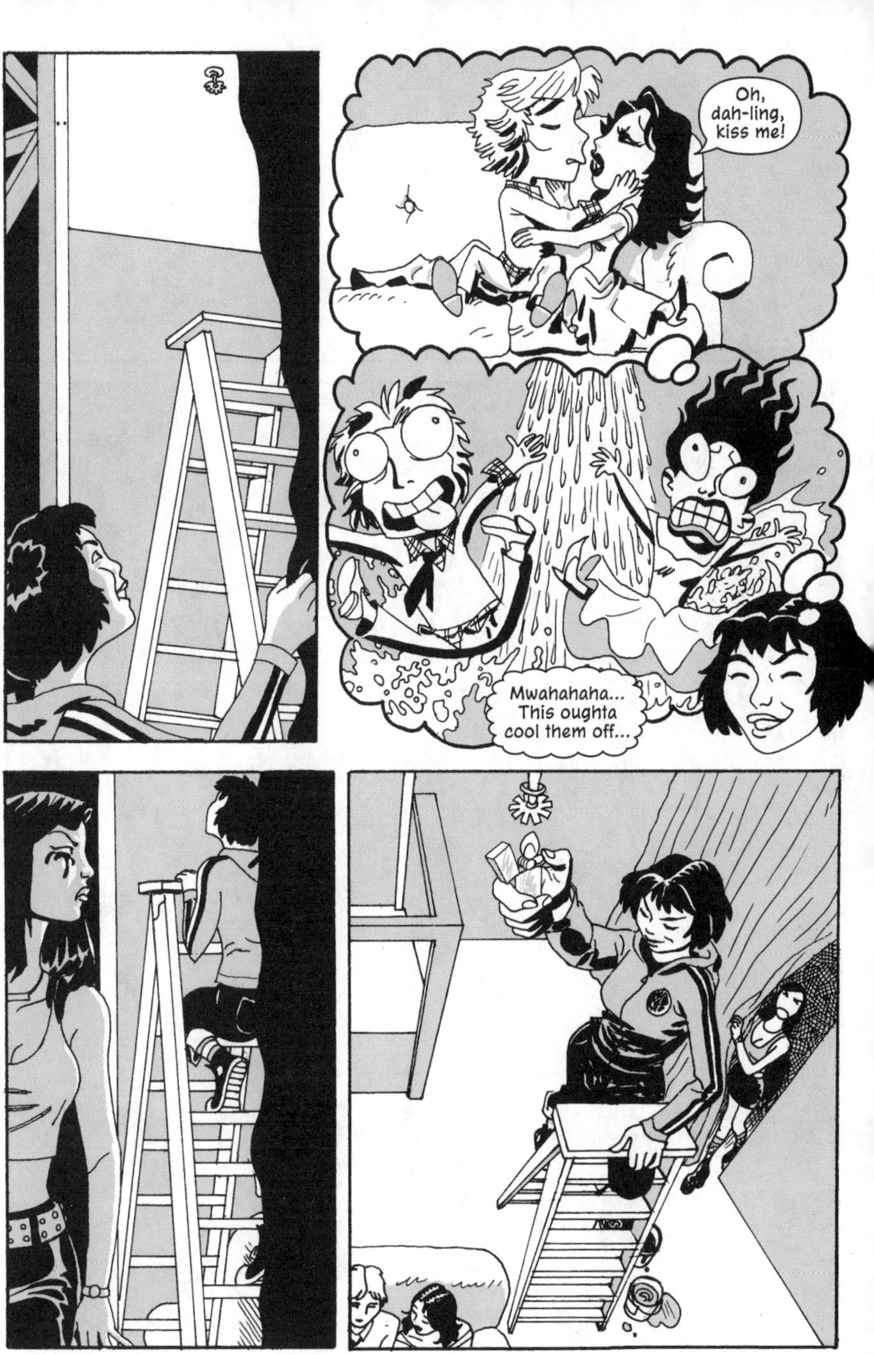
Oh, dah-ling, kiss me!
Mwahahaha... This oughta cool them off...

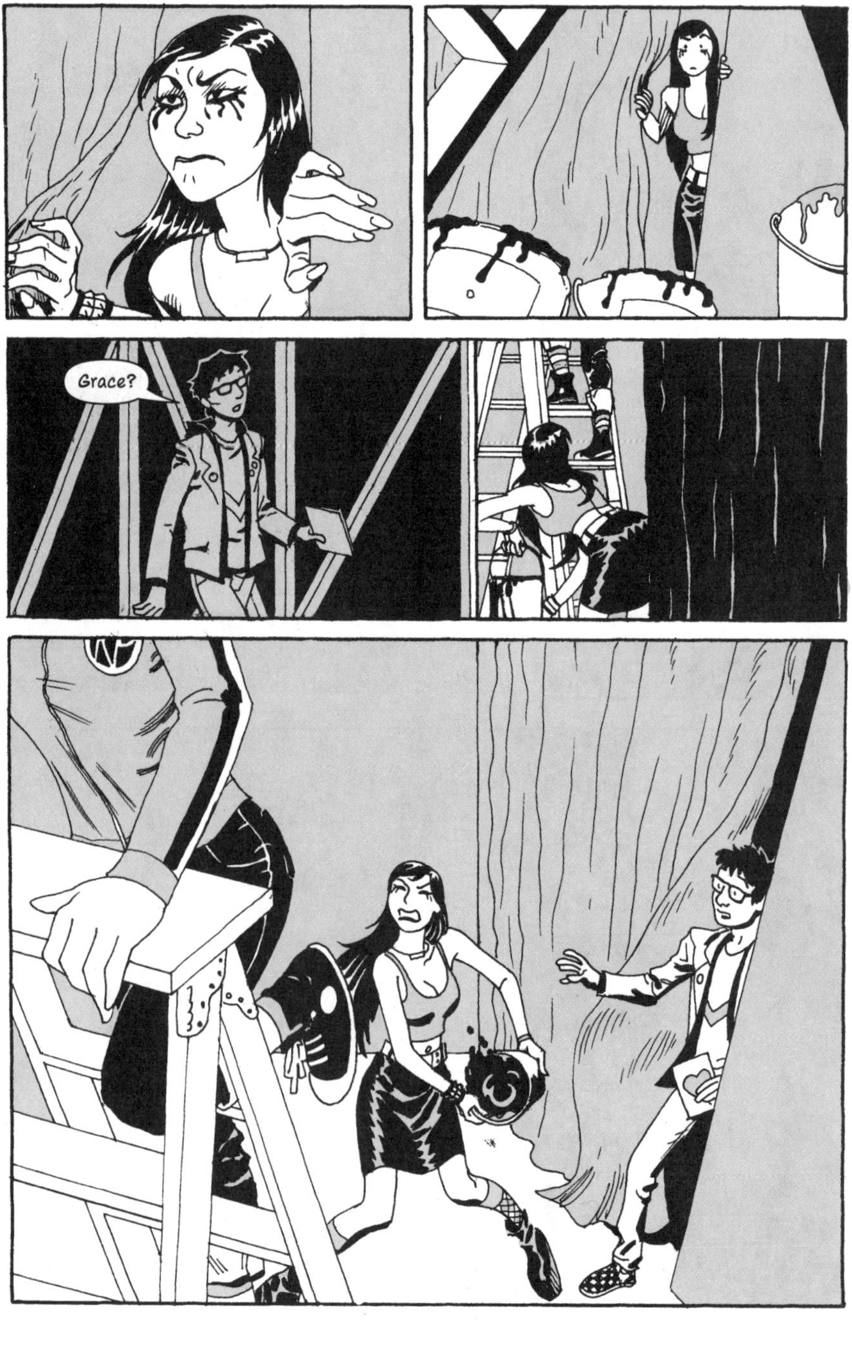
Grace?

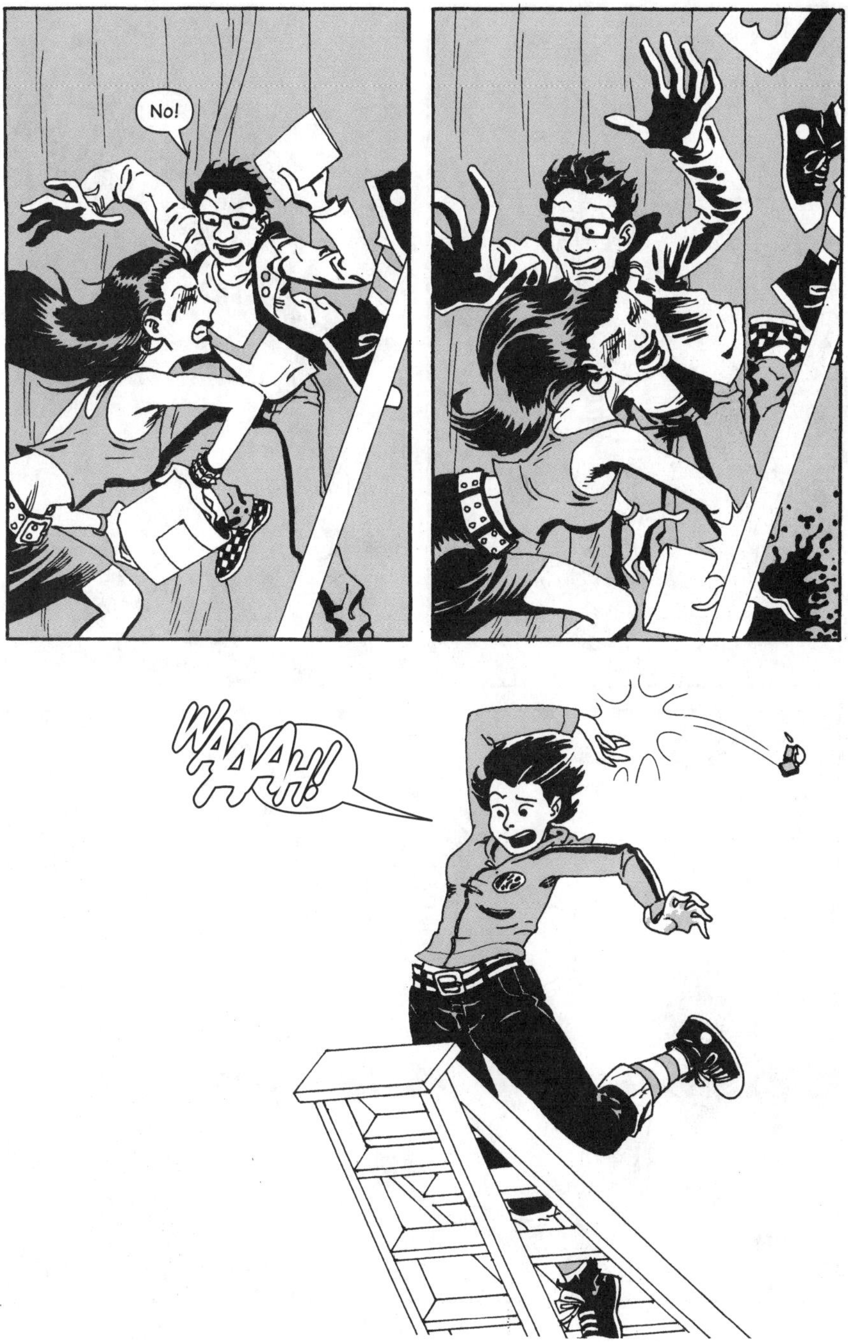
No!
WAAAH!

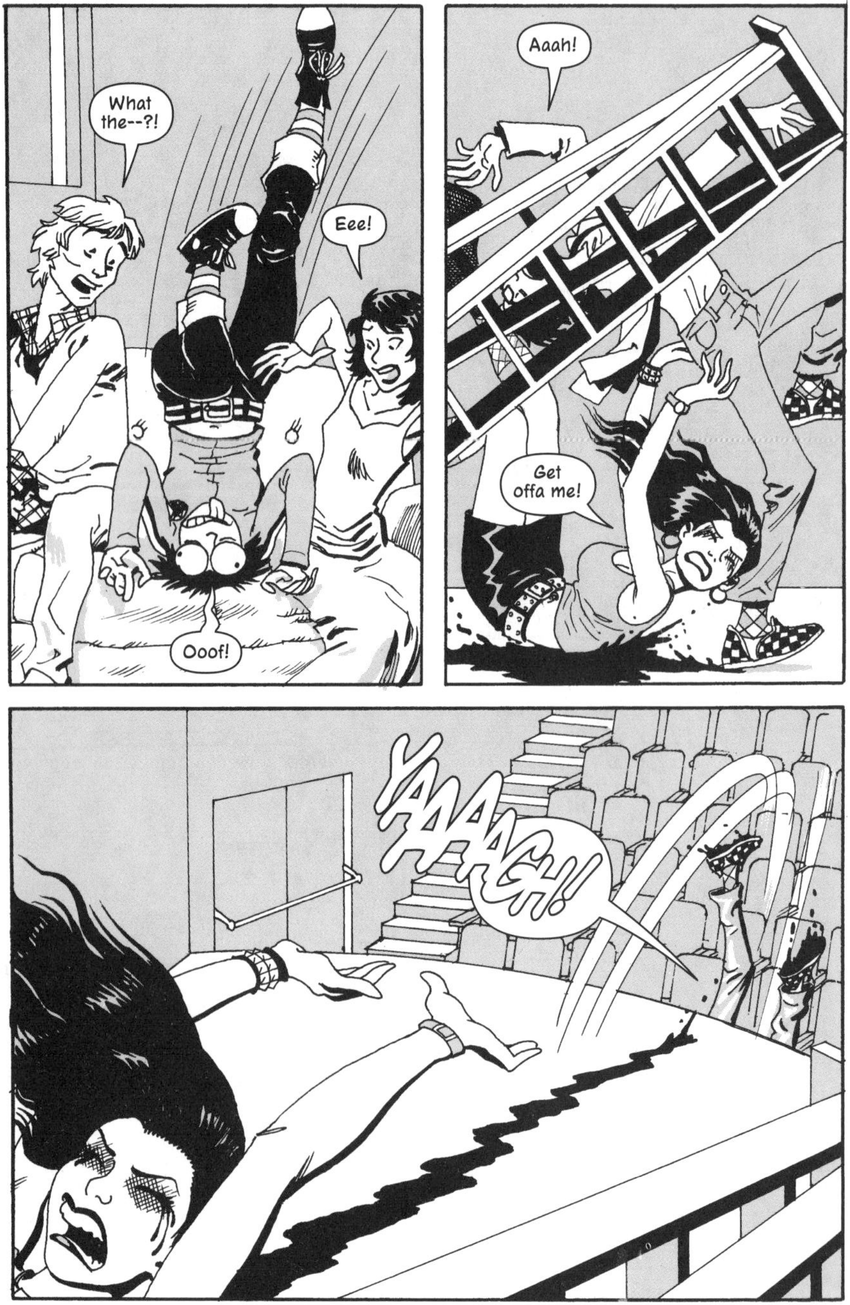
What the--?!
Eee!
Ooof!
Aaah!
Get offa me!
YAAAAAGH!!

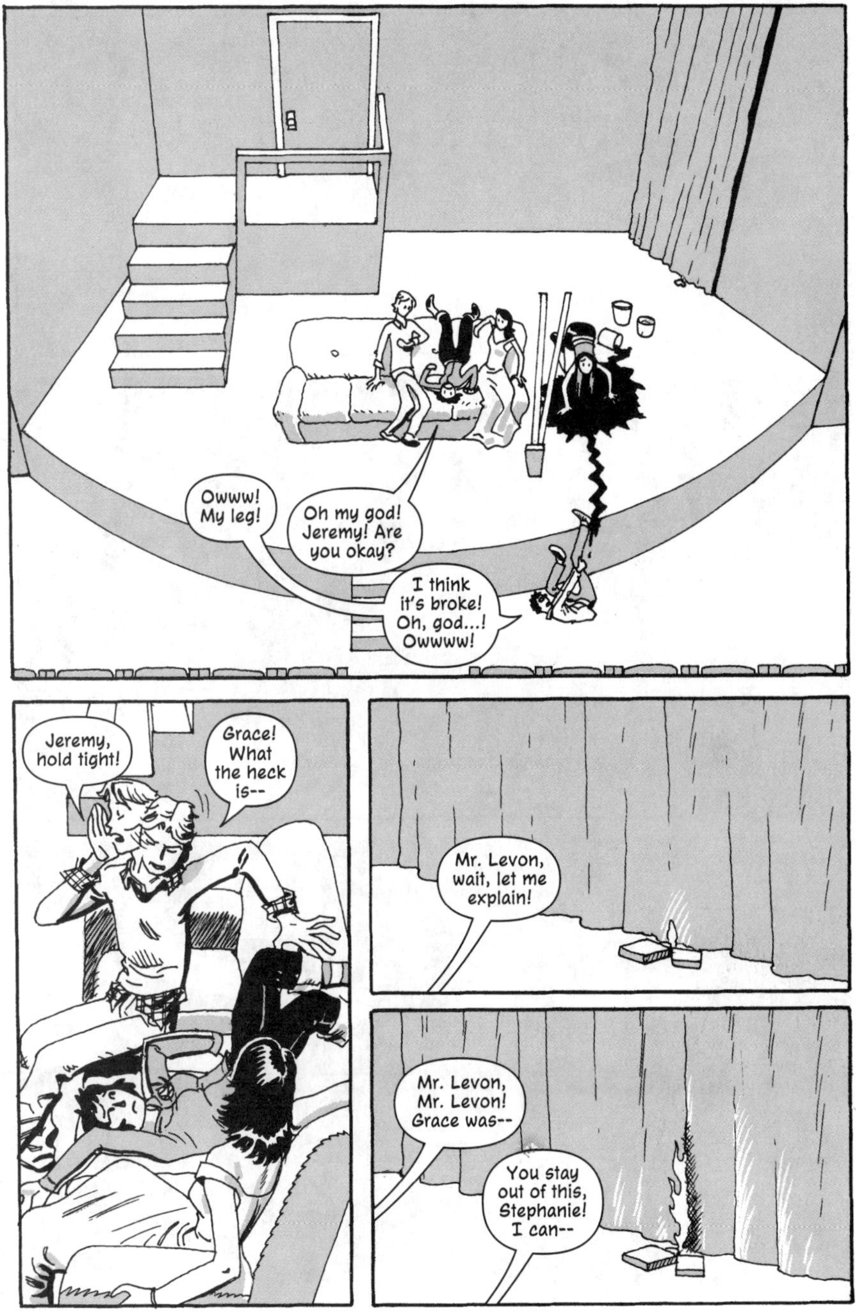
Owww! My leg!
Oh my god! Jeremy! Are you okay?
I think it's broke! Oh, god...! Owwww!
Jeremy, hold tight!
Grace! What the heck is--
Mr. Levon, wait, let me explain!
Mr. Levon, Mr. Levon! Grace was--
You stay out of this, Stephanie! I can--

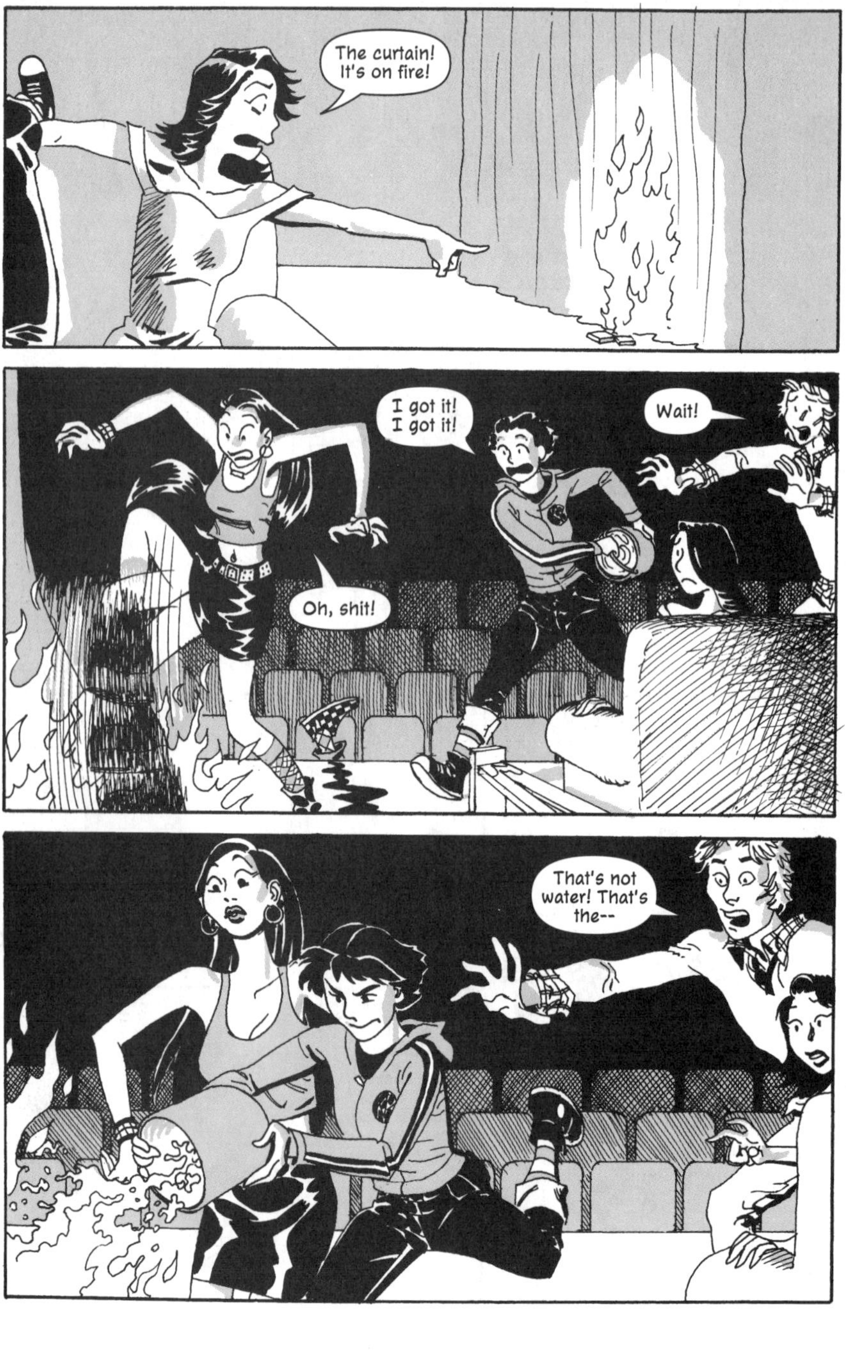
The curtain! It's on fire!
Oh, shit!
I got it! I got it!
Wait!
That's not water! That's the--

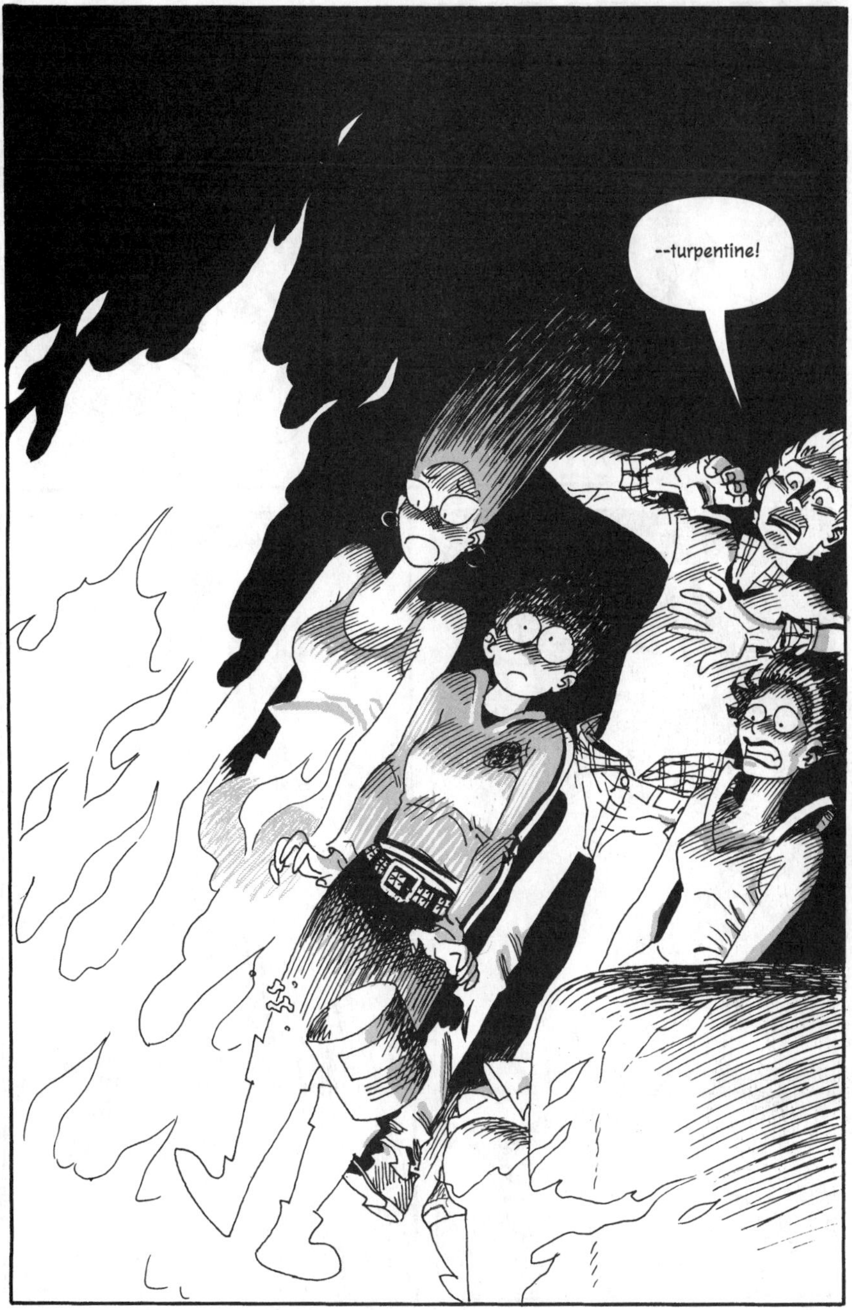
--turpentine!

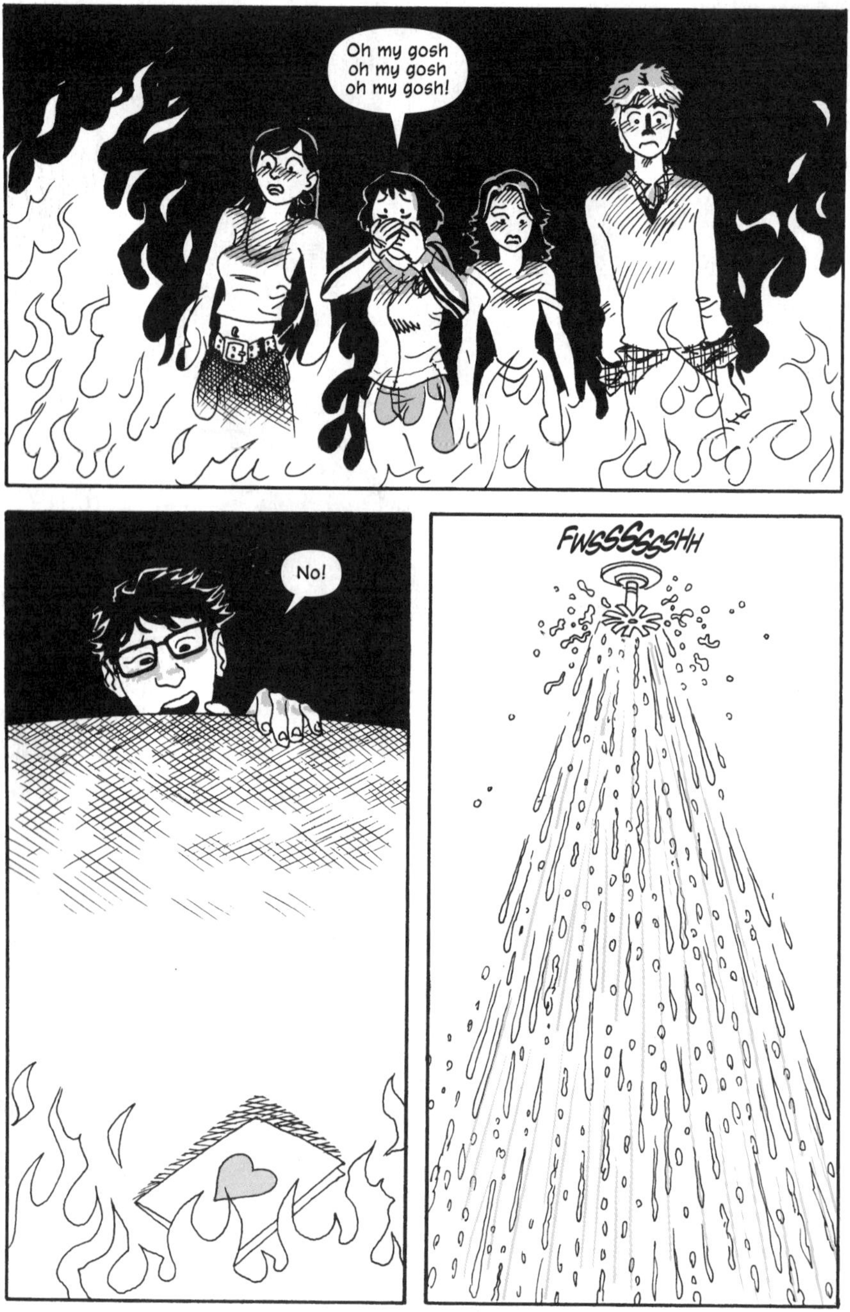
Oh my gosh
oh my gosh
oh my gosh!
No!
FWSSSSSSHH

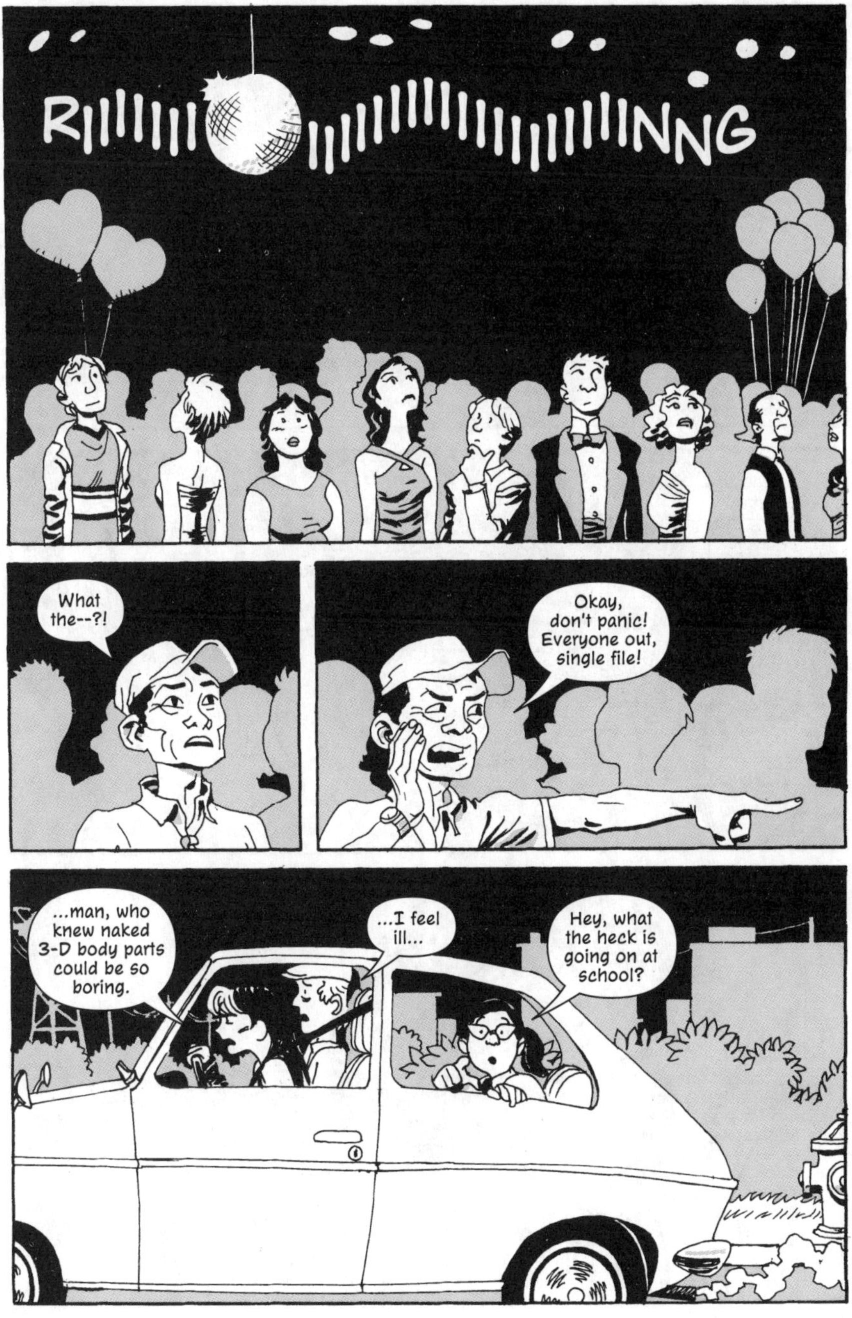
RIIIIIIIIIIIIIIIIIIIIIIIIIIINNG
What the--?!
Okay, don't panic! Everyone out, single file!
...man, who knew naked 3-D body parts could be so boring.
...I feel ill...
Hey, what the heck is going on at school?

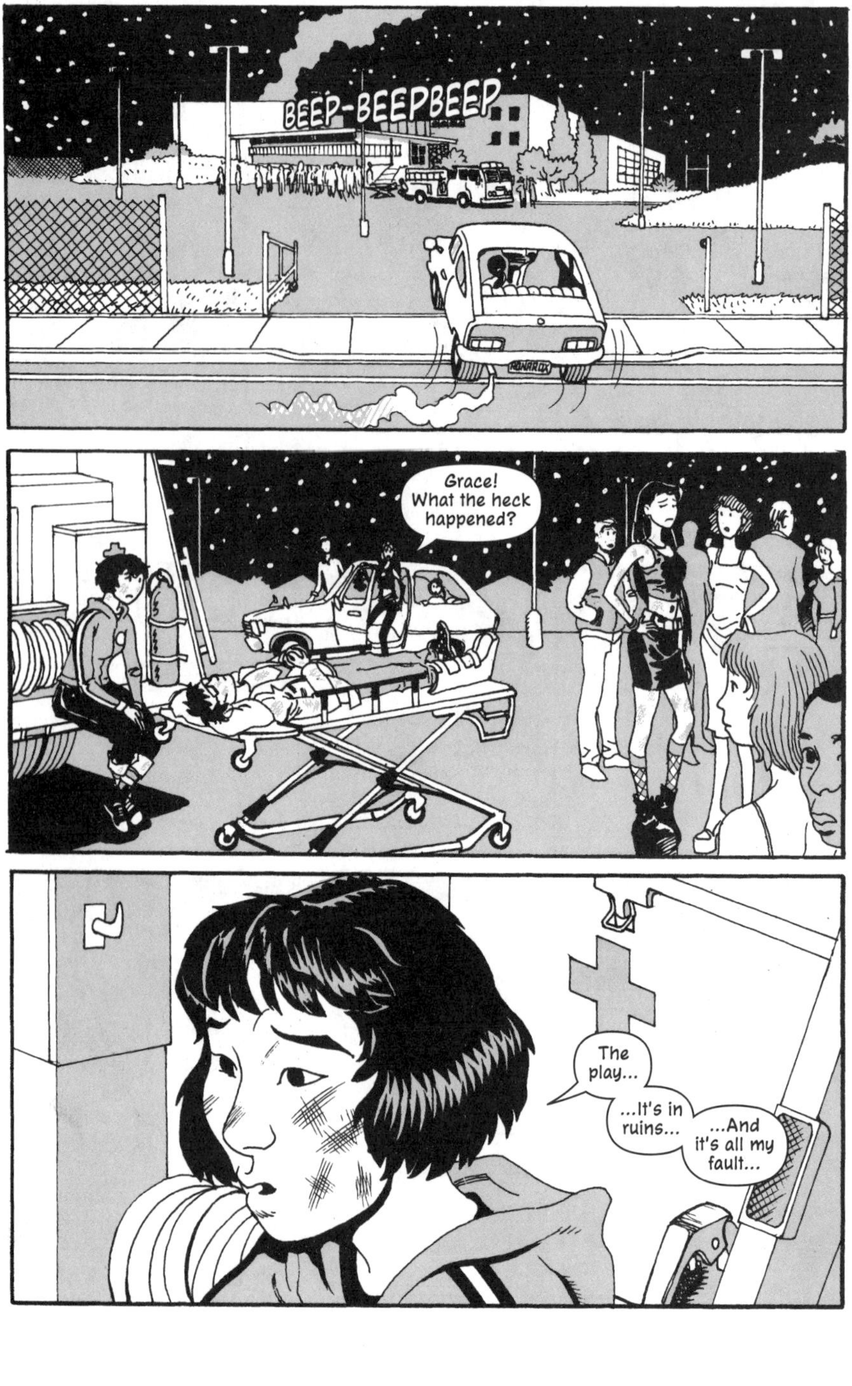
BEEP-BEEPBEEP
Grace! What the heck happened?
The play...
...It's in ruins...
...And it's all my fault...

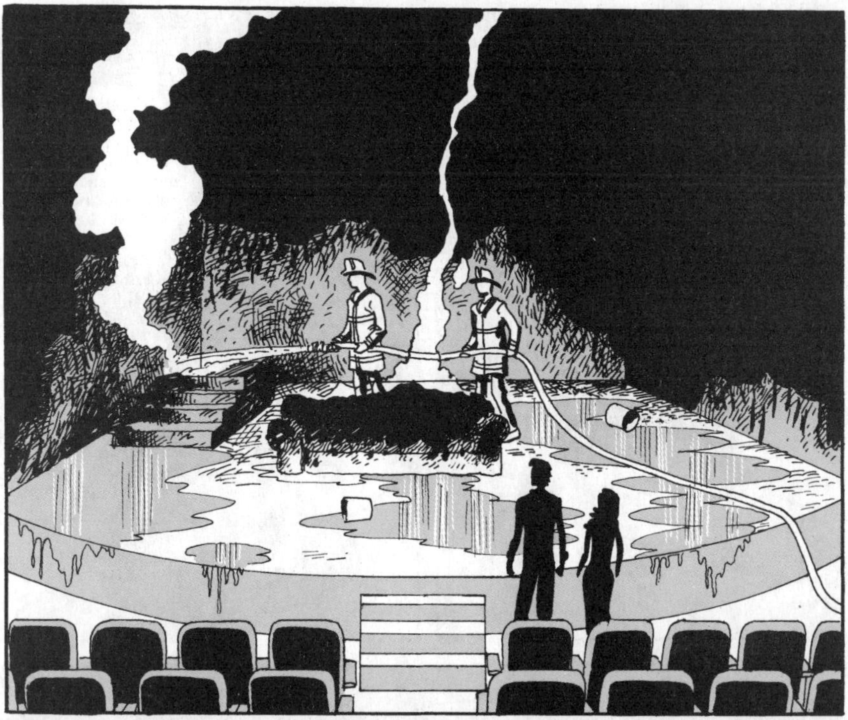

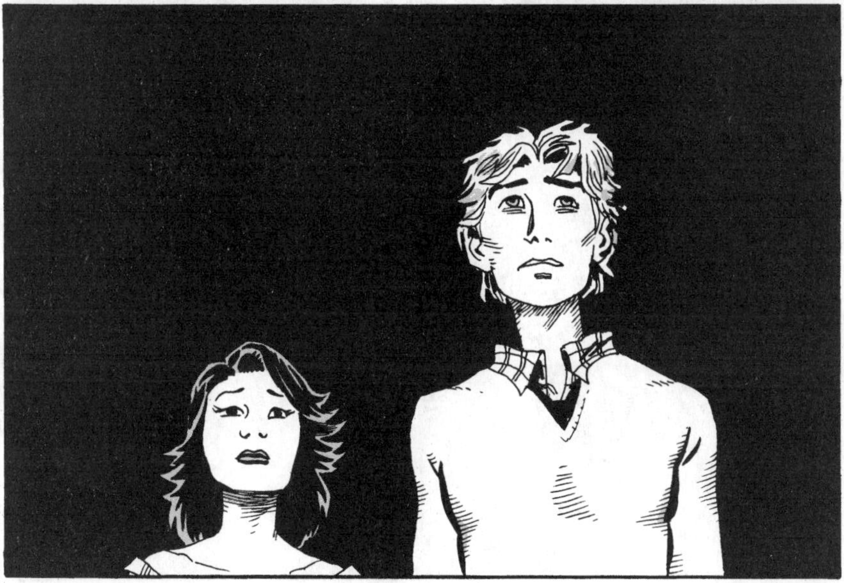

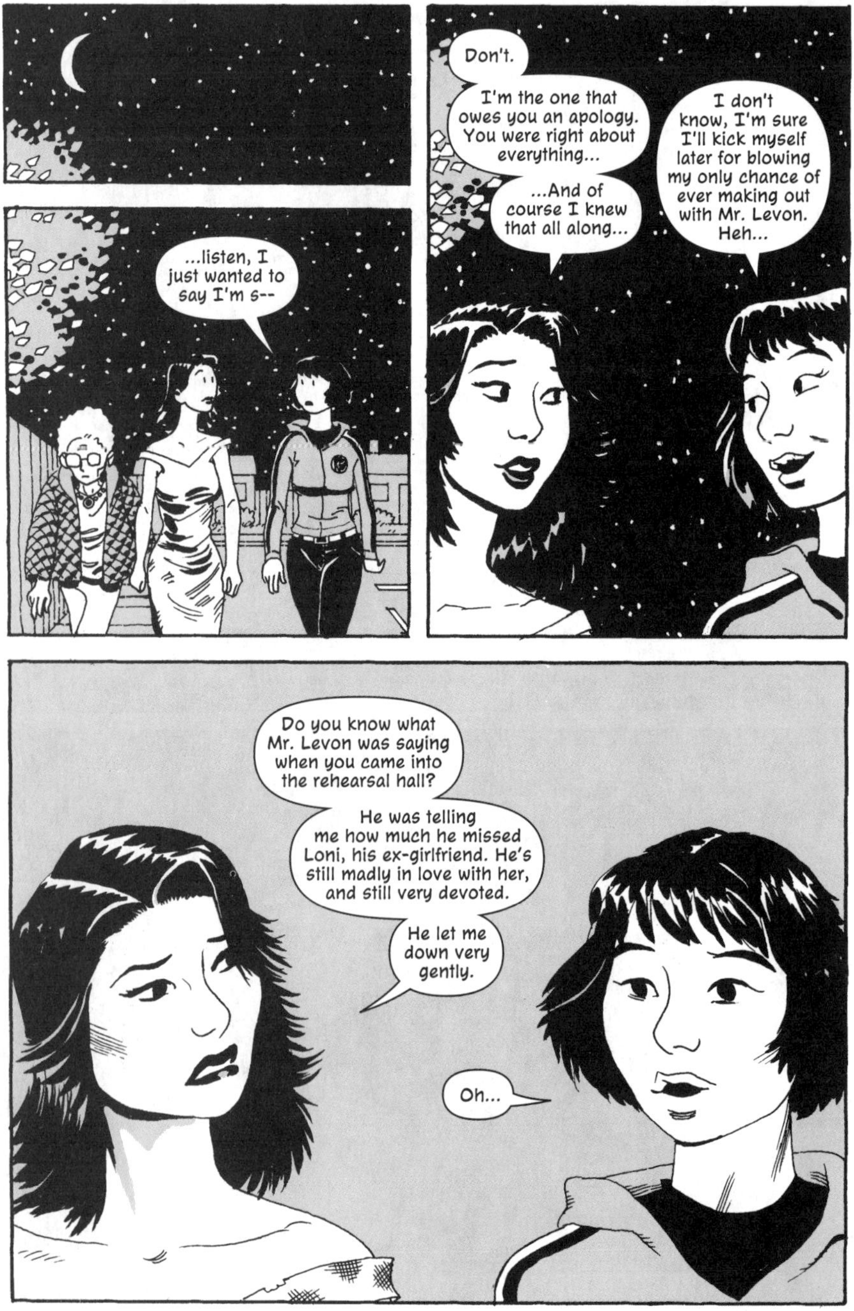
...listen, I just wanted to say I'm s--
Don't.
I'm the one that owes you an apology. You were right about everything...
...And of course I knew that all along...
I don't know, I'm sure I'll kick myself later for blowing my only chance of ever making out with Mr. Levon. Heh...
Do you know what Mr. Levon was saying when you came into the rehearsal hall?
He was telling me how much he missed Loni, his ex-girlfriend. He's still madly in love with her, and still very devoted.
He let me down very gently.
Oh...

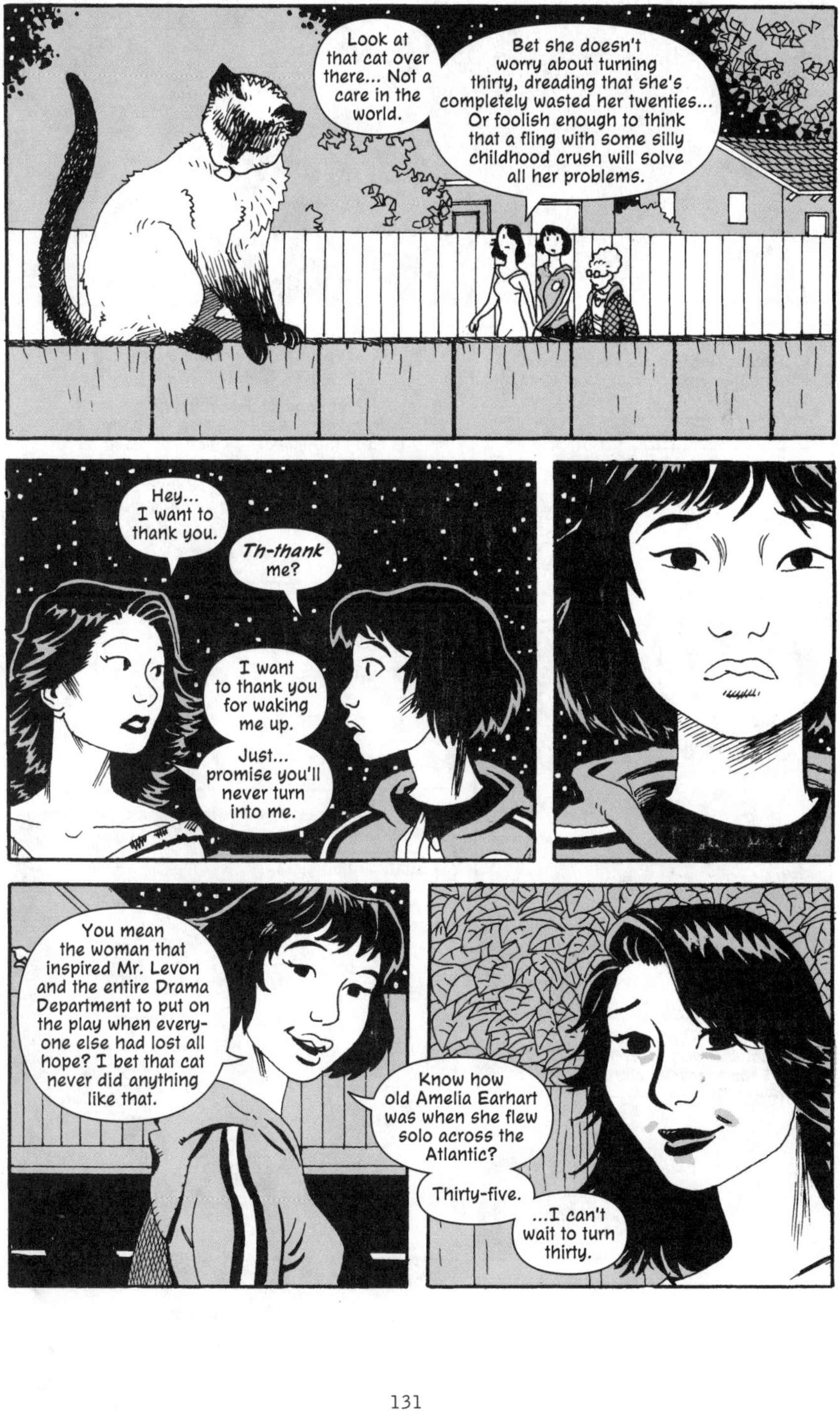
Look at that cat over there... Not a care in the world.
Bet she doesn't worry about turning thirty, dreading that she's completely wasted her twenties... Or foolish enough to think that a fling with some silly childhood crush will solve all her problems.
Hey... I want to thank you.
Th-thank me?
I want to thank you for waking me up.
Just... promise you'll never turn into me.
You mean the woman that inspired Mr. Levon and the entire Drama Department to put on the play when every-one else had lost all hope? I bet that cat never did anything like that.
Know how old Amelia Earhart was when she flew solo across the Atlantic?
Thirty-five.
...I can't wait to turn thirty.

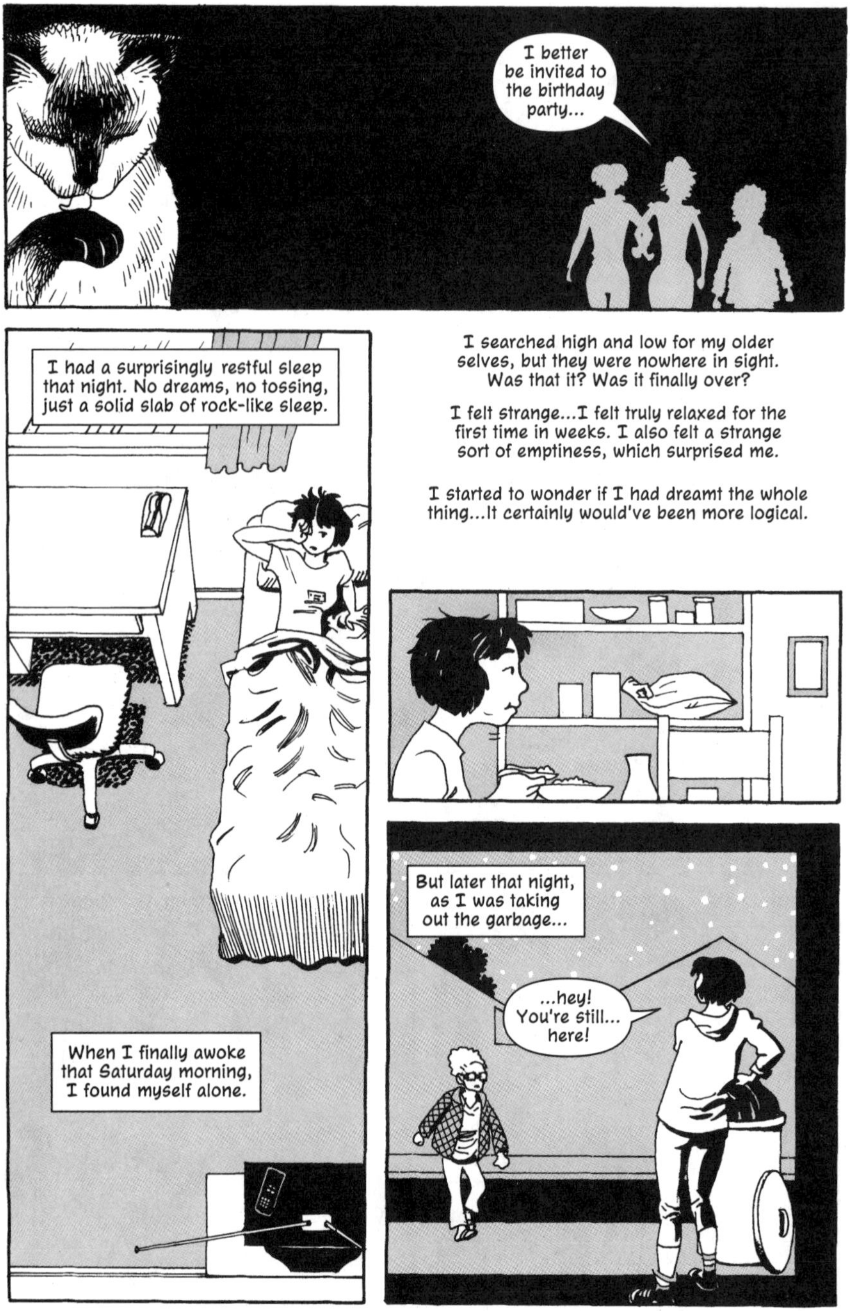

I better be invited to the birthday party...
I had a surprisingly restful sleep that night. No dreams, no tossing, just a solid slab of rock-like sleep.
When I finally awoke that Saturday morning, I found myself alone.
I searched high and low for my older selves, but they were nowhere in sight. Was that it? Was it finally over?
I felt strange...I felt truly relaxed for the first time in weeks. I also felt a strange sort of emptiness, which surprised me.
I started to wonder if I had dreamt the whole thing...It certainly would've been more logical.
But later that night, as I was taking out the garbage...
...hey! You're still... here!

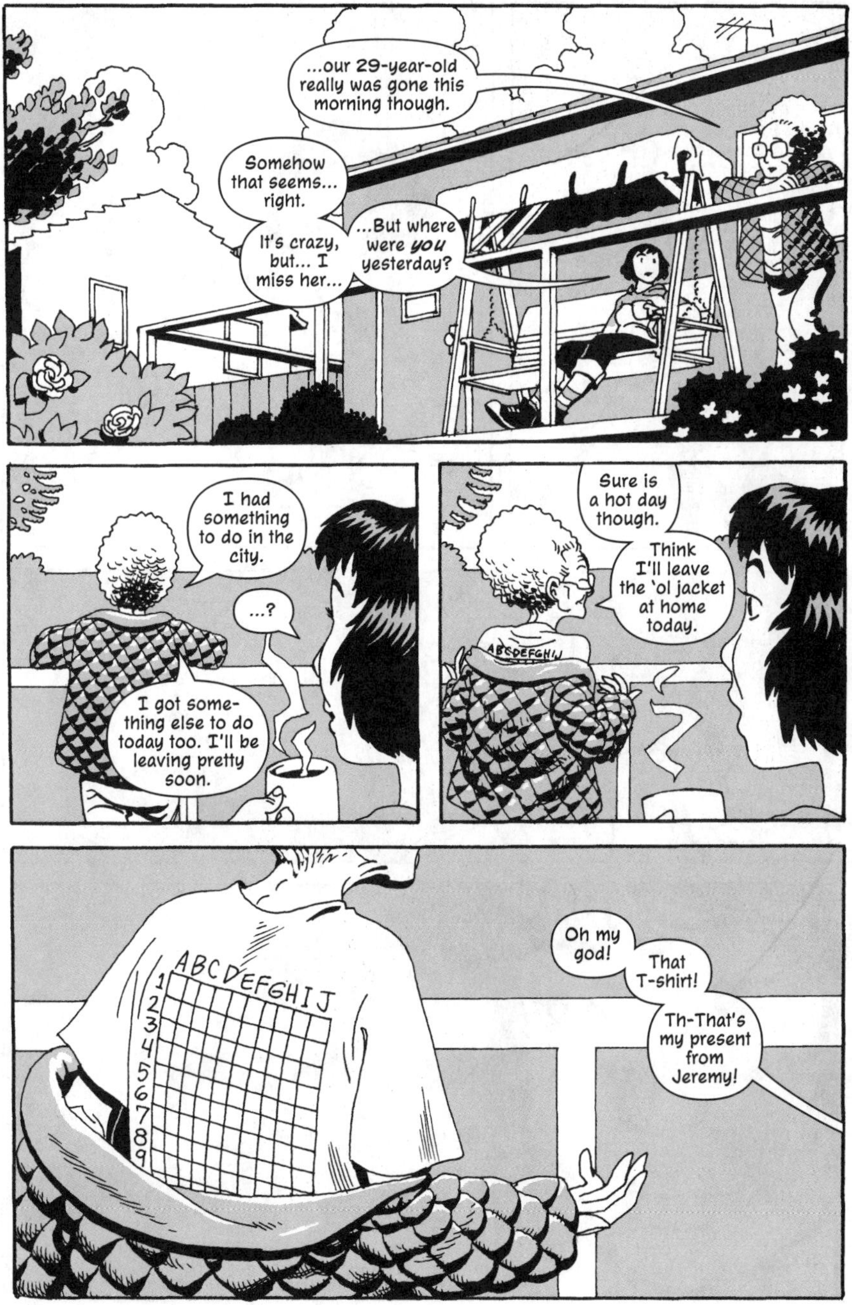

...our 29-year-old really was gone this morning though.
Somehow that seems... right.
It's crazy, but... I miss her...
...But where were *you* yesterday?
I had something to do in the city.
...?
I got something else to do today too. I'll be leaving pretty soon.
Sure is a hot day though.
Think I'll leave the 'ol jacket at home today.
ABCDEFGHIJ
ABCDEFGHIJ
1
2
3
4
5
6
7
8
9
Oh my god!
That T-shirt!
Th-That's my present from Jeremy!

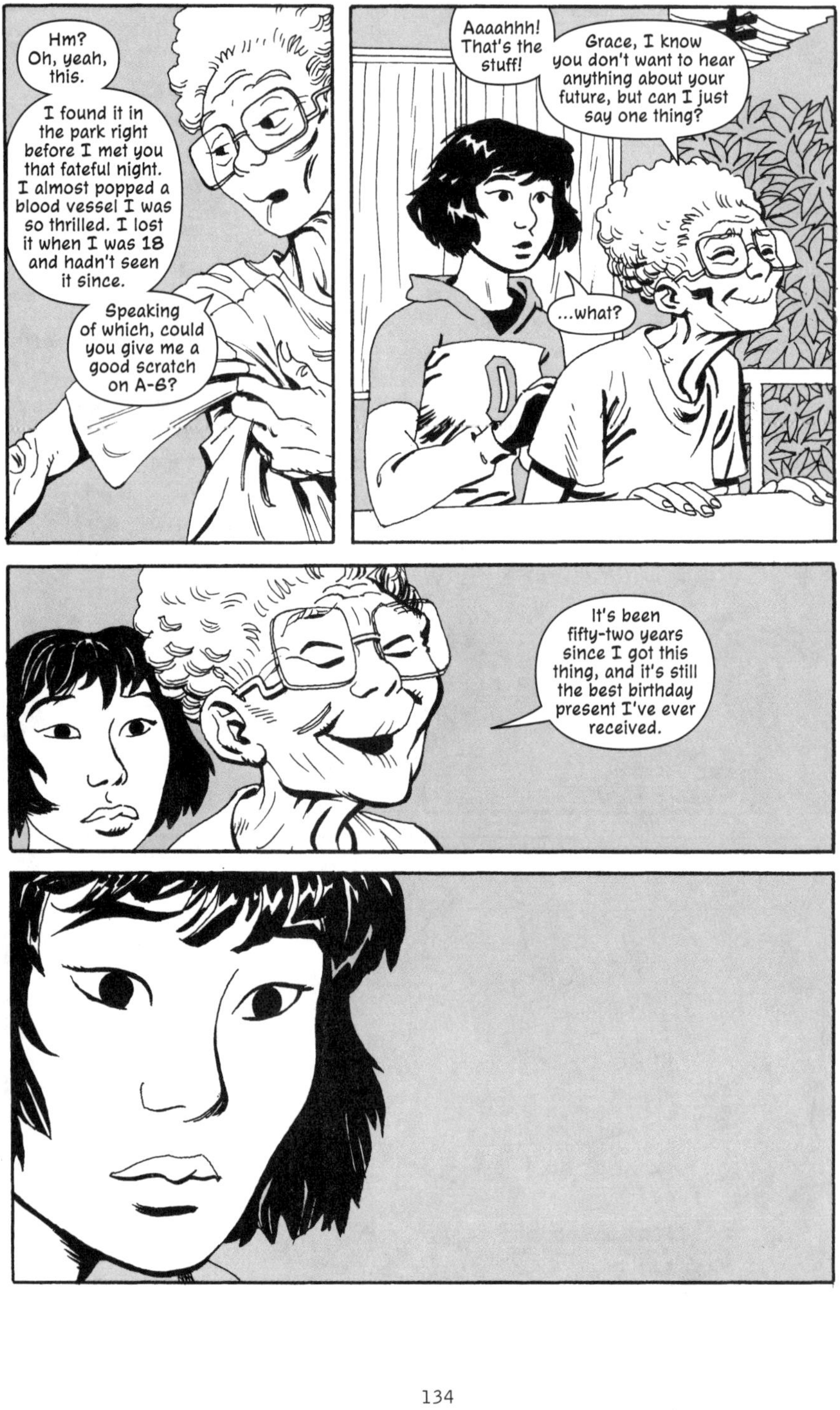
Hm? Oh, yeah, this.
I found it in the park right before I met you that fateful night. I almost popped a blood vessel I was so thrilled. I lost it when I was 18 and hadn't seen it since.
Speaking of which, could you give me a good scratch on A-6?
Aaaahhh! That's the stuff!
Grace, I know you don't want to hear anything about your future, but can I just say one thing?
...what?
It's been fifty-two years since I got this thing, and it's still the best birthday present I've ever received.

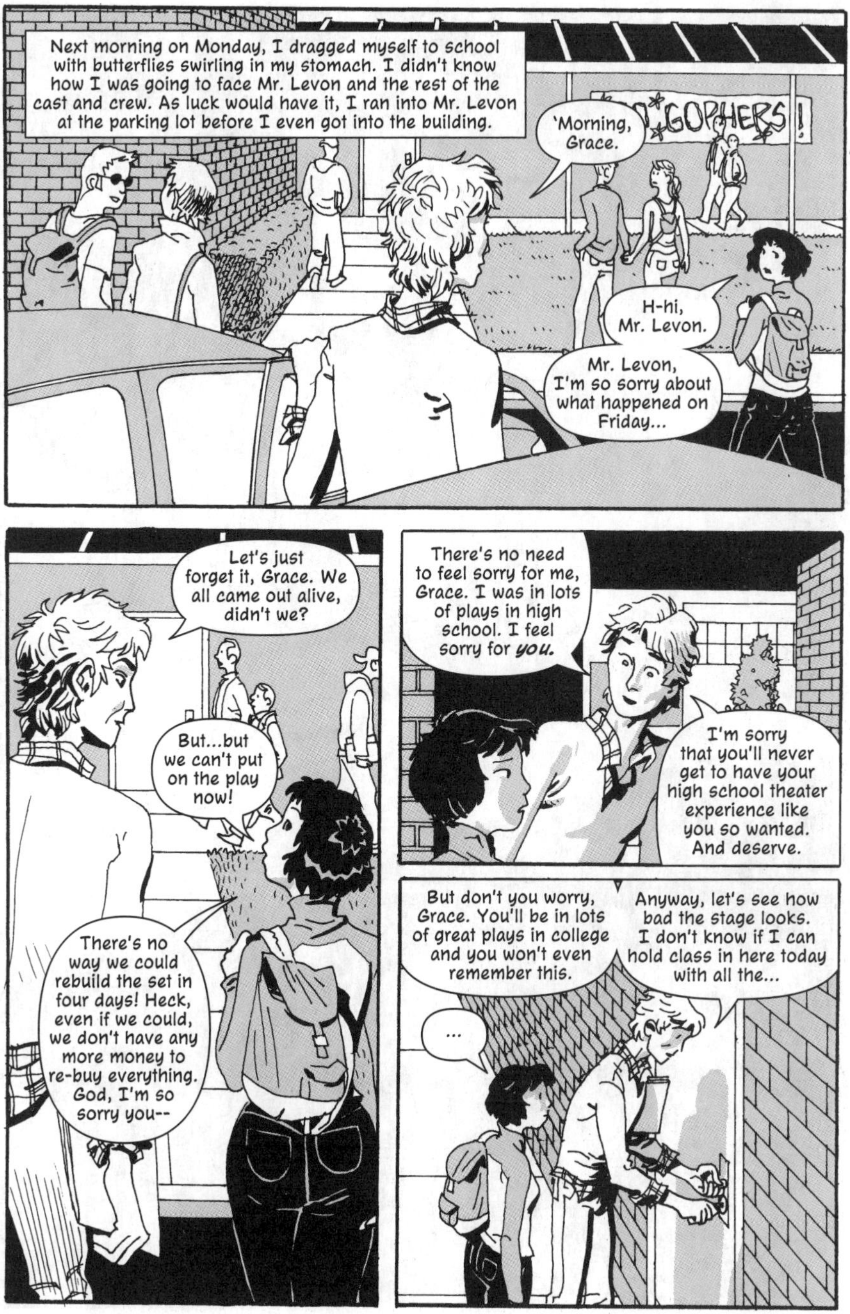
Next morning on Monday, I dragged myself to school with butterflies swirling in my stomach. I didn't know how I was going to face Mr. Levon and the rest of the cast and crew. As luck would have it, I ran into Mr. Levon at the parking lot before I even got into the building.
'Morning, Grace.
H-hi, Mr. Levon.
Mr. Levon, I'm so sorry about what happened on Friday...
Let's just forget it, Grace. We all came out alive, didn't we?
But...but we can't put on the play now!
There's no way we could rebuild the set in four days! Heck, even if we could, we don't have any more money to re-buy everything. God, I'm so sorry you--
There's no need to feel sorry for me, Grace. I was in lots of plays in high school. I feel sorry for *you.*
I'm sorry that you'll never get to have your high school theater experience like you so wanted. And deserve.
But don't you worry, Grace. You'll be in lots of great plays in college and you won't even remember this.
Anyway, let's see how bad the stage looks. I don't know if I can hold class in here today with all the...
...

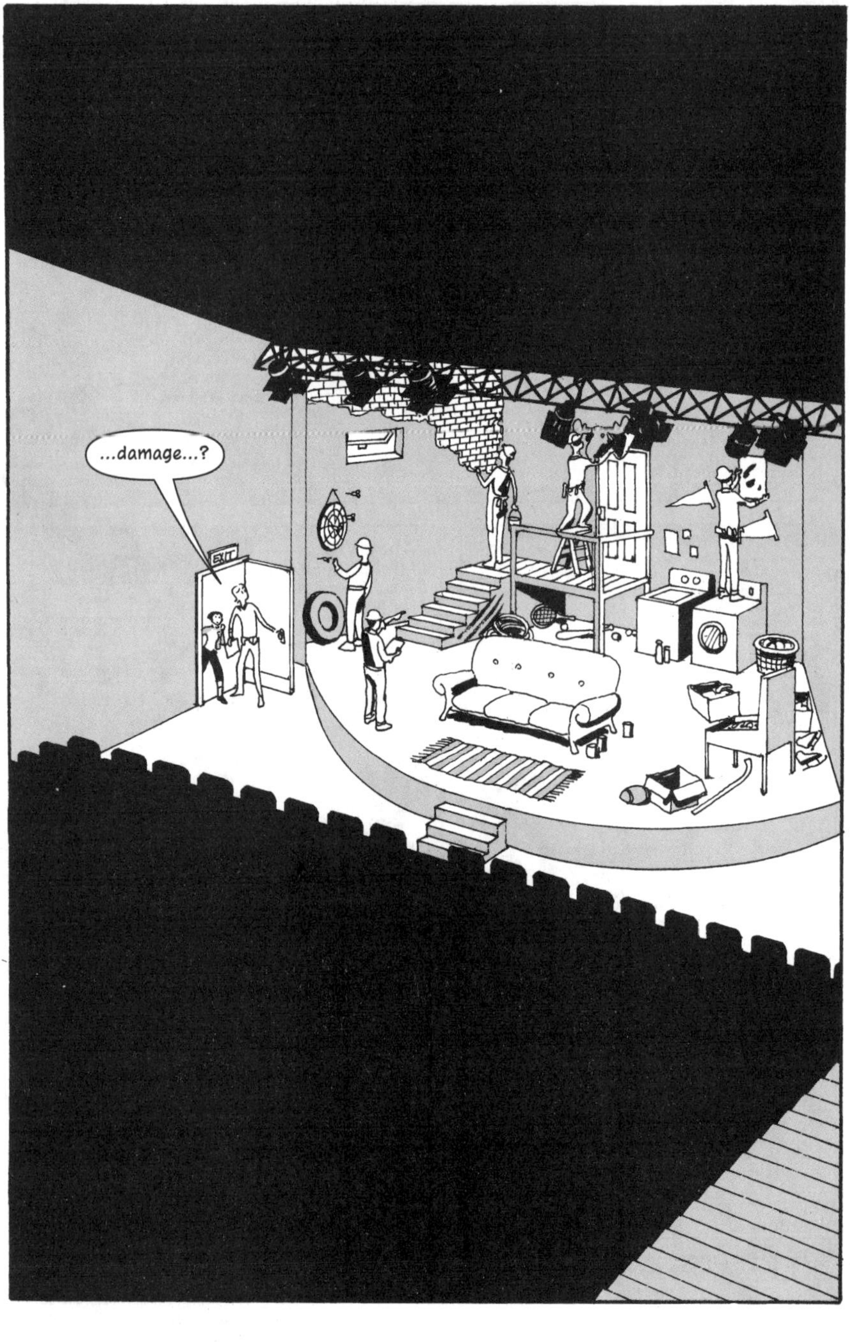
...damage...?
EXIT

E-Excuse me, what's going on here?

Well, an old Asian lady came to me yesterday morning and gave me $30,000 in cash to finish this set by tonight.

Didn't know if we could pull it off, but I couldn't pass up that kinda money!

We've been working all day and night. Hope it looks okay so far...

...uh huh...

E-Excuse me...What was the old lady's name?

Said her name was "Jessica Kwon."

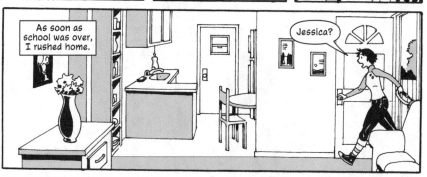

As soon as school was over, I rushed home.

Jessica?

Jessica?

Wha...?

TO ME
FROM GRACE

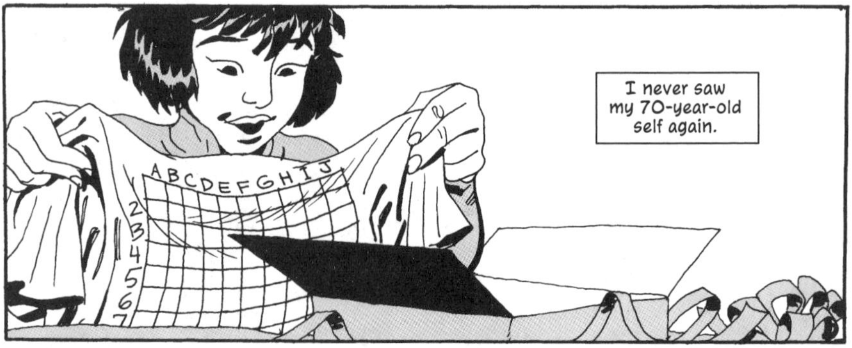
I never saw my 70-year-old self again.
A B C D E F G H I J
2 3 4 5 6 7

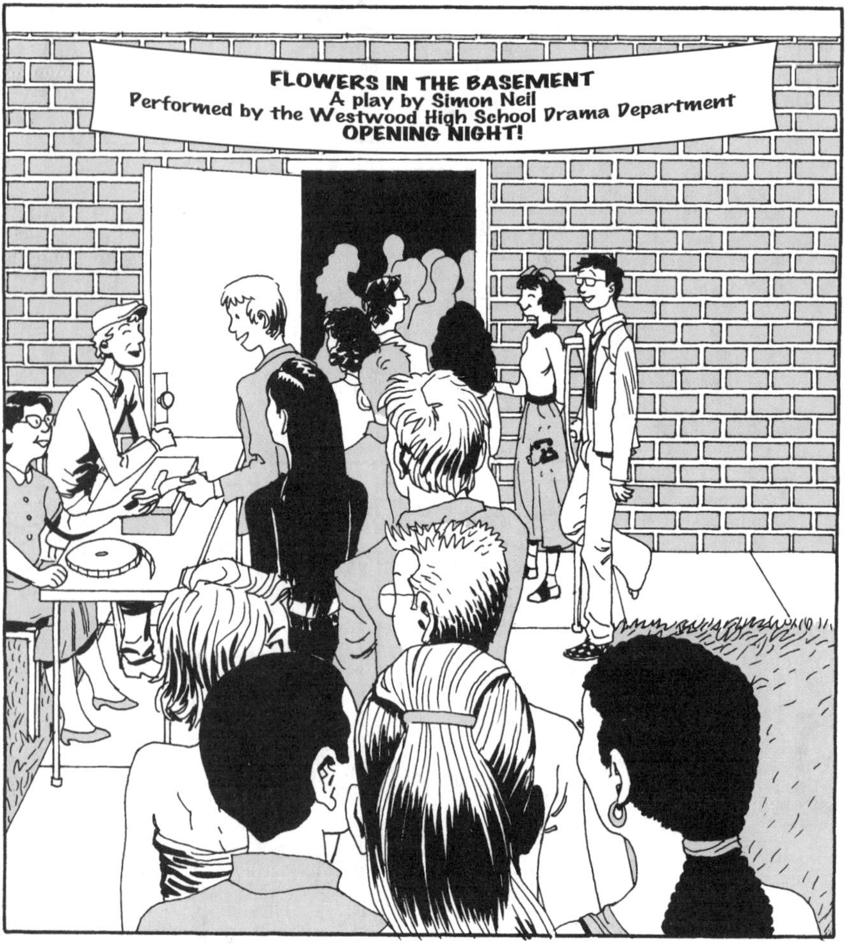
FLOWERS IN THE BASEMENT
A play by Simon Neil
Performed by the Westwood High School Drama Department
OPENING NIGHT!

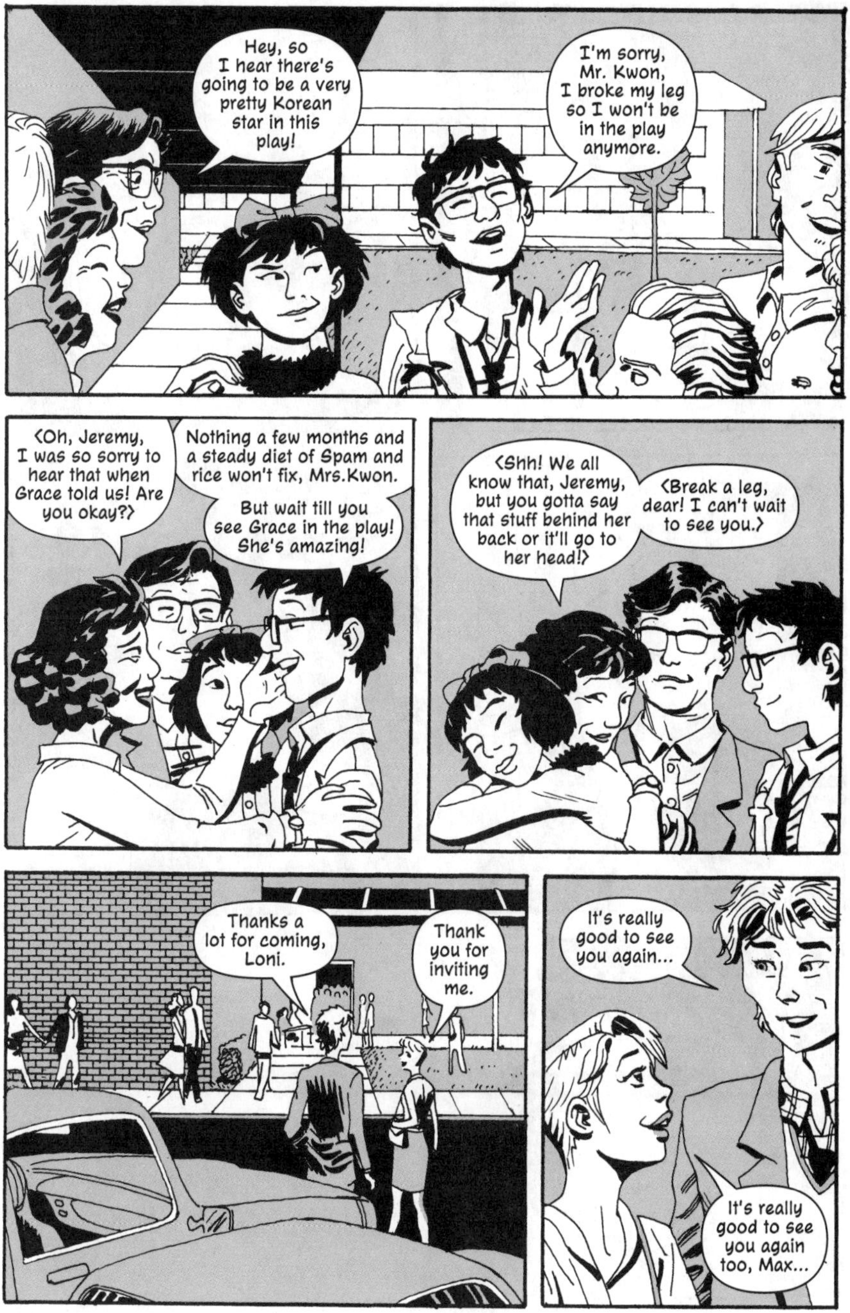
Hey, so I hear there's going to be a very pretty Korean star in this play!
I'm sorry, Mr. Kwon, I broke my leg so I won't be in the play anymore.
<Oh, Jeremy, I was so sorry to hear that when Grace told us! Are you okay?>
Nothing a few months and a steady diet of Spam and rice won't fix, Mrs.Kwon.
But wait till you see Grace in the play! She's amazing!
<Shh! We all know that, Jeremy, but you gotta say that stuff behind her back or it'll go to her head!>
<Break a leg, dear! I can't wait to see you.>
Thanks a lot for coming, Loni.
Thank you for inviting me.
It's really good to see you again...
It's really good to see you again too, Max...

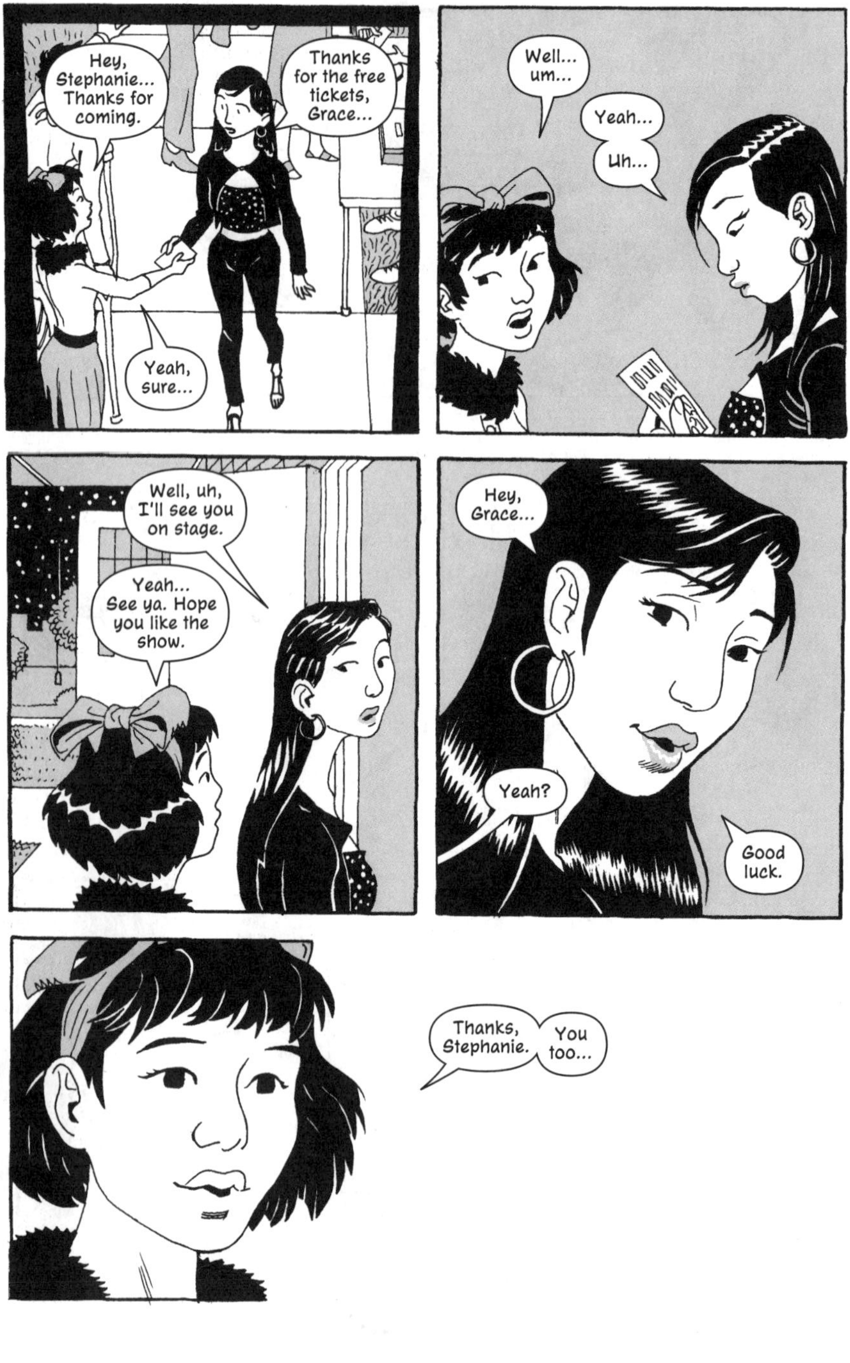
Hey, Stephanie... Thanks for coming.
Thanks for the free tickets, Grace...
Yeah, sure...
Well... um...
Yeah...
Uh...
Well, uh, I'll see you on stage.
Yeah... See ya. Hope you like the show.
Hey, Grace...
Yeah?
Good luck.
Thanks, Stephanie.
You too...

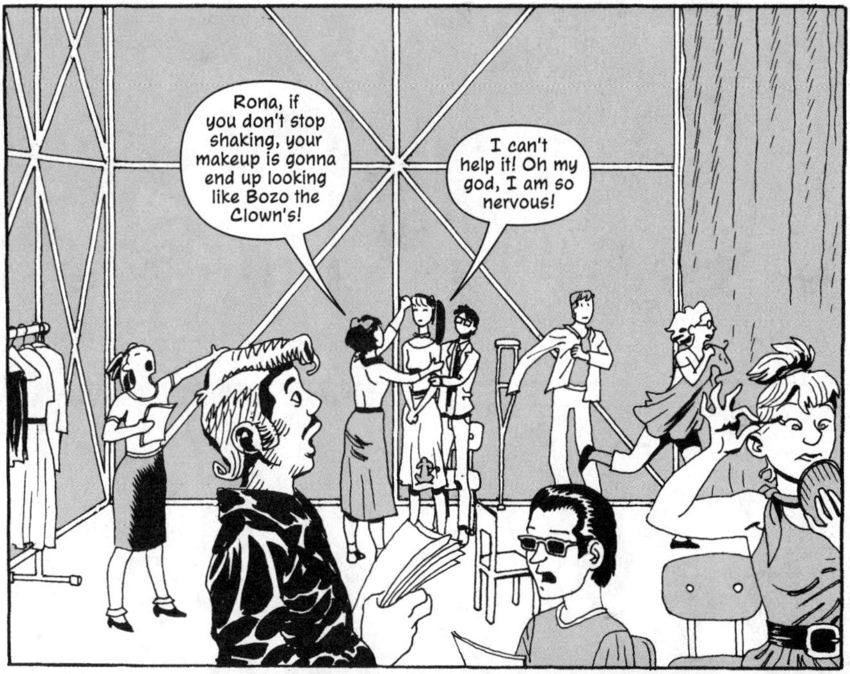
Rona, if you don't stop shaking, your makeup is gonna end up looking like Bozo the Clown's!
I can't help it! Oh my god, I am so nervous!

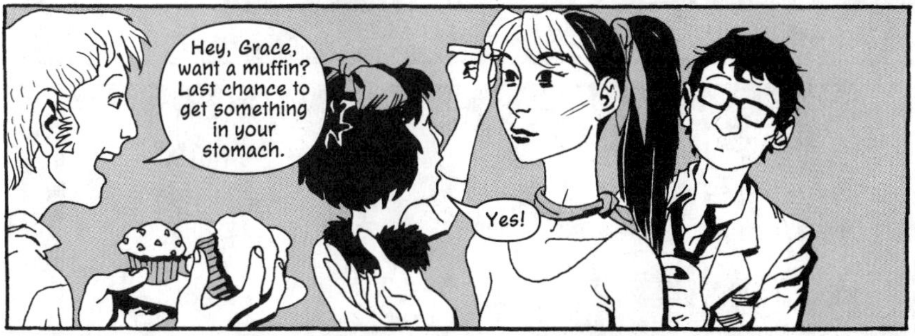
Hey, Grace, want a muffin? Last chance to get something in your stomach.
Yes!

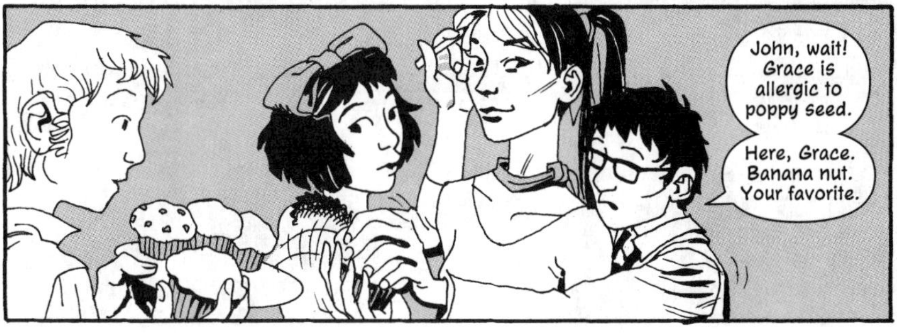
John, wait! Grace is allergic to poppy seed.
Here, Grace. Banana nut. Your favorite.

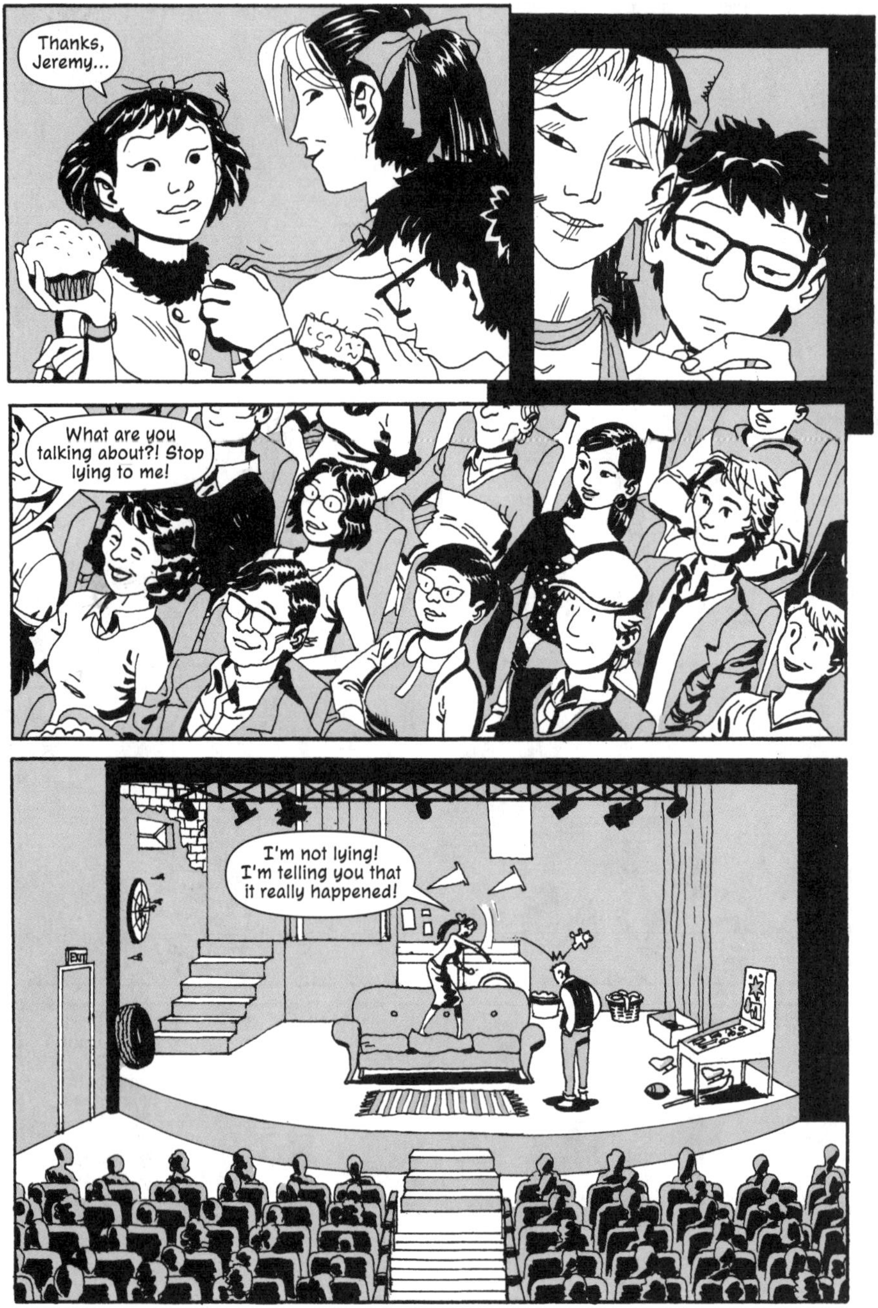
Thanks, Jeremy...
What are you talking about?! Stop lying to me!
I'm not lying! I'm telling you that it really happened!
EXIT

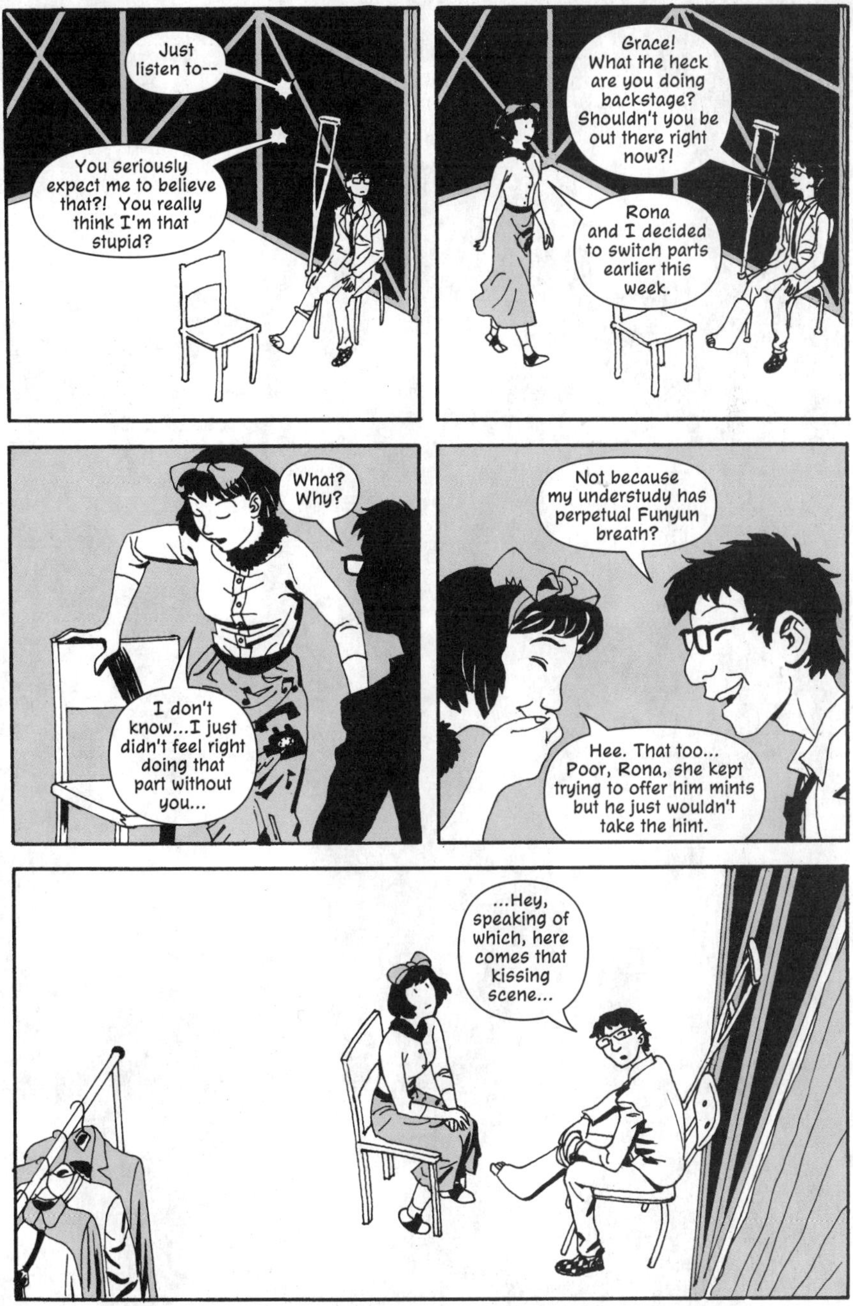
Just listen to--
You seriously expect me to believe that?! You really think I'm that stupid?
Grace! What the heck are you doing backstage? Shouldn't you be out there right now?!
Rona and I decided to switch parts earlier this week.
What? Why?
I don't know...I just didn't feel right doing that part without you...
Not because my understudy has perpetual Funyun breath?
Hee. That too... Poor, Rona, she kept trying to offer him mints but he just wouldn't take the hint.
...Hey, speaking of which, here comes that kissing scene...

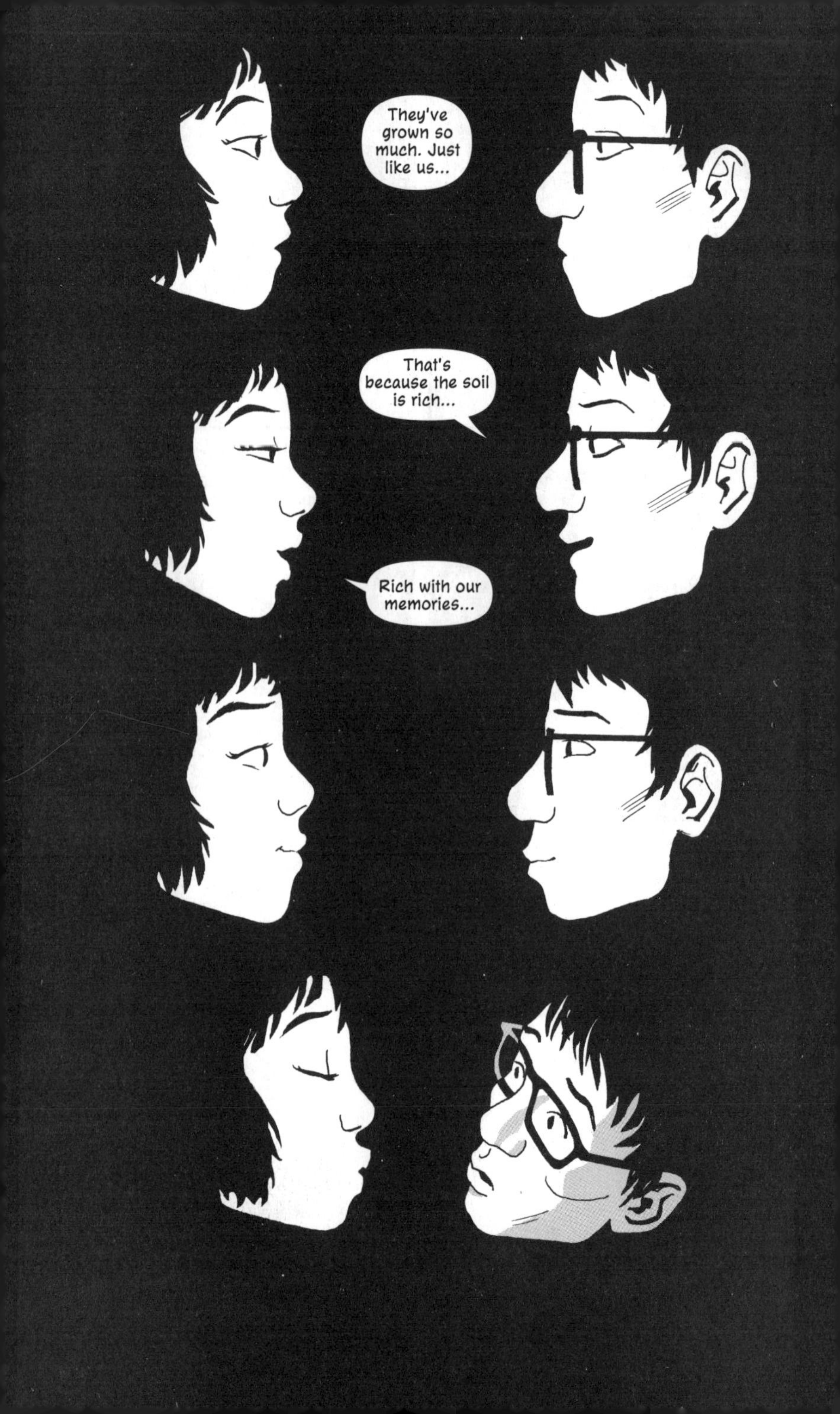
They've grown so much. Just like us...
That's because the soil is rich...
Rich with our memories...

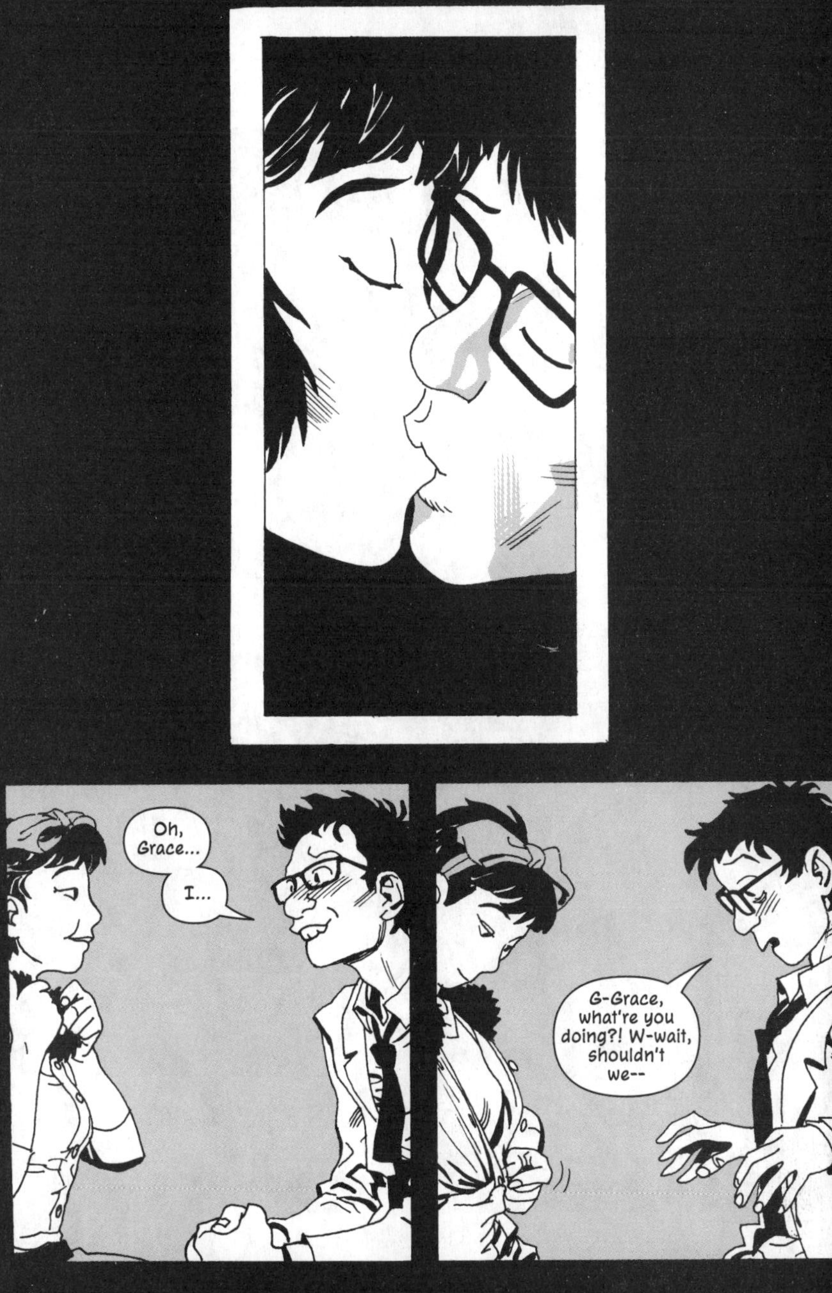
Oh, Grace...
I...
G-Grace, what're you doing?! W-wait, shouldn't we--

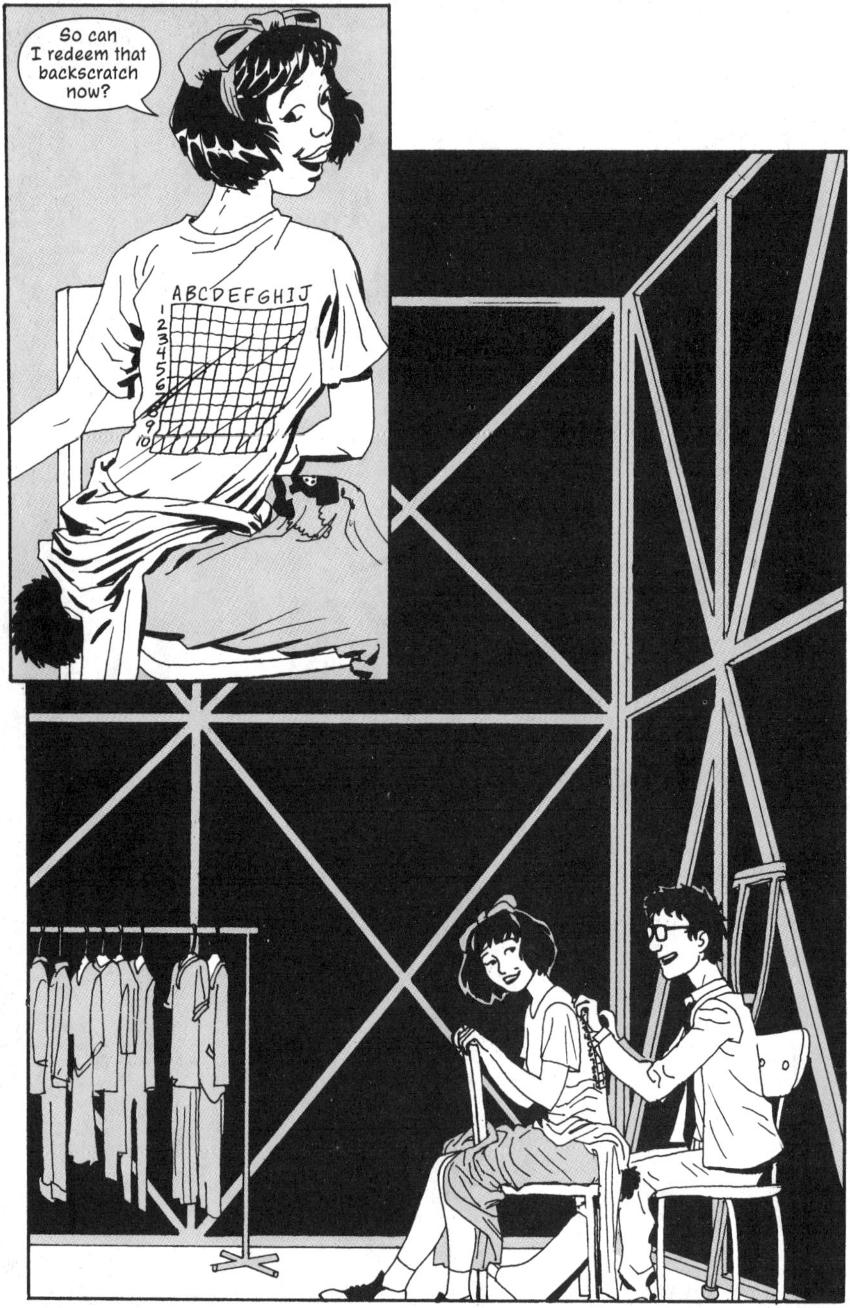
So can I redeem that backscratch now?
ABCDEFGHIJ
1
2
3
4
5
6
7
8
9
10

...is an extraordinary necklace! Jessica, this is the finest piece of jewelry I've seen in the four years I've been with Antiques Streetshow.

How did this dazzler end up in your possession?

Oh, it's been in the family for generations. My mother passed it down to me shortly before she passed away.

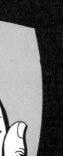

Well, you're very lucky she did. This very specific motif in the rim surrounding the ruby here is proof that this is a genuine 12th century Korean necklace.

Jewelry of this quality can only have been made for royalty-- probably the queen. Also, if you'll take a close look at the inscription on the--

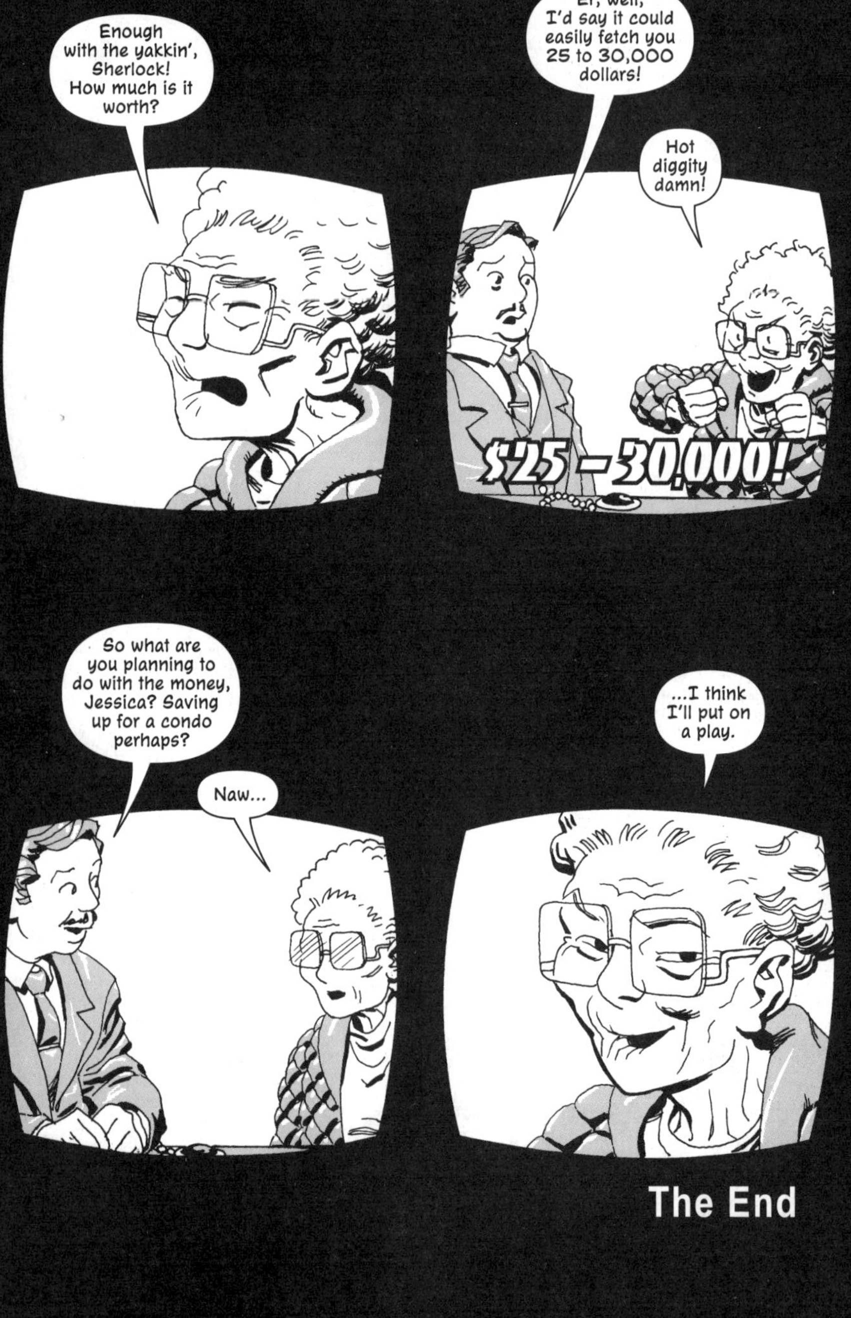

Enough with the yakkin', Sherlock! How much is it worth?
Er, well, I'd say it could easily fetch you 25 to 30,000 dollars!
Hot diggity damn!
$25 - 30,000!
So what are you planning to do with the money, Jessica? Saving up for a condo perhaps?
Naw...
...I think I'll put on a play.

The End

DEREK KIRK KIM

Derek scored the "triple crown"
with his debut graphic novel,
Same Difference and Other Stories,
winning all three industry awards—
the Eisner, Harvey, and Ignatz. It was
also selected as one of the best books
of 2003 by **Publishers Weekly**.
Currently, he is collaborating
with Gene Yang on a book for
First Second Books. He likes Tabasco
sauce on everything.

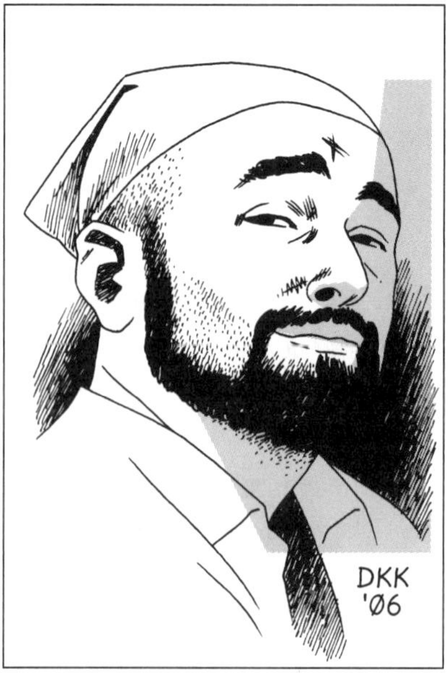
DKK
'Ø6

JESSE HAMM

Jesse's cartooning has appeared in various mini-comics and anthologies and on the web. GOOD AS LILY is his first mainstream project. His interests include old movies, pulp fiction, and Christian theology. Jesse lives near Portland, Oregon with his wife, Anna, and her cat.

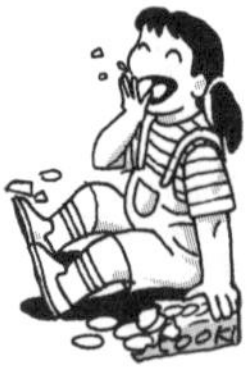

SPECIAL BACKSTAGE PASS:

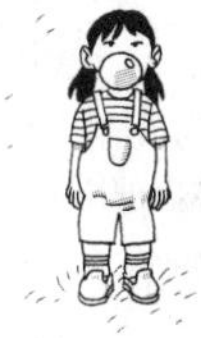

If you liked the story you've just read, fear not: Other MINX books will be available in the months to come. MINX is a line of books that's designed especially for you — someone who's a bit bored with straight fiction and ready for stories that are visually exciting beyond words — literally. In fact, we thought you might like to get in on a secret, behind-the-scenes look at a few of the new MINX titles that will aid in your escape to cool places this fall. So hurry up and turn the page already! And be sure to check out other exclusive material at

minxbooks.net

If there were a category in the Olympics for blabbing, Tasha Flanagan

would blab for her country. And when her mom brings home a

creepy boyfriend and his deadpan daughter, Tasha's dysfunctional family

is headed for a complete mental meltdown.

COMING IN SEPTEMBER 2007

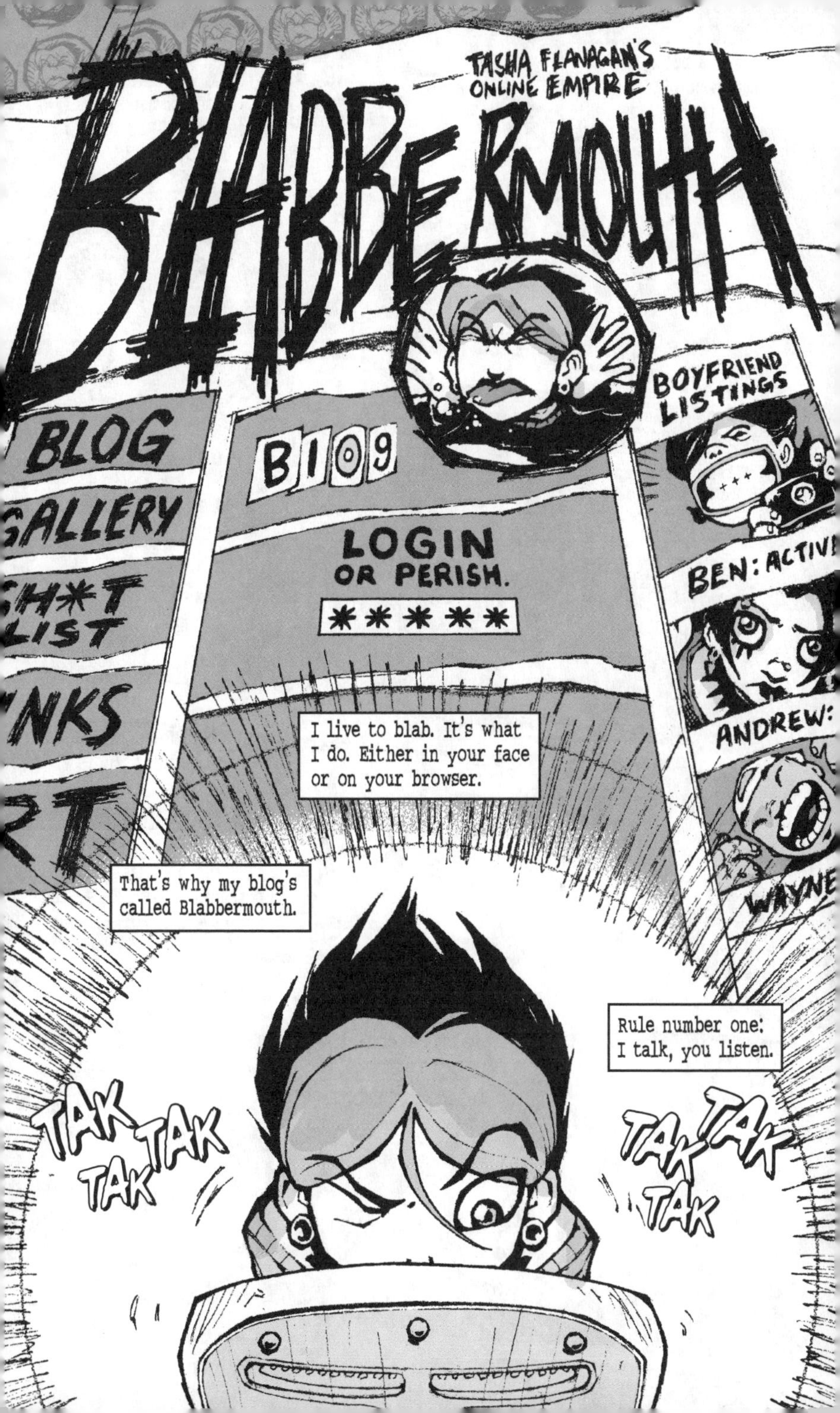
TASHA FLANAGAN'S ONLINE EMPIRE
BLABBERMOUTH
BLOG
GALLERY
SH*T LIST
BIO
LOGIN OR PERISH.
*****
BOYFRIEND LISTINGS
BEN: ACTIVE
ANDREW:
WAYNE
I live to blab. It's what I do. Either in your face or on your browser.
That's why my blog's called Blabbermouth.
Rule number one: I talk, you listen.
TAK TAK TAK
TAK TAK TAK

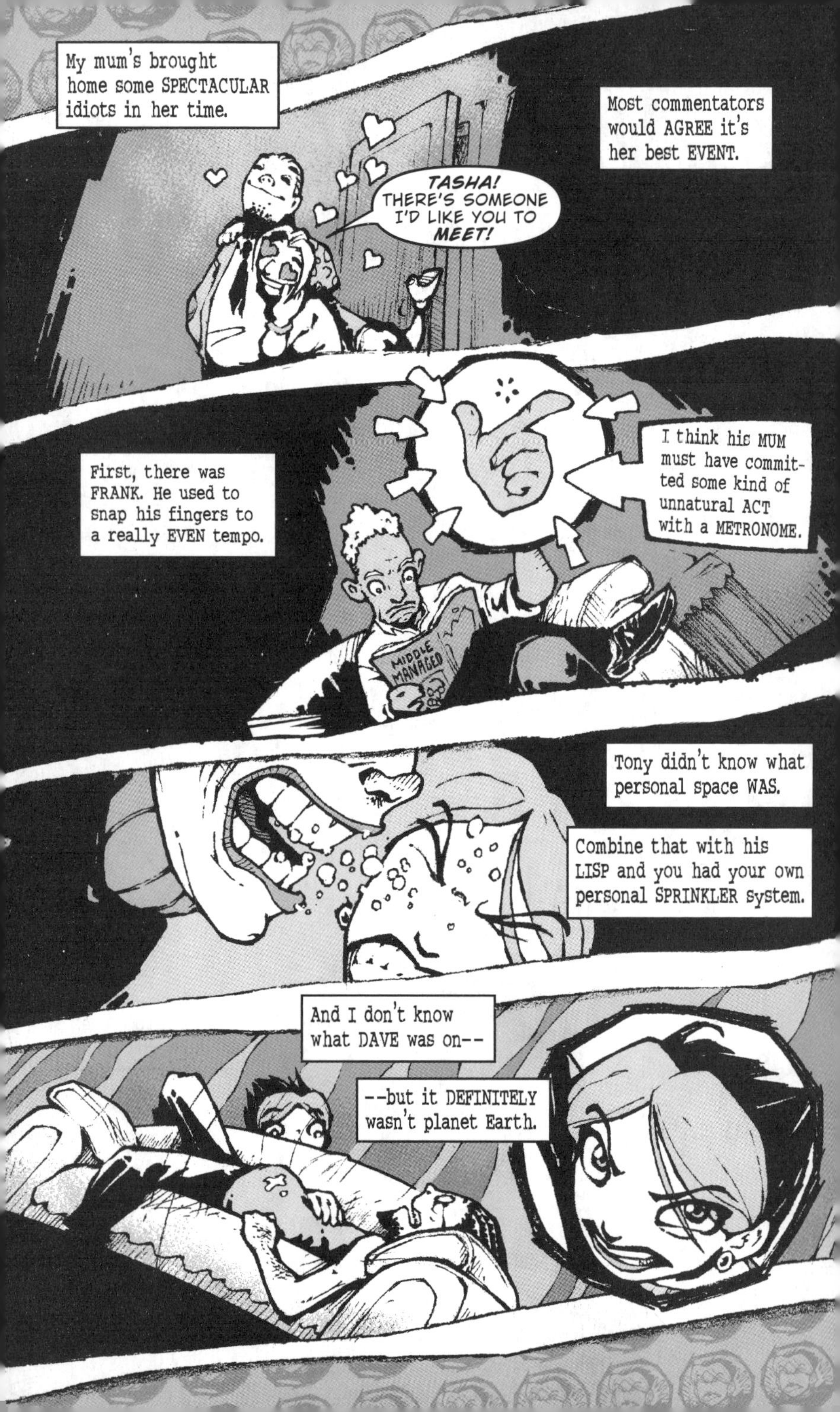
My mum's brought home some SPECTACULAR idiots in her time.
Most commentators would AGREE it's her best EVENT.
TASHA! THERE'S SOMEONE I'D LIKE YOU TO MEET!
First, there was FRANK. He used to snap his fingers to a really EVEN tempo.
I think his MUM must have commit-ted some kind of unnatural ACT with a METRONOME.
MIDDLE MANAGED
Tony didn't know what personal space WAS.
Combine that with his LISP and you had your own personal SPRINKLER system.
And I don't know what DAVE was on--
--but it DEFINITELY wasn't planet Earth.

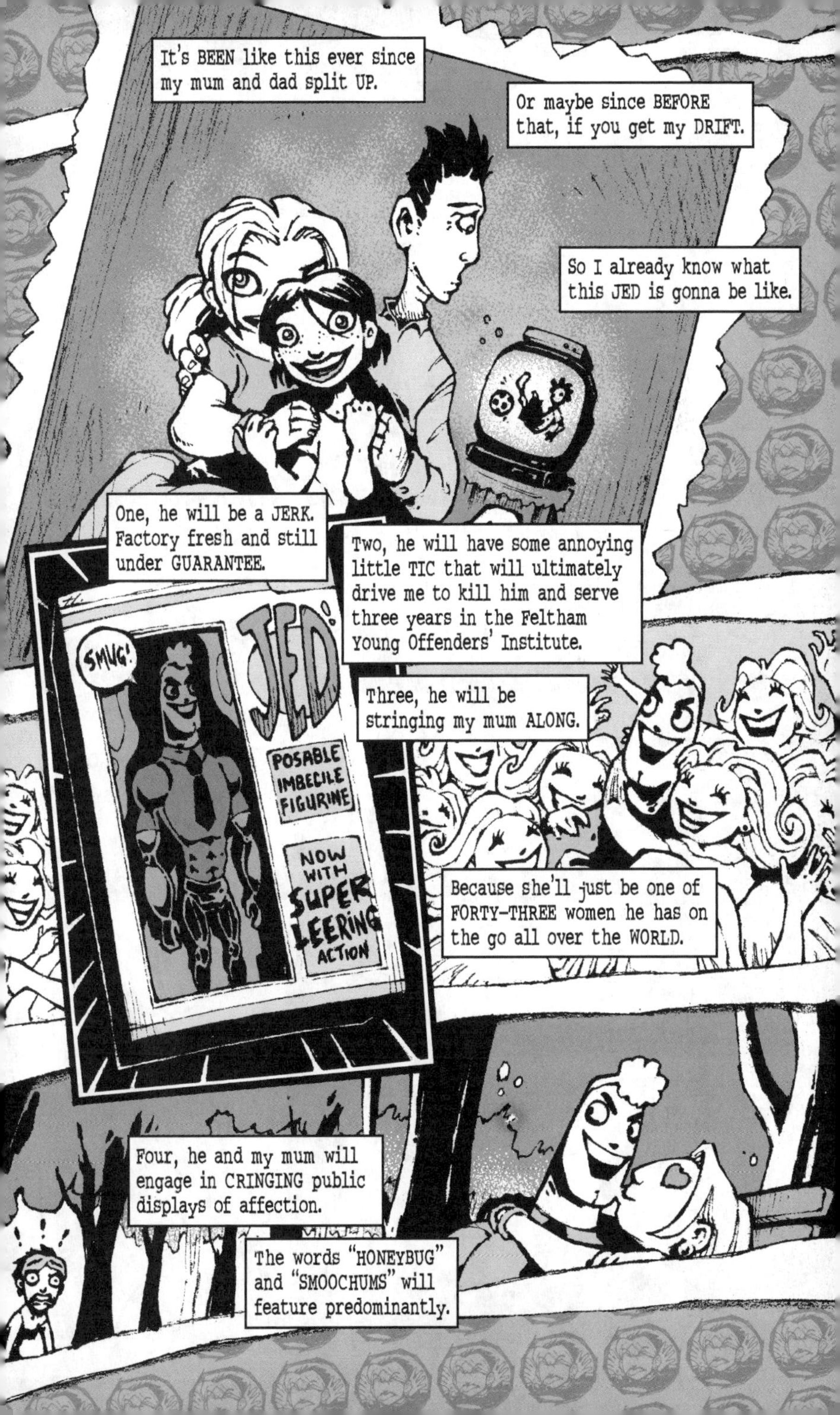
It's BEEN like this ever since my mum and dad split UP.
Or maybe since BEFORE that, if you get my DRIFT.
So I already know what this JED is gonna be like.
One, he will be a JERK. Factory fresh and still under GUARANTEE.
Two, he will have some annoying little TIC that will ultimately drive me to kill him and serve three years in the Feltham Young Offenders' Institute.
SMUG!
JED
POSABLE IMBECILE FIGURINE
NOW WITH SUPER LEERING ACTION
Three, he will be stringing my mum ALONG.
Because she'll just be one of FORTY-THREE women he has on the go all over the WORLD.
Four, he and my mum will engage in CRINGING public displays of affection.
The words "HONEYBUG" and "SMOOCHUMS" will feature predominantly.

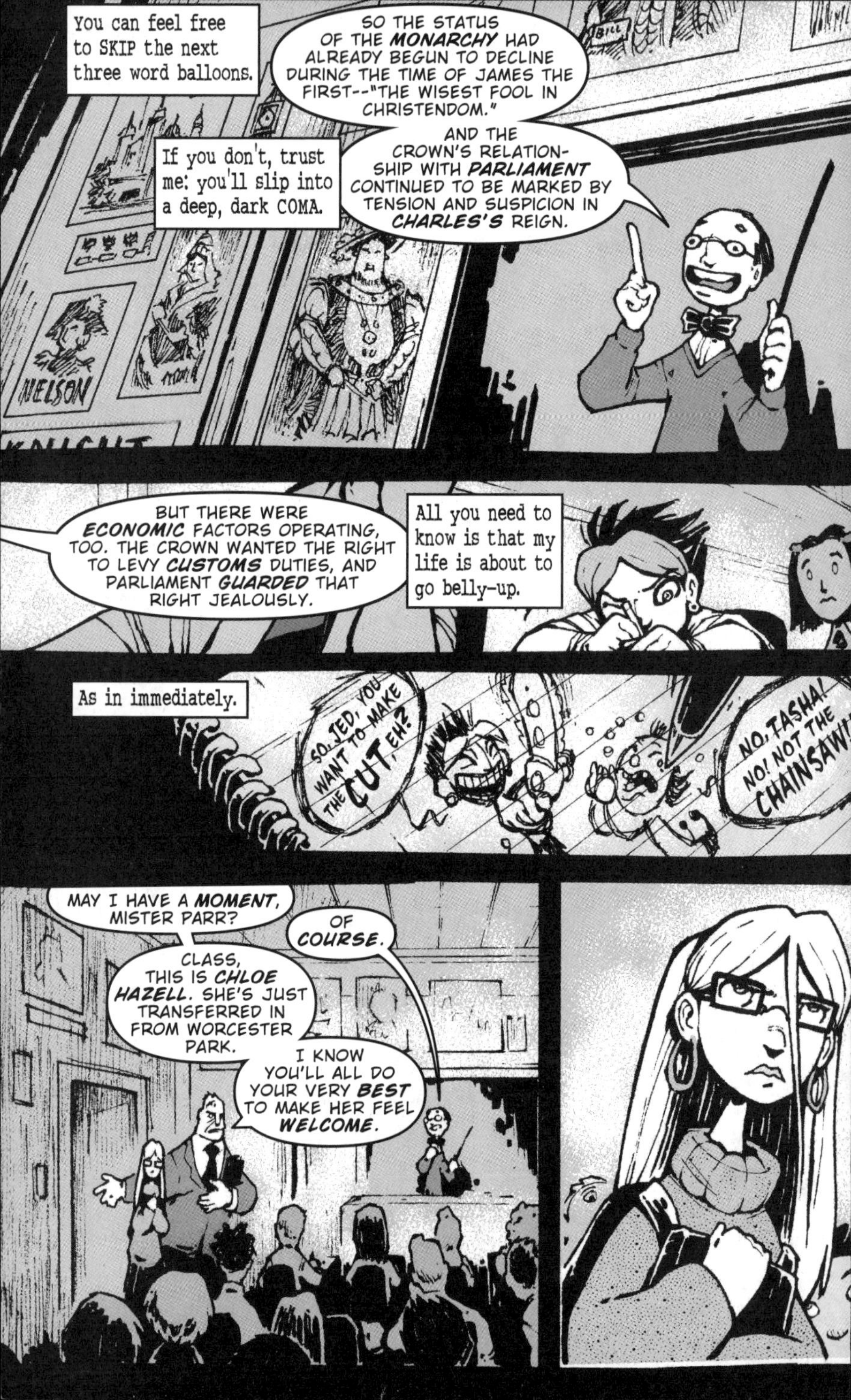
You can feel free to SKIP the next three word balloons.
SO THE STATUS OF THE MONARCHY HAD ALREADY BEGUN TO DECLINE DURING THE TIME OF JAMES THE FIRST--"THE WISEST FOOL IN CHRISTENDOM."
If you don't, trust me: you'll slip into a deep, dark COMA.
AND THE CROWN'S RELATIONSHIP WITH PARLIAMENT CONTINUED TO BE MARKED BY TENSION AND SUSPICION IN CHARLES'S REIGN.
NELSON
BUT THERE WERE ECONOMIC FACTORS OPERATING, TOO. THE CROWN WANTED THE RIGHT TO LEVY CUSTOMS DUTIES, AND PARLIAMENT GUARDED THAT RIGHT JEALOUSLY.
All you need to know is that my life is about to go belly-up.
As in immediately.
SO, JED, YOU WANT TO MAKE THE CUT, EH?
NO, TASHA! NO! NOT THE CHAINSAW!
MAY I HAVE A MOMENT, MISTER PARR?
OF COURSE.
CLASS, THIS IS CHLOE HAZELL. SHE'S JUST TRANSFERRED IN FROM WORCESTER PARK.
I KNOW YOU'LL ALL DO YOUR VERY BEST TO MAKE HER FEEL WELCOME.

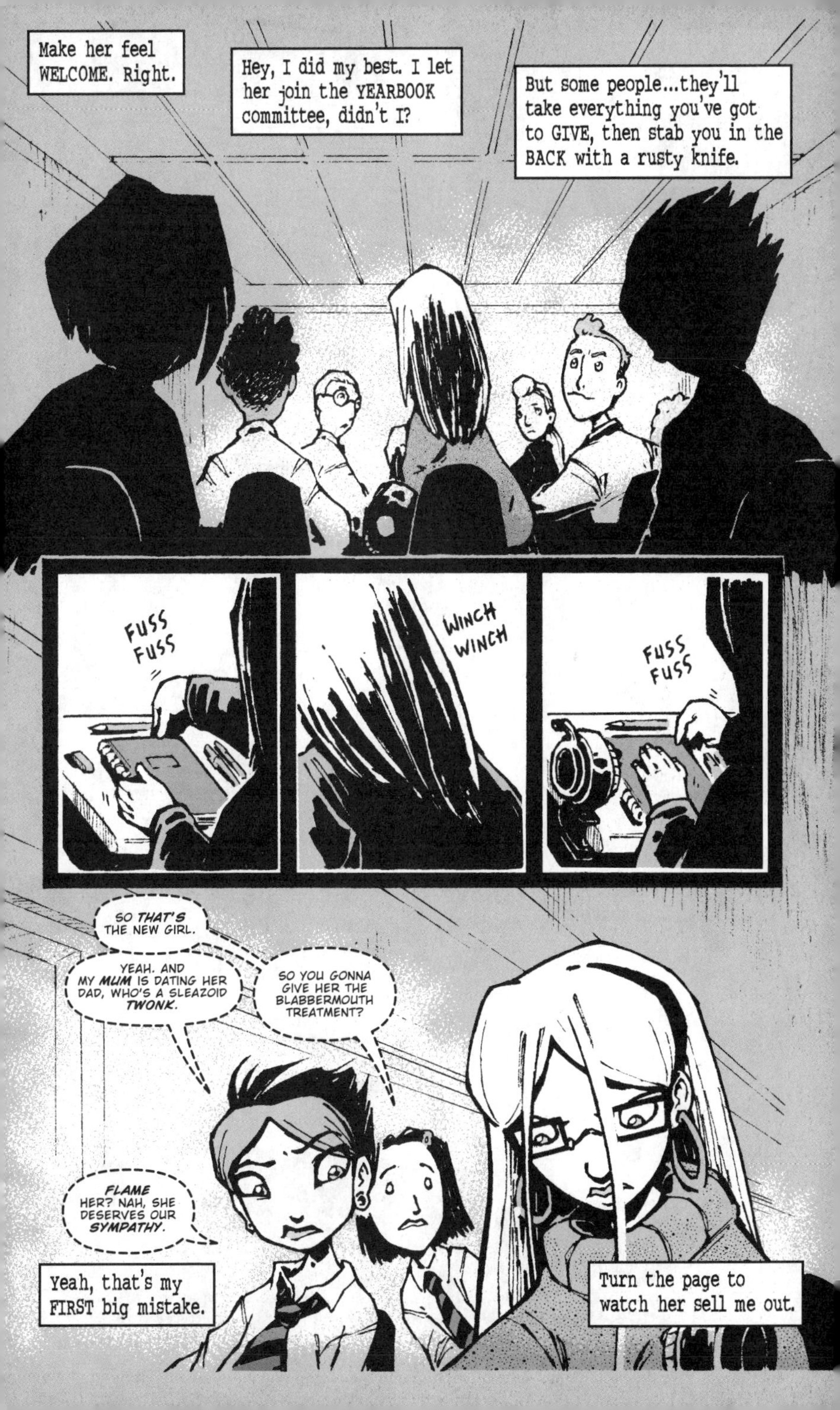
Make her feel WELCOME. Right.
Hey, I did my best. I let her join the YEARBOOK committee, didn't I?
But some people...they'll take everything you've got to GIVE, then stab you in the BACK with a rusty knife.
FUSS FUSS
WINCH WINCH
FUSS FUSS
SO THAT'S THE NEW GIRL.
YEAH. AND MY MUM IS DATING HER DAD, WHO'S A SLEAZOID TWONK.
SO YOU GONNA GIVE HER THE BLABBERMOUTH TREATMENT?
FLAME HER? NAH, SHE DESERVES OUR SYMPATHY.
Yeah, that's my FIRST big mistake.
Turn the page to watch her sell me out.

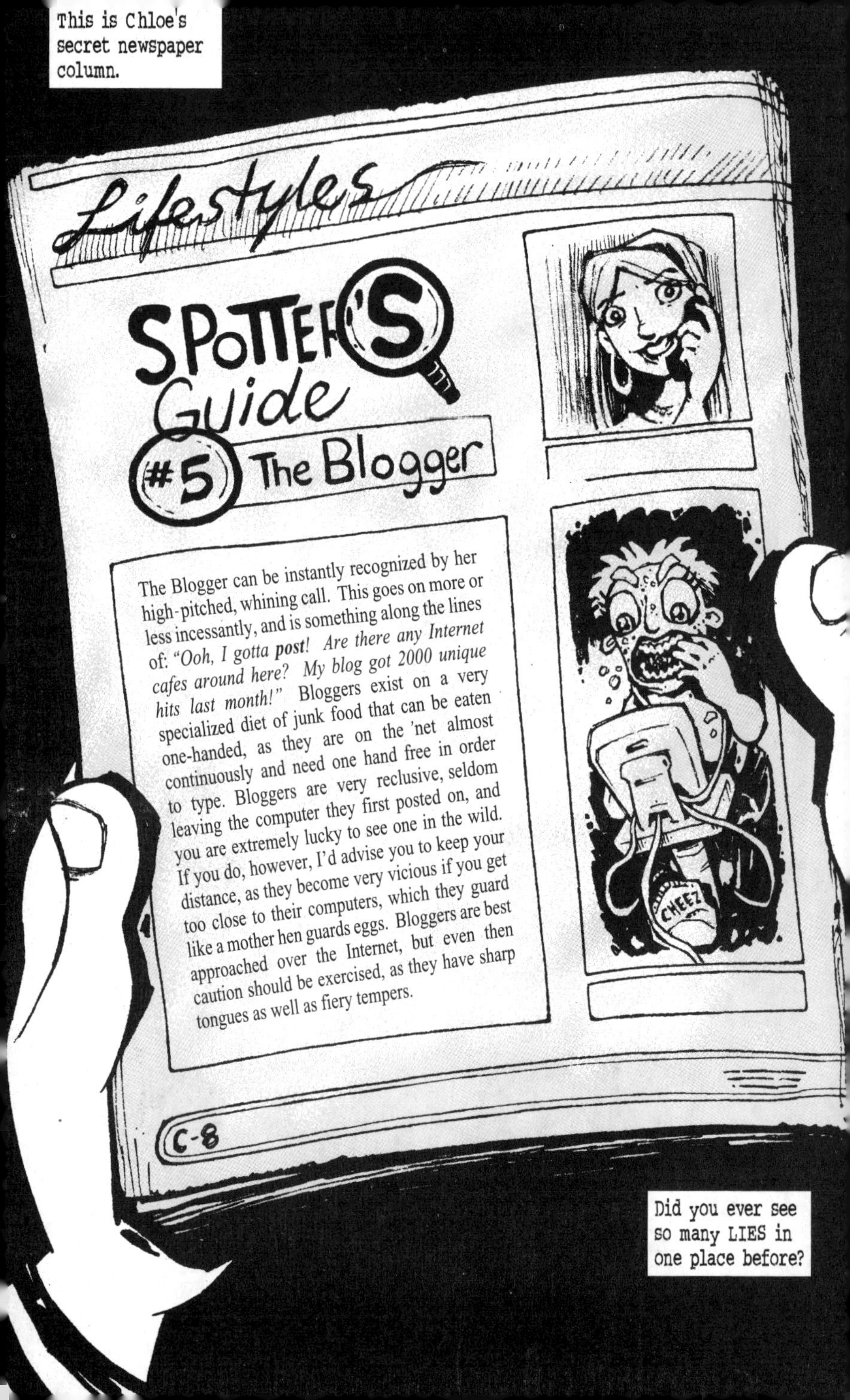
This is Chloe's secret newspaper column.
Lifestyles
SPOTTER'S Guide
#5 The Blogger
The Blogger can be instantly recognized by her high-pitched, whining call. This goes on more or less incessantly, and is something along the lines of: "Ooh, I gotta post! Are there any Internet cafes around here? My blog got 2000 unique hits last month!" Bloggers exist on a very specialized diet of junk food that can be eaten one-handed, as they are on the 'net almost continuously and need one hand free in order to type. Bloggers are very reclusive, seldom leaving the computer they first posted on, and you are extremely lucky to see one in the wild. If you do, however, I'd advise you to keep your distance, as they become very vicious if you get too close to their computers, which they guard like a mother hen guards eggs. Bloggers are best approached over the Internet, but even then caution should be exercised, as they have sharp tongues as well as fiery tempers.
CHEEZ
C-8
Did you ever see so many LIES in one place before?

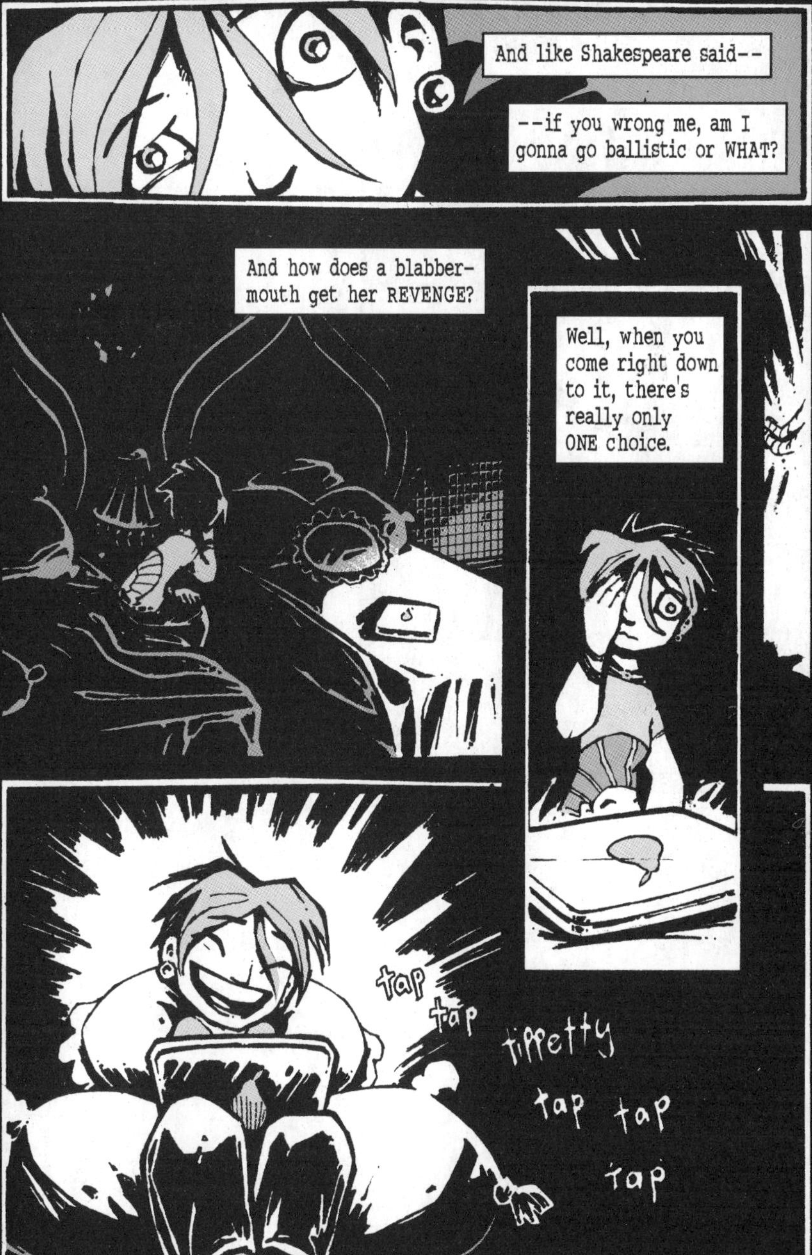

And like Shakespeare said--
--if you wrong me, am I gonna go ballistic or WHAT?
And how does a blabber-mouth get her REVENGE?
Well, when you come right down to it, there's really only ONE choice.
tap
tap
tippetty
tap tap
tap

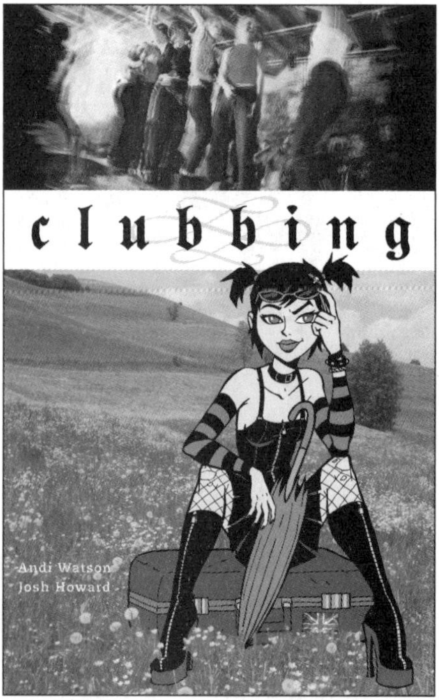
clubbing
Andi Watson
Josh Howard

A spoiled, rebellious London teenager conquers the stuffy English countryside when she solves a murder mystery on the 19th hole of her grandparents' golf course.

AVAILABLE NOW!

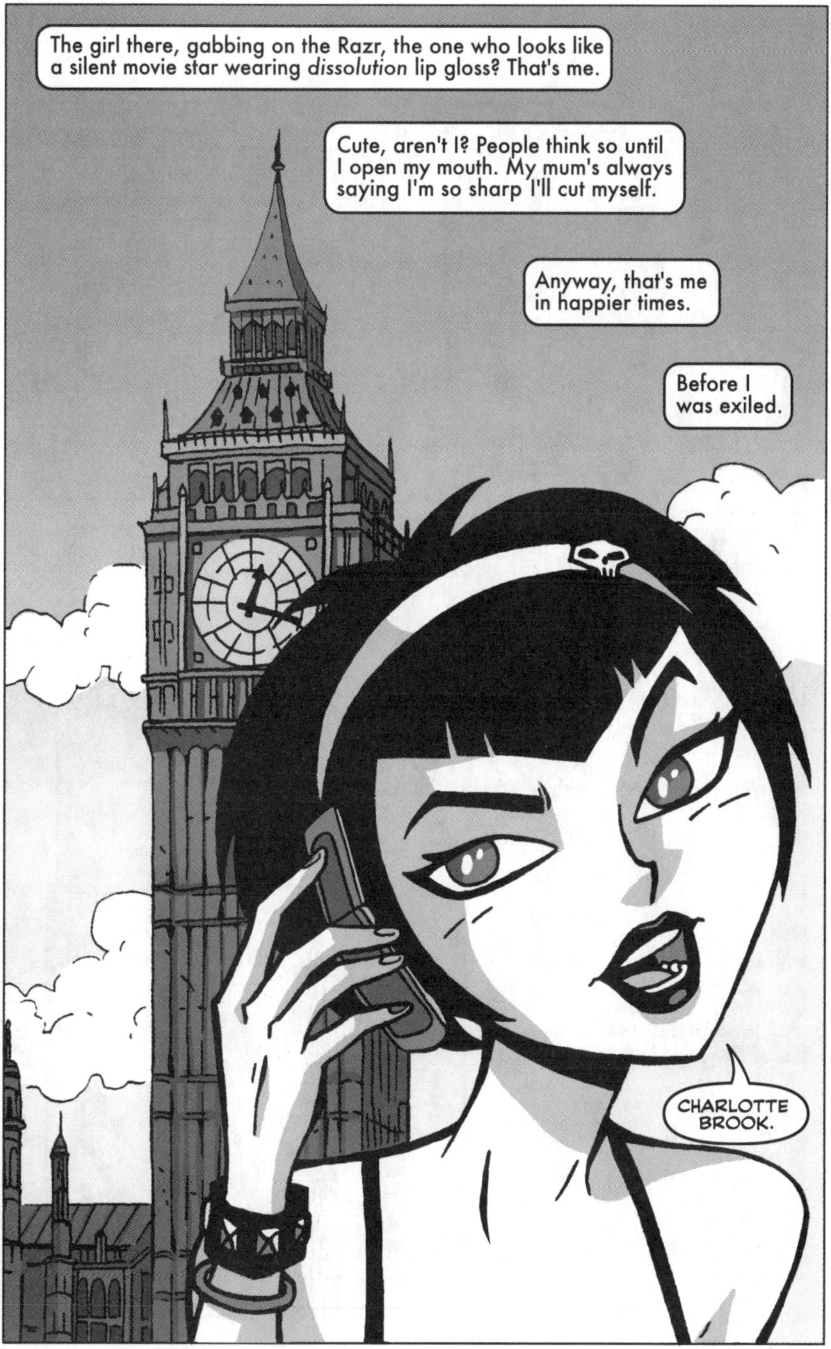
The girl there, gabbing on the Razr, the one who looks like a silent movie star wearing *dissolution* lip gloss? That's me.
Cute, aren't I? People think so until I open my mouth. My mum's always saying I'm so sharp I'll cut myself.
Anyway, that's me in happier times.
Before I was exiled.
CHARLOTTE BROOK.

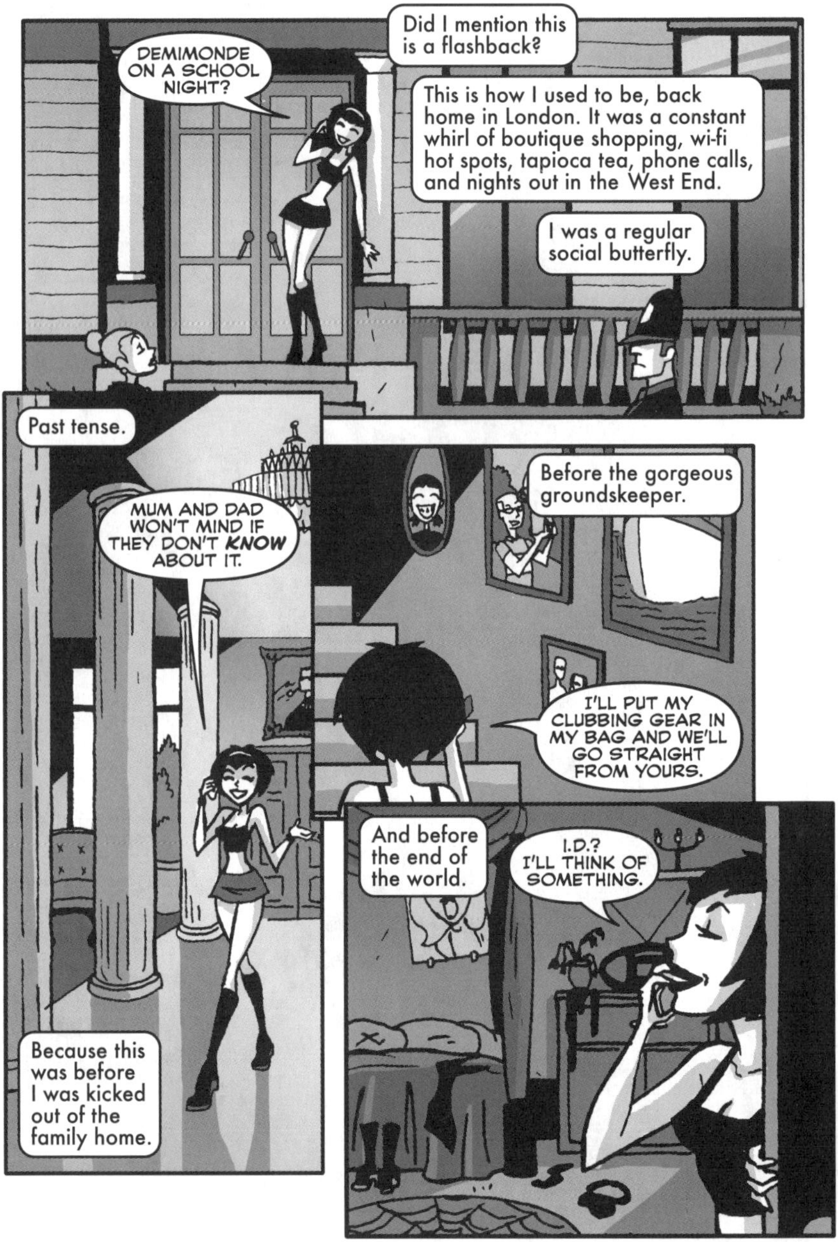

DEMIMONDE ON A SCHOOL NIGHT?
Did I mention this is a flashback?
This is how I used to be, back home in London. It was a constant whirl of boutique shopping, wi-fi hot spots, tapioca tea, phone calls, and nights out in the West End.
I was a regular social butterfly.
Past tense.
MUM AND DAD WON'T MIND IF THEY DON'T ***KNOW*** ABOUT IT.
Because this was before I was kicked out of the family home.
Before the gorgeous groundskeeper.
I'LL PUT MY CLUBBING GEAR IN MY BAG AND WE'LL GO STRAIGHT FROM YOURS.
And before the end of the world.
I.D.? I'LL THINK OF SOMETHING.

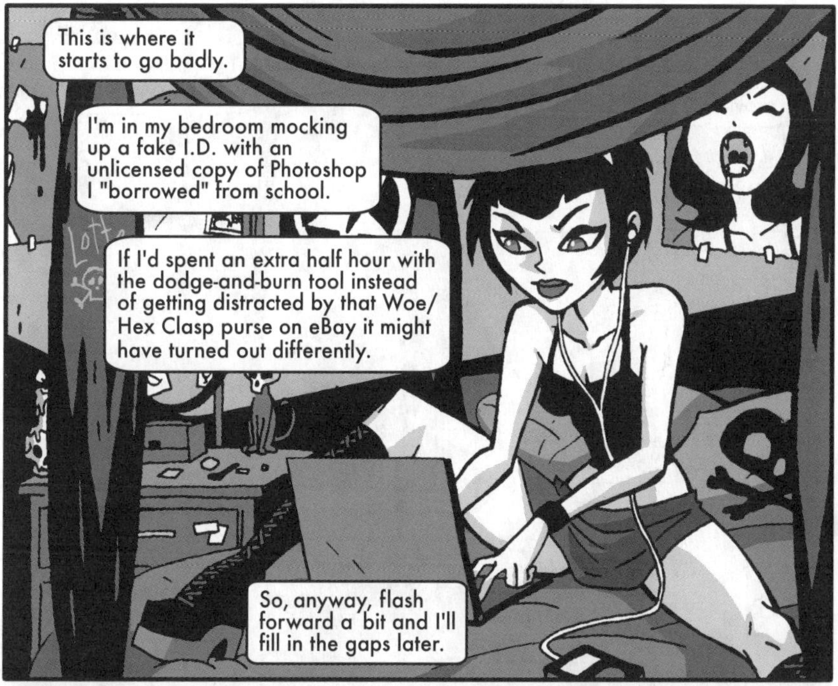
This is where it starts to go badly.
I'm in my bedroom mocking up a fake I.D. with an unlicensed copy of Photoshop I "borrowed" from school.
If I'd spent an extra half hour with the dodge-and-burn tool instead of getting distracted by that Woe/Hex Clasp purse on eBay it might have turned out differently.
So, anyway, flash forward a bit and I'll fill in the gaps later.

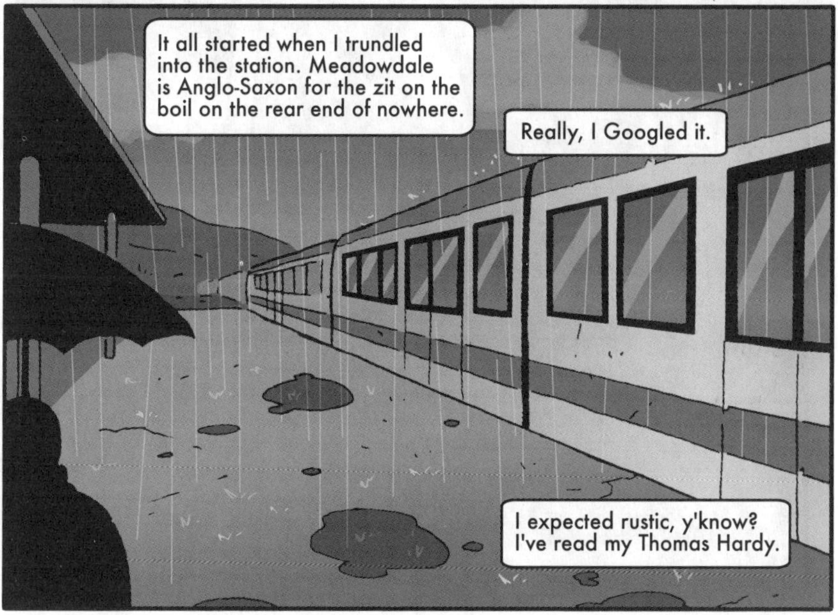
It all started when I trundled into the station. Meadowdale is Anglo-Saxon for the zit on the boil on the rear end of nowhere.
Really, I Googled it.
I expected rustic, y'know? I've read my Thomas Hardy.

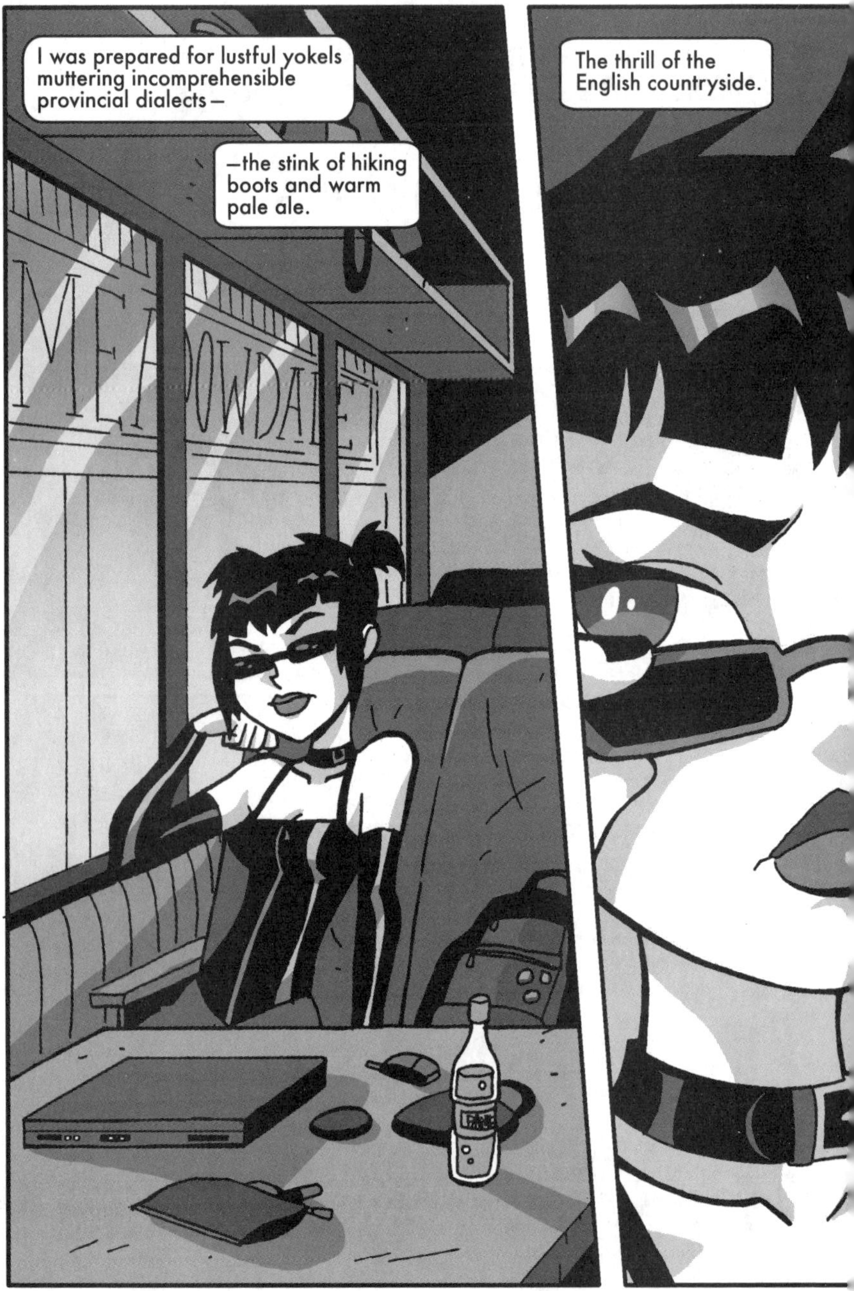

I was prepared for lustful yokels muttering incomprehensible provincial dialects–
–the stink of hiking boots and warm pale ale.
The thrill of the English countryside.

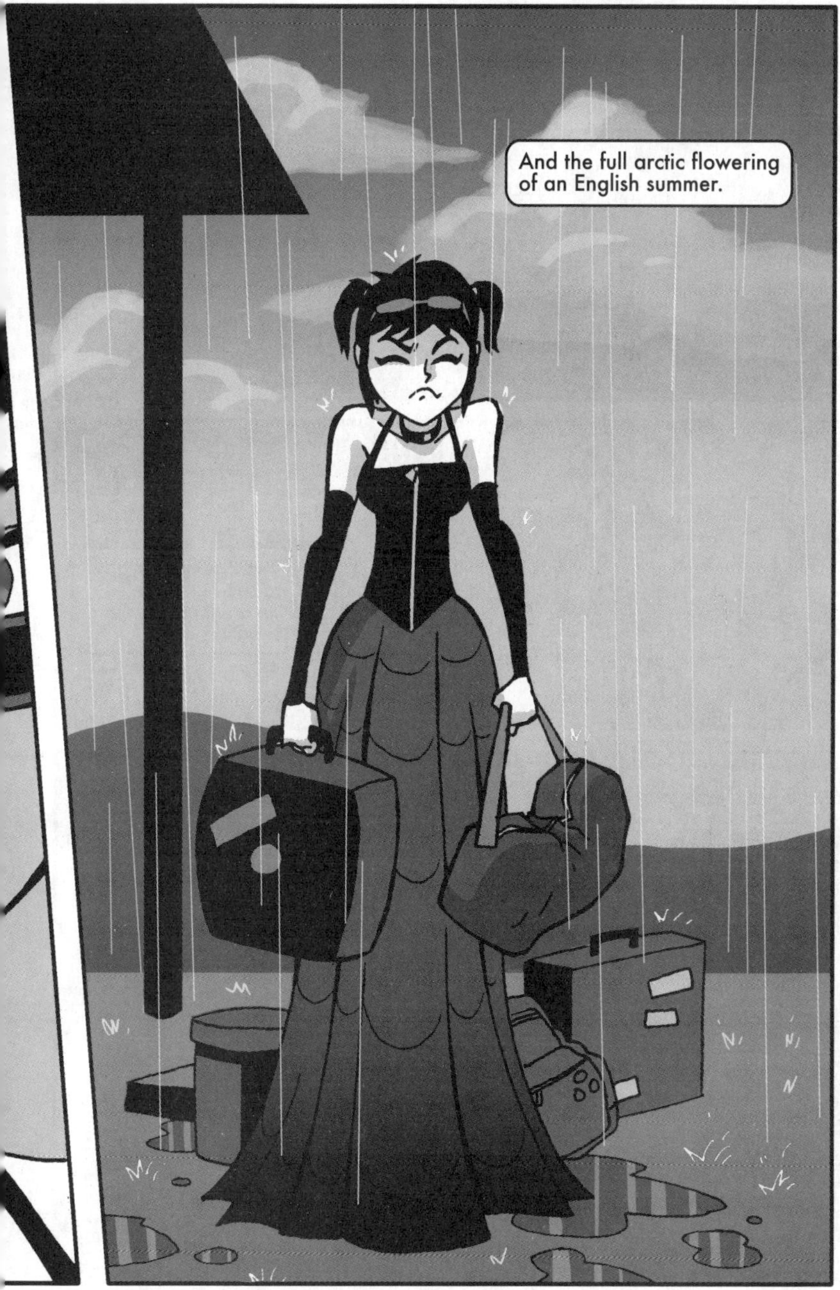
And the full arctic flowering of an English summer.

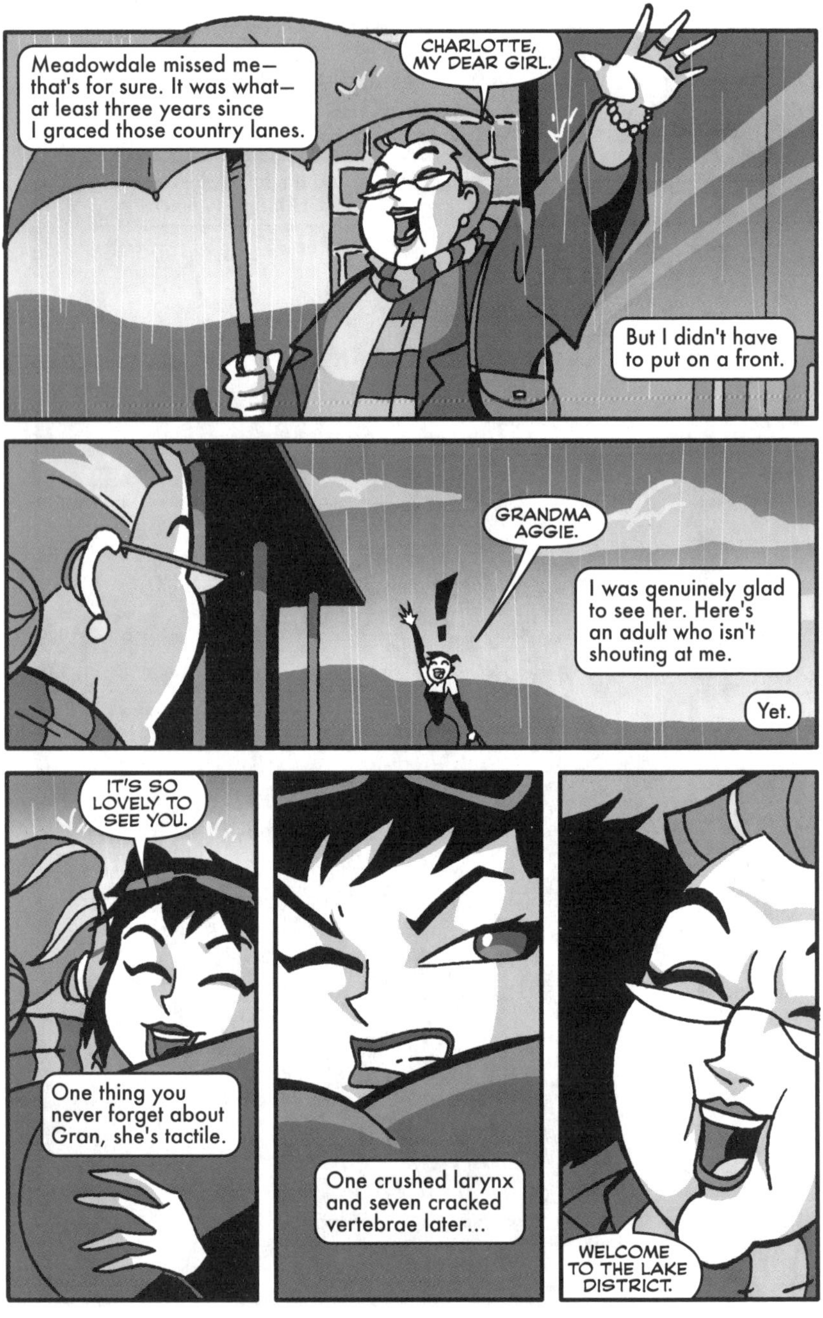
Meadowdale missed me—that's for sure. It was what—at least three years since I graced those country lanes.
CHARLOTTE, MY DEAR GIRL.
But I didn't have to put on a front.
GRANDMA AGGIE.
I was genuinely glad to see her. Here's an adult who isn't shouting at me.
Yet.
IT'S SO LOVELY TO SEE YOU.
One thing you never forget about Gran, she's tactile.
One crushed larynx and seven cracked vertebrae later...
WELCOME TO THE LAKE DISTRICT.

Follow a technosavvy teenager as she navigates the neonlit trenches

of an online VR lair to locate the legendary Kimmie66, the world's

first digital girl.

COMING IN NOVEMBER 2007

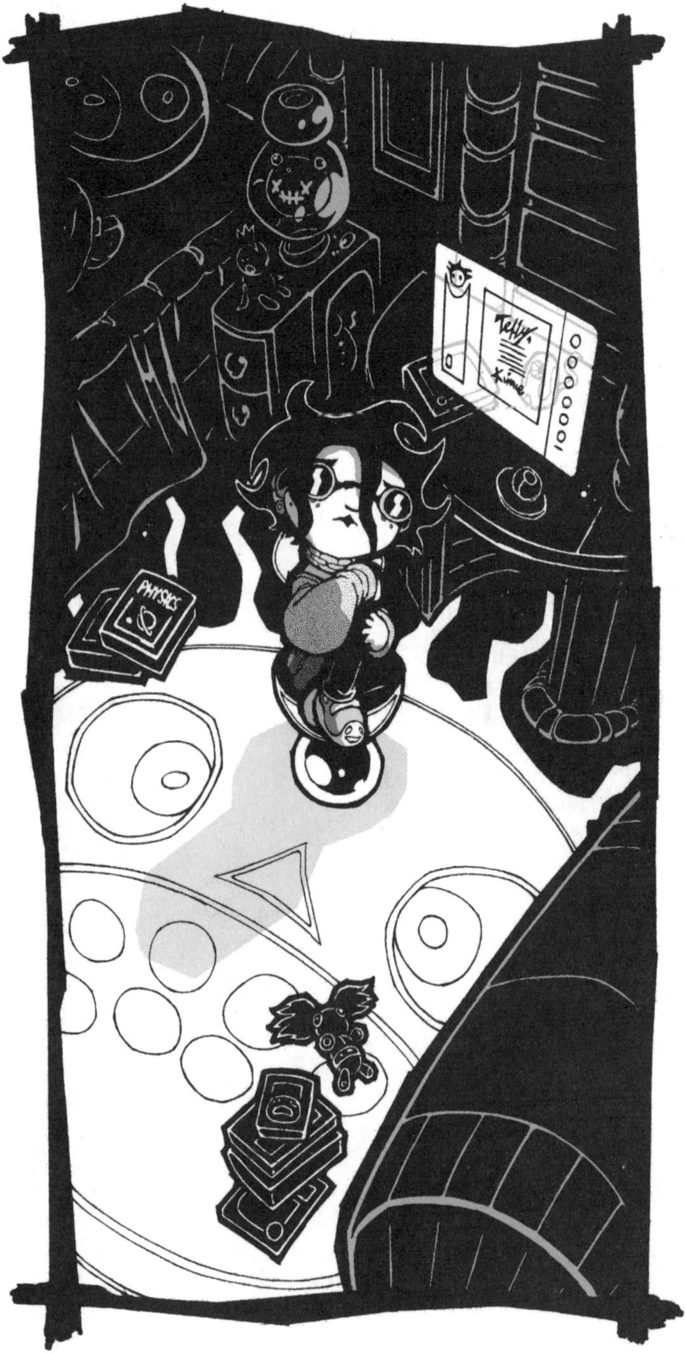
PHYSICS

HOO.

BOY.

IT'S SUCH A PAIN IN THE BUTT WHEN YOU DON'T KNOW YOUR FRIENDS' REAL NAMES. I MEAN, PEOPLE WHO LIVE OUTSIDE THE LAIRS JUST DON'T HAVE PROBLEMS LIKE THIS, DO THEY?

IT'S LIKE... *UM*...

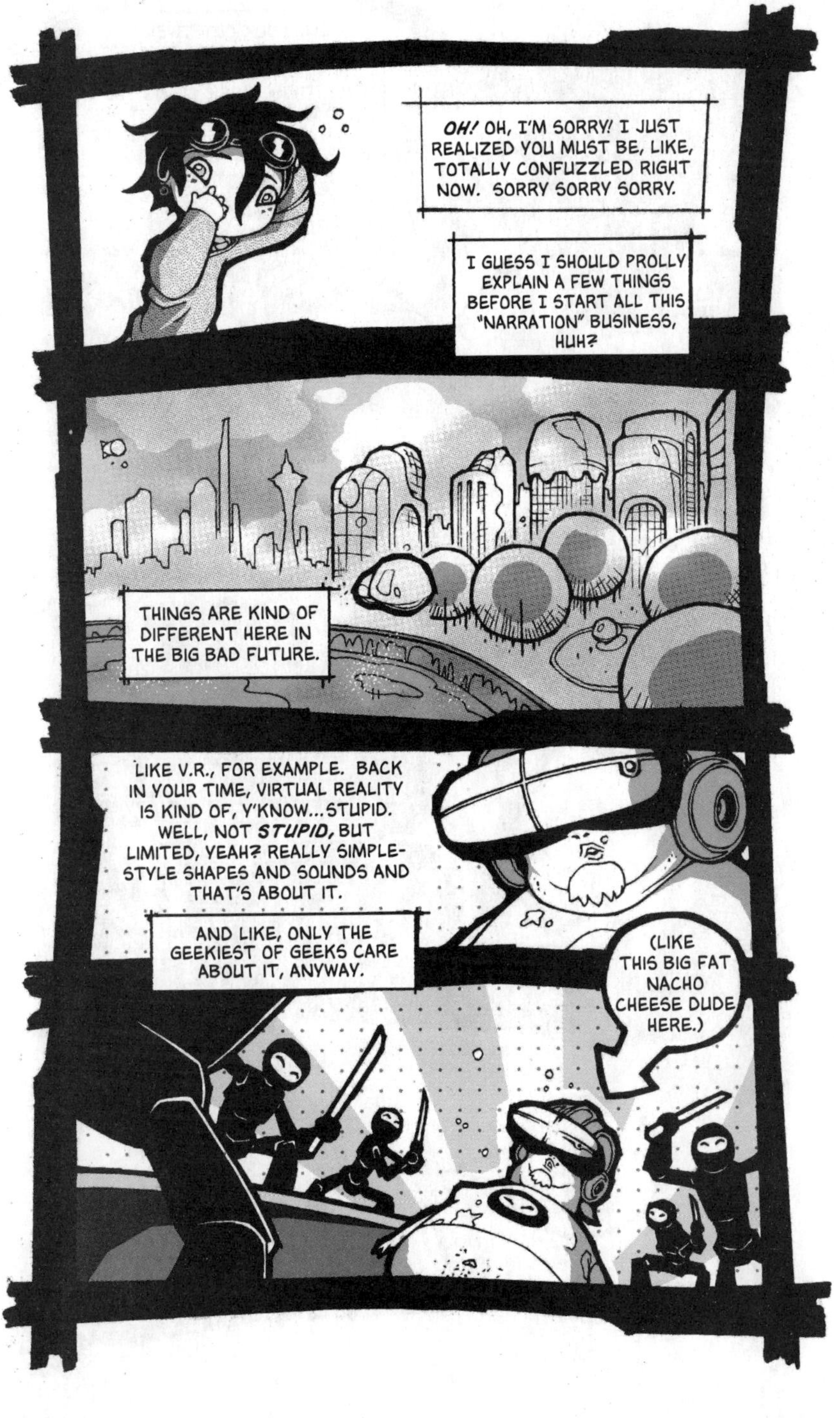
OH! OH, I'M SORRY! I JUST REALIZED YOU MUST BE, LIKE, TOTALLY CONFUZZLED RIGHT NOW. SORRY SORRY SORRY.
I GUESS I SHOULD PROLLY EXPLAIN A FEW THINGS BEFORE I START ALL THIS "NARRATION" BUSINESS, HUH?
THINGS ARE KIND OF DIFFERENT HERE IN THE BIG BAD FUTURE.
LIKE V.R., FOR EXAMPLE. BACK IN YOUR TIME, VIRTUAL REALITY IS KIND OF, Y'KNOW... STUPID. WELL, NOT STUPID, BUT LIMITED, YEAH? REALLY SIMPLE-STYLE SHAPES AND SOUNDS AND THAT'S ABOUT IT.
AND LIKE, ONLY THE GEEKIEST OF GEEKS CARE ABOUT IT, ANYWAY.
(LIKE THIS BIG FAT NACHO CHEESE DUDE HERE.)

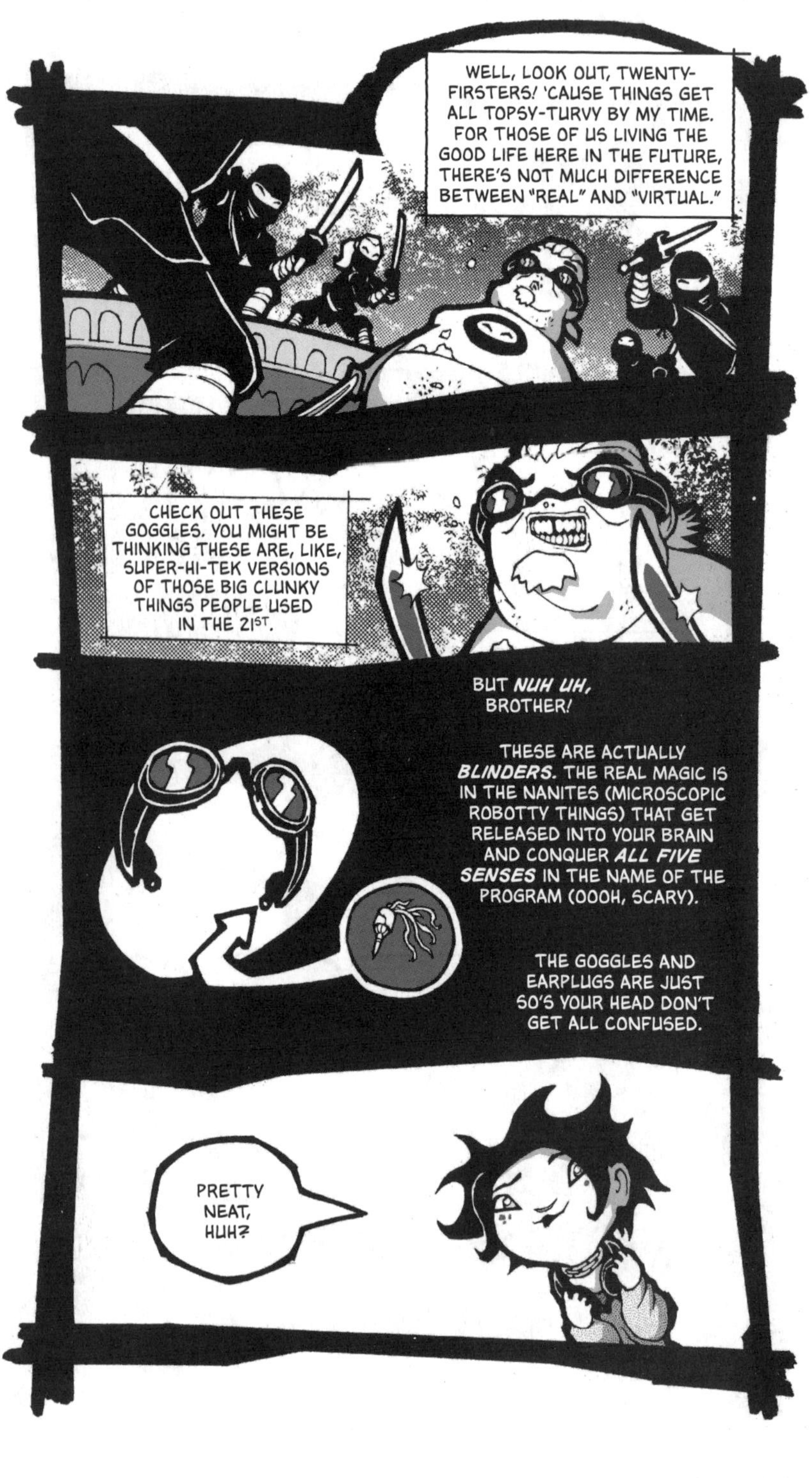
WELL, LOOK OUT, TWENTY-FIRSTERS! 'CAUSE THINGS GET ALL TOPSY-TURVY BY MY TIME. FOR THOSE OF US LIVING THE GOOD LIFE HERE IN THE FUTURE, THERE'S NOT MUCH DIFFERENCE BETWEEN "REAL" AND "VIRTUAL."
CHECK OUT THESE GOGGLES. YOU MIGHT BE THINKING THESE ARE, LIKE, SUPER-HI-TEK VERSIONS OF THOSE BIG CLUNKY THINGS PEOPLE USED IN THE 21ST.
BUT NUH UH, BROTHER!
THESE ARE ACTUALLY BLINDERS. THE REAL MAGIC IS IN THE NANITES (MICROSCOPIC ROBOTTY THINGS) THAT GET RELEASED INTO YOUR BRAIN AND CONQUER ALL FIVE SENSES IN THE NAME OF THE PROGRAM (OOOH, SCARY).
THE GOGGLES AND EARPLUGS ARE JUST SO'S YOUR HEAD DON'T GET ALL CONFUSED.
PRETTY NEAT, HUH?

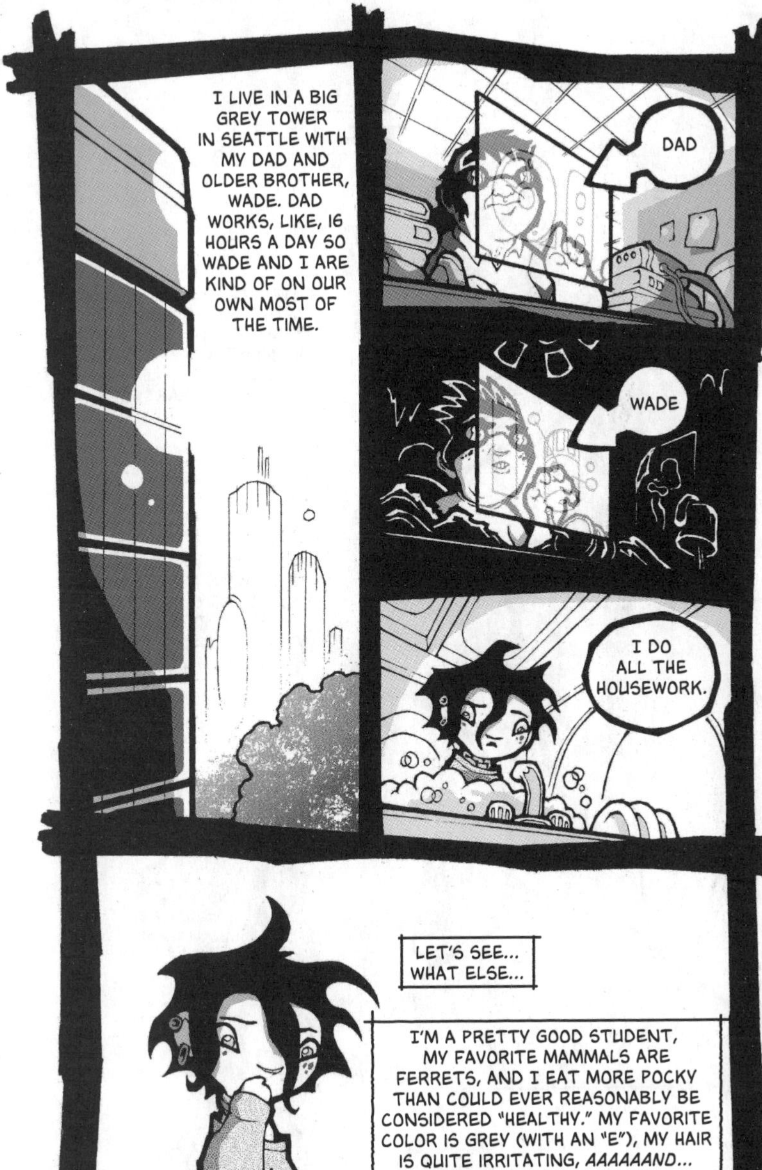
I LIVE IN A BIG GREY TOWER IN SEATTLE WITH MY DAD AND OLDER BROTHER, WADE. DAD WORKS, LIKE, 16 HOURS A DAY SO WADE AND I ARE KIND OF ON OUR OWN MOST OF THE TIME.
DAD
WADE
I DO ALL THE HOUSEWORK.
LET'S SEE... WHAT ELSE...
I'M A PRETTY GOOD STUDENT, MY FAVORITE MAMMALS ARE FERRETS, AND I EAT MORE POCKY THAN COULD EVER REASONABLY BE CONSIDERED "HEALTHY." MY FAVORITE COLOR IS GREY (WITH AN "E"), MY HAIR IS QUITE IRRITATING, *AAAAAAND...*

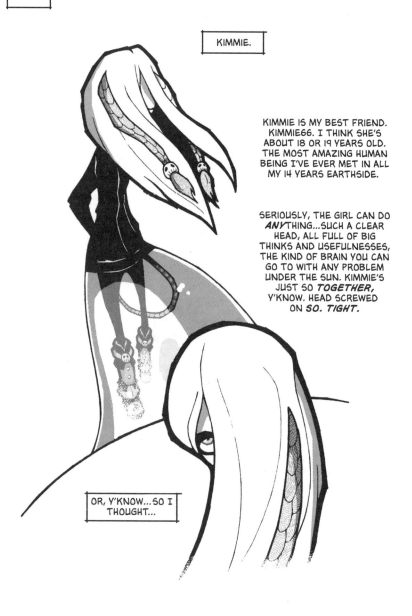

...

KIMMIE.

KIMMIE IS MY BEST FRIEND. KIMMIE66. I THINK SHE'S ABOUT 18 OR 19 YEARS OLD. THE MOST AMAZING HUMAN BEING I'VE EVER MET IN ALL MY 14 YEARS EARTHSIDE.

SERIOUSLY, THE GIRL CAN DO *ANY*THING...SUCH A CLEAR HEAD, ALL FULL OF BIG THINKS AND USEFULNESSES, THE KIND OF BRAIN YOU CAN GO TO WITH ANY PROBLEM UNDER THE SUN. KIMMIE'S JUST SO *TOGETHER*, Y'KNOW. HEAD SCREWED ON *SO. TIGHT.*

OR, Y'KNOW...SO I THOUGHT...

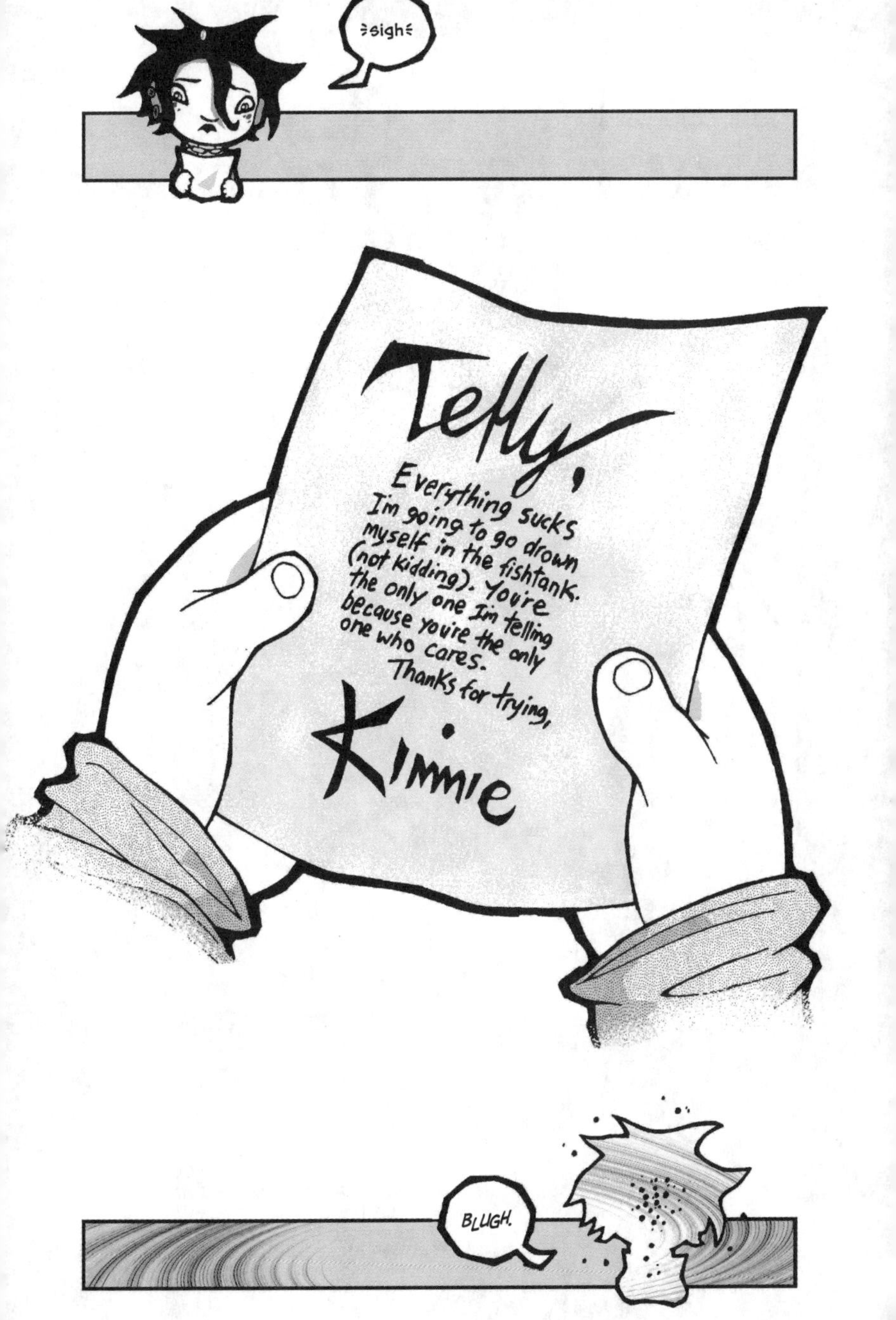
sigh
Telly,
Everything sucks
I'm going to go drown
myself in the fishtank.
(not kidding). You're
the only one I'm telling
because you're the only
one who cares.
Thanks for trying,
Kimmie
BLUGH.

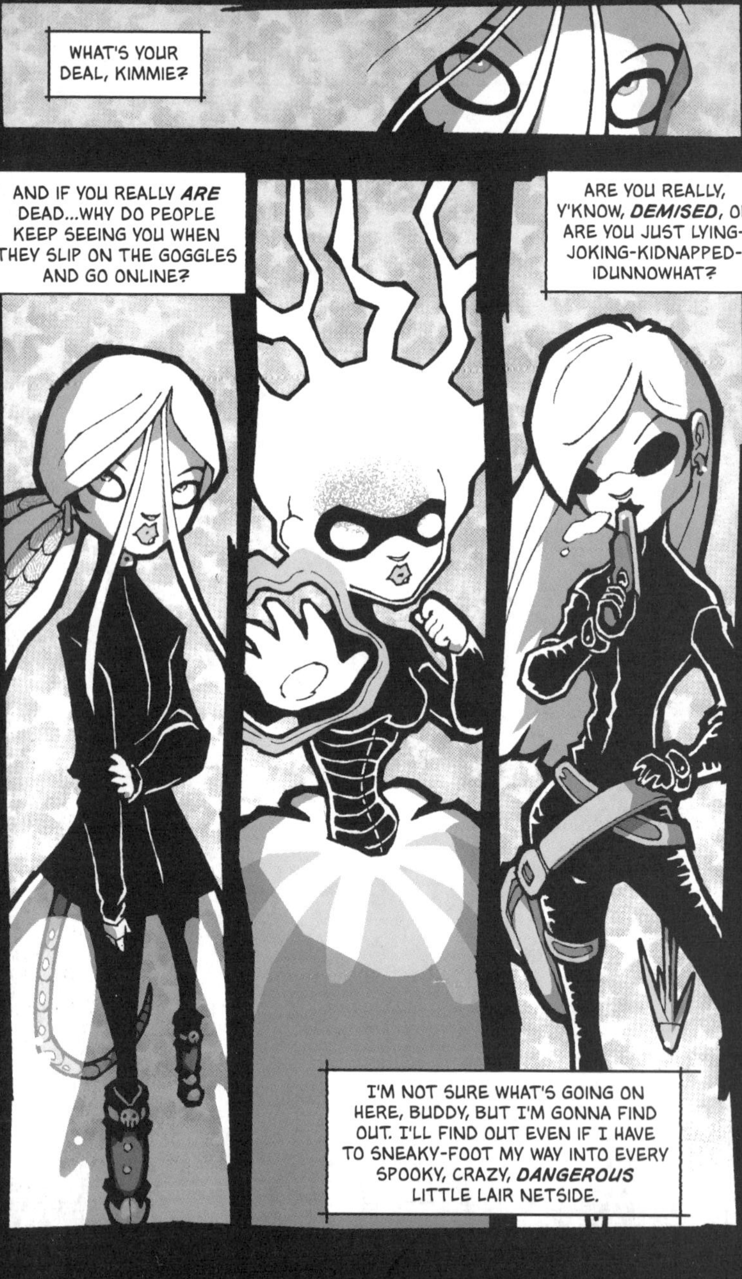
WHAT'S YOUR DEAL, KIMMIE?
AND IF YOU REALLY ARE DEAD...WHY DO PEOPLE KEEP SEEING YOU WHEN THEY SLIP ON THE GOGGLES AND GO ONLINE?
ARE YOU REALLY, Y'KNOW, DEMISED, OR ARE YOU JUST LYING-JOKING-KIDNAPPED-IDUNNOWHAT?
I'M NOT SURE WHAT'S GOING ON HERE, BUDDY, BUT I'M GONNA FIND OUT. I'LL FIND OUT EVEN IF I HAVE TO SNEAKY-FOOT MY WAY INTO EVERY SPOOKY, CRAZY, DANGEROUS LITTLE LAIR NETSIDE.